PENGUIN BOOKS

SEXUAL BEHAVIOUR IN BRITAIN

Kaye Wellings is a medical sociologist and a graduate of London University, with master's degrees from London University Institute of Education and Bedford College, London. She has worked in the field of education and sexual health for fifteen years and has written widely in this area. Her previous employment has included posts at the Open University, the Family Planning Association and the Health Education Authority and she is currently Senior Research Fellow in the Academic Department of Public Health at St Mary's Hospital Medical School and at the London School of Hygiene and Tropical Medicine.

Julia Field is a Research Director at Social and Community Planning Research (SCPR), the independent social research institute responsible for carrying out the Survey. She has worked at SCPR for eighteen years and has been responsible for surveys on a wide range of topics, including health and exercise, diet and sex education. She has a BA in sociology and social anthropology from Rhodes University, South Africa, and was born and brought up in Zambia.

Anne Johnson is a medical epidemiologist. She was educated at Newnham College, Cambridge, and the University of Newcastle-upon-Tyne. After qualifying in medicine, she trained in general practice and subsequently in public health at the London School of Hygiene and Tropical Medicine. She has worked in research in the epidemiology of HIV and sexual health since 1985 and has published many scientific papers in the field. She is currently Senior Lecturer in Epidemiology at UCL Medical School and Honorary Consultant in Public Health Medicine.

Jane Wadsworth is Senior Lecturer in Medical Statistics in the Academic Department of Public Health at St Mary's Hospital Medical School, where she has been working since 1983. She is a graduate of St Andrews University and has a master's degree from the London School of Hygiene and Tropical Medicine. She has previously held posts at St Bartholomew's Hospital and Bristol and Exeter universities, and has worked on several multi-disciplinary teams investigating social and behavioural influences on health. She has published widely in the fields of child health and education and sexual health.

Sally Bradshaw is Associate Research Fellow in the Department of Genito-Urinary Medicine at University College London. After graduating in human geography from Bristol University in 1981 she joined the Research Unit at Tesco Stores and was involved in locational research and customer survey design and analysis. In 1987 she completed an M.Sc. in Social Statistics at Southampton University and then worked as a statistician for ICI Agrochemicals before becoming involved in the National Survey of Sexual Attitudes and Lifestyles in 1988.

Sexual Behaviour in Britain

The National Survey of Sexual Attitudes and Lifestyles

Kaye Wellings, Julia Field, Anne Johnson and
Jane Wadsworth

With Sally Bradshaw

PENGUIN BOOKS

PENGUIN BOOKS

Published by the Penguin Group
Penguin Books Ltd, 27 Wrights Lane, London W8 5TZ, England
Penguin Books USA Inc., 375 Hudson Street, New York, New York 10014, USA
Penguin Books Australia Ltd, Ringwood, Victoria, Australia
Penguin Books Canada Ltd, 10 Alcorn Avenue, Toronto, Ontario, Canada M4V 3B2
Penguin Books (NZ) Ltd, 182–190 Wairau Road, Auckland 10, New Zealand

Penguin Books Ltd, Registered Offices: Harmondsworth, Middlesex, England

First published 1994
10 9 8 7 6 5 4 3 2 1

The artwork for all the figures throughout this book was prepared by Capricorn Design

Filmset in 10/12.5pt Monotype Bembo
Typeset by Datix International Limited, Bungay, Suffolk
Printed in England by Clays Ltd, St Ives plc

Contents

Foreword

by Sir Donald Acheson

I regard it as a privilege to have been invited to write the foreword to this crucial book and I commend the courage and determination of the pioneers who have brought it to a successful conclusion.

As the authors point out, the emergence in the 1980s of a lethal epidemic of sexually transmitted infection focused attention on our profound ignorance about many aspects of sexual behaviour. Not only was there no reliable baseline against which the success of efforts to reduce risky behaviour could be judged, but we lacked a firm base from which to predict the future course of the epidemic. The results of this survey have gone a long way towards filling these gaps.

But the importance of *Sexual Behaviour in Britain* goes beyond HIV and AIDS. The high response rate shows beyond a peradventure that most members of the public will accept and cooperate with the efforts of responsible people working to protect and improve their health in the sensitive area of sex. This was also the experience of my predecessor as Chief Medical Officer, Sir Wilson Jamieson, who during the Second World War first used the mass media (BBC National Radio News) to give advice on 'venereal disease', and was later my own experience. Neither of us received complaints or criticisms for discussing frankly in public subjects previously regarded as taboo.

It is well known that the Government declined to finance the survey and that the Wellcome Trust speedily came to the rescue. Ironically, according to my notes written at the time, the

Government's door was still ajar when on 10 September 1989 an article entitled 'Thatcher halts survey on sex' hit the front page of *The Sunday Times*. It certainly closed with a bang the following week!

But time moves on and attitudes change. In the Government's Strategy for Health in England published in 1992[1] the nettle has been grasped in no uncertain way. HIV/AIDS and sexual health figure in it as one of only five areas selected as key priorities for action, and targets have been set to reduce the frequency of risky behaviours. The work described in this book will form the basis for monitoring progress in this area, and will encourage others abroad to do likewise.

Sir Donald Acheson
Chief Medical Officer, Department of Health, and Chief Medical Adviser, HM Government 1983–91

[1] 'The Health of the Nation' A Strategy for Health in England. London HMSO 1992.

Preface

This detailed account of the British National Survey of Sexual Attitudes and Lifestyles is the culmination of nearly eight years' work. Through this period lessons have been learned, friendships formed and alliances forged. We have each gained experience of one another's disciplines and have drawn strength from this multi-disciplinary approach.

Without question, the HIV epidemic has provided the impetus, the rationale and the legitimation for the survey. Some will say it also created the funding opportunities. The emergence of the HIV pandemic, and attendant concern to assess and control its spread, have heralded a new era of sexual research throughout the world. This has led to greater openness in public discussion of sexual matters. Yet because of the heightened profile of work in this area, constraints have been too often political rather than scientific.

The study has been a challenge intellectually, scientifically and politically. We have tried to broaden out the scope of inquiry to include a range of aspects of sexual attitudes and lifestyle of interest to all those concerned with social, epidemiological and health aspects of the field. This also reflects our varied interests and training, in the fields of epidemiology, sociology, social survey research and statistics. Deciding how to draw boundaries round the scope of the survey; how to sustain a broad view while recognizing that public acceptability was likely to be limited to those questions essential to public health concerns; how to maximize response, understanding, consistency and validity, has all taught us a great deal about the problems and limitations of large-scale survey research into sensitive topics.

Once the scientific and political hurdles were overcome through the generous financial support of the Wellcome Trust the main survey was completed, without major problems, despite the concerns of many about attempting an inquiry of such a sensitive nature among a random population sample.

This book provides an account of the process of the research and of some of the major findings. The study has generated a rich and complex dataset and, even in a full-length book, there is space to present only a broad overview of the major results. The dataset lends itself to almost limitless inquiry and it is our hope that it will provide a major resource for many different types of scientific analysis. The results presented provide an account of sexual lifestyles in Britain at the end of the twentieth century. 18,876 men and women aged 16–59 participated in the survey in an inquiry that ranged across early education and experience, the extent of homosexual experience, patterns of sexual partnership formation, sexual practices and attitudes to sexual expression. *Sexual Behaviour in Britain* is a shortened edition of the full report of the survey. The longer text is published by Blackwell Scientific Publications as *Sexual Attitudes and Lifestyles* and includes a fuller account of the methodology together with more detailed tables.

The survey is, as much as any previous research in the field, a product of its own time. Probably as many questions remain unanswered as were asked, and certainly many areas of sexual expression remain unexplored. In compiling this account of the largest representative sample survey of sexual lifestyles ever undertaken in the British population, we hope we are at the starting point rather than the finishing post, and that the study opens the field to other avenues of inquiry.

Acknowledgements

The preparation, execution and completion of the survey has been a genuinely collaborative venture and we wish to thank a large number of people.

For financial support, we are indebted to the Wellcome Trust, especially for its speedy processing of our application when public funding was declined. In particular, we thank David Gordon for support and encouragement over the years. We also wish to thank the Economic and Social Research Council and the Health Education Authority for financial support of the development work.

At Social and Community Planning Research (SCPR), many people were involved in all stages of the survey. Special thanks are due to Liz Spencer and Jill Keegan, the principal actors in the qualitative work for the questionnaire design; to Peter Lynn for sample design and statistical advice; to Margaret Weatherby, field controller for the survey; to Sally Harford one of the senior interviewers who came to play a key role in briefing interviewers; to over 500 members of the SCPR fieldforce of specially trained interviewers whose commitment to the project ensured the quality of the data; to Ann Palmer, who masterminded the clerical editing and coding and her team; and to Jo Periam, computer programmer responsible for the final editing of the data. Because of its size and high public profile, the survey tended to dominate the life of SCPR for a long time and few staff escaped some involvement. Our thanks go to them all.

Carol Morgan had sole responsibility for all graphical material presented throughout the book. Kay Stratton prepared a substantial part of the manuscript. We thank them for their diligence and patience in the seemingly endless redrafts prepared.

Many people have provided practical help, encouragement and intellectual advice, particularly when the project looked close to being mothballed. In particular, we thank the project's advisory group: Mike Adler, Roy Anderson, Roger Jowell and David Miller. In addition, we are very grateful to the following people for their helpful contributions: Sir Donald Acheson, Valerie Beral, Toni Belfield, Graham Bird, Mildred Blaxter, Lindsay Brook, Manuel Carballo, Margaret Chekry, Tony Coxon, Sir David Cox, Nicholas Day, Caroline Gardner, Graham Hart, Keith Hatfield, Lord Kilmarnock and the All-Party Parliamentary Group on AIDS, Peter Linthwaite, John McEwan, Sally MacIntyre, Klim McPherson, Charles Turner, John Watson, Jeffrey Weeks and Daniel Wight. We wish also to thank Stuart Taylor, our editor at Blackwell's, and Ravi Mirchandani at Penguin for their tolerance and patience with missed and ever tighter deadlines.

Our greatest debt is to the 18,876 participants in the survey who gave freely of their time, and allowed us to inquire into one of the most intimate areas of their lives.

Glossary

ACORN A classification of residential neighbourhoods: a way of classifying small geographical areas, based on census data, such as type of housing and the age profile of residents.

Adjusted Odds Ratio An odds ratio (see below) which has been adjusted in a standard way to control for other factors.

Bivariate Analysis A collective term for statistical analysis to investigate the relationship between two variables.

Centile See percentile.

DHSS Department of Health and Social Security (before August 1988).

DoH Department of Health (from August 1988).

ER Electoral Register.

ESRC Economic and Social Research Council.

FPA Family Planning Association.

GHS General Household Survey.

GUM Genito-urinary medicine.

HEA Health Education Authority.

IUD Intrauterine contraceptive device.

Logistic Regression One type of multivariate analysis (see below), which investigates the relationship between the probability of occurrence of a characteristic and two or more other variables.

Mean The sum of a set of values divided by the number of values (commonly known as the average).

Median The median divides a set of values which have been listed in order into two subgroups of equal size. Half of the values will be larger and half smaller than the median. The median is often preferred to the mean (see above) as it is not sensitive to extreme values.

MRC Medical Research Council.

Multivariate Analysis A collective term for statistical analysis which investigates relationships between three or more variables simultaneously. The advantage of multivariate analysis over bivariate analysis (see above) is that one can establish a relationship between two variables after allowing for the fact that they are both related to a third variable.

Odds The ratio of the number of individuals with a particular characteristic to the number without that characteristic.

Odds Ratio The ratio of odds for two different subgroups (e.g. men and women). For example, an odds ratio of 2:1 for men versus women for a particular characteristic means that the odds for men are twice that for women. The results of logistic regression (see above) can be expressed as odds ratios.

OPCS Office of Population Censuses and Surveys.

PAF Postcode Address File.

Percentile An ordered set of values can be divided into 100 groups of equal size. The division points are known as Percentiles and the 50th percentile is the median (see above).

PHLS Public Health Laboratory Service.

Quartile An ordered set of values can be divided into 4 groups of equal size. The division points are known as quartiles and the second quartile is the median (see above).

SCPR Social and Community Planning Research.

Skewness The extent to which the values in a distribution are concentrated at the upper or lower end of the range of values.

STD Sexually transmitted disease.

UCMSM/UCLMS University College and Middlesex School of Medicine, renamed University College London Medical School in 1993.

Variance A measure of the extent to which a set of values is dispersed around their mean (see above). If the values are all close to the mean, the set of values is said to have low variance; the more spread out they are, the higher the variance.

95% Confidence Interval The range of values of some measure (e.g. odds ratio, see above) within which there is a 95% probability that the true value lies.

CHAPTER I

Studying Sexual Lifestyles

The amount of speculation and discussion of sexual behaviour stands in stark contrast to the lack of reliable empirical evidence. Despite the apparent trend towards greater openness in sexual matters, this remains one of the most underdeveloped fields in the human sciences. Scholars from many disciplines have contributed to the understanding of sexuality and its expression, but their insights have been limited by the difficulty of investigative work in the area. Research has seldom been conducted without controversy, and researchers who have ventured into the area have rarely avoided suspicion and constraint.

As a result, important questions have gone largely unanswered. What proportion of people have homosexual experience, have exclusive relationships, are celibate, have visited prostitutes? When do men and women first become sexually active? What factors influence the range and regularity of sexual practices? How are attitudes to sex and sexuality changing and how are they associated with behaviour? What evidence is there for generational trends in behaviour and what are the social and demographic correlates of variability in sexual lifestyle?

The emergence in the 1980s of a worldwide epidemic of a predominantly sexually acquired infection, human immunodeficiency virus (HIV), sharply focused these gaps in knowledge, and served to demonstrate the need for research into sexual lifestyles. Efforts to mount effective public health education campaigns, to predict the likely extent and pattern of the spread of HIV, and to plan services for those affected were all hampered by the absence of reliable data on sexual behaviour.

Although the HIV epidemic highlighted the dearth of information on sexual lifestyles, the need for robust research has been recognized for some time. The lack of reliable information on the subject has long handicapped those specializing in the fields of sexual and reproductive health, as well as those in the broader disciplines of education and medicine. Reliable quantitative data are essential for understanding fertility patterns, contraceptive use and the epidemiology of sexually transmitted diseases, and are fundamental to informed debate about the timing and content of sex education.

Information is needed not only about current sexual behaviour but also about the dynamics of change and its possible explanations. The forces that fashion human sexual behaviour are as yet imperfectly understood, but factors that influence change over time include technological and demographic changes, population mobility, advances in control of fertility and sexually transmitted diseases (STDs), the emergence of new diseases, changing theories of sexuality, in addition to changes in the moral climate and the law.

Examples of such forces in the recent past are easily instanced. In the past thirty years, reliable contraception has increasingly separated sex from its procreative function and diminished the fear of unwanted pregnancy. Modern medicine has improved control of venereal diseases such as syphilis and gonorrhoea, reducing further the adverse consequences of sexual expression. Public discussion of studies of sexual satisfaction may have increased expectations of sexual performance and pleasure (Masters and Johnson, 1966; Masters and Johnson, 1970). Successive acts of legislative and statutory reform have liberalized aspects of sexual behaviour: the legalization of homosexuality and abortion, for example, and the provision of contraceptive advice and supplies to single women. More recently, with the emerging HIV epidemic and concerns about other sexually acquired conditions resistant to cure, such as genital herpes and invasive cervical cancer, new forces may be affecting sexual behaviour. The influence of these factors on patterns of behaviour has gone largely uncharted.

THE ABSENCE OF DATA

Little reliable information has been available on the sexual behaviour of the general population based on random probability samples. The AIDS epidemic resulted in a proliferation of interest in the subject but the investigative focus at the start of the epidemic was chiefly on specific subgroups of the population identified as being at particularly high risk of HIV infection: homosexual men, injecting drug users and prostitutes, for example, (Winkelstein *et al.*, 1987; Johnson, 1988; Wodak and Moss, 1990). These studies have generally been based on clinic and volunteer samples of individuals, selected on the basis of a particular lifestyle.

Invaluable as these surveys undoubtedly are in describing features of interest in specific groups, they cannot be used to assess the extent of that particular behaviour in the whole population. Estimates of behaviours in a national representative sample are necessary to set other studies in context, as well as to assess whether purposive samples typify the wider populations they are chosen to represent.

At the start of the AIDS epidemic those needing information were thrown back on the data gathered by Alfred Kinsey and his colleagues in the United States (Kinsey *et al.*, 1948; Kinsey *et al.*, 1953) some fifty years earlier. Pioneering though these surveys were, they used largely volunteer samples recruited from a variety of sources: from colleges, prisons, the armed forces and all kinds of informal networks. The findings, showing widespread diversity in sexual lifestyles, had a major effect on the lives of ordinary men and women in America, but since the sample was not representative of the US population, the findings could not be generalized to that wider population (Cochran *et al.*, 1953). The use of Kinsey's data in the context of AIDS/HIV, despite its flaws, testified to the absence of reliable data from other sources.

The application of modern survey methods to the study of human sexual behaviour began to gather momentum in the 1960s and 1970s, but studies undertaken in that period were often small or limited to specific subsets of the population (Reinisch *et al.*, 1990). On occasions their usefulness was limited for other reasons. Data from a US survey of over 3000 adults carried out in 1970 by the

National Opinion Research Centre (NORC) using a combination of random and quota sampling were not published for nearly twenty years because of a dispute between the investigators – a cautionary tale for all involved in such enterprises (Fay *et al.*, 1989).

In Britain, too, there has been a similar lack of quantitative data gathered from surveys using probability sampling methods. The Mass Observation studies of the 1930s and 1940s (England, 1950) represent an early attempt to study sexual attitudes and behaviour in the British population, but few data were ever published from these investigations. Other surveys were either not based on strictly random samples (Chesser, 1956) or else insufficiently detailed to be of general relevance (Gorer, 1971), and in any case they were out of date by the time information was needed in the context of the HIV epidemic.

More recent research has benefited from improvements in survey methodology and computer technology has simplified the selection of representative samples of the general population. Yet surveys of sexual behaviour have generally been undertaken in response to a particular social or health problem, investigation being legitimized by the policy relevance of the findings. The apparent increase in sexual activity among young people in the 1960s, for example, prompted the Health Education Council to sponsor the first national surveys of teenage sexual behaviour (Schofield, 1965; Schofield, 1973), and the increasing incidence of teenage pregnancy motivated studies of young people's experience of sex education and knowledge of birth control in the 1970s (e.g. Farrell, 1978). Material relevant to sexual behaviour has also been collected in large-scale studies of family formation and family planning (Bone, 1978; Bone, 1986; Dunnell, 1979; OPCS, 1985) but this has been confined to women of reproductive age and to factors relevant in the context of those inquiries.

The potential disadvantages of linking scientific surveys with specific contemporary social and health issues are clear. General applicability is limited by too narrow a focus or too limited a sample. An awareness that this is a charge that may also be levelled at this survey in the future led to attempts to broaden its scope beyond the specific need for information related to HIV and AIDS.

THE RATIONALE FOR THE SURVEY

Undeniably the emergence of the HIV epidemic provided the impetus, the legitimation and the funding opportunities for this study. Every aspect of the survey, from the theoretical framework and the measurement objectives to the size of the sample and the content of the questionnaire, necessarily reflects the aims of the survey and the uses to which the data are to be put. The study was conceived in the context of the need for information that would help in assessing and preventing the future spread of HIV. Two of the main purposes of the survey were to provide data that would increase understanding of the transmission patterns of HIV and other sexually transmitted infections, and would aid the selection of appropriate and effective health education strategies for epidemic control.

Both these objectives required information on patterns of sexual behaviour in the population. Epidemiological evidence indicated that the virus behaved like many other sexually acquired infections. Once it was introduced into a community, the likelihood of an individual becoming infected in the early stages of the epidemic increased with the number of sexual partners (homosexual or heterosexual) with whom unprotected intercourse had taken place (Johnson, 1988). Spread outside the populations initially affected was likely to depend on the proportion of the population engaging in high-risk activities, the pattern and frequency of partner change in the population and the extent of mixing between different groups (Johnson, 1992; Anderson *et al.*, 1986; Potts *et al.*, 1991). A series of studies aimed at estimating the potential spread of HIV in the UK were commissioned through the Department of Health (Report of a Working Group, 1989 and 1990), but although attempts were made to assess the prevalence of risk behaviours from available data sources, it became evident that too little was known about key behavioural variables that could determine current prevalence or future transmission.

There were, for example, no estimates of the proportion of men who had homosexual partners. It was not known how representative were clinic-based or volunteer samples of homosexual men (Coxon, 1988; McManus and McEvoy, 1992), how homosexuality should be defined, what was the extent of same-gender contact in the population, nor what proportion engaged in practices that were risky for the transmission of HIV (primarily anal intercourse). Similar concerns arose in relation to the heterosexual population. Little was known about the overall pattern of sexual behaviours, in particular the pattern of heterosexual partner change in the population and the frequency and prevalence of different sexual practices.

A large sample size was required in order to represent and characterize these patterns adequately, and to obtain sufficient representation of more unusual kinds of behaviour. Some high-risk practices, such as injecting drug use and homosexual anal intercourse, involve only a small minority of the population. Similarly, a relatively small proportion of the population has very large numbers of sexual partners, but may contribute disproportionately to the spread of STDs (Hethcote and Yorke, 1984).

Reliable data on sexual behaviour were also essential for those concerned with developing an effective policy for prevention. In particular it was necessary to describe the socio-demographic and attitudinal characteristics of those with different sexual lifestyles. Success in limiting further spread of the virus is currently dependent on the ability of educational and other interventions to establish norms of safer sex. Advice on risk reduction must be presented in a form acceptable to sexually active populations. A sound understanding of patterns of human sexuality is a necessary prerequisite for the design of preventive interventions, since it is difficult to focus interventions or to monitor their impact over time in the absence of such data. This survey sought to collect data that could help to define target populations for specific interventions, to determine those risk-reduction messages that are most likely to meet with acceptance, to identify preferred educational agencies, to identify needs for information, and to provide baseline data for monitoring and evaluating the impact of interventions.

To a considerable extent, the public-health implications of the HIV epidemic have dictated the direction of research. But while such concerns have both stimulated and in some sense limited the scope of the survey, every attempt has been made to extend its relevance to other areas of health and human behaviour. An understanding of sexual experience in the population is of importance to many disciplines: to social historians documenting generational changes in sexual behaviour, to anthropologists concerned with cross-cultural comparisons, to educationalists requiring a more realistic understanding of contemporary teenage sexual experience in order to design effective sex education programmes, to demographers concerned with changing patterns of family formation, and to health workers in many fields. As a result, while the need for data for use in the context of the AIDS epidemic remained high on the research agenda, the questionnaire was designed to be sufficiently durable and broad-based for it to be relevant to a range of disciplines concerned with sexuality, sexual health and reproduction.

The desire to provide data of broad interest had to be balanced against concern to maximize response on the key issues of contemporary importance, and to avoid jeopardizing the acceptability of the survey by widening its scope too far. Future historians may wonder at the absence of information on the psychological and pleasurable nature of sexual relationships. The omissions must remain the responsibility of the researchers, but, in mitigation, the acceptability of detailed inquiry into sexual behaviour in the general population was largely unknown when this work began, and the sensitivities of funding bodies spending government money were made clear at a relatively early stage.

Theoretical Framework for the Study

The rationale for the survey has shaped its theoretical perspective as well as its investigative focus. This perspective is centrally and fairly exclusively social and epidemiological. Certainly the aims of the survey would not have been served by the kind of narrowly biological perspective that has characterized much writing on the subject. The belief that the determinants of sexual expression are to be found in instinct has – as Weeks points out – a long provenance, dating from Plato and Aristotle and reappearing in the Middle Ages in the concept of natural law (Weeks, 1985). The concept of sex as a natural urge is a recurrent theme in the writing of the sexologists of the late nineteenth century; Havelock

Ellis, for example, described it as an 'impulse', and Freud as a 'drive' (Freud, 1953). The biological imperative is hinted at in the choice of terms used in the accounts of Kinsey's research, in the term 'outlet' for example (Kinsey *et al.*, 1948; Kinsey *et al.*, 1953) and certainly the attempt to develop a taxonomy of human sexual behaviours, carefully categorized in a manner characteristic of the natural sciences, very much reflected Kinsey's background in biology.

Biological determinants of sexual behaviour cannot be ignored. Any theory of sexuality will have recourse to an understanding of anatomical and biological potential and limits which provide the preconditions for human sexuality (Weeks, 1985). But while the biological human sexual capacity is universal, its expression is influenced by socio-cultural forces (Carballo *et al.*, 1989). Sexuality is defined, regulated, and given meaning through cultural norms. While biological and psychological causes may be central when comparing individuals, they are not of first importance when comparing societies. Biology explains little of the variation between population groups. If sexuality were solely biologically determined, then forms of sexual expression would vary little cross-culturally or historically, and the evidence suggests that they do (Ford and Beach, 1952). Narrowly biological explanations are inadequate when research questions concern social trends and variations between different populations and subgroups.

It is in the potential of sexuality for diversity that the seeds of hope may be found in the selection of sexual health strategies. Human relationships offer an enormous range of choices in terms of sexual expression. We owe a debt to Kinsey for demonstrating this to be so. In the search for a healthy lifestyle, a perspective that sees in sexuality opportunities for choice and diversity is of greater value than one that sees sexual behaviour as immutably fixed by biological forces.

Progress and Politics of the Survey

Late in 1986, a group of epidemiologists and statisticians from University College and Middlesex School of Medicine, St Mary's Hospital Medical School and Imperial College (including Anne Johnson and Jane Wadsworth) met to consider the possibility of undertaking a large random-sample survey in Britain with the prime interest of measuring the distribution of sexual behaviours in the population, and particularly patterns of partner change, in order to assist in measuring the current and future magnitude of the HIV epidemic. Their focus was almost entirely behavioural. A questionnaire was developed and Gallup International was commissioned to undertake a pilot study of nearly 800 randomly selected adults aged 16–64 (Johnson *et al.*, 1989). This study allowed valuable progress to be made in the development of the survey methodology, but the response rate was disappointing.

In June 1987, in response to a meeting of the Chief Scientist's group at the Department of Health and Social Security (DHSS) an internal discussion paper was prepared on the possibility of developing a National Study of Sexual Attitudes and Lifestyles with the dual objectives of facilitating the development of a well-targeted and effective educational campaign and enabling more accurate estimates of the possible future spread of HIV. This document was discussed at the meeting of the DHSS Behavioural Change Group in September 1987, where it was decided that the Health Education Authority should take forward a survey with a predominant emphasis on the first of the two aims. A protocol based on a proposal drafted earlier by Kaye Wellings (then at the Family Planning Association (FPA), later Senior Research Officer at the HEA) and Julia Field (Social and Community Planning Research (SCPR)) was approved by the Department of Health in the HEA's Operational Plan in October 1987. Development work on the HEA survey began in January 1988 when the research institute, SCPR, was commissioned to carry out the work. A three-stage development programme was proposed. This was to begin with a qualitative phase, consisting of a series of unstructured, exploratory interviews aimed at guiding the design of a structured questionnaire. This was to be followed by a period of testing the structured questionnaire through small-scale piloting, culminating in a large-scale feasibility study with a random sample large enough to give reasonably accurate measures of response rates and prevalence of particular behaviours within the population. Progress to the main stage depended on the success of the feasibility work.

The shared interests of the HEA and epidemiological groups became evident to senior research management at the Department of Health and Social Security (DHSS). In December 1987 a meeting was organized by the Medical Research Council (MRC) under the chairmanship of Sir Richard Doll to discuss the possibility of a large-scale random-sample survey of sexual lifestyle in Britain. Present at this meeting were scientists involved in the pilot study undertaken by Gallup, and representatives from the MRC, the Economic and Social Research Council (ESRC), the HEA and the DHSS. It was agreed that any government funding for such a study should be channelled through the ESRC and the HEA, and that any funding through the DHSS would be subject to ministerial approval.

The advantages of combining the two studies were now self-evident and collaboration between the two research teams began in earnest. There were sound reasons for the merger of the projects, not least a concern for economies of human and financial resources and a desire to pool expertise and share experience. In early May 1988, a research proposal for a feasibility study of 1000 individuals was prepared and submitted to the ESRC. It was agreed that funding should be shared by the ESRC and the HEA. In July, the ESRC agreed its share of the feasibility phase of the study. Through the period, much work was done by the combined team to develop questionnaires and decide on sampling methodology. A series of pre-pilots was run through the summer.

In the autumn of 1988, 977 interviews were carried out with men and women aged 16–59 in Great Britain. The hoped-for response rate (65%) was achieved and the study was approved by the DHSS in the HEA's operational plan for 1989/90, and by the ESRC Council at the end of January 1989. In the same month, the HEA's Project Review Committee sanctioned release of funds for the years 1988/89 and 1989/90 for the purpose of funding the survey. The study was discussed with senior members of Research Management of the Department of Health and the scientific merits of the study again endorsed. The team was promised a decision on funding before the end of February 1989, with a view to starting fieldwork for the main stage in April 1989.

In the event, no such decision was forthcoming. In March 1989, the Chief Executive of the HEA was instructed to delay the start of the fieldwork for an estimated two months until the matter had been discussed in a higher Cabinet committee. Some work continued in expectation of a decision in April, but plans were now seriously disrupted as deadlines passed and fieldwork timetables were interrupted. By the end of June, concern at the delay was being raised elsewhere, by the Medical Research Council, for example, and by the All-Party Parliamentary Group on AIDS. A letter from the study's advisory group members to the Minister (at that time David Mellor) in July requesting a meeting to discuss the study met with no response. Effectively, the survey had been put on ice without explanation.

The next bulletin was provided by *The Sunday Times*. The newspaper ran a lead story on the survey on 10 September 1989 with the headline, 'Thatcher Halts Survey on Sex'. The reasons for the decision to ban the survey, reportedly made from Downing Street, were threefold. According to reports, it was felt that such an inquiry represented an invasion of public privacy, that it would be unlikely to produce valid results and, since numerous AIDS-related surveys of sexual behaviour were already underway, this further investment would be an inappropriate use of public funds. But the source of the decision as described in the press was never communicated directly to the researchers.

The veto was followed by widespread discussion in the press and other media, and the ban incurred considerable disquiet not only among the researchers involved but also the scientific community in general. Protests were voiced against scientific decisions being made on apparently political grounds. In late September, the ESRC wrote to inform the applicants that the ESRC had received a letter from the Department of Health stating that 'in all the circumstances it is not appropriate for the Government to support it and, more generally, that it would not be right for the Government to sponsor the survey', and expressing regret that the ESRC would not be able to provide support.

After inquiries had been made, the survey team learned that the Wellcome Trust would be willing to consider an application for funding the proposed study. The Trust undertook peer review of the proposal with unprecedented speed and, on 15 October 1989, the Wellcome Trust announced a grant of £900,000 to be awarded to researchers at SCPR, St Mary's Hospital, Imperial College, and University College and Middlesex School of Medicine (UCMSM).

The stage was set for the main survey, but time had been lost and work carried out in the spring in the hope of DoH funding was wasted. Much of the work on sampling and interviewer recruitment had to be repeated. The main study was in the field by May 1990 when the first interview was completed. By November 1991, the last interview was filed, bringing the final sample to 18,876.

The political sensitivity concerning research into this area of human behaviour is by no means a problem unique to late twentieth-century Britain. Examples of hindrance, obstruction and discouragement are legion in the history of sex research. Questionnaires have been seized as pornographic, researchers slanderously attacked and their findings suppressed. Kinsey, for example, faced hostility from colleagues and threats of dismissal from his college (Kinsey *et al.*, 1953), while Lanval, a Belgian researcher working in the 1930s, was forced to work at night to avoid police raids on his data (Lanval, 1950).

By demonstrating the clear need for data, the HIV epidemic has legitimized scientific research in the area and this may have considerably eroded political resistance and softened public attitudes to such endeavours. Research has proceeded apace in the wake of the epidemic, particularly in Europe where surveys have been conducted in several European countries: in Norway, Denmark, the Netherlands, France and Finland, for example (Sundet *et al.*, 1988; Melbye and Biggar, 1992; ACSF Investigators, 1992). A Concerted Action has been established by the European Community (EC) to co-ordinate the findings of these European surveys (1990) and a research protocol for surveying sexual lifestyles developed by the World Health Organization (WHO) is being used in several developing countries (Carballo *et al.*, 1989).

Yet, despite this obvious progress, the British experience finds close parallels in several other countries. Although considerable headway has been made in response to the AIDS epidemic, researchers in many countries have still been frustrated in their attempts to set up studies. US efforts to launch a national survey of sexual behaviour foundered on opposition from the Bush Administration and from conservative lawmakers which resulted in the withdrawal of funding (Aldhous, 1992) – although scaled-down versions of the original proposals have had some success in attracting alternative sources of financial support. Also in Sweden, widely regarded as a sexually very tolerant country, plans for a national survey were thwarted. In 1991, the Swedish Board of Statistics approached one of the country's leading sexologists to develop a feasibility survey for a national survey, but retracted when the time came to make these plans public (Lewin, personal communication, 1992). In Switzerland, the country with one of the highest AIDS incidence rates in Europe, a proposal in 1991 for a survey of sexual behaviour failed to receive financial support. Even the French team encountered some testing hurdles as the proposal went through appropriate ethical committees.

It might seem surprising that political reservations have persisted in the face of such a serious health problem. The nature of the demand for data could have been expected to confer legitimacy on investigation in this area. Sex research has traditionally achieved respectability through its association with the medical profession. Besides which, scientific endeavour is generally concerned with aiding an explanation and understanding of patterns of sexual behaviours, and not with whether the conclusions will lead to more or less societal prejudice or tolerance, licence or restraint, or any other change in sexual ethics (Reiss, 1986). But although there may be nothing in science that favours or opposes any form of sexuality, it would nevertheless be naïve to ignore or underestimate the political importance of data on sexual behaviour. As Weeks points out, 'The production in sexological discourse of a body of knowledge that is apparently scientifically neutral ... can become a resource for utilization in the production of normative definitions that limit and demarcate erotic behaviour' (Weeks, 1985).

The impact of Kinsey's data testifies precisely to this. The exposure of sexual diversity in the US in the mid-twentieth century had major implications for sexual ethics in the US. Most people at the time understood that the official norms of sexuality did not quite match practice in American society, but also understood that sexual conduct that did not match those norms was harshly judged. The publication of the Kinsey volumes exposed to an entire society the difference between official dogma and the actuality of people's lived experience (Gagnon, 1988). Some of the political disquiet surrounding surveys of sexual behaviour must be associated with the power of statistical norms to change moral norms, and the difficulty of maintaining ethical values in the face of evidence that a considerable proportion of the populace feels or behaves differently.

THE SURVEY METHODOLOGY

Defining the Objectives

The investigative focus of the study needed to reflect its aims, which were, as already stated, to assist in the prevention of further spread of the virus and in the planning and provision of health-care services for those already affected. Since this survey was originally expected to draw extensively on public funds, and since there was no certainty that these funds would be available on a regular basis, the research instrument was designed to provide data that would assist health-care professionals working in many areas of sexual health – psycho-sexual counselling, the prevention of sexually transmitted disease, and family planning, for example. This was the policy-driven objective but, although of most practical urgency, it was not the only one guiding the content of the survey. In addition, the hope was that the survey would stimulate further social inquiry in this field, addressing questions raised by previous research and posing fresh ones by generating new hypotheses.

The measurement objectives of the study were defined as follows:

1. To quantify components of sexual history, such as numbers of partners in particular time intervals and age at first sexual intercourse, in a representative sample of the British population
2. To measure the prevalence and distribution of different patterns of sexual orientation
3. To measure the frequency and extent of experience of particular risk practices
4. To measure attitudes towards sexual behaviour, knowledge of possible associated health risks and to examine their relationship with behaviour
5. To determine the demographic characteristics of those whose current sexual lifestyle puts them at greatest risk of HIV and other STDs
6. To assess changes in sexual lifestyles through generational comparisons of sexual histories

Development Work

The study of sexual behaviour undoubtedly presents certain methodological challenges and a number of methodological issues had to be resolved at the start of the survey. In addition to formulation of the measurement objectives, decisions needed to be taken on the mode of data collection, the size and nature of the sample and the form and content of the questionnaire. To help make these decisions, several stages of fieldwork took place during the course of a two-year development and pilot phase of the research leading to the implementation of the main stage.

Method of Data Collection

Decisions about the method of data collection centred on the breadth and complexity of the information sought, and its sensitive and personal nature. The advantages of face-to-face interviewing in terms of establishing rapport with the respondent and providing opportunities for clarification had to be balanced against the possibly greater opportunities for bias due to interviewer effect and reduced anonymity.

The amount of data to be collected favoured a personal interview survey. The length of the interviews planned (on average, just under an hour for a quarter of the sample, and 40–45 minutes for the remainder) is less acceptable for postal or telephone surveys than for face-to-face interviews. The complexity of the data to be sought, and the need for careful definition of terms and extensive filtering and routing instructions also militated against a postal method. The restriction on interview techniques, chiefly the impossibility of using show-cards, militated against a telephone survey. An additional problem with a telephone survey is that the interviewer has little control over whether the interview is conducted in comfort or out of earshot of other household members.

Both postal (Sundet *et al.*, 1988) and telephone surveys (ACSF Investigators, 1992; McQueen, 1991) on the subject have been carried out successfully in surveys of sexual behaviour in Britain and in other countries. But the high proportion of individuals without telephones in Britain, particularly young people, and the lack of an efficient sampling method for telephone interviewing, discouraged the use of this method (Collins and Sykes, 1987; Foreman and Collins, 1991). The use of personal interview seemed best suited to the specific objectives and social context of this study.

Qualitative Research to Guide Questionnaire Design

The first phase of fieldwork consisted of a series of 40 in-depth interviews carried out with men and women from a wide age range, all social classes and both urban and rural areas (Spencer *et al.*, 1988). A topic guide was used to control the content of the interviews, which were otherwise unstructured and lasted over an hour. The main aims of these exploratory interviews were to discover the extent of sexual information that members of the public were willing to disclose, the source of any discomfort, the terminology preferred and understood, and the accuracy with which people were able to recall sexual experiences, such as numbers of partners, lengths of relationships and when they occurred.

Designing the Questionnaire

Format

Having decided on a personal interview, a decision was needed on whether to use face-to-face delivery, or self-completion – or both and in what combination. This was guided by a concern to minimize interview bias, to maximize clarity, and to provide a sequence of questions that would lead to reliable responses. In making the choice, the advantages of face-to-face presentation of questions in terms of opportunities for clarification and facilitating a good rapport between respondent and interviewer were obvious. On the other hand, a self-completion component containing the more sensitive questions allowed privacy of reporting, with consequent advantages for validity. The challenge lay in finding a mix that optimally combined the merits of both.

Evidence of greater willingness to report sensitive sexual behaviours on self-administered questionnaires in other surveys was confirmed in the qualitative stage of development work, which revealed some discomfort on the part of both interviewer and respondent at face-to-face disclosure of more intimate information. The decision was taken to combine a face-to-face component with a self-completion booklet. The first part of the schedule, conducted as a face-to-face interview, included questions of a less personal nature – on general health, family circumstances, etc. – moving on to family background and then into memories of sex education and early sexual experiences. Relatively neutral questions led gently on to more intimate and sensitive ones, such as those on first heterosexual experiences and sexual orientation (responses to which were needed in order to decide whether a booklet should be given at all). Answers to the more personal questions asked in the face-to-face part of the interview were elicited through the use of show-cards.

More sensitive questions on, for example, numbers of sexual partners, frequency and nature of different sexual practices, history of contact with prostitutes and injecting drug use were included in a booklet unseen by the interviewer, sealed by the respondent and identified only by a number. Only where problems of literacy or language made self-completion impossible did the interviewer read the questions to the respondent. Respondents aged under 18 with no experience of heterosexual intercourse and those of any age with no sexual experience at all were not asked to complete the booklet.

Questions on attitudes were placed towards the end of the questionnaire, on the basis that it would be easier for respondents to report their own behaviours before making judgement on behaviour in general. The final part of the interview collected information on demographic characteristics. Two versions of the questionnaire were developed. The longer version, containing a full module of attitude questions and more detailed questions on family background and influences, first intercourse and sex education, was given to a quarter of the sample (a fully representative random subset of the total selected) and a reduced module to the remaining three-quarters.

The use of a combined instrument afforded opportunities to compare responses on items repeated in both self-completion and face-to-face interview (e.g. homosexual experience).

Wording the Questions

Of crucial importance to the acceptability and validity of the survey is the way in which questions are phrased and posed. Misreporting of sensitive personal information is often as much a function of question design as of unwillingness or inability to report (Marquis *et al.*, 1986). Discomfort with, and misunderstanding of, the language used will jeopardize both willingness to respond and the ability to produce accurate responses.

An early decision was needed on whether or not the questionnaire should be fully standardized or whether there should be some flexibility to allow respondents to use their own language. Several surveys have successfully adopted this latter formula (Kinsey *et al.*, 1948; AIMN, 1988) and researchers, including Kinsey, have cautioned against the use of a standardized questionnaire and neutral terminology, counselling instead the use of the vernacular. Our own preparatory work failed to instil confidence that the use of the respondent's own language would provide the required standardization.

Sexual behaviour is rarely spoken about publicly and as a result the language used to describe it is inadequate and inappropriate. Many terms used in the vernacular in the English language double also as terms of abuse and their use in the research setting may cause offence. The use of terms describing sexual experience, their meaning and respondents' preferences for use, were all explored in the course of the qualitative phase of development work. This revealed a wide diversity of language styles used to describe sexual behaviour, ranging from the biblical ('couple', 'copulate', 'fornicate') to the vernacular ('screw', 'fuck'), from the euphemistic ('doing it', 'having it') to the romantic ('making love'), and from lay terms ('having sex', 'sexual intercourse') to the scientific ('coitus'). Because of the variability, meanings were far from precise enough for research purposes.

The development work also unearthed a problem of misunderstanding. The meaning of many terms – 'vaginal sex', 'oral sex', 'penetrative sex', 'heterosexual' – were unclear to a sizeable enough number of people to threaten substantially the overall validity of response. A starting point for quantitative estimates is to ensure that common definitions are attached to specific acts. Yet there was wide variation in the meaning attached to crucial variables such as 'sexual partner' and 'having sex'. Some respondents discounted their spouse as a 'sexual partner', for example. For heterosexual respondents, the term 'having sex' was generally equated with vaginal intercourse, while homosexual respondents included in the definition a broader repertoire of sexual acts.

In the qualitative, in-depth interviews, respondents were asked to state explicitly their preferences for terms and style of language. A general consensus emerged for use of fairly formal terms ('sexual intercourse', 'penis', 'vagina', etc.) with explanations provided where necessary. There was some evidence of discomfort on the part of respondents and interviewers alike with the use of the vernacular. The decision was therefore to use standard neutral terms throughout the questionnaire, both in the face-to-face interview and the self-completion booklet, with a glossary. Terms were defined not simply according to dictionary definitions, but in concrete practical terms. For example, 'partners' were defined as 'people who have had sex together just once, or a few times, or as regular partners, or as married partners'. (The text of the glossary can be found in full on pp. xiii–xv.) In the face-to-face section of the interview schedule, interviewers were provided with explanations to offer to respondents.

Questionnaire Piloting

Draft versions of the structured questionnaire were tested in several rounds of small-scale pilots. These pilot stages enabled the questionnaire to be refined in readiness for the feasibility survey and provided valuable experience which was to guide other aspects of the study, such as introducing the survey on the doorstep, wording introductory letters and training interviewers.

Reliability and Validity

Attempts at obtaining quantitative data on sexual behaviour must rely on self-reports and there are few opportunities for checking information obtained against that from other sources. For these reasons the need to ensure reliability (the potential of the research instrument to replicate the results, and the extent to which findings are generalizable to the population as a whole) and validity (whether the question measures what is intended to be measured) were paramount in designing the research instrument.

Two important and related aspects of reliability and validity are the twin problems of veracity and recall. One of the chief concerns voiced over the legitimacy of value of research in this area of behaviour is whether people will give honest responses. Yet the problem is not exclusive to research into sexual behaviour. Problems relating to people's ability to report reliably and accurately beset investigation into many aspects of human behaviour. Topics on which people might be tempted to give less than honest replies include drinking and smoking behaviour, frequency of having a bath or shower, disclosure of earnings, views on racial minorities, etc. (Belson, 1981). Researchers display few reservations about investigating these areas of behaviour on the grounds of doubtful disclosure.

Nevertheless this is an area in which the presence of an interviewer effect could threaten validity of response. Some of the behaviours respondents were asked to reveal are not only socially disapproved, but are actually illegal in this country (anal sex between a man and a woman, for example). A guarantee of confidentiality can also do much to ensure veracity of response. Reassuring respondents of the confidentiality of the survey was of greatest importance in relation to the self-completion booklet which contained the more intimate and personal questions. A non-judgemental approach on the part of the interviewer and a guarantee of confidentiality were also essential. A firm understanding on the part of the respondent of the urgent need for the data and the credentials and integrity of the originators also does much to overcome this problem. In this respect the introduction was made easier by a reference to health and AIDS and the need for the information.

The use of neutral questions, the avoidance of stigmatizing labels and judgemental questions also aided candid disclosure. Finally, the authority of the funding and investigative agencies was significant in motivating honesty. Respondents were asked, at the end of the in-depth interview, whether they had answered truthfully and whether they believed others would do so, and the majority claimed that they themselves had done so because of the urgent need for the data and the credentials of the originators.

The problem of accuracy of recall, in common with that of veracity, is not exclusive to research into sexual behaviour. Social-survey researchers regularly rely for their data on the memories of respondents. The two problems are often related since forgetting may be as much a process of active blocking as passive memory decay, and so the problem responds to the same kinds of methodological devices designed to deal with the problem of honesty.

Large-scale quantitative surveys have, however, particular limitations in eliciting data that is difficult to recall. Recall can be more a process of gradual reminiscence than instant recollection, and techniques involving a slow, careful process of retrieval are more likely to facilitate this. Design features that can facilitate the process of recall included scheduling the question order in such a way that the early section includes a number of life-stage questions ('When did you first . . . ?'), providing respondents with a framework in which to locate less easily recalled experiences and triggering associations between life events. The feasibility survey provided the opportunity to experiment with some of these strategies.

Feasibility Study

A feasibility study developed from the qualitative and pilot work was carried out by SCPR to assess the acceptability of the survey, the extent to which it would produce valid and reliable results, and the sample size needed to obtain accurate estimates of minority behaviours. This was a large-scale test of the instrument and sampling strategy, the target being an achieved sample of around 1000 interviews. The design was a multi-stage random sample stratified by socio-economic characteristics of the neighbourhood within the Registrar General's Standard Regions (Acorn groupings). Each address was approached by an interviewer and all members of the household aged 16–59 enumerated. From this, one individual was chosen by a random selection procedure and invited for interview. The target response rate (65%) was achieved and experiments on question wording and order successfully resolved the remaining design dilemmas. The results, which included extensive searches of internal and external consistency, reported in some detail elsewhere (Wellings *et al.*, 1990), formed the basis of the application for funding of the main study.

Sample Size and Type

A major criticism of surveys that have depended on volunteer samples is that they may self-select according to the variable under investigation, in this case sexual behaviour, and this is especially likely where there may be sensitivity surrounding the subject-matter. A random sample reduces the likelihood of this occurring and also ensures that the sample has a similar structure to that of the general population in terms of key demographic variables such as age, gender and social class.

A further sampling consideration concerned the aims of the survey, one of which was to provide reliable estimates of the prevalence of relatively uncommon behaviours, such as paying for sex, injecting drugs, etc. On the basis of random sampling, adequate precision was required to estimate prevalence of behaviours as uncommon as one in a hundred even within subgroups of the population. These considerations pointed to a need for a general population sample, randomly selected from a reliable sampling frame, with a target of around 20,000 achieved interviews, and this was confirmed by feasibility study findings.

A key consideration concerned the lower and upper limits of the age range of the sample. A lower age range of 16 was agreed on the assumption (borne out by the feasibility study) that a sizeable proportion of young adults would already be sexually experienced, representing an important group for health education targeting. The questionnaire was, nevertheless, carefully designed to protect sexually inexperienced respondents from being asked questions that were not relevant to them.

A decision relating to an upper age limit was more difficult. Qualitative work had shown that older people found the subject more intrusive and were less willing than younger people to agree to be interviewed. This was borne out by the fact that the response rate in the feasibility study among the oldest eligible age group

(45–59) was slightly below average. The decision to impose a cut-off point of 59 years for inclusion in the survey was also guided by the measurement objectives of the survey. The feasibility survey revealed more difficulties of recall and co-operation among older people but, more importantly, many of the topics for which data were collected are known not to affect older people greatly. Sexually transmitted infections are rarely found among older people, and problems of infertility and unwanted pregnancy no longer affect older women at least. Intrusion into this personal area of life was therefore less justified for older people, and excluding them allowed concentration of resources on the groups of most urgent concern at the present time.

Sampling Frame

The selection of personal interview as the data collection method narrowed the choice of sampling frame to a choice between the Electoral Register and the Post Office small-users Postcode Address File (PAF), each of which has advantages and disadvantages (Lynn and Lievesley, 1992). The Electoral Register (ER), a list of individuals eligible to vote in the UK, is available for use approximately six months after collection of the information. Because of the estimated 10% change in registrations each year due to deaths, new entrants and home-movers (Butcher, 1988; OPCS, 1987), it quickly becomes outdated. The coverage of addresses is incomplete and young people, members of ethnic minorities and the highly mobile are more likely to live at addresses not on the Register (Todd and Butcher, 1982). Recently, the number of registered electors has fallen, due possibly to failure to register because of fears about the Community Charge.

The small-users Postcode Address File, a regularly updated computer-held file of largely residential addresses, is free from problems of failure to register or of mobility of residents; coverage of residential addresses is superior to that of the ER and the few omissions are more likely to be random and not biased in any particular direction (Dodd, 1987) and so are less likely to be directly related to any of the variables of interest to the study. The major disadvantage of the PAF is that it contains no information about individuals resident at each address; that is, it does not list the names of residents or how many there are. Consequently addresses can be selected only with equal probabilities. A sampling procedure that requires that only one person per household is interviewed means that those who live alone have a higher chance of selection than do individuals who live in larger households. In order to derive population estimates from such a sampling strategy it becomes essential to weight the data to take account of these differential selection probabilities.

Both the PAF and the ER exclude the homeless and the PAF also excludes some elements of the institutionalized population. However, less than 1% of the population is resident in institutions and the majority of these are elderly people who would not have been eligible for this survey. The PAF was chosen for this survey mainly on the grounds of its superior coverage of private residential addresses. The biased coverage of the ER would be particularly serious in this case because sexual behaviour is likely to be associated with the known correlates of coverage such as age and mobility.

The Main Stage of the Survey

Following the development work, a number of tasks remained to be completed before the main stage could begin. The sample design needed to be specified, the fieldwork organized and conducted, and procedures established for preparing data for analysis. The quality of the data needed to be assessed, particularly with regard to the response rate and the representativeness of the achieved sample.

Fieldwork

SCPR-trained interviewers were briefed at a series of briefing conferences. Interviewing began in May 1990 and was completed in November 1991. Nearly two-thirds of the work was completed before the end of 1990. The last few months of fieldwork (July–November 1991) were needed to complete the last 10% of the work, which included reissues and addresses that were difficult to reach or contact.

Interviewers approached listed addresses to establish whether the address was residential and occupied, and if so whether the household contained an eligible resident (i.e., aged 16–59). One individual was randomly selected from households with more than one member using a standard technique for this purpose, the Kish Grid (Kish, 1949). The survey was fully explained to the selected individual and briefing documents left with them describing the survey. Interviewers were instructed to make at least four calls to each address, but in practice often made many more. Most of the total of 488 interviewers who carried out the 18,876 interviews were women (421), and this reflected the preferences of the majority of both men and women at the qualitative stage of fieldwork (Spencer *et al.*, 1988). However, respondents who seemed doubtful about taking part were offered a choice of gender of interviewer. Standard quality-control procedures used by SCPR in any survey were carried out, including supervision of interviewers in the field, random checkbacks on selected interviews, careful editing of questionnaires, etc. All completed questionnaires were subjected to a thorough clerical editing and coding stage before the data were keyed into computer. The edit inspection looked for missing information and inconsistencies, which were dealt with. Once clerical editing was complete and the data keyed to computer, a computer edit programme was applied, checking for missing data, correct routing and for correct code ranges for each variable.

Response Rate

The response rate for any survey is important in assessing the representativeness of the sample and hence the extent to which the survey findings can be generalized to the population as a whole. Refusal to take part is especially important if it is related to the subject-matter of the survey. At the point of contact every sample is voluntary since respondents cannot be forced to take part, but every effort was made to increase the response rate in order to enhance reliability. As noted above, repeated calls were made to addresses in order to secure interviews, and those that were not achieved by one interviewer were reissued to another in the hope, and often realization, of eventual success.

One implication of using the small-user Postcode Address File is that a proportion of addresses will be out of scope or will be the homes of individuals who are not eligible to take part. Figure 1.1 represents the process, by which the final sample was arrived at. Of the 50,010 addresses selected, 5,980 (12.0%) were found to be businesses and non-residential institutions or residential but vacant, derelict or not yet built, and so out of scope. At 14,228 (28.5%) there were no eligible residents, i.e., aged 16–59. Removing these out-of-scope and ineligible addresses left 29,802 potentially eligible addresses constituting the basic response-rate denominator. Of these no contact was made at 1,027 (3.5%) after repeated calls, and at 1,761 (5.9%) the person with whom contact was made refused to give information needed to allow the selection of a household member to take place. At 562 (1.9%) addresses the selected person was ill or away or unable to speak English, and at 7,517 (25.2%) the selected person refused to participate. Refusal was not necessarily direct. In some cases the selected respondent broke appointments and could not be recontacted (often tantamount to a refusal); other refusals were made by proxy on behalf of the selected person by another. Interviews were completed with 18,876 respondents, giving an overall response rate of 63.3%. When adjusted for the likely proportions of addresses with no eligible resident at addresses where no contact could be made, the response rate is 64.7%. In households where an eligible respondent could be identified and interviewed the acceptance rate was 71.5% (18,876 out of 26,393).

Weighting

Two sources of bias were likely to result from the choice of sampling method. Since the sample was selected from a register of addresses, individuals in single-occupation dwellings were more likely to be selected than those living in multi-occupation (though in fact this bias was limited since those who live alone are more likely to be over the age of 60 and therefore ineligible for inclusion). The second source of potential bias resulted from differences in response to the survey across different geographical areas – in rural as opposed to urban areas, for example. The response rate was lowest in London.

These potential sources of error in providing population estimates were dealt with by weighting the data; firstly by constructing

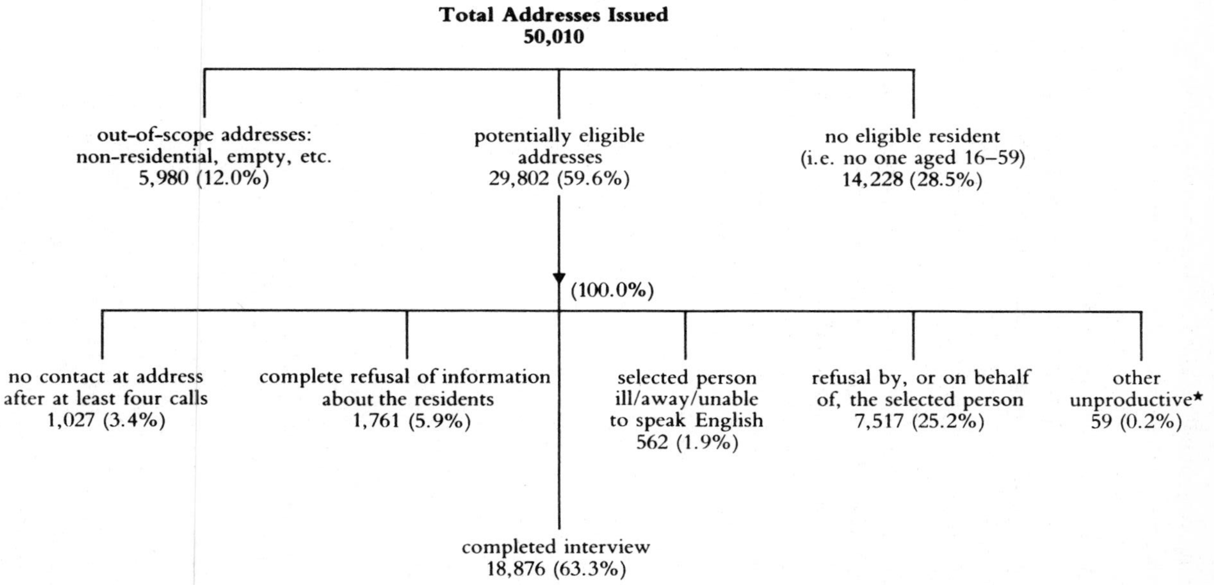

*lost in post, rejected as unusable

Figure 1.1 Outcome of sampling. Source: Address Record Form

weights proportional to the number of eligible residents per household, and secondly by applying a regional weight directly proportional to the response rate for each of 31 regions stratified into population density bands. The final weight was a product of the regional weight and the household size weight scaled to the actual sample size, 18,876. All study results are presented on weighted data; the quoted bases are rounded to the nearest whole number.

Population Representativeness

Comparative data are not available for the variables at the core of this study (i.e., population-based estimates of sexual behaviour), so that there are no means of assessing the extent to which the sample population is representative of the total population in terms of sexual lifestyle. Nevertheless, the extent to which the achieved sample is representative of the general population in terms of age, social class, marital status and ethnicity, etc., was easily assessed using available demographic data. Compared with the Census figures for 1991 (OPCS, 1993), a slight deficit of men is found overall. Comparing the age distribution, small differences were observed (Figure 1.2). The most marked deficit was an under-representation of the oldest age group of men and women, aged 55–59 balanced by over-representation of those in younger age groups. A higher refusal rate on the part of older people, particularly older men, is common to other studies from other countries and confirms the decision to restrict the survey to those under the age of 60.

Otherwise, the demographic characteristics of the sample corresponded well with those of census estimates. The achieved sample was compared with other Office of Population Censuses and Surveys (OPCS) data sets for ethnic group, marital status and socio-economic group.

Internal and External Validity

Because sexual behaviour takes place largely in private, there are few possibilities for objective verification. In addition, disclosures may include acts that are socially disapproved if not actually illegal. One measure of data validity is that of internal consistency between

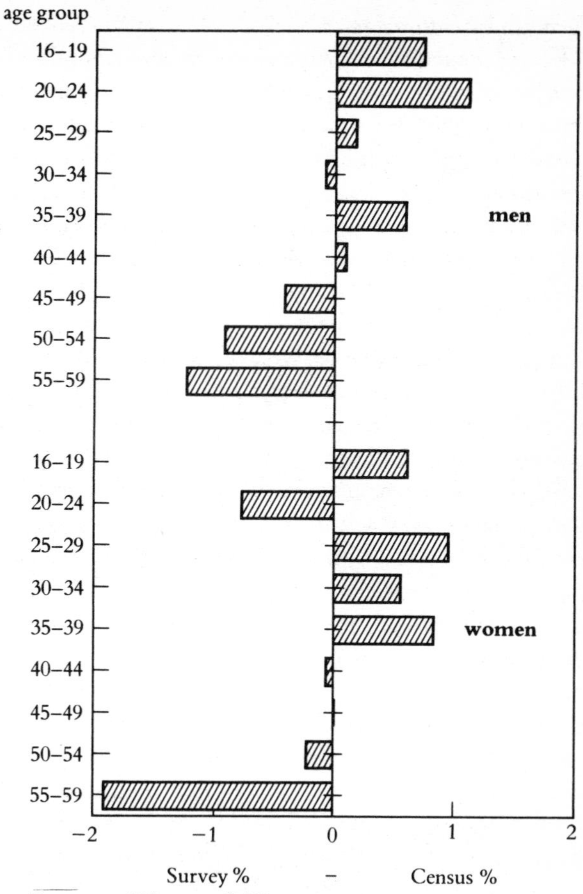

Bases = men 8384; women 10,942

Figure 1.2 Age distribution of survey sample compared with data from the 1991 Census

responses to different questions in the questionnaire. Internal consistency checks are particularly useful in checking on recall, and the consistency with which respondents completed questions was encouraging. In all, 185 inconsistency checks were carried out on each questionnaire. In the region of 80% had no inconsistencies at all (Wadsworth, *et al.*, 1993).

A check on the external validity of data from social surveys can be made by comparing responses with independent data sets, such as STD clinic attendance, abortion statistics, etc. One such check concerned height, weight and body mass, which respondents to this survey described in whatever units they chose. Comparison of these data with those from a survey in which qualified nurses weighed and measured people using standardized scales (Cox, 1987) revealed only small discrepancies. Comparison of national data on rates of therapeutic abortion again showed a close approximation between the two sets of data (Wadsworth, *et al.*, 1993).

This study, like any other large-scale survey, has emerged from a lengthy period of design and development. Unlike other studies, there was doubt about whether it could or should be done. But the achieved sample is broadly representative of the population of Great Britain aged 16–59 in terms of standard demographic variables. The response rate is similar to that of other surveys, including those on sexual behaviour. Internal and external validity checks and comparison of self-completion and face-to-face approaches were used to validate the data and these showed the design to be robust. As with all social surveys, measurement error and possible bias cannot be ruled out. Where problems of measurement error arise, these have been discussed in the relevant chapters.

Note: the methodology is described more fully by Johnson *et al.* (1994).

REFERENCES

ACSF Investigators (1992). 'AIDS and Sexual Behaviour in France', *Nature*, 360: 407–9

AIMN (1988). *AIDS in a Multicultural Neighbourhood.* Bayview-Hunter's Point Foundation for Community Improvement, 6025 Third Street, San Francisco, California

Aldhous, P. (1992). 'French Venture where US Fear to Tread', *Science*, 257: 25

Anderson, R. M., G. F. Medley, R. M. May, and A. M. Johnson (1986). 'A Preliminary Study of the Transmission Dynamics of the Human Immunodeficiency Virus (HIV), the Causative Agent of AIDS', *Journal of Maths, Applied Medicine and Biology, 3*, 229–63

Belson, W. A. (1981). *The Design and Understanding of Survey Questions*. London: Gower

Bone, M. (1978). *Family Planning Services: Changes and Effects*. London: HMSO

Bone, M. (1986). 'Trends in Single Women's Sexual Behaviour in Scotland', *Population Trends*, 43 (spring 1986)

Butcher, R. (1988). 'The use of the Postcode Address File as a sampling frame', *Statistician*, 37: 15–24

Carballo, M., J. Cleland, M. Carael, and G. Albrecht (1989). 'A Cross National Study of Patterns of Sexual Behaviour', *Journal of Sex Research*, 26, 3, 287–99

Chesser, E. (1956). *The Sexual, Marital and Family Relationships of the English Woman*. London: Hutchinson's Medical Press

Cochran, W. G., F. Mostelier, and J. W. Tukey (1953). 'Statistical Problems of the Kinsey Report', *Journal of the American Statistical Association, 48*, 673–716

Collins, M., and W. Sykes (1987). 'The Problems of Non-coverage and Unlisted Numbers in Telephone Surveys in Britain', *Journal of the Royal Statistical Society*, series A, 150 (3), 241–53

Cox, B. (1987). 'Body Measurement (Heights, Weights, Girth, etc.)', chapter 4 in B. D. Cox, M. Blaxter, A. L. S. Buckle *et al.* (eds), *The Health and Lifestyle Survey*. London: Health Promotion Research Trust

Coxon, A. (1988). 'The Numbers Game', in P. Aggleton and H. Homans (eds), *Social Aspects of AIDS*. Lewes: Falmer Press

Dodd, T. (1987). 'A Further Investigation into the Coverage of the Postcode Address File', in *Survey Methodology Bulletin 21*. London: OPCS

Dunnell, K. (1979). *Family Formation 1976*. London: HMSO

England, L. (1950). 'A British Sex Survey', *International Journal of Sexology*, 3: 148–56

Farrell, C. (1978). *My Mother Said . . . The Way Young People Learn about Sex and Birth Control*. London: Routledge and Kegan Paul

Fay, R. E., C. F. Turner, A. D. Klassen, and J. H. Gagnon (1989). 'Prevalence and Patterns of Same Gender Sexual Contact among Men', *Science, 243*, 338–48

Ford, C. S., and F. A. Beach (1952). *Patterns of Sexual Behaviour.* London: Eyre and Spottiswoode

Foreman, J. and M. Collins (1991). 'The Viability of Random Digit Dialling in the UK', *Journal of the Market Research Society*, 33, 3, 218–27

Freud, S. (1953). 'Introductory Lectures on Psychoanalysis', lecture 12 in James Strachey, (ed.), *The Standard Edition of the Complete Psychological Works of Sigmund Freud*, vol. 16, p. 323. London: Hogarth Press and the Institute of Psychoanalysis, 24 vols (1953–74).

Gagnon, J. H. (1988). 'Sex Research and Sexual Conduct in the Era of AIDS', *Journal of AIDS*, 1: 593–601

Gorer, G. (1971). *Sex and Marriage in England Today.* London: Nelson

Hethcote, H. W., and J. A. Yorke (1984). 'Gonorrhoea: Transmission Dynamics and Control. Lecture Notes', *Biomathematics*, *56*, 1–105

Johnson, A. M. (1988). 'Social and Behavioural Aspects of the HIV Epidemic – A Review', *Journal of Royal Statistical Society,* series A, 151, 99–114

Johnson, A. M. (1992). 'Epidemiology of HIV Infection in Women', in F. D. Johnstone (ed.), *Bailliere's Clinical Obstetrics and Gynaecology*, 6th edn, pp. 13–31. London: Bailliere Tindall

Johnson, A. M., J. Wadsworth, P. Elliott, *et al.* (1989). 'A Pilot Study of Sexual Lifestyle in a Random Sample of the Population of Great Britain', *AIDS*, *3*, 135–41

Johnson, A. M., J. Wadsworth, K. Wellings, and J. Field (1994). Sexual Attitudes and Lifestyles. Oxford: Blackwell Scientific

Kinsey, A. C., W. B. Pomeroy, and C. E. Martin (1948). *Sexual Behaviour in the Human Male.* Philadelphia: W. B. Saunders

Kinsey, A. C., W. B. Pomeroy, C. E. Martin, and P. H. Gebhard (1953). *Sexual Behaviour in the Human Female.* Philadelphia: W. B. Saunders

Kish, L. (1949). 'A Procedure for Objective Respondent Selection within the Household', *Journal of the American Statistical Association*, 44: 380–87

Lanval, M. (1950). *An Inquiry into the Intimate Lives of Women.* New York: Cadillac Publishing Company

in Great Britain. London: Social and Community Planning Research

McManus, T. J., and M. McEvoy (1987). 'Some Aspects of Male Homosexual Behaviour in the United Kingdom, *British Journal of Sexual Medicine*, 14, 110–20

McQueen, D. V., B. J. Robertson, L. Nisbet (1991). *Data-Update: AIDS-Related Behaviour, Knowledge and Attitudes, Provisional data*. No. 27. RUHBC, University of Edinburgh

Marquis, K. H., S. Marquis, M. Pollitch (1986). 'Response Bias and Reliability in Sensitive Topic Surveys', *Journal of the American Statistical Association*, 394: 381–9

Masters, W., and V. Johnson (1966). *Human Sexual Response*. London: Churchill

Masters, W., and V. Johnson (1970). *Human Sexual Inadequacy*. London: Churchill

Melbye, M., and R. J. Biggar (1992). 'Interactions between Persons at Risk for AIDS and the General Population in Denmark', *American Journal of Epidemiology*, *135*, 593–602

Office of Population Censuses and Surveys (1985). *General Household Survey 1983*. London: OPCS

Office of Population Censuses and Surveys (1987). *Central Postcode Directory Guide*. Titchfield, Hants: OPCS

Office of Population Censuses and Surveys (1993). *1991 Census. Age, Sex and Marital Status*. London: HMSO

Potts, M., R. Anderson, and M.-C. Boily (1991). 'Slowing the Spread of Human Immunodeficiency Virus in Developing Countries', *Lancet*, *338*, 608–12

Reinisch, J. M., M. Ziemba-Davis, and S. A. Sanders (1990). 'Sexual Behaviour and AIDS: Lessons from Art and Sex Research', in B. Voeller, J. M. Reinisch, and M. Gottlieb (eds), *AIDS and Sex: An Integrated Biomedical and Biobehavioural Approach*, pp. 37–80. Oxford: Oxford University Press

Reiss, I. L. (1986). *Journey into Sexuality: An Exploratory Voyage*. New Jersey: Prentice Hall

Report of a Working Group (Chairman D. Cox) (1989). *Short term prediction of HIV infection and AIDS in England and Wales*. London: HMSO

Report of a Working Group (Chairman N. E. Day) (1990). 'AIDS in England and Wales to end 1993. Projections using Data to end September 1989', *Communicable Diseases Report*, 1–12

Schofield, M. (1965). *The Sexual Behaviour of Young People*. London: Longman

Schofield, M. (1973). *The Sexual Behaviour of Young Adults*. London: Allen Lane

Spencer, L., A. Faulkner, and J. Keegan (1988). *Talking about Sex*. London: Social and Community Planning Research

Sundet, J. M., I. L. Kvalem, P. Magnus, and L. S. Bakketeig (1988). 'Prevalence of Risk-prone Behaviour in the General Population of Norway', in A. F. Fleming, M. Carballo and D. F. Fitzsimons (eds), *The Global Impact of AIDS*. London: Alan R. Liss

Todd, J., and B. Butcher (1982). *Electoral Registration in 1981*. London: OPCS

Wadsworth, J., J. Field, A. M. Johnson, S. Bradshaw, and K. Wellings (1993). 'Methodology of the National Survey of Sexual Attitudes and Lifestyles', *Journal of the Royal Statistical Society*, series A, 156:3: 407–21

Weeks, J. (1981). *Sex, Politics and Society: The Regulation of Sexuality since 1800*. New York: Longman

Weeks, J. (1985). *Sexuality and its Discontents*. London: Routledge and Kegan Paul

Wellings, K., J. Field, J. Wadsworth, A. M. Johnson, R. M. Anderson, and S. A. Bradshaw (1990). Sexual Lifestyles under Scrutiny', *Nature*, *348*, 276–8

Winkelstein, W., D. M. Lyman, N. Padian, *et al.* (1987). 'Sexual Practices and Risk of Infection by the Human Immunodeficiency Virus', *Journal of American AIDS*, *257*, 321–5

Wodak, A., and A. Moss (1990). 'HIV Infection and Injecting Drug Users: From Epidemiology to Public Health', *AIDS*, *4*, S105–9

CHAPTER 2

First Intercourse between Men and Women

There seems little doubt that first sexual intercourse remains an event of immense social and personal significance. The status of virginity, which is still of considerable cultural and legal importance, is technically defined in terms of experience of sexual intercourse. The apparent ease with which individuals are able to recall the first occasion on which coitus takes place (fewer than 1% of respondents were unable to do so) also testifies to the fact that it is a memorable event. In addition, the event has clear health implications, since it marks initiation into the sexual act which, unprotected, carries a risk of adverse outcomes such as unplanned pregnancy and sexually transmitted infection. The importance of collecting robust data on early sexual experience to guide provision of services and the design of educational and preventive strategies is particularly important in Britain, where levels of teenage pregnancy are higher than in other countries in Europe (Jones *et al.*, 1985).

In relation to early sexual experience, the occurrence of first intercourse – its timing, the circumstances that surround it, and its consequences – is therefore of central interest in the context of this study. At the same time, this one event alone is likely to be an unreliable indicator of the onset of sexual activity generally. Sexual behaviour involves a variety of practices that do not necessarily culminate in intercourse. Sexual practices that may be seen as preliminary to intercourse for many older adults may, for younger people, be an end in themselves. To reflect this, data were collected on age at first sexual experience as well as age at first sexual intercourse. This chapter describes only first heterosexual experiences. The timing of homosexual experiences is discussed in Chapter 5.

QUESTIONS ASKED

Two questions were asked in the face-to-face section of the questionnaire eliciting reports of early sexual behaviour. Respondents were handed show-cards on which were printed the questions:

How old were you when you *first* had sexual intercourse with someone of the opposite sex, or hasn't this happened?

and

How old were you when you first had *any* type of experience of a sexual kind – for example, kissing, cuddling, petting – with someone of the opposite sex (or hasn't this happened either)?

In addition, respondents were asked the age of their partner at the time, whether it was also their first time and whether contraception was used. Additional questions probing the nature of the relationship, the circumstances surrounding the event and feelings about its occurrence were asked of only those receiving the longer version of the questionnaire. This accounts for the major differences in bases throughout this chapter.

It was not one of the aims of this survey to explore the extent and circumstances of sexual intercourse occurring in childhood, and the research instrument used would have been inadequate and inappropriate to this task. Consequently, although respondents were initially asked when they had sexual intercourse for the first time *ever*, they were asked to confine subsequent accounts to their first experience of intercourse *after* the age of 13. (1.2% of men and 0.4% of women reported experiencing sexual intercourse before the age of 13.) All the following analysis in this chapter refers to intercourse that took place after the age of 13.

AGE AT FIRST INTERCOURSE

By Current Age

Since first intercourse occurs only once in a lifetime, analysis of the data from successive birth cohorts in the sample allows secular trends to be described with some confidence. Experience of the event cannot change throughout a person's lifetime (though reflections on and attitudes towards the reporting of it can). The existing literature on the subject provided evidence of major changes in age of first sexual intercourse during recent decades (Schofield, 1965; Dunnell, 1979; Farrell, 1978). Three trends were identified: a progressive reduction over the years in the age at which first intercourse occurs, an increase in the proportion of young women who have had sexual intercourse before the age of sexual consent, and a convergence in the behaviour of men and women.

[*a*] *The Decline in the Age at which First Intercourse Occurs*

As Table 2.1 and Figure 2.1 clearly show, one of the most striking trends to emerge from these data is the strong relationship between current age and age at first intercourse. Age at first intercourse decreases with the current age of the respondent, becoming successively lower in the more recent birth cohorts.

Analysis by five-year age groups (Table 2.1) shows clearly the pattern of decline. Among women aged 55–59 at the time of interview, born between 1931 and 1935, the median age at first sexual intercourse was 21 years. For women aged 50–54, born between 1936 and 1940, it falls to 20 years and further still to 19 for those born between 1941 and 1945. Thereafter, the median age continues to decline with decreasing current age, though less dramatically. The median age at first intercourse for the youngest birth cohort, those aged 16–24 and born between 1966 and 1975, was 17.[1]

[1] Median rather than mean ages have been used throughout this chapter. The mean, particularly for the younger age group, may be artificially lowered since it can be based only on reports from those who have already had sexual intercourse and excludes those who have not yet done so. Further, for a respondent reporting first

	1st	median	3rd	*base*
		men		
16–19	15	17	19	*551*
20–24	15	17	18	*924*
25–29	16	17	19	*1212*
30–34	16	17	19	*1128*
35–39	16	18	20	*1076*
40–44	16	18	20	*1035*
45–49	16	18	21	*779*
50–54	17	19	22	*646*
55–59	18	20	23	*629*
		women		
16–19	16	17	19	*704*
20–24	16	17	18	*1163*
25–29	16	18	19	*1673*
30–34	16	18	19	*1563*
35–39	17	18	20	*1355*
40–44	17	19	21	*1214*
45–49	18	19	21	*971*
50–54	18	20	22	*972*
55–59	19	21	23	*994*

Table 2.1 Quartiles for age at first heterosexual intercourse by age group. Source: Interview Question 19a

Thus the median age at which the youngest women in the sample, aged 16–19, experienced first sexual intercourse was some four years earlier than for those born four decades earlier. This striking trend is also marked for men: the median age at first intercourse for men aged 16–19 is 17, 3 years earlier than for those aged 55–59.

---

intercourse at, for example, 16, the event could have occurred at any time during the 12 months after the sixteenth birthday, and without more precise information the mean cannot be reliably calculated.

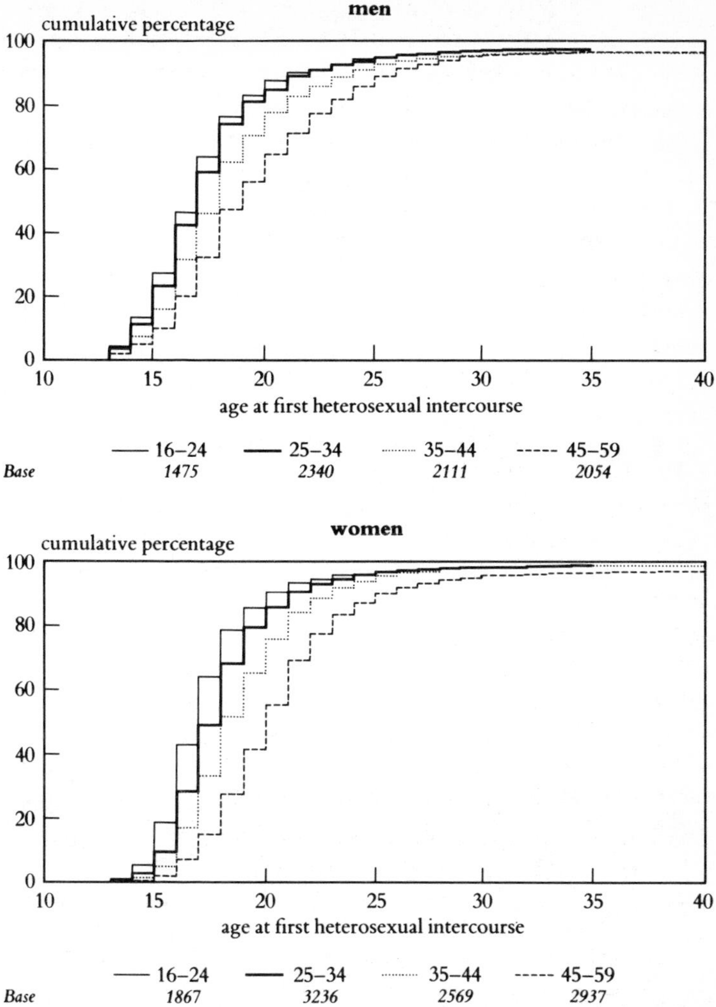

Figure 2.1 Cumulative proportions of age at first heterosexual intercourse after age 13 by age group. Source: Interview Question 19

Data from surveys of young people carried out in the early 1960s and 1970s (Schofield, 1965, 1973; Farrell, 1978) show a similar pattern, as do all age surveys in which comparisons of the behaviour of successive birth cohorts are possible (Dunnell, 1979; Bone, 1986). These surveys provide the opportunity for a validation exercise, in so far as attempts can be made to assess the degree of correspondence between women's recollections in this survey and those collected contemporaneously in others. In 1964, 14% of the boys and 5% of the girls in Schofield's sample of young people aged 15–19 reported having had sexual intercourse by the age of 16. In the corresponding sample aged 41–45 at the time of interview in this survey, 14% of the men and 4% of the women had had sexual intercourse by the age of 16. Similarly, 31% of the boys and 12% of the girls in Farrell's sample of young people aged 15–19 in 1974 reported having had intercourse by the age of 16, compared with 21% of the men and 9% of the women in the corresponding age group (those aged 31–35) in our sample. (Farrell notes a possible tendency for boys to exaggerate their sexual experience at the time of reporting.)

The dramatic decrease in age at first intercourse over recent decades is equally marked for age at first sexual experience (Table 2.2); the median age has dropped from 16 to 14 for women and from 15 to 13 for men through successive age cohorts from 45–59 to 16–24. The data indicate that sexual experience in the broader sense tends to precede sexual intercourse by some time. While only 2.7% of the women and 9.3% of the men of all ages had experienced sexual intercourse before the age of 15, 33.8% and 55.8% respectively reported having had some sexual experience before this age. Not surprisingly, as Table 2.3 shows, the age at which first sexual experience occurs tends to be strongly associated with age at first intercourse. For men whose first sexual experience occurred before the age of 13, the median age at first intercourse was 16, compared with a median of 19 for those for whom it occurred between 16 and 17.

The time period between first experience and first intercourse seems to be diminishing over time, more markedly for women than men (Table 2.2). The median time lapse between the two events for women in the age group 45–59 was 4 years or more, 2 years longer than for women aged 16–24, and for men 4 years for those in the oldest age group, and 3 for those in the youngest.

	median age at: first experience (1)	*base*	first intercourse (2)	*base*	median timelag in years between 1 and 2	*base*
men						
16–24	13	*1462*	17	*1475*	3	*1397*
25–34	14	*2336*	17	*2340*	3	*2299*
25–44	14	*2105*	18	*2111*	3	*2070*
45–59	15	*2046*	19	*2054*	4	*2000*
women						
16–24	14	*1842*	17	*1867*	2	*1795*
25–34	15	*3223*	18	*3236*	2	*3192*
35–44	15	*2558*	18	*2569*	3	*2537*
45–59	16	*2916*	20	*2937*	4	*2822*

Table 2.2 Age at first experience and first intercourse by age group.
Source: Interview Question 19

age at first experience	1st	median	3rd	*base*
men				
< 13 yrs	15	16	18	*1982*
13–15	16	17	18	*3571*
16–17	18	19	21	*1452*
18–19	19	21	24	*461*
20–24	22	24	26	*229*
25+ yrs	26	28	30	*83*
women				
< 13 yrs	15	17	18	*818*
13–15	16	17	19	*4599*
16–17	17	19	21	*3373*
18–19	19	20	22	*1103*
20–24	21	22	24	*432*
25+ yrs	26	28	33	*88*

Table 2.3 Quartiles for age at first intercourse by age at first experience.
Source: Interview Question 19

[b] *First Intercourse before the Age of 16*

Alongside a decline in the median age of first intercourse can be seen a parallel increase in the proportion of young people experiencing sexual intercourse before the age of 16 (Figure 2.1 and Table 2.4). (16 is the age for a woman before which a man is acting unlawfully if he has sexual intercourse with her. See p. 236.)

	women		men	
	%	*base*	%	*base*
age at interview				
16–19	18.7	*971*	27.6	*827*
20–24	14.7	*1251*	23.8	*1137*
25–29	10.0	*1519*	23.8	*1126*
30–34	8.6	*1349*	23.2	*1012*
35–39	5.8	*1261*	18.4	*982*
40–44	4.3	*1277*	14.5	*1042*
45–49	3.4	*1071*	13.9	*827*
50–54	1.4	*933*	8.9	*684*
55–59	0.8	*716*	5.8	*603*

Table 2.4 First sexual intercourse before the age of 16 by current age.
Source: Interview Question 19a

A sizeable minority of young people are now sexually active before the age of 16 (Table 2.4). 18.7% of women aged 16–19 had experienced sexual intercourse before the age of 16 compared with fewer than 1% of those aged 55–59; for men the equivalent proportions are higher: 27.6% of men in the youngest age group compared with 5.8% of men aged 55–59 (Table 2.4 and Figure 2.2). Higher proportions of sexually active teenagers sometimes cited may result from estimates based on non-random samples, or calculations using a different denominator. A recent quota-sample survey of young people in the South-West of England, for example, showed 41% of young people aged 16–24 to have had intercourse before the age of 16 (Ford, 1993) but this calculation was based on young people already sexually active at the time of interview, and so cannot be

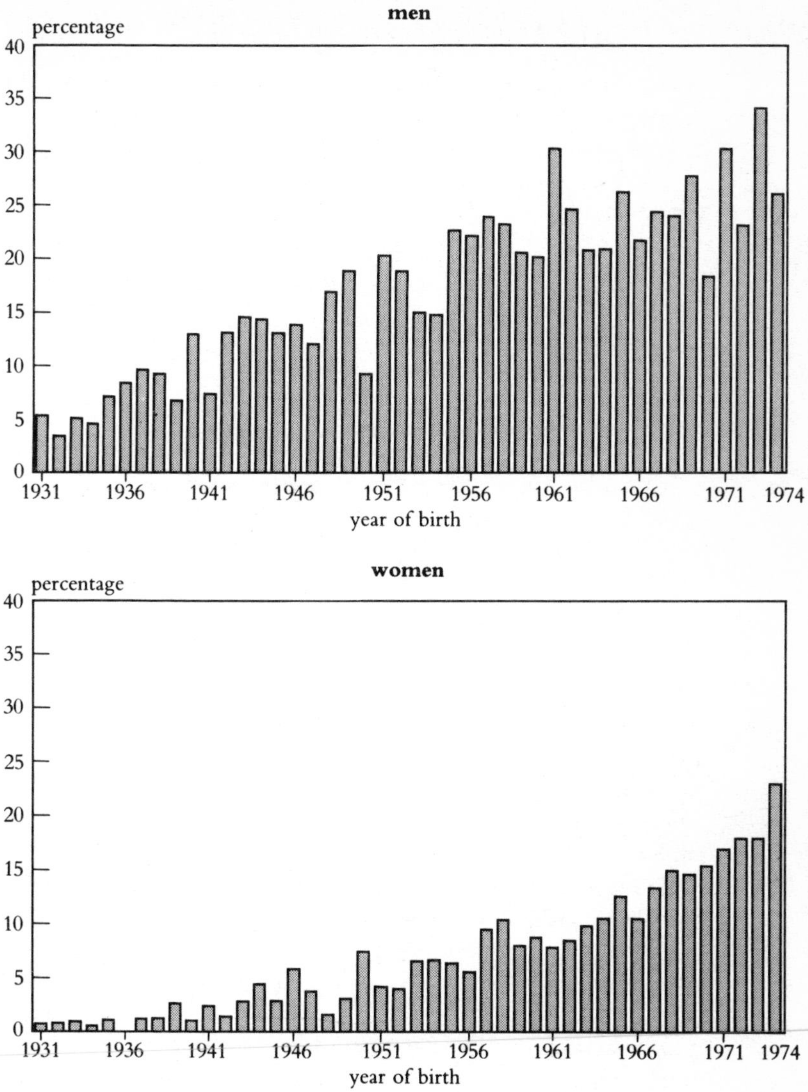

Figure 2.2 Proportion having first intercourse before 16 years of age by year of birth. Source: Interview Question 19a

extrapolated to a population including virgins. Data from a random sample of 18-year-olds in Scotland shows 24% of men and 7% of women aged 18 to have experienced intercourse before the age of 16 (West *et al.*, 1993).

[*c*] *Gender Differences in Age at First Experience*

There is a widespread belief that men differ from women in sexual behaviour, that they have a higher sex drive, lower tolerance of sexual abstinence and are more easily sexually aroused (Bancroft, 1989). However, a shift towards greater convergence between the sexes is documented in recent literature on the subject, particularly that from the US. Several studies in the past two decades have shown a decline in differences in attitudes and behaviour between men and women, towards a single standard for both (Christiansen and Gregg, 1970; Robinson and Jedlicka, 1982; Orr *et al.*, 1989).

This trend seems to be broadly confirmed in this survey, though the convergence between men and women is more apparent in the data for first intercourse than for first sexual experience (Table 2.2). First intercourse still takes place later for women than men, but the gap between the sexes has been closing in recent years. For those over the age of 25 at the time of interview, the median age for men is one year earlier than it is for women, while for those under the age of 25 the median is the same for both sexes. The gap between men and women also narrows with respect to the proportions reporting first intercourse under the age of 16 (Table 2.4). Compared with women, the proportion of men who are sexually active before 16 is higher in all age groups, but the ratio of men to women who experienced intercourse before the age of 16 has narrowed from 7:1 in the oldest age group (55–59) to 3:2 in the youngest (16–19).

The data for first intercourse for successive birth cohorts then shows a consistent pattern of decreasing age at first occurrence, together with an increase in the proportions with experience before the age of 16, and some convergence in the behaviour of men and women over time. This trend is likely to reflect a combination of maturational effects and social influences on sexual behaviour.

Although it is not possible from these data to attempt any conclusive explanation of these trends, some attempt can be made to assess the interplay between biological and cultural factors.

Biological Effects

A trend towards earlier physical maturity together with a progressive relaxation in social mores governing sexual intercourse would result in the effects of biological and cultural influences being additive. An attempt was made to separate biological-maturational from social-historical effects. Although there is no single reliable marker of sexual maturation in men, the onset of menstruation (menarche) offers a useful indicator in women. If biological readiness played a major role then some correlation between age at first intercourse and age of menarche together with a decline in the age of menarche in recent decades could be expected. In contrast to some US studies which have shown little association between age at menarche and onset of sexual activity except among black teenagers (Kantner and Zelnick, 1972; Udry *et al.*, 1986), these data show a significant correlation between the two events (Tables 2.5 and 2.6). Median age at first sexual experience and sexual intercourse for women who first menstruate at 15 or older is a year later than for those who do so under the age of 15.

Over the past century, age at menarche has declined in most developed countries. In 1900, the average age was probably around 14 years (Tanner, 1962), and it has decreased steadily since, levelling off in recent generations. These data show a small but statistically significant fall in the mean age of menarche (Table 2.7)

	1st	median	3rd	*base*
age at menarche				
10 or younger	14	15	16	*394*
11–12 years	14	15	16	*3615*
13–14 years	14	15	17	*4615*
15 or older	15	16	17	*1564*

Table 2.5 Quartiles for age at first sexual experience by age at menarche. Source: Interview Question 33b; Booklet Question 21

	1st	median	3rd	*base*
age at menarche				
10 or younger	16	18	20	*397*
11–12 years	16	18	20	*3637*
13–14 years	17	18	20	*4638*
15 or older	17	19	21	*1579*

Table 2.6 Quartiles for age at first sexual intercourse by age at menarche Source: Interview Question 33b; Booklet Question 21

	mean age at menarche	95% confidence interval	*base*
age at interview			
16–24	13.40	13.33–13.47	*2172*
25–34	13.42	13.37–13.47	*2810*
35–44	13.41	13.35–13.47	*2481*
45–59	13.54	13.48–13.60	*2606*

Table 2.7 Mean age at menarche by age group. Source: Interview Question 33b; Booklet Question 21

between the oldest age group (45–59) and women under 45.[2] 18.8% of women aged 45–59 began menstruating after their 15th birthday, compared with 12.6% of those aged 16–24. However, the percentage of women in this older age group who reported menstruating before the age of 11 was also greater than for the youngest age group (Figure 2.3).

The fall in the age of menstruation is not on a scale sufficient to explain the scale of the changes in age at first intercourse. Despite the relationship between biological readiness and age at occurrence, the decline in the age at menstruation with successive age groups is

[2] Analysis of variance showed a significant difference at the 1% level between the mean age at menarche for the age group 45–49 and the three younger age groups. Half a year was added to the reported age at menarche when the means were calculated to take account of the fact that menarche reported at age 13, for example, could have occurred at any time between the ages of 13 and 14 years.

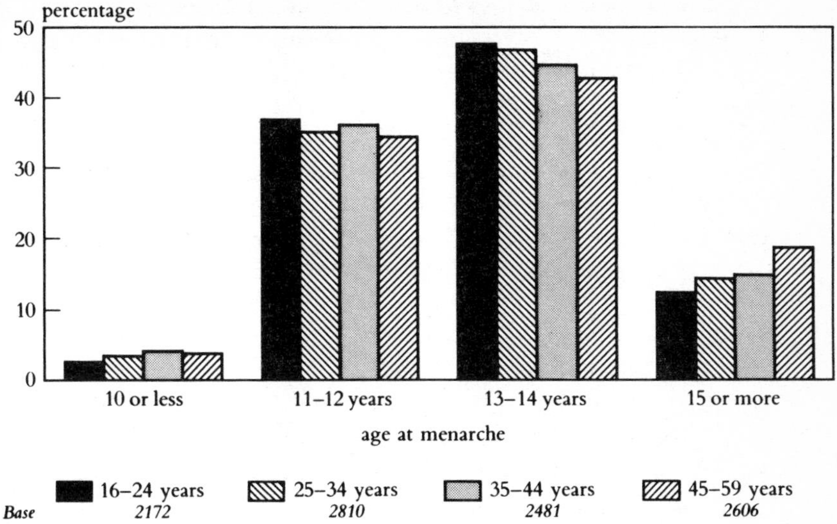

Figure 2.3 Age at menarche by age group. Source: Interview Question 33b; Booklet Question 21

not large enough to account for much of the decline in age at first intercourse in recent decades.[3]

Cultural Influences

Given the importance of social factors in determining the start of sexual experience, the historical backcloth against which these changes have taken place is of interest here. Among other things, the past three decades have seen marked changes in the employment status of women, a series of legal reforms in the 1960s liberalizing sexual behaviour (the Abortion Law Reform Act in 1967, for

[3] Combining the effect of current age and age at menarche in a life-table analysis shows that both are significant but the log rank Chi-square statistics (1213 and 64) show that the effect of current age is stronger. In a stepwise analysis current age entered the model first (Chi-square = 1213) followed by age at menarche (Chi-square = 56), indicating a strong association between current age and age at first intercourse and in addition a weaker association between age at menarche and age at first intercourse.

example), the advent of effective contraception and the extension of family planning services. Of these, the factor often held to be of paramount importance in explaining trends in first sexual intercourse is the availability of reliable birth control, in particular oral contraception.

A number of empirical studies carried out in the 1970s found no association between pill use and sexual activity (Black and Sykes, 1971; Settlage *et al.*, 1973; Garris *et al.*, 1976; Akpom *et al.*, 1976; Reichelt, 1978). A more recent survey of Scottish women favours an explanation of the fall in age at first intercourse according to factors other than oral contraception (Bone, 1986), and these survey data seem to support those conclusions. As Table 2.1 shows, age at first intercourse has declined progressively through each age group, but not uniformly so. As noted above, the fall is most marked for the older age groups. Median age at first intercourse is 2 years higher, at 21 years, for women aged 55–59 than it is for those 10 years younger. Thus the steepest decline occurred during the 1950s. Median age of first intercourse fell as much during this one decade as it was to do over the next 30 years. This irregular pattern is also apparent in the data for men.

A common assumption is that the advent of reliable birth-control methods (in the form of oral contraception) preceded and probably facilitated a lowering of age at first intercourse, by removing one of the most powerful deterrents – the fear of unwanted pregnancy – from the sexual act. Yet although the pill was prescribed as early as 1961, it was not available in practice for unmarried women until 1972, and it was not available regardless of ability to pay until 1975, so that the women in the sample whose experience contributed to the most dramatic fall in age at first intercourse would have been largely unaffected by these events. This is not to say that efficient and accessible contraception has not been influential in the lowering of age at first intercourse, but we must look to other factors to explain the steep decline during the 1950s. It seems as likely that legal and technological advance has occurred in response to changing sexual mores as vice versa.

These data provide no evidence of a sexual revolution co-terminous with the decade of the 1960s; rather the major changes seem to have occurred in the previous decade.

THE INFLUENCE OF SOCIAL CLASS AND EDUCATION

Table 2.8 indicates marked variation with social class, particularly for men. The median age at first intercourse for men of all ages in social class I is 19, 3 years later than for men in social class V, and for women in social class I it is 20, 2 years later than for women in social class V. This relationship is not easily interpreted since social class is measured at the time of interview, following a varying interval since first intercourse. In the case of older respondents, occupation recorded, on which social classification is based, is the current one and will almost invariably be different from occupation at the time of first intercourse. Younger respondents still in full-time education will be categorized as students so that their social-class status will be as yet undetermined.

Findings of previous studies are equivocal on the relationship between social class and age at first intercourse. Kinsey's data (1948; 1953) indicate striking social-class differences; working-class adolescents experienced sexual intercourse at an earlier age than those from the middle classes. Yet more recent US studies have noted a lessening of social-class influences over time (Kantner and Zelnick, 1972; Fisher and Byrne, 1981). Surveys of young German workers and students carried out at roughly the same time similarly indicate the disappearance of social-class differences in age at onset of sexual experience (Schmidt and Sigusch, 1971; 1972).

In the UK, however, social-class differences seem to have persisted later than in the US and elsewhere in Europe. Studies in the 1970s found age at first intercourse to be earlier among young people from working-class backgrounds compared with those from middle-class backgrounds (Dunnell, 1979; Farrell, 1978), as have more recent studies (Forman and Chilvers, 1989; West *et al.*, 1993). Certainly stratification of these data by age group (Table 2.8) shows no clear evidence of any lessening of social-class effect through successive age cohorts, except perhaps for the oldest age group of men aged 45–59 at interview, among whom the social-class effect was more marked than for men aged under 45.

There is evidence here that the trend towards diminishing differ-

	age group and social class							
	16–24 years							
	I	II	III NM	III M	IV	V	other	*base*
men	18	17	17	16	16	16	18	*1472*
women	18	17	17	17	16	16	17	*1863*
	25–34 years							
	I	II	III NM	III M	IV	V	other	*base*
men	18	17	17	16	16	16	18	*2337*
women	19	18	18	17	17	17	17	*3230*
	35–44 years							
	I	II	III NM	III M	IV	V	other	*base*
men	19	18	18	17	18	17	16	*2108*
women	19	19	18	18	18	18	18	*2565*
	45–59 years							
	I	II	III NM	III M	IV	V	other	*base*
men	21	19	19	18	18	17	18	*2047*
women	22	20	20	19	20	20	20	*2933*

Table 2.8 Median age at first intercourse by social class within age group. Source: Interview Question 19

NM = non-manual; M = manual

ences between men and women in age at first intercourse identified above (page 37) may, in common with many other behavioural trends, have begun earlier among those in upper social-class groups. For those aged 45–59, the median age at first intercourse for women in all social-class groups is higher than it is for men but the difference is greater the lower the social class. The gender difference is 3 years in social class V and 1 year in social classes I–III. By contrast, median age at first intercourse is the same for both men and women in the 16–24-year age range, regardless of social class (with the exception of social class III M). We see here another indication of a trend hinted at elsewhere in this book, of a general convergence in the sexual behaviour of men and women.

The relationship between age at first intercourse and social class is of interest in the context of cervical cancer. Epidemiological studies have suggested the importance of early sexual experience with multiple partners in the aetiology of this disease, the incidence of which is higher among women in lower social-class groups (Boyd and Doll, 1964; Wynder, 1969). Recent studies exploring this relationship have found that although working-class women experienced sexual intercourse earlier, social class had no obvious impact on numbers of sexual partners – if anything working-class women accumulated fewer sexual partners than middle-class women – suggesting that early age at first intercourse, rather than multiple partners, may be a more useful focus in explaining the higher incidence of cervical cancer among working-class women (Harris *et al.*, 1980; Brown *et al.*, 1984; Mant *et al.*, 1988). The data from this survey on the relationship between social class and both age at first intercourse and numbers of sexual partners (Chapter 3) add further support to these conclusions.

US data show age at first sexual intercourse also increases with educational level (Klassen *et al.*, 1981). The interaction between age at first intercourse, education, social class and current age of respondent is complex. Social class and education are clearly interrelated and both are related to current age as people acquire qualifications and move through social grades during their lifetime. At the same time educational level also decreases with increasing age, since younger people are more likely to spend longer in full-time

	age group and education					
	16–24 years					
	degree	A level	O level/CSE	other	none	*base*
men	18	17	16	17	16	*1471*
women	18	17	17	17	16	*1862*
	25–34 years					
	degree	A level	O level/CSE	other	none	*base*
men	18	17	17	17	16	*2334*
women	19	18	17	18	17	*3228*
	35–44 years					
	degree	A level	O level/CSE	other	none	*base*
men	19	18	17	17	17	*2104*
women	20	19	18	18	18	*2566*
	45–59 years					
	degree	A level	O level/CSE	other	none	*base*
men	21	19	19	18	18	*2041*
women	21	21	20	20	20	*2931*

Table 2.9 Median age at first intercourse by education within age group. Source: Interview Question 19a

education. It is assumed that educational level will influence age at first intercourse. Yet in many cases young people will experience first intercourse before completing their education and it might equally be the case that the age at which the event occurs might itself wield an effect on level of educational achievement.

The differential according to educational level is apparent for all ages and both sexes (Table 2.9). Median age at first intercourse increases with educational level, and the effect is particularly marked for graduates. The major difference between graduates and non-graduates is also manifest in the analysis for intercourse before the age of 16. Compared with their graduate peers, non-graduate men are more than three times as likely to have sex before their 16th birthday, and non-graduate women nearly twice as likely. Only one in four male graduates had experienced sexual intercourse before the age of 18 compared with more than half non-graduates.

Multivariate analysis was used to assess the strength of the relationship between first intercourse before 16 and current age, social class and educational level. Although education and social class are related, they each have an independent effect on age at first intercourse, once the effects of current age have been accounted for, that of education being stronger than that of social class. This analysis confirmed the association between education to at least O-level standard and a reduced likelihood of intercourse before 16. The relationship between social class and age at first intercourse is likely to be more tenuous since social class measures current rather than contemporary socio-economic status.

The Influence of Ethnic Group

The relationship between racial origin and age at first intercourse is similarly complex. Ethnic influences appear to have an important effect on adolescent sexual behaviour through cultural or contextual mechanisms but they may also operate through structural factors influencing family income and marital status. Table 2.10 shows the relationship between race and religion and first intercourse before 16. As can be seen, those of Pakistani, Bangladeshi and Indian origin

	men		women	
	%	*base*	%	*base*
ethnic group				
white	18.9	*7749*	8.0	*9760*
black	26.3	*157*	9.6	*218*
Pakistani, Bangladeshi, Indian	10.7	*186*	1.1	*189*
other	14.0	*120*	5.0	*139*
all ethnic groups	18.8	*8212*	7.9	*10307*
religion				
Church of England	13.4	*2039*	5.1	*3403*
Roman Catholic	19.5	*731*	5.1	*1171*
other Christian	14.6	*882*	5.7	*1538*
non-Christian	10.8	*342*	4.6	*383*
none	22.7	*4240*	12.3	*3834*
all religious groups	18.8	*8234*	7.8	*10329*

Table 2.10 Proportion of respondents who first had sexual intercourse before age 16 by ethnicity and religion. Source: Interview Question 19a

are much less likely to report sexual intercourse having occurred before the age of 16 than are those from other ethnic groups, and this is especially marked for women, little more than 1% of whom report first intercourse before this age. Black men and women are more likely to report sexual intercourse before the age of 16, though the excess for women is more marginal. US data have also shown that black Americans begin sexual experience earlier than white (Klassen *et al.*, 1981; Hofferth, 1988).

Not surprisingly given these figures, median age at first intercourse is higher for Asian groups and lower for blacks, compared with whites. What is of interest is that gender differences are more pronounced for minority ethnic groups. While the median age at first intercourse for those who are white is 18 for both men and women; for those who are black it is 17 for men and 18 for women, and for Asians 20 for men and 21 for women.

The relationship between religion and early intercourse is also explored in Table 2.10. Those reporting no religious affiliation were more likely to experience intercourse before the age of 16, and the differences are more marked for women than men. Respondents belonging to the Church of England or other Christian religions (excluding Roman Catholic) were less likely to experience sexual intercourse before the age of 16, and those from non-Christian religions even less likely to do so. More surprisingly perhaps, given the position of the Roman Catholic Church on sexual behaviour, those reporting RC affiliation are no less likely than those reporting another religious affiliation to report intercourse before the age of 16, and if anything slightly more so. It is possible that the effects of religious beliefs and sexual behaviour are reciprocal. Sexual behaviour may reflect the influence of religion, but the converse might also be true as religious beliefs that do not support a preferred pattern of behaviour may be allowed to lapse. These bivariate relationships are likely to be confounded by other effects and particularly those of age, since trends in religious affiliation have changed over time along with falling age at first intercourse.

A logistic regression model was used to look at the relationship between current age, religion, race and educational qualifications, and the likelihood of first intercourse occurring before the age of 16. The adjusted odds ratios and their 95% confidence intervals are shown in Figure 2.4a. Social class was not included in this analysis because of its close association with educational qualifications, and the possibly greater relevance of education to early intercourse. For both men and women age remained the most important factor; increasing age at interview was associated with decreasing likelihood of reporting of first sexual intercourse before the age of 16. For both men and women, intercourse before the age of 16 is less likely to have occurred if the respondent was educated at least to O level or if s/he acknowledged any religious affiliation (except Roman Catholic for men and non-Christian religions for women). First sexual intercourse before 16 was less likely for women of Pakistani, Indian or Bangladeshi racial origin (the confidence intervals are wide due to the relatively small numbers in this category) and more likely for men who were black.

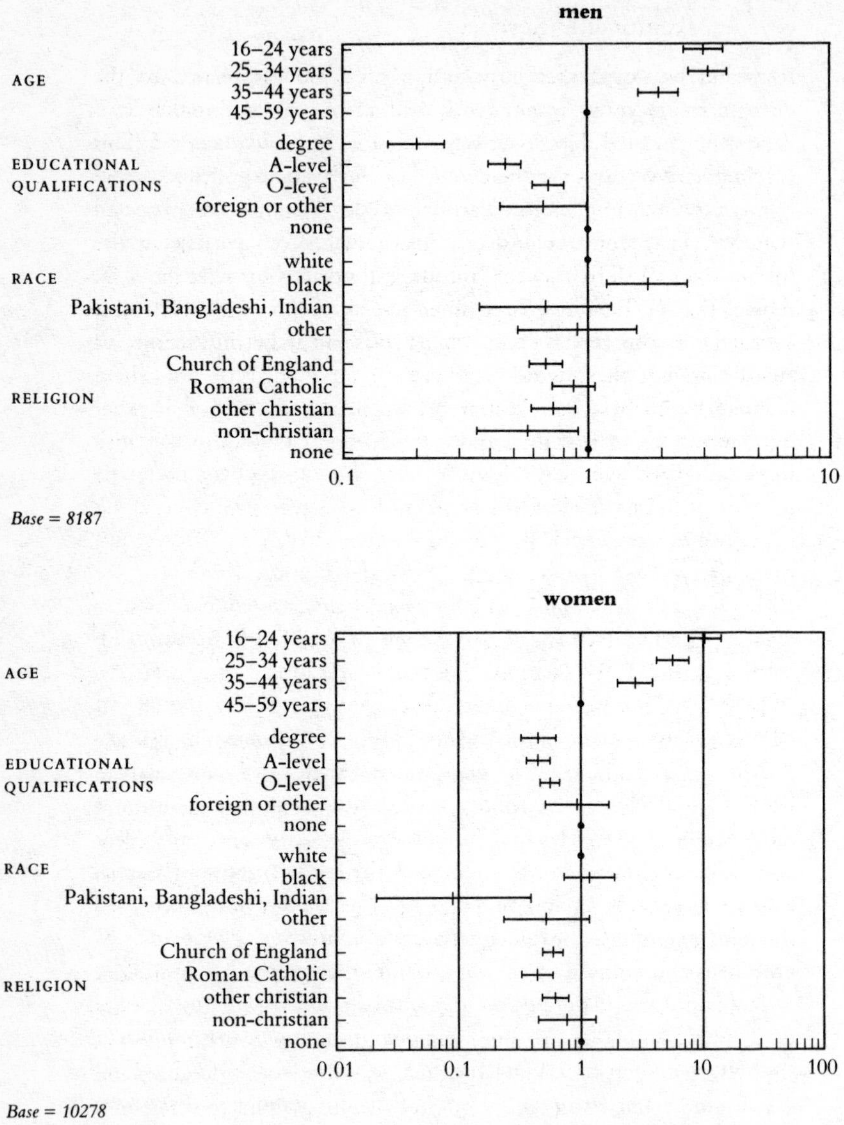

Figure 2.4 Adjusted odds ratios with 95% confidence intervals for first intercourse before the age of 16. Source: Interview Question 19a

Regional Differences

It should be noted that information on region is related to the current residence of respondents, and in a mobile population it cannot be assumed that this is where first intercourse occurred. This might partly account for the absence of clear regional differences in the data. According to popular stereotypes, it might be expected that first intercourse would take place earlier on average in the 'permissive' south than in the 'puritanical' north. Our data show no sign of this. Median age for women in East Anglia and Scotland is 1 year later than for those in other areas, and these differences are significant, but there is no clear pattern for men. Nor does there seem to be in these data a clear rural/urban divide found in other data, where age at first intercourse is earlier in cities compared with the country (Klassen *et al.*, 1981; Ford and Bowie, 1989). While there is some slight evidence of this for women, again there is no clear pattern for men.

CONTRACEPTION AT FIRST INTERCOURSE

The risks of unplanned pregnancy among the young make the question of contraception at first intercourse an important focus in the context of sexual health. Contraceptive use at first intercourse varies both with current age and with age at which the event occurred. Since, as we have seen, there is also a relationship between current age and age at first intercourse, there is clearly the potential for some confounding of these effects.

As Figure 2.5 shows, men are more likely than women, and older respondents more likely than younger ones, to report not having used contraception at first intercourse. Non-use of contraception at first intercourse has declined steadily over the recent decades, and was reported by fewer than a quarter of women and fewer than a third of men aged 16–24. Failure to use contraception does not necessarily signify risk of unplanned pregnancy; a proportion of respondents – higher in older age groups (see page 71) – were married at first intercourse and may have intended to become

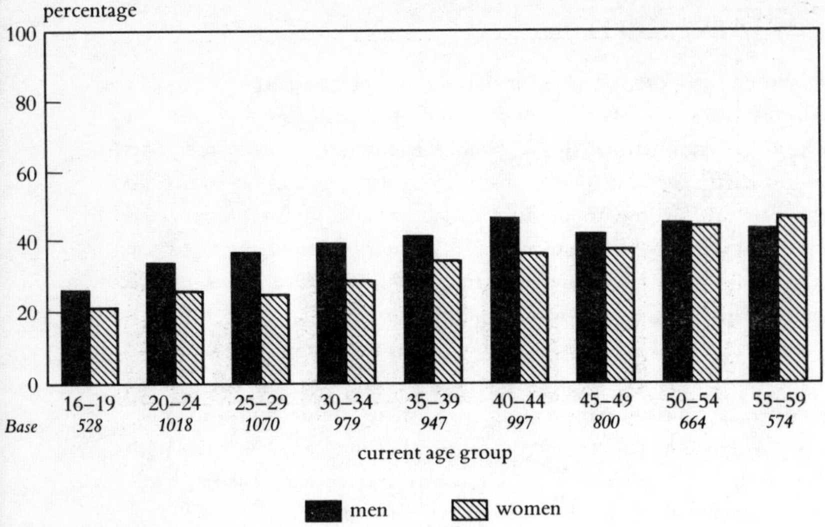

Figure 2.5 Proportion using no contraception at first intercourse by current age. Source: Interview Question 23

pregnant. Failure to recall contraceptive practice at first intercourse is low for all respondents and only marginally higher for the older respondents.

The likelihood of no contraception being used also varies with age at first intercourse (Figure 2.6). Where intercourse occurs before the age of 16, nearly half of young women and more than half of young men report no method used either by themselves or by a partner. This proportion falls sharply to 32% of women and 36% of men aged 16 and over at first intercourse. This might reflect lack of confidence in seeking contraceptive supplies or advice or, alternatively, the sporadic nature of sexual activity in this age group. This emphasizes the particular vulnerability of this group to unplanned pregnancy.

With regard to specific methods, the evidence is that the condom is the most commonly used method of contraception at first intercourse, and that its use has been increasing over recent years. Condoms are more commonly used by young people aged 16–24 than by those in any other age group. Half of all women and nearly

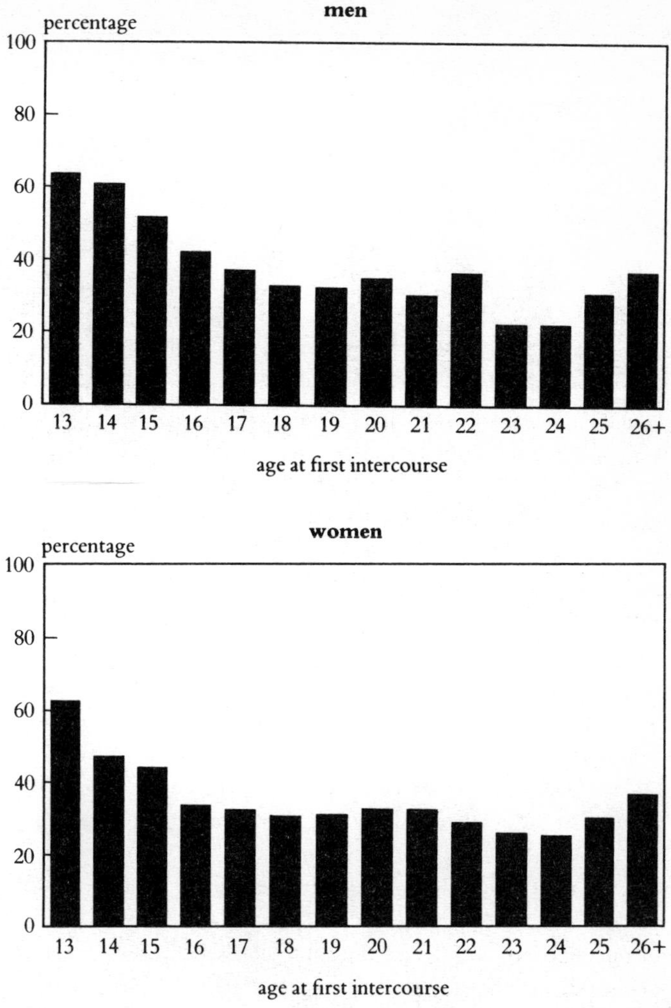

Figure 2.6 Proportion using no contraception at first intercourse by age at first intercourse. Source: Interview Questions 19a, 23

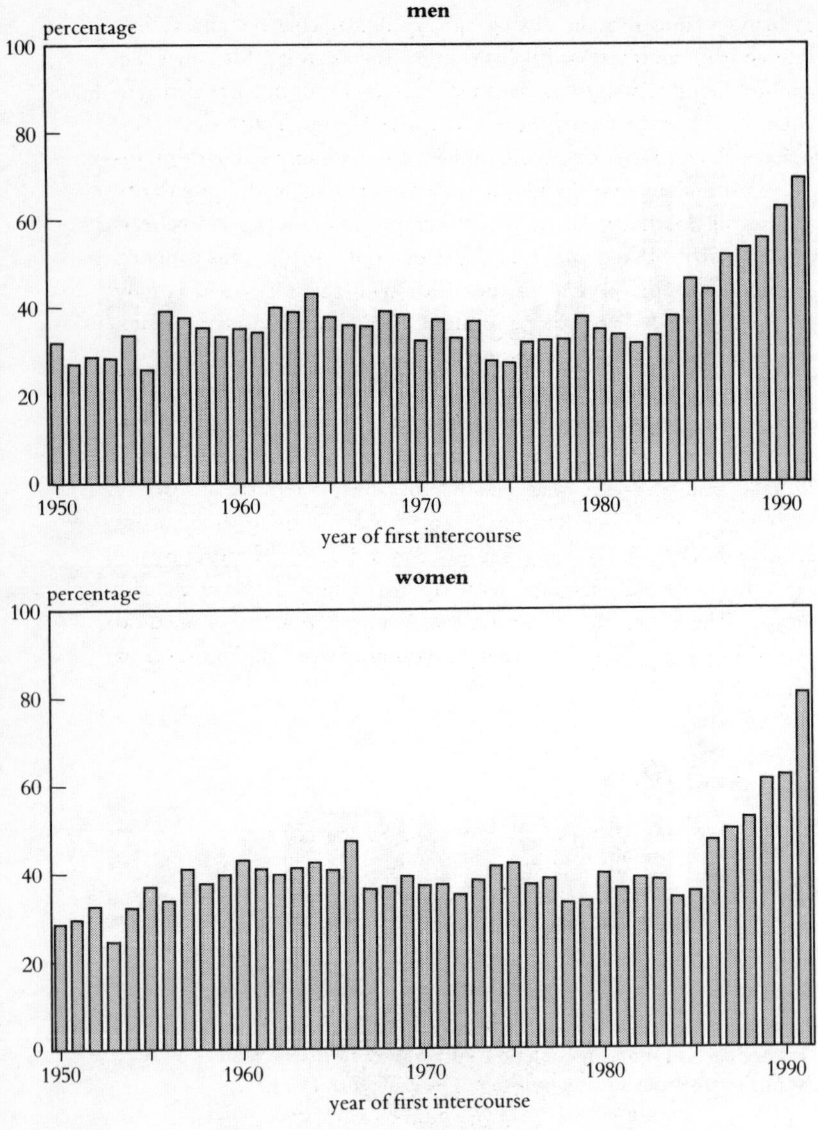

Note: Figures for 1991 based on data for 5 months

Figure 2.7 Proportion using a condom at first intercourse by year of first intercourse. Source: Interview Questions 19a, 23

as many young men in this age group report condom use at first intercourse, compared with little more than a third for other age groups. Figure 2.7 shows a recent sharp increase in the prevalence of condom use at first intercourse. The rise began in the mid-1980s, before which time condom use remained remarkably stable throughout the previous two decades despite fluctuations in the popularity of the pill in the wake of reports of possible adverse side-effects (RCGP, 1977; Pike *et al.*, 1983; Vessey *et al.*, 1977). This supports the view that the revival of the method in the 1980s was largely attributable to AIDS public education, suggesting considerable success in motivating public response.

The use of 'other method' (predominantly oral contraception) is highest among women now aged 25–34, 28% of whom used this method of contraception at first intercourse. The proportion falls to 20% of 16–24-year-olds, possibly because of reports of adverse side-effects of oral-contraceptive use among young nulliparous women (Pike *et al.*, 1983) (Figures 2.8a and 2.8b). Reports of use of 'other method' increase with age at which first intercourse occurs. The necessity for professional consultation for a medical prescription may be a deterrent to younger women (Figures 2.9a and 2.9b).

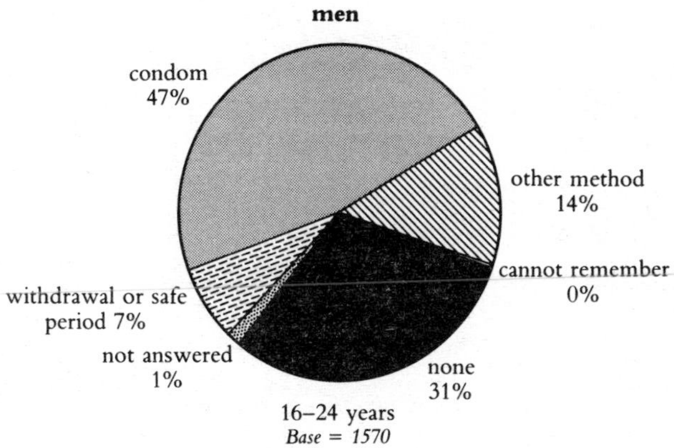

Figure 2.8 *continued overleaf*

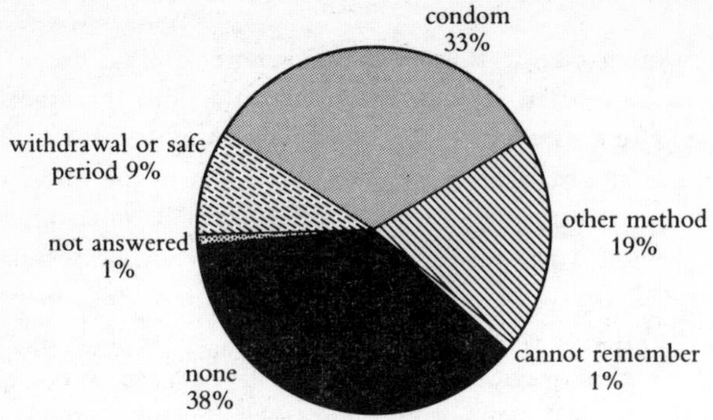

25–34 years
Base = 2081

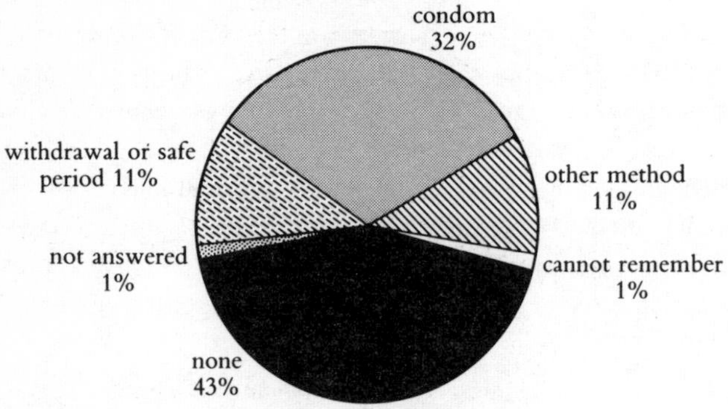

35–44 years
Base = 1996

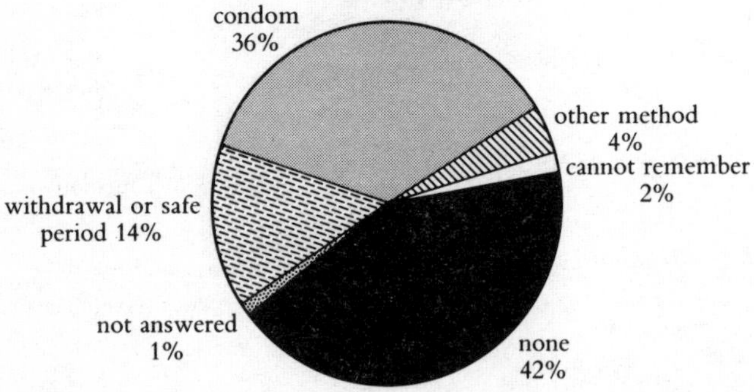

45–59 years
Base = 2096

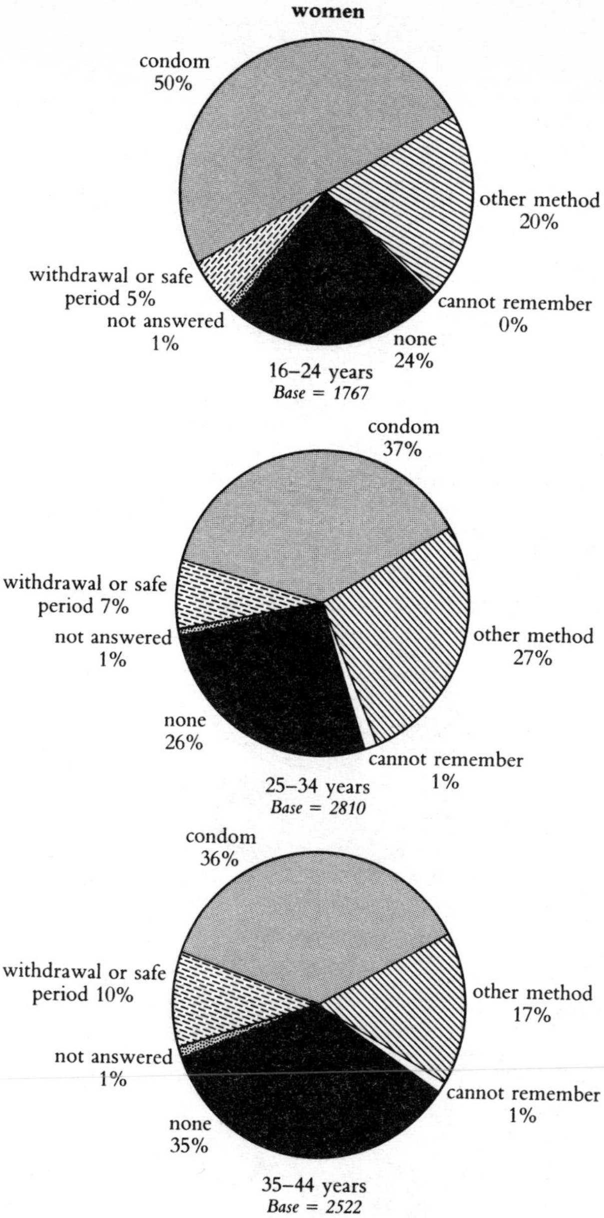

Figure 2.8 *continued overleaf*

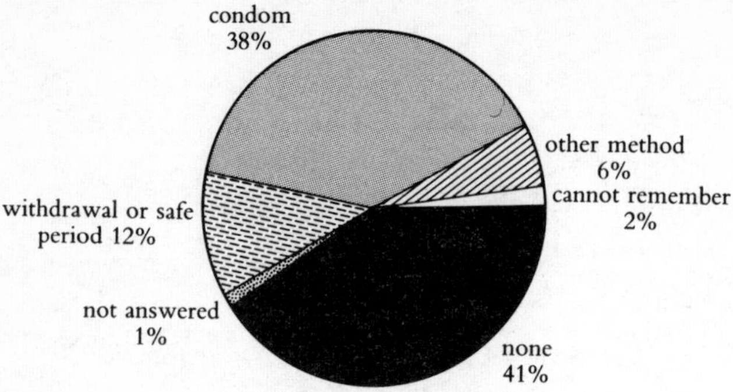

45–59 years
Base = 2683

Figure 2.8 Contraceptive use at first intercourse by current age. Source: Interview Question 23

men

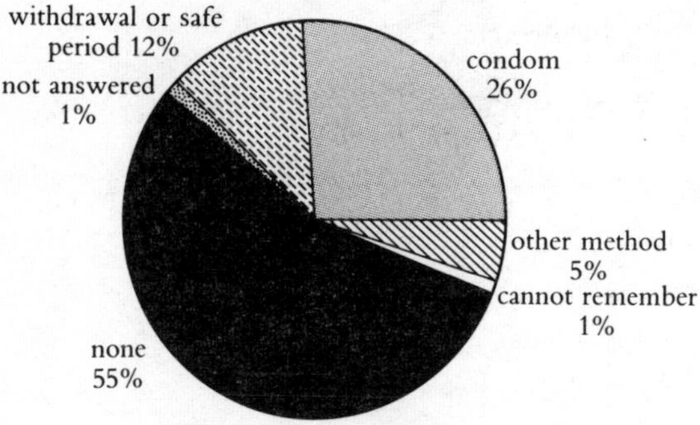

13–15 years
Base = 1543

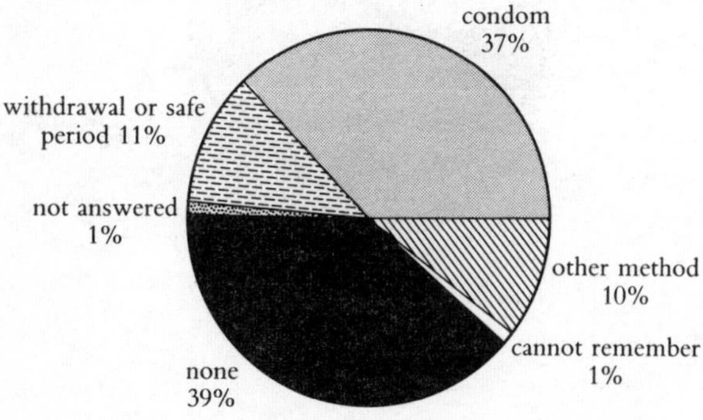

16–17 years
Base = 2552

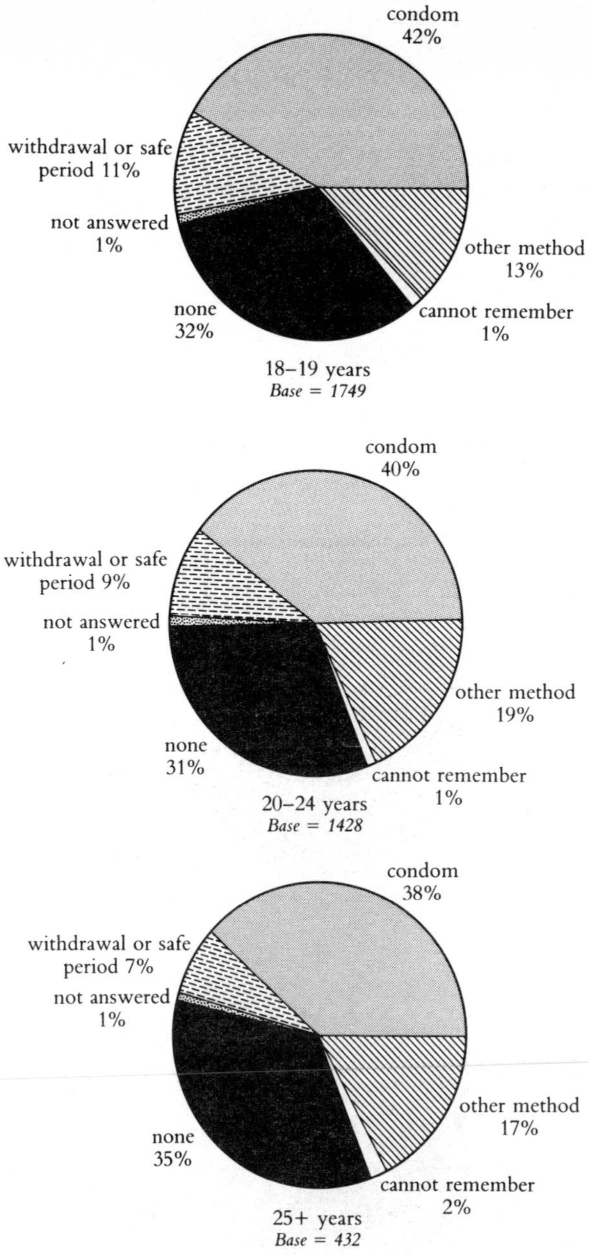

Figure 2.9 *continued overleaf*

women

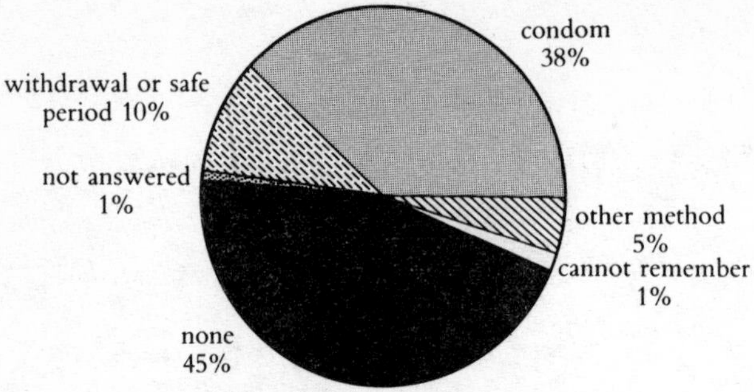

13–15 years
Base = 815

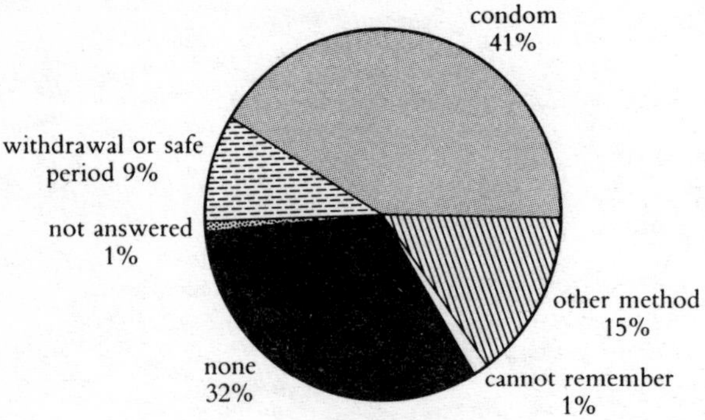

16–17 years
Base = 3125

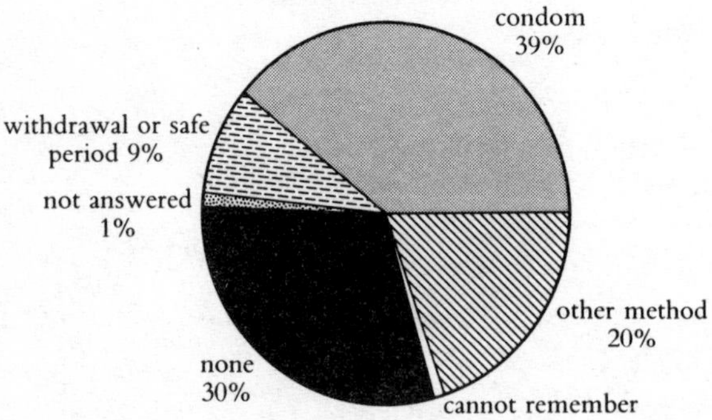

18–19 years
Base = 2774

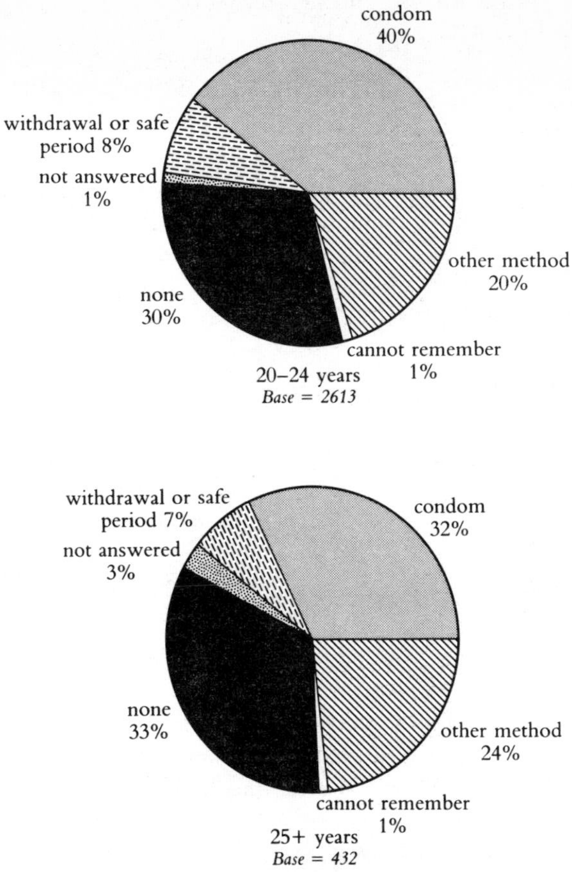

Figure 2.9 Contraceptive use at first intercourse by age at first intercourse. Source: Interview Questions 19a, 23

EXPERIENCE OF FIRST INTERCOURSE

Relatively little is known about the context in which first sexual intercourse occurs; the stimulus to the event, influences on decision-making, the nature of the relationship with the first partner and the feelings provoked by the experience. The circumstances in which first intercourse occurs vary widely and this study cannot provide more than superficial insights into this important event. Some of the contextual data from the survey is discussed below, together with its implications for the age at which first intercourse occurs and whether contraception is used.

Age of Partner

All respondents were asked the age of the person with whom they first had sexual intercourse and whether or not it was the first time for them. Only 2% of men and fewer than 1% of women reported never having known how old their first partner was, while 13% of women and 14% of men had no knowledge of whether or not they were also virgins. The younger men were at first intercourse, the less likely they were to have known whether or not their partners were also virgins, while for women the reverse is true. Similar findings have been reported by Zelnick and Shah (1983).

Men's partners at first intercourse tend to be roughly the same age as themselves (Figure 2.10). This holds even for those who reported early intercourse; nearly two-thirds of men aged under 16 at first intercourse had partners who were also under 16. (The possibility that men believed their partners to be older than they actually were cannot be ruled out, particularly where the woman was under 16.) Where men's partners were of discordant age, whether they were older or younger varied with the age at which first intercourse occurred. The older the man at first intercourse the more likely it is to have taken place with a partner younger than himself and vice versa. But there is no evidence of widespread initiation of young men into sex by older women.

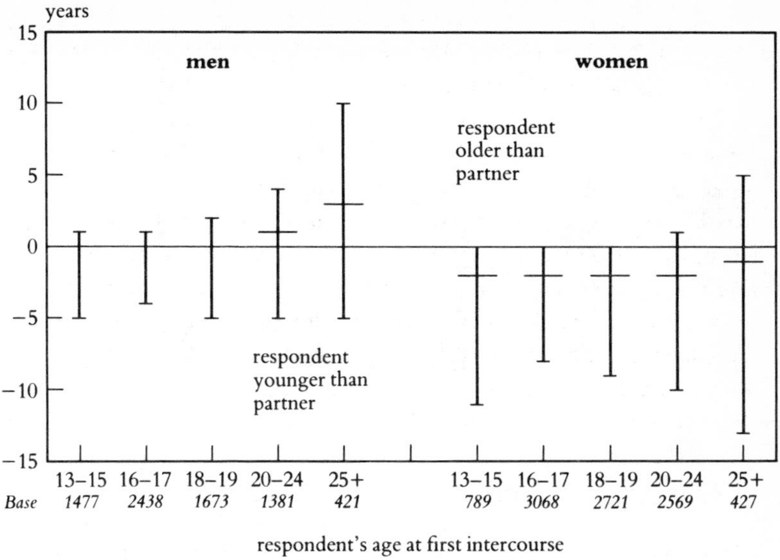

Figure 2.10 Difference between respondent's and partner's age at first intercourse. Source: Interview Questions 19a, 21a

For women the pattern is different. An older partner at first intercourse is the norm. 75% of women aged 13–17 at first intercourse had partners older than themselves, and 75% of those aged 18–24 at first occurrence had partners who were the same age or older. Only women who delayed first intercourse until after the age of 24 were more likely to have had partners closer in age to themselves.

All respondents were also asked whether it was the first experience of intercourse for their partner (Figure 2.11). Not surprisingly, given the age differences described above, more men reported their partners to have been virgins than did women. Overall, 37% of women had first intercourse with someone for whom it was also the first time, while 51% did so with an experienced partner. For men, the proportions were 47% and 39% respectively. Regardless of gender, the younger the respondent at first intercourse, the less likely it was to have also been the inaugural occasion for their partner.

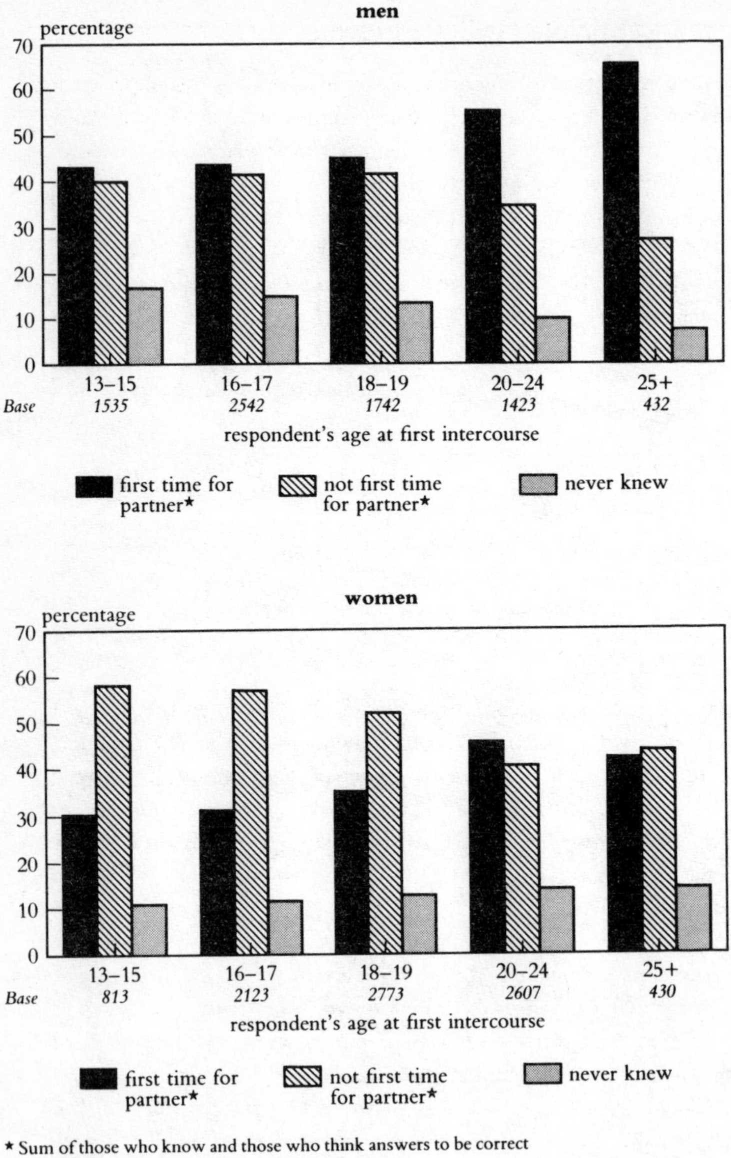

Figure 2.11 Age at first intercourse and whether first time for partner.
Source: Interview Questions 19, 21b

Relationship with First Partner

The evidence is that the majority of people have their first experience of intercourse in an established relationship. For 42.9% of men and 51.4% of women in the sample, the event took place with someone with whom they had a steady relationship, and for 28.6% of men and 16.5% of women with someone known for some time though not in a steady relationship (Table 2.11). It is uncommon, and increasingly so, for first intercourse to take place within marriage, or with someone to whom marriage is planned. Overall, 6.1% of

	first intercourse before age 16		total	
	men %	**women** %	**men** %	**women** %
nature of relationship				
prostitute (men only)	1.2	—	1.6	—
met for first time	4.6	3.3	4.4	0.8
met recently	15.8	8.7	13.1	3.8
known but not steady	42.0	28.6	28.6	16.5
steady	35.5	57.9	42.9	51.4
cohabiting	0.4	0.0	0.4	0.8
engaged	0.6	1.3	3.0	10.5
married	0.0	0.0	6.1	15.9
rape (women only)	—	0.3	—	0.3
base	391	217	1909	2405
*planning**				
spur of the moment	44.2	38.0	31.1	25.6
expected soon	28.9	37.9	39.1	43.4
expected then	10.5	9.2	10.9	12.1
planned then	2.7	2.0	3.8	3.5
planned in advance	13.7	12.9	14.5	15.5
base	*392*	*216*	*1784*	*2002*

Table 2.11 *continued overleaf*

* excludes those married at first intercourse

	first intercourse before age 16		total	
	men	**women**	**men**	**women**
	%	%	%	%
feelings				
too soon	24.4	58.5	12.3	25.5
waited too long	1.8	1.6	7.1	3.1
about right	73.8	39.9	80.6	71.4
base	*381*	*214*	*1864*	*2344*
*main factor**				
curiosity	40.5	23.2	27.1	14.1
carried away	11.0	11.2	10.0	8.6
peer group	13.9	9.4	8.4	4.4
natural course	15.9	8.8	26.0	24.3
drunk	3.6	6.7	4.0	2.7
lose virginity	9.0	1.2	7.1	1.1
in love	6.2	39.5	17.3	44.9
base	*387*	*195*	*1748*	*1924*

Table 2.11 Context of first intercourse by age at occurrence. Source: Interview Questions 19a, 24, 25, 26b, 28

* excludes those married at first intercourse

men's and 15.9% of women's first experience of intercourse was with wife or husband, and this proportion decreases markedly with the current age of the respondent (Table 2.12). Fewer than 1% of men and women aged 16–24 were married at the time of their first sexual intercourse. (In much of the past literature on teenage sexual activity premarital sex has been a major preoccupation, as some of the earlier titles in the references testify. These data show premarital sex to be nearly universal. This represents a major shift in behaviour in recent decades, but indicates that there is little value in focusing on its prevalence in contemporary studies.)

Women are more likely than men to report a steady relationship with their partner at first intercourse and this greater commitment on the part of women, compared with men, has been noted by others (Zelnick and Shah, 1983; Christopher and Cate, 1985; Faulkenberry *et al.*, 1987). However, the data for women in different age groups shows clearly that the small proportion reporting first intercourse with someone met for the first time or only recently, has been increasing over recent decades.

Very few men report their first experience to have been with a prostitute, and the proportion decreases with successive birth cohorts. First intercourse with a prostitute was reported by 3.4% of men aged 45–59, and by none aged 16–24 (Table 2.12). This decline no doubt reflects a relaxation in social rules governing sexual relationships, which removes the need to have to pay for sexual initiation. This is further discussed in Chapter 3.

Bivariate analysis also shows contraceptive use at first intercourse to vary with the nature of the relationship and this has been reported in other surveys (West *et al.*, 1993). Failure to use any contraception at first intercourse was less common among those for whom the experience took place with a regular partner (Table 2.13).

The high proportion of women who were married at first intercourse who reported no contraceptive use probably reflects a tendency to marry in order to start a family (Table 2.13). More than two-thirds of women whose partner at first intercourse was someone they had met for the first time used no contraception, and nearly half of those for whom it was someone they had met recently, and fewer than a third in a steady relationship. The increased likelihood of lack of contraceptive protection with a non-steady partner may be a cause for concern as this is the group most likely to suffer and least likely to welcome an unplanned pregnancy.

Factors Associated with First Intercourse

Respondents receiving the long questionnaire were asked to choose from a selection of response options relating to the circumstances surrounding first intercourse. The selection of these was guided partly by the early development work for the survey, and partly by the desire to achieve some comparability with Schofield's survey of young people, in which this question was also asked (Schofield, 1965). Respondents were asked to mention any of several factors

	16–24		25–34		35–44		45–59	
	men	**women**	**men**	**women**	**men**	**women**	**men**	**women**
	%	%	%	%	%	%	%	%
nature of relationship								
prostitute	0.0	—	0.9	—	1.7	—	3.4	—
met for first time	4.3	1.9	5.5	0.7	3.6	1.1	4.4	0.2
met recently	17.0	6.9	14.0	5.1	11.5	3.0	10.5	1.2
known but not steady	29.5	23.3	28.3	18.6	31.6	14.2	25.1	12.1
steady	48.3	62.5	46.8	61.7	40.5	51.1	36.7	33.8
cohabiting	0.4	1.7	0.3	0.9	1.0	0.8	0.0	0.1
engaged	0.6	2.8	1.6	7.8	3.6	15.5	5.7	13.6
married	0.0	0.8	2.6	5.3	6.7	13.8	14.2	38.5
rape	—	0.1	—	0.0	—	0.5	—	0.5
base	*393*	*428*	*520*	*698*	*518*	*614*	*477*	*665*
*planning**								
spur of the moment	27.1	24.0	30.7	20.8	29.9	26.4	37.1	33.8
expected soon	40.4	40.2	38.3	42.1	44.3	46.1	34.9	45.2
expected then	12.2	12.9	10.6	13.2	8.1	11.5	13.6	10.2
planned then	5.0	5.3	2.8	3.0	3.6	3.3	4.2	2.8
planned in advance	15.3	17.5	17.6	20.9	14.2	12.7	10.3	8.0
base =	*393*	*424*	*507*	*656*	*481*	*520*	*403*	*401*

feelings								
too soon	15.6	36.9	10.1	29.4	12.5	24.3	11.7	15.3
waited too long	3.1	0.8	6.7	1.6	9.2	3.8	8.8	5.5
about right	81.3	62.4	83.1	69.0	78.3	71.9	69.6	79.3
base	*388*	*413*	*508*	*689*	*507*	*601*	*451*	*641*
*main factor**								
curiosity	30.7	23.6	32.5	15.1	23.7	8.4	20.8	9.5
carried away	4.5	6.3	8.2	6.6	12.6	8.3	14.6	14.5
peer group	7.2	4.1	7.2	6.3	8.8	3.8	10.5	2.5
natural course	23.1	23.2	25.0	6.9	29.7	25.7	25.6	19.8
drunk	6.6	5.2	3.8	2.0	2.3	2.8	3.9	1.1
lose virginity	11.2	0.2	8.8	1.6	6.3	1.1	2.2	1.0
in love	16.7	37.5	14.4	41.5	16.7	49.9	22.4	51.6
base	*387*	*409*	*492*	*632*	*474*	*488*	*395*	*396*

Table 2.12 Context of first intercourse by age group of respondent. Source: Interview Questions 19a, 24, 25, 26b, 28

Excludes respondents unable to recall, uncertain or with no opinion

* excludes those married at first intercourse

	% using no contraception			
	men		women	
	%	*base*	%	*base*
nature of relationship				
prostitute	75.4	*30*	—	—
just met for the first time	46.8	*85*	67.6	*19★*
met recently	40.0	*244*	47.7	*90*
known but not steady	49.1	*540*	43.6	*394*
steady relationship	29.8	*809*	30.1	*1218*
cohabiting	—	*8★*	30.6	*20*
engaged to be married	37.5	*54*	32.4	*248*
married	29.1	*115*	38.5	*377*
other	—	*8★*	65.5	*15★*
planning†				
spur of the moment	54.4	*551*	56.5	*510*
expected soon	34.3	*693*	32.5	*854*
expected then	35.2	*194*	23.0	*241*
planned then	32.8	*68*	19.3	*67*
planned in advance	24.9	*258*	13.4	*307*
feelings				
too soon	50.0	*226*	47.6	*594*
waited too long	33.7	*128*	34.4	*70*
about right	36.6	*1483*	29.5	*1654*
main factor†				
curiosity	43.9	*468*	34.8	*269*
carried away	50.2	*174*	46.3	*161*
peer group	52.6	*146*	45.2	*83*
natural course	26.2	*449*	25.5	*466*
drunk	63.2	*69*	64.2	*51*
lose virginity	40.4	*120*	31.2	*20*
in love	30.1	*300*	31.4	*851*

Table 2.13 Proportion using no contraception at first intercourse by nature of the relationship. Source: Interview Questions 23, 24, 25, 26b, 28

Excludes respondents unable to recall, uncertain or with no opinion

★ note small base.

† excludes those married at first intercourse

they considered to apply to themselves, and then to try to identify the single main factor obtaining at the time. Show-cards providing precoded responses contained the following statements:

I was curious about what it would be like
I got carried away by my feelings
Most people in my age group seemed to be doing it
It seemed like a natural 'follow on' in the relationship
I was a bit drunk at the time
I wanted to lose my virginity
I was in love
Other particular factor (*specify*)
None of these applied

The question assumes both awareness and accurate recall of contributory and motivating factors at the time. Both assumptions are questionable and we need to accept that many of the responses may well be rationalizations after the event. It is also possible that a response bias is operating here too, since some options – e.g. being drunk – are less socially acceptable than others.

Factors most commonly associated with first intercourse were curiosity (cited by 55% of men and 42% of women), and that it seemed a natural progression in the relationship (cited by 45% men and 50% women). There were, however, marked gender differences in the choice of factors. While curiosity was the factor most commonly selected by men, for women it was 'being in love'. 58% of women reported this as an associated factor, compared with only 30% of men. These findings are similar to those in other studies (Reiss, 1967; Kraft *et al.*, 1989).

Looking at the *main* factor associated with first intercourse (Figure 2.12), there is little evidence of any return to an age of romanticism, certainly among women. The proportion of women who mention being in love as the main precipitating factor continues a slow decline through all age groups, from more than half the sample of 45–59-year-olds (51.6%) to little more than a third (37.5%) of women aged 16–24. Men gave this as the main factor in first intercourse far less commonly than women, and the proportion doing so, after falling from 22.4% of 45–59-year-olds to 14.4% of 25–34-year-olds, rises slightly to 16.7% of 16–24-year-olds.

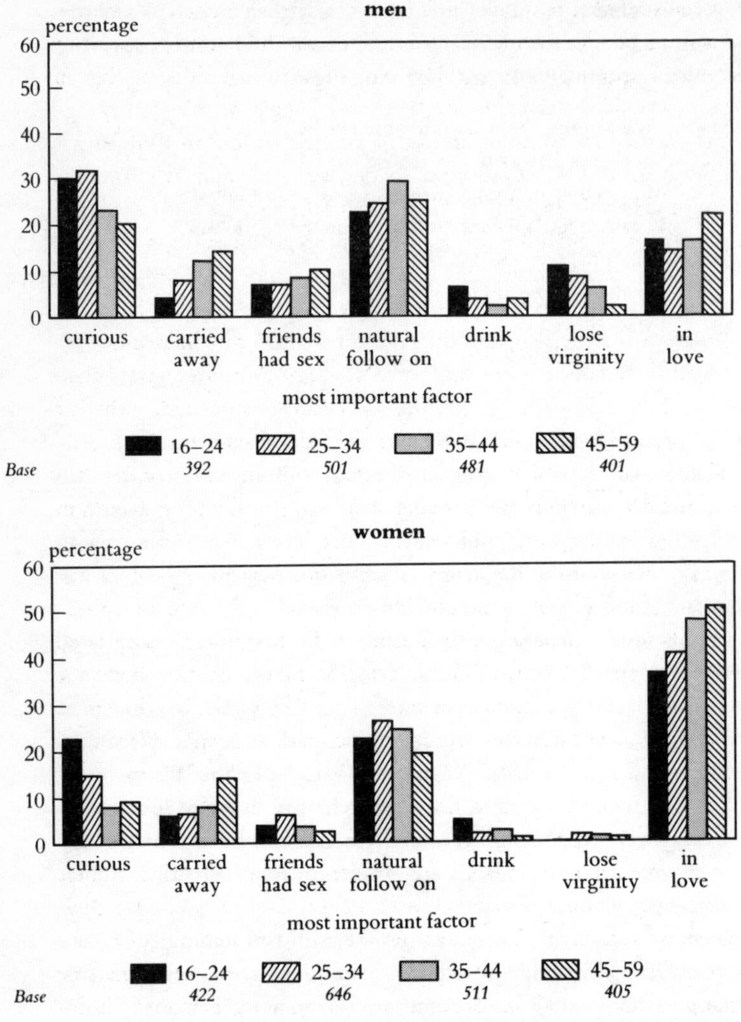

Figure 2.12 Most important factor associated with first intercourse by current age. Source: Interview Question 26b

Social pressure, particularly from peers, has been cited as a reason for young people having intercourse for the first time (Delameter and MacCorquodale, 1979). The two measures of this variable in the questionnaire relate to the responses, 'Most people in my age group seemed to be doing it' and 'I wanted to lose my virginity'. While it is not a key factor for either sex, men seem more susceptible to the 'herding instinct' than women: 8.4% of men and 4.4% of women mention the prevailing peer-group norm as the most important factor (though this is an option respondents might have been least aware of at the time). There seems also to be more motivation for men to lose their virginity, and this increases with younger birth cohorts. For men aged 16–24 at interview, more than 1 in 10 gave this as the most important factor associated with first intercourse, compared with only 1 in 50 of those aged 45–59.

The use of alcohol is often associated with first intercourse but there is little evidence of it being a major precipitating factor in these data. Younger respondents are more likely than older ones to report having been a 'bit drunk' at first intercourse, yet only 5.2% of women and 6.6% of men in the youngest age group of 16–24-year-olds report being slightly drunk as the main factor associated with their loss of virginity (Table 2.12), and 14% of men and 10% of women as a contributory factor. This factor is more likely to be cited by women for whom intercourse occurred before 16 (Table 2.11).

First intercourse seems to have been characterized by more planning and less spontaneity in recent years. Younger women in the sample were less likely than older women to report first intercourse having been mainly associated with being 'carried away by their feelings' (Table 2.12). This is consistent with the findings of recent US studies which have shown that many adolescents see their first experience of sexual intercourse as a conscious personal choice (Bigler, 1989; Coles and Stokes, 1985).

Contraception at first intercourse was far more likely to be used by either partner if intercourse was planned than if it was unplanned. While more than half of women (56.5%) who reported that intercourse had occurred 'on the spur of the moment' reported no contraceptive use by themselves or their partner, only 14.5% of those who had planned the event did so.

Feelings about First Intercourse

The majority of respondents recall their first intercourse as an event that both they and their partner agreed to, though there are some discrepancies between the perceptions of men and women. Men were more likely to report having been the more willing partner at first intercourse than women (8% cf. 2%), and more likely to claim that both they and their partner were equally willing (85% cf. 74%). Women were more likely to report having been persuaded than men (16% cf. 1.5%). This may be influenced by women's expectations about the social appropriateness of compliance. Again, retrospective data need to be cautiously interpreted. Respondents, in indicating what they felt about first intercourse, may have unconsciously justified that long-ago decision by choosing responses that reflect their present-day morality. Reported incidence of coercion at first intercourse is rare, but it is more common for women than for men (1.7% cf. 0.2%). (The phrasing here was, 'Would you say ... that you were forced' (see Appendix: Long Questionnaire, Question 22).

Most people, more than two-thirds of women and more than three-quarters of men, judged their first intercourse to have been well timed (Table 2.11). There are marked gender differences among those who did not. 25.5% of women reported feeling that the event took place too soon compared with 12.3% of men, and 7.1% men said they waited too long compared with 3.1% women. Predictably, these views relate strongly to age at first intercourse. More than half (58.5%) of women for whom first intercourse occurred under the age of 16 judged this to have been too soon, but less than a quarter of men (24.4%) did. Interestingly, a higher proportion of both men and women in the youngest age group (16–24) considered their first experience of intercourse to have been too soon (Table 2.12). The median age at first intercourse for men for whom it was 'about right' was 17; for those for whom it was 'too soon', 16, and for those who felt they had waited too long, 19. For women, the comparable figures are 19, 16 and 20 (Table 2.14).

	1st	median	3rd	*base*
		men		
too soon	15	16	17	*209*
waited too long	18	19	22	*133*
about right	16	17	19	*1431*
don't know/no opinion	15	17	18	*47*
		women		
too soon	16	16	18	*600*
waited too long	19	20	22	*82*
about right	17	19	21	*1672*
don't know/no opinion	17	18	20	*59*

Table 2.14 Quartiles of age at first intercourse by feelings about first intercourse. Source: Interview Questions 19a, 28

Multivariate Analysis

The combined effects of factors surrounding first intercourse, of current age and education on likelihood of first intercourse before the age of 16 and contraceptive use were explored using logistic regression. The likelihood of first intercourse under the age of 16 (Figure 2.13) was strongly related to current age, as expected, but for both men and women the effects of education were attenuated by factors surrounding the experience. Intercourse under the age of 16 was more likely to take place with a new partner than a steady one and to be motivated by curiosity rather than being in love. Alcohol played a minor role for women but not for men.

When contraceptive use at first sexual intercourse was considered using similar variables (Figure 2.14) both age and education remained highly significant with the youngest respondents and those with educational qualification at least to O-level standard being more likely to use contraception than older or less educated respondents. Alcohol was strongly associated with failure to use contraception, an effect that has been documented elsewhere (Wight, 1993). Sex under the age of 16 and lack of planning are also associated

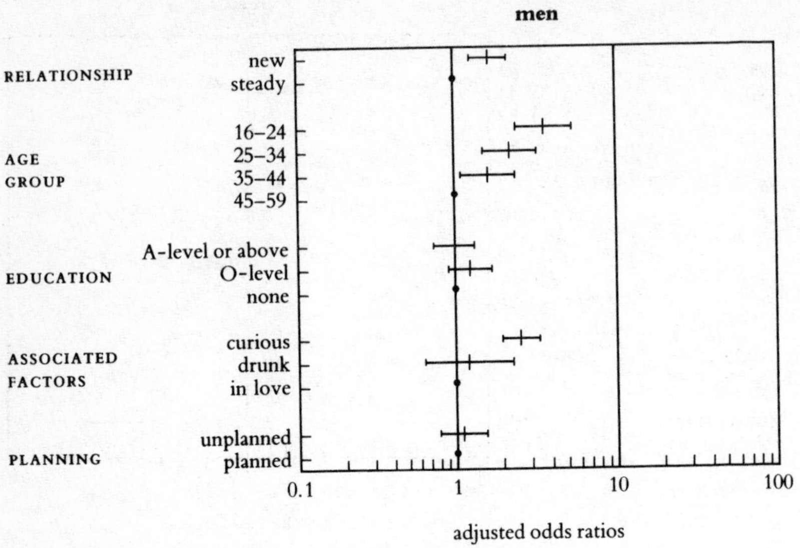

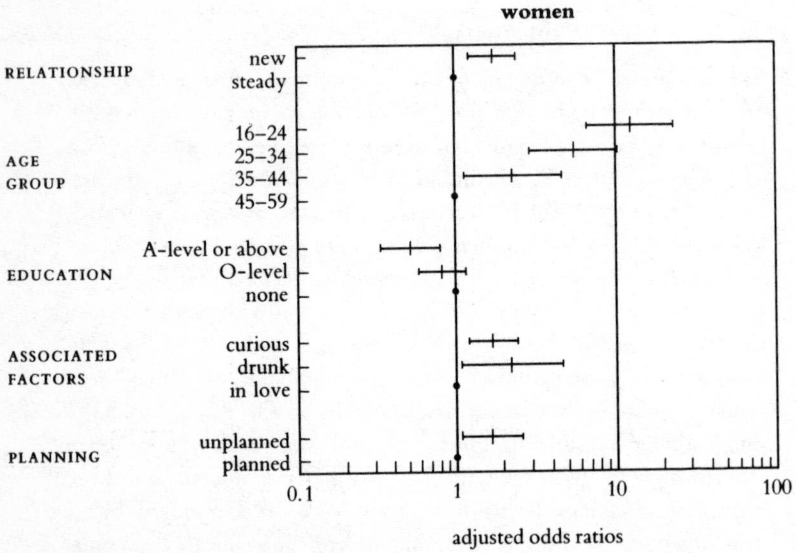

Response options were grouped into categories for this model

Figure 2.13 Adjusted odds ratios for first intercourse before age 16.*
Source: Interview Question 19a

* excludes those who have never had sexual intercourse

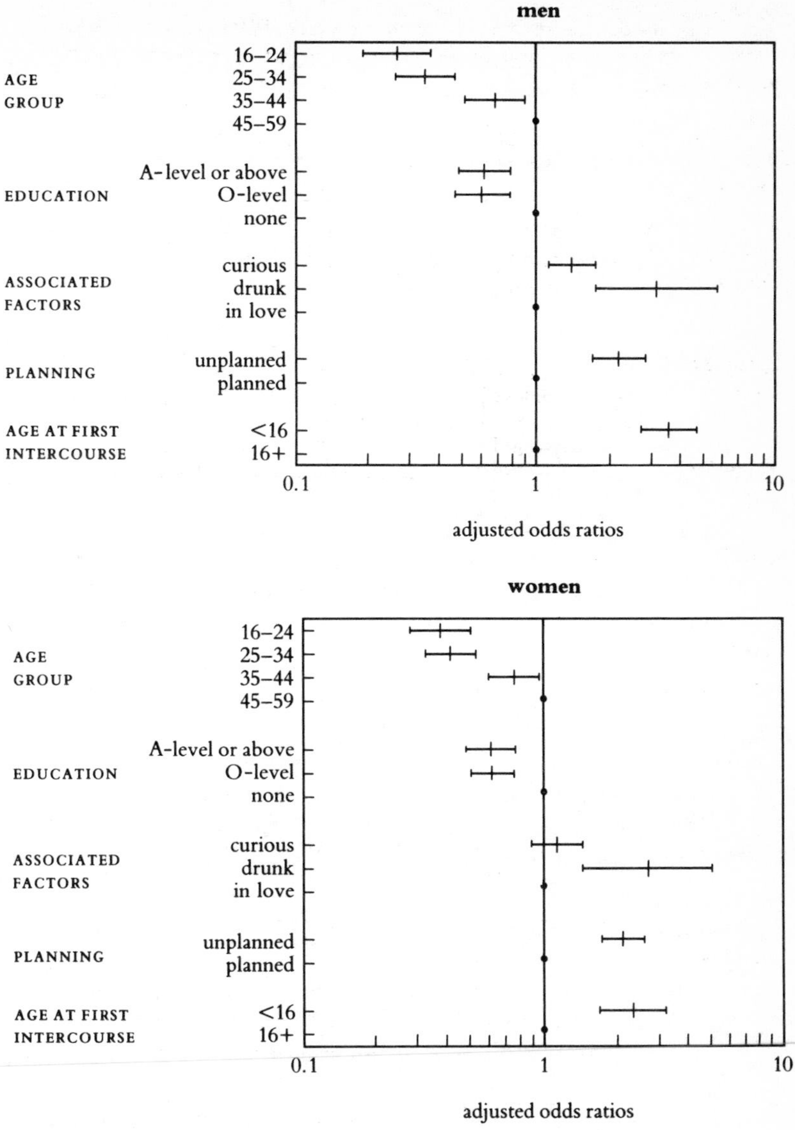

Response options were grouped into categories for this model

Figure 2.14 Adjusted odds ratios for no contraceptive use at first intercourse*. Source: Interview Question 19

* excludes those who have never had sexual intercourse

with no contraceptive use, again an effect noted elsewhere (Zelnick and Shah, 1983). In this context, the apparent trend towards greater planning noted above has positive implications for contraceptive use.

The comparison of these models is interesting. Whether or not first intercourse happens before the age of 16 is strongly associated with current age and weakly associated with the circumstances at the time. However, although the use of contraception on the first occasion is also associated with current age, it is strongly associated with factors surrounding the event itself. It is particularly striking that while those aged 16–24 are most likely to have intercourse under the age of 16, this is also the age group least likely to have intercourse without contraception.

SUMMARY

The data for first heterosexual intercourse show a pattern of decreasing age at occurrence together with an increase in the proportions reporting experience before the age of 16 and some convergence in the behaviour of men and women over time. Perhaps the most notable of these trends is the sharp fall in the age at which first intercourse occurs. In the past four decades, the median age at first heterosexual intercourse has fallen from 21 to 17 for women and from 20 to 17 for men, while the proportion reporting its occurrence before the age of 16 has increased from fewer than 1% of women aged 55 and over to nearly one in five of those now in their late teens.

This change seems to have coincided with a period in which the traditional constraints on early sexual expression – social disapproval of sex before marriage, negative attitudes towards teenage sexuality and a fear of pregnancy – have been gradually lifted. These changes need to be seen in the context of liberalizing legal reform, a relaxation of sexual attitudes and advances in medical technology. There is no evidence that any one factor is paramount in terms of explanatory importance.

Early intercourse is still associated with lower social class and educational level, but these effects seem to be weakening. The general impression is one of increasing homogeneity with respect to gender, occupational and educational level, and other sociodemographic variables.

Younger respondents are more likely to report early intercourse but more likely to report contraceptive use than are older respondents. The earlier first intercourse occurs, the less likely it is to be protected, yet there is no evidence that a fall in the age of first intercourse has been accompanied by increased risk-taking in this respect. Young people today are more likely to be using contraception (most commonly the condom) at their first experience of sexual intercourse than were those of the previous generation.

The event of first heterosexual intercourse is associated with more planning and less spontaneity than was formerly the case, and contraceptive use tends to be associated with the former.

The majority of people have their first experience of sexual intercourse in an established relationship. Young women seem to be initiated by an older male partner while men's first heterosexual partners tend to be age peers. It is uncommon, and increasingly so, for first sexual intercourse to take place within marriage, and very rare for men's first experience of this to be with a prostitute.

REFERENCES

Akpom, C. A., K. L. Akpom, and M. Davis (1976). 'Prior Sexual Behaviour of Teenagers Attending Rap Sessions for the First Time', *Family Planning Perspective*, 8: 203–6

Bigler, M. O. (1989). 'Surveys of American Adolescents Have Found that the Average Age of First Intercourse Ranges from 16–16.9 years', *Siecus*, October–November, 6–9

Black, S., and M. Sykes (1971). 'Promiscuity and Oral Contraception: The Relationship Examined', *Social Science and Medicine*, 5:637–43

Bone, M. (1986). 'Trends in Single Women's Sexual Behaviour in Scotland', *Population Trends*, 43: 7–14

Boyd, J. T., and R. Doll (1964). 'A Study of the Aetiology of Carcinoma of the Cervix Uteri', *British Journal of Cancer*, 18: 419–34

Brown, S., M. Vessey, and R. Harris (1984). 'Social Class, Sexual

Habits and Cancer of the Cervix', *Community Medicine*, 6: 281–6

Christiansen, H. R., and C. F. Gregg (1970). 'Changing Sex Norms in America and Scandinavia', *Journal of Marriage and the Family*, 32: 616–27

Christopher, F. S., and R. M. Cate (1985). 'Anticipated Influences on Sexual Decision-making for First Intercourse', *Family Relations*, 34: 265–70

Coles, R., and G. Stokes (1985). *Sex and the American Teenager*. New York: Harper and Row

De Buono, B. A., S. Zinner, M. Daamen, and W. M. McCormack (1990). 'Sexual Behaviour of College Women in 1975, 1986 and 1989', *New England Journal of Medicine*, 322 (12), 821–5

Delameter, J., and P. MacCorquodale (1979). *Premarital Sexuality*. Madison: University of Wisconsin Press

Dunnell, K. (1979). *Family Formation 1976*. London: HMSO

Farrell, C. (1978). *My Mother Said . . . The Way Young People Learn about Sex and Birth Control*. London: Routledge and Kegan Paul

Faulkenberry, J. R., M. Vincent, A. James, and W. Johnson (1987). 'Coital Behaviors, Attitudes and Knowledge of Students who Experience Early Coitus', *Adolescence*, 22: 321–32

Fisher, W., and D. Byrne (1981). 'Social Background, Attitudes and Sexual Attraction', in M. Cook (ed.), *The Bases of Human Attraction*. London: Academic

Ford, N. (1993). 'The Sexual and Contraceptive Lifestyles of Young People: Parts I and II', *British Journal of Family Planning*, 18: 52–5; 119–22

Ford, N., and C. Bowie (1989). 'Urban–Rural Variations in the Level of Heterosexual Activity of Young People', *AREA* 21, (3): 237–48

Forman, D., and C. Chilvers (1989). 'Sexual Behaviour of Young and Middle-aged Men in England and Wales', *British Medical Journal*, 298: 1137–41

Garris, L., A. Steckler, and J. R. McIntyre (1976). 'The Relationship between Oral Contraceptives and Adolescent Sexual Behaviour', *Journal of Sex Research* 12 (2): 135–46

Harris, R. W. C., L. A. Brinton, R. H. Cowdell, *et al.* (1980).

'Characteristics of Women with Dysplasia or Carcinoma in situ of the Cervix Uteri', *British Journal of Cancer*, 42: 359–69

Hofferth, S. L. (1988). 'Trends in Adolescent Sexual Activity, Contraception and Pregnancy in the United States', in J. Bancroft and J. Reinisch (eds), *Adolescence and Puberty: Third Kinsey Symposium*. New York: Oxford University Press

Jones, E. F., J. D. Forrest, N. Goldman, *et al.* (1985). 'Teenage Pregnancies in Developed Countries: Determinants and Policy Implications', *Family Planning Perspectives*, 17: 53–63

Kantner, J. F., and M. Zelnick (1972). 'Sexual Experience of Young Unmarried Women in the United States', *Family Planning Perspectives*, 4: 9–18

Kinsey, A. C., W. B. Pomeroy, and C. E. Martin (1948). *Sexual Behavior in the Human Male*. Philadelphia: W. B. Saunders

Kinsey, A. C., W. B. Pomeroy, C. E. Martin, and P. H. Gebhard (1953). *Sexual Behavior in the Human Female*. Philadelphia: W. B. Saunders

Klassen, A. D., C. J. Williams, and E. E. Levitt (1981). *Sex and Morality in the US*. Middletown, Connecticut: Wesleyan University Press

Kraft, P., J. Rise, and J. K. Gronnesby (1989). 'Prediction of Sexual Behaviour in a Group of Norwegian Adults', *NIPH Annals*, 12(2): 27–44

McCabe, M. P., and J. K. Collins (1983). 'The Sexual and Affectional Attitudes and Experiences of Australian Adolescents During Dating: The Effects of Age, Church Attendance, Type of School and Socioeconomic Class', *Archives of Sexual Behaviour*, 12: 525–40

Mant, D., M. Vessey, and N. Loudon (1988). 'Social Class Differences in Sexual Behaviour and Cervical Cancer', *Community Medicine*, 10 (1): 52–6

Orr, D. P., M. L. Wilbrandt, C. J. Brack, S. P. Raunch and G. M. Ingersoll (1989). 'Reported Sexual Behaviours and Self-esteem among Young Adolescents', *American Journal of Diseases of Children*, 143: 86–90

Pike, M. C., D. E. Henderson, M. D. Krailo, *et al.* (1983). 'Breast Cancer in Young Women and Use of Oral Contraceptives: Possible Modifying Effect of Formulation and Age of Use', *Lancet*, ii: 926–30

RCGP (1977). 'Mortality among Oral Contraceptive Users', Royal College of General Practitioners' Oral Contraception Study, *Lancet*, 2 (8041) 727–31

Reichelt, P. A. (1978). 'Changes in Sexual Behaviour among Unmarried Women Utilizing Oral Contraception', *Journal of Population*, 1: 1: 57–68

Reiss, I. L. (1967). *The Social Context of Premarital Sexual Permissiveness*. New York: Rinehart and Winston

Robinson, I. E., and D. Jedlicka (1982). 'Changes in Sexual Attitudes and Behaviour of College Students from 1965 to 1980: A Research Note', *Journal of Marriage and the Family*, 44: 237–40

Schmidt, G., and V. Sigusch (1971). 'Patterns of Sexual Behaviour in West German Workers and Students', *Journal of Sex Research*, 7: 89–106

Schmidt, G., and V. Sigusch (1972). 'Changes in Sexual Behaviour among Young Males and Females between 1960 and 1970', *Archives of Sexual Behaviour*, 2: 27–45

Schofield, M. (1965). *The Sexual Behaviour of Young People*. London: Longman

Schofield, M. (1973). *The Sexual Behaviour of Young Adults*. London: Allen Lane

Settlage, D. S. F., S. Baroff, and D. Cooper (1973). 'Sexual Experience of Younger Teenage Girls Seeking Contraceptive Assistance for the First Time', *Family Planning Perspectives*, 5: 223–6

Tanner, J. M. (1962). *Growth at Adolescence*, 2nd edn. Oxford: Blackwell

Udry, J. R., L. M. Talbert, and N. M. Morris (1986). 'Bio-social Foundations for Adolescent Female Sexuality', *Demography*, 23: 217–27

Vessey, M. P., K. McPherson and B. Johnson (1977) 'Mortality among Women Participating in the Oxford/FPA Contraceptive Study', *Lancet*, ii: 731–3

West, P., D. Wight, and S. MacIntyre (1993). 'Heterosexual Behaviour of 18-year-olds in the Glasgow Area', *Journal of Adolescence*, forthcoming

Wight, D. (1993). 'Constraints or Cognition? Young Men and Safer Heterosexual Sex', in P. Aggleton, P. Davies, and G. Hart (eds), *AIDS: The Second Decade*, Basingstoke: Falmer Press

Wynder, E. L. (1969). 'Epidemiology of Carcinoma in situ of the Cervix', *Obstetric and Gynecological Surveys*, 24: 697–711

Zelnick, M., and J. F. Kantner (1980). 'Sexual Activity, Contraceptive Use and Pregnancy among Metropolitan-area Teenagers: 1971–79', *Family Planning Perspectives*, 12: 230–37

Zelnick, M., and F. K. Shah (1983). 'First Intercourse among Young Americans', *Family Planning Perspectives*, 15: 64–70

CHAPTER 3

Heterosexual Partnerships

INTRODUCTION

Patterns of sexual partnership may vary markedly. At any point in time, variation may occur between individuals, between social groups and between societies. For each individual the nature and stability of sexual partnership may vary with life stage. Within a society, sexual lifestyle may alter through historical time (Weeks, 1981).

Previous work for this study and that carried out by other observers in the late twentieth century provide evidence of the striking variability in numbers of sexual partners reported by individuals over a given time period. While many people report one or few partners, a small proportion report many partners (Johnson *et al.*, 1989; Centers for Disease Control, 1988; ACSF Investigators, 1992; Johnson *et al.*, 1992). In this chapter, the variability in numbers of heterosexual partners in different time intervals is described, and some of the possible influences on variation discussed. Patterns of homosexual partnership are described in Chapter 5.

As in describing other aspects of sexual behaviour, such as sexual practices (Chapter 4), it is logical to assume that a number of factors may influence the formation of sexual partnerships. These include, for example, age and marital status. Those embarking on their sexual careers may be passing through a sexually experimental phase and experience a number of partner changes before establishing a longer term and more committed relationship. Later in life, separation, divorce or widowhood may lead to loss of a stable partnership and a return either to the formation of new partnerships or to a period of sexual abstinence. The life course may thus substantially influence patterns of relationships. This influence must be distinguished from changes in sexual behaviour in historical time (or birth-cohort effects) whereby cultural norms and behaviour are influenced by the changing social climate, legislative, medical, demographic or other factors (Weeks, 1981). It is perhaps worth emphasizing again, with a future historian's eye, that the study has been undertaken at the end of a period of at least 30 years of rapid change in sexual mores, the availability of reliable contraception, effective treatment for most of the traditional sexually transmitted diseases (STDs), a growth in international travel, a relaxation of legal constraints on male homosexuality, abortion and divorce, and a more open attitude to sexual expression (see Chapter 1) (Dunnell, 1979). In addition to studying current behaviour patterns, the data have therefore been examined for evidence of temporal trends, in so far as this is possible from retrospective information.

An understanding of patterns of partnerships is of interest to many different disciplines. From the anthropological point of view, comparisons between societies may allow conclusions to be drawn about the relative influences of nature and nurture on human sexual behaviour. From the sociological viewpoint, patterns of sexual partnership and family formation are a key component of social relations in contemporary Britain, while secular changes are an important aspect of the social history of the twentieth century. For the educationalist, an understanding of the extent of sexual experience and of age at sexual début (Chapter 2) can inform sex education policy. For the epidemiologist, measurement of the frequency of partner change can improve understanding of the relationship between demographic characteristics and sexual behaviour as well as the dynamics of STD transmission. Patterns of partner change are a key concern in the latter context since the risk of acquiring a sexually transmitted infection, including HIV, increases with the number of sexual partners with whom an individual has unprotected intercourse (Holmes and Aral, 1991; May and Anderson, 1987). In addition, the spread of STD is influenced by the extent to which those with many partners mix with those with few partners, an area that is more difficult to study from survey data (Hethcote and Yorke, 1984; Potts *et al.*, 1991). Some limited aspects of sexual mixing have been analysed in this study, including patterns of age mixing and the extent to which men pay for sexual contact with women.

QUESTION FORMAT

This chapter draws largely on the questions about number and type of heterosexual partnership, all of which were asked in the self-completion booklet. Question 7 asked about the number of opposite-sex partners in a series of different time intervals. Questions 10–12 asked for details of the most recent 3 partnerships in the last 5 years for those with more than one partner in that time. In addition, men were asked whether they had ever paid money for sex with a woman (Question 13), as well as the number of women paid.

Qualitative research for this survey as well as that of others (Spencer *et al.*, 1988; Hunt *et al.*, 1991) indicates that the definition of a sexual partner may vary considerably between individuals. Some may include as partners only those with whom penetrative vaginal intercourse took place, while others may include relationships that did not involve penetrative sex or involved only oro-genital contact. The pilot work raised the suspicion that a small minority of respondents failed to include their spouse when assessing numbers of sexual partners. For these reasons, specific instructions were given to respondents in the question about number of partners: 'Please include everyone you have ever had sex with, whether it was just once, a few times, a regular partner or your husband (wife).' Heterosexual partners were defined as partners of the opposite sex with whom the respondent had had vaginal, oral or anal sexual intercourse.

ITEM NON-RESPONSE AND CODING ASSUMPTIONS

Questions on numbers of sexual partners were asked of all but a small minority of respondents who did not complete the booklet. 4.1% of women and 3.8% of men declined to complete the booklet and gave insufficient information in the face-to-face interview for any assumptions to be made about the numbers of heterosexual partners. For those who answered in the face-to-face interview that they had never had sexual intercourse and were not eligible to complete the booklet, the number of partners was assumed to be zero in the calculation of population estimates.

Item non-response varied according to each question and was greatest for self-completion Questions 10–12, which required further information for those with multiple partnerships in the last 5 years, a level of detail it was difficult for some people to supply. For numbers of partners the non-response was in general below 5%.

MEASUREMENT PRECISION

Questions about numbers of heterosexual partners were asked over 5 different time periods: 1 month, 1 year, 2 years, 5 years and lifetime. It is important to collect data over several different time periods in order to capture the variability in sexual behaviour, to assess patterns of partner change, as well as to identify possible secular trends. These are difficult to measure if data are restricted to relatively short time periods such as 1 year. However, the longer the time interval, the greater the problems of recall error. This is particularly true for 'lifetime' partners (so far). This summary statistic is complex since it is influenced by the number of years of sexual experience of the respondent, which is highly variable. It includes respondents who are embarking on their sexual careers and those who may form many new partnerships in the future as well as those whose sexual careers are complete. It is also potentially the most inaccurate measure, especially for those in the older age groups who have a long period both to recall and to acquire partners, and who are likely to be those for whom the most active period is the most distant. However, lifetime partners are perhaps the most useful way of examining cohort effects in the data since, among the older age groups, this was the only measurement made in the survey of sexual behaviour many years ago.

NUMBER OF HETEROSEXUAL PARTNERS IN DIFFERENT TIME INTERVALS

Table 3.1 shows the numbers of partners reported in the last year, in the last 5 years and ever (so far) stratified by age group and gender. One of the striking features of these data is the marked variability between individuals in the number of partners reported, and the extreme skewness of the distribution. For example, over the last 5 years 65.2% of men and 76.5% of women reported 0 or 1 sexual partner. At the other end of the scale, 1% of men reported more than 22 partners and 1% of women reported more than 8 partners. The maximum reported lifetime partners exceeded 4,500 for men and 1000 for women. The corresponding 5-year estimate was 500 for men and 100 for women; and in the last year 200 for men and 25 for women. There was marked digit preference for multiples of ten, indicating the considerable difficulties that arise in accurately recording large numbers of partners, and the inherent inaccuracies that are likely to arise in reporting by these respondents, particularly if there is any bias resulting from rounding up or down.

Correspondingly, the mean and variance are strongly influenced by those reporting a very large number of partners. For example, for men the mean number of reported partners ever is 9.9, with a variance of 6575. The median for the same distribution is 4. Such extreme skewness may be unduly influenced by memory error, particularly among people with long and varied sexual careers, making the mean an unstable and potentially unreliable summary statistic. The shape of the distribution implies decreasing precision as time intervals increase, and the period of recall lengthens, while the greatest inaccuracy is likely to occur among those with the largest number of partners. This high degree of variability has been commented on previously and is a finding common to studies in many other populations (Centers for Disease Control, 1988; ACSF Investigators, 1992; Johnson *et al.* 1992; Wadsworth and Johnson, 1991; Anderson and Johnson, 1990).

Recent attention has been drawn to the potential importance of those with particularly high numbers of partners (sometimes called

	age group				
	16–24 %	25–34 %	35–44 %	45–59 %	all %
			men		
lifetime					
0	20.4	3.1	1.9	1.5	6.6
1	16.3	15.0	20.5	30.5	20.6
2	9.8	9.2	10.7	12.6	10.6
3–4	19.4	18.2	17.1	18.9	18.4
5–9	17.9	23.1	20.9	15.8	19.4
10+	16.2	31.4	28.9	20.8	24.4
99th centile	45	86	75	100	75
last 5 years					
0	20.6	4.6	4.5	5.7	8.7
1	20.1	51.7	72.6	80.6	56.5
2	11.8	12.4	9.4	6.4	10.0
3–4	20.2	15.9	7.5	4.7	12.0
5–9	16.1	9.6	4.2	1.9	7.9
10+	11.2	5.8	1.7	0.7	4.8
99th centile	35	25	12	6	22
last year					
0	26.9	8.6	6.8	10.8	13.1
1	46.2	76.8	84.1	83.8	73.0
2	14.3	8.6	6.1	4.2	8.2
3–4	9.1	4.1	2.1	1.1	4.1
5+	3.5	1.9	0.8	0.1	1.5
99th centile	10	5	4	3	6
base	*1984*	*2167*	*2051*	*2182*	*8384*

Table 3.1 *continued overleaf*

	age group				
	16–24 %	25–34 %	35–44 %	45–59 %	all %
			women		
lifetime					
0	20.7	2.1	0.7	1.5	5.7
1	27.0	30.8	40.7	57.7	39.3
2	14.7	18.3	17.7	16.6	16.9
3–4	18.8	22.5	18.5	12.9	18.2
5–9	14.1	16.7	13.9	7.4	13.0
10+	4.6	9.7	8.5	3.8	6.8
99th centile	18	25	28	20	25
last 5 years					
0	20.8	3.1	3.3	11.3	9.1
1	33.1	67.6	82.4	81.9	67.4
2	16.3	14.3	9.0	4.9	11.0
3–4	16.9	10.3	4.3	1.7	8.1
5–9	10.5	3.8	0.9	0.2	3.6
10+	2.5	0.8	0.2	0.04	0.8
99th centile	15	8	5	3	8
last year					
0	23.9	6.7	7.4	19.3	13.9
1	60.5	86.8	88.4	78.9	79.4
2	10.0	4.9	3.3	1.6	4.8
3–4	4.5	1.3	0.8	0.2	1.6
5+	1.0	0.3	0.1	0.0	0.4
99th centile	7	3	2	2	3
base	*2246*	*2899*	*2576*	*2771*	*10492*

Table 3.1 Distribution of numbers of heterosexual partners in various time intervals by gender and age group. Source: Booklet Questions 7a, 7b, 7d

'core groups') in the maintenance of transmission of sexually transmitted organisms in a population (Holmes and Aral, 1991); and the influence of mixing between those with many partners and those with few in transmission dynamics (Hethcote and Yorke, 1984). The extreme skewness of the distribution lends support to the existence of such a high-activity group and an understanding of the characteristics of those with very large numbers of partners is of great importance to STD epidemiologists. Nevertheless, such minorities in the population are not static, and the individuals in the upper centiles of the distribution may vary over time in response to influences of marriage, parenthood, divorce, ageing, sexual fashion and availability of partners.

RESPONDENT'S CURRENT AGE AND HETEROSEXUAL PARTNERSHIPS

Table 3.1 demonstrates marked variability in the distribution of number of partners by age group. These effects are most marked over recent time periods (1–5 years). Men and women in the age group 16–24 are consistently those reporting the greatest numbers of sexual partners, despite being the group with the highest proportion of respondents who have not yet experienced heterosexual intercourse (20.7% of women and 20.4% of men). Among those aged 16–24, 11.2% of men and 2.5% of women reported 10 or more partners in the last 5 years. This higher number of partners per unit time is reflected in statistics for STD clinics, which indicate that the highest incidence of reported STD occurs in those aged 20–24 (PHLS, 1992).

The age differences in reported numbers of partners may be influenced by two factors. First, the youngest age groups are starting on their sexual careers, and may explore a series of relationships before (in the future) adopting a long-term relationship with a monogamous lifestyle. Second, age differences may reflect genuine generational changes in sexual behaviour influenced by the many different social and legislative issues previously discussed.

Examination of generational changes is more difficult from the data set, since there are differential problems of recall according to the length of time that an individual has been sexually active. For older people it may be more difficult to remember what happened 30 years ago than for the youngest age group to reflect over only a 5-year period. Since the questions asked related to fixed time periods, rather than precise calendar years, it is not possible to reconstruct the precise sexual histories of older respondents when they were in their teens and twenties.

Nevertheless, some evidence of temporal changes in sexual behaviour is available from the data on lifetime numbers of partners. Not surprisingly, the youngest age group (16–24) report fewer lifetime partners than those aged 25–44 because they have had less time to acquire many partners. For women and men, both the median number of partners (3 and 5 respectively), and the proportion reporting more than 10 partners (9.7% and 31.4% respectively) peak in the 25–34-year-old group, with a marked decline to 3.8% of women and 20.8% of men reporting more than 10 partners in the 45–59-year-old group (Table 3.1). Despite having a longer period in which to form sexual partnerships, the 45–59 age group reports fewer lifetime partners than those aged 25–44.

The trend in the overall distribution of number of lifetime partners is shown in Figure 3.1 by 5-year age group. The proportion of respondents reporting no partners rapidly declines with age, as individuals become sexually active, while the proportion who report only one lifetime partner increases steadily for women from the age of 25 and for men (less markedly) from the age of 35. The proportion with larger numbers of partners shows an increase followed by a decrease with age, the peak being around the age of 30–34. This confirms the increasing change from a pattern of a single sexual partner for life to acceptance of a number of partner changes throughout the life course.

This suggests that there have been genuine generational changes, reflected not only in younger age of sexual intercourse (Chapter 2), but also in increasing numbers of sexual partners. Figure 3.2 shows this effect, where the proportion of men and women reporting 10 or more partners in their lifetime (so far) is shown by calendar year of first sexual intercourse. This shows a steady increase over time in the proportion of respondents reporting 10 or more lifetime part-

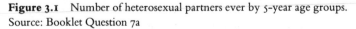

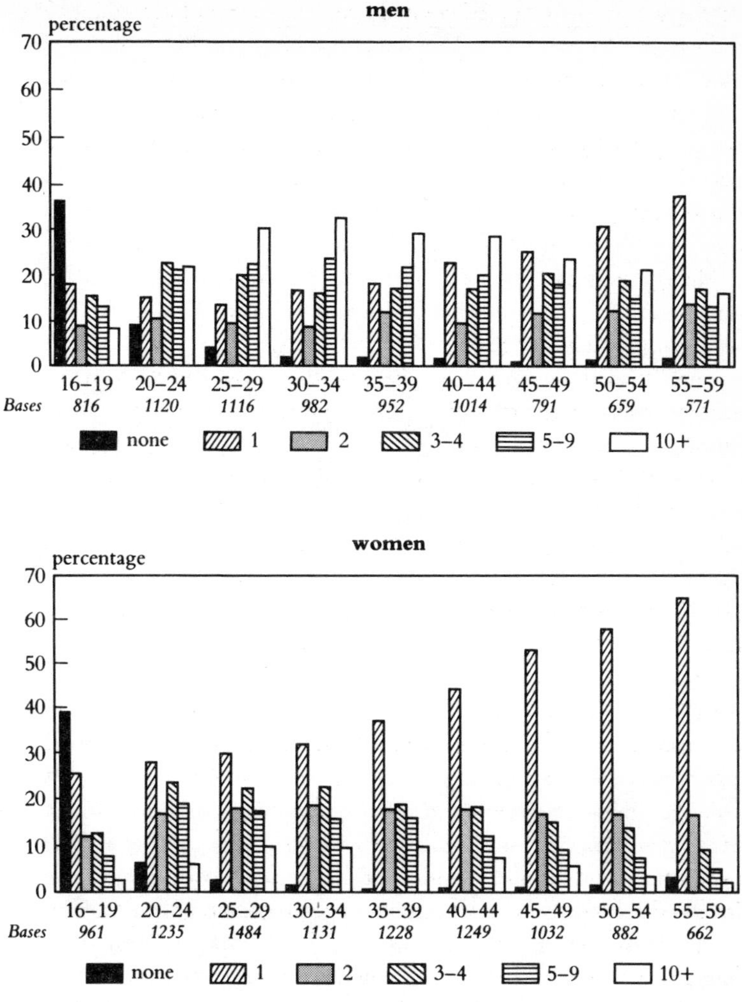

Figure 3.1 Number of heterosexual partners ever by 5-year age groups. Source: Booklet Question 7a

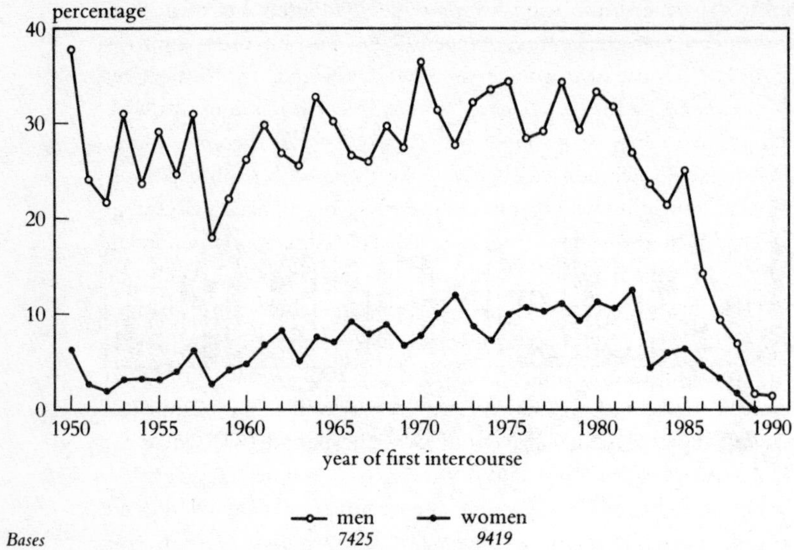

Figure 3.2 Proportion of respondents reporting 10 or more heterosexual partners ever by year of first sexual intercourse. Source: Interview Question 19a; Booklet Question 7a

ners, an effect that is more marked for women than men. Around 3% of women whose sexual début occurred in the 1950s reported 10 or more lifetime partners. The equivalent figure is over 10% for those commencing intercourse in the 1970s. The decline in this proportion after the early 1980s is probably an effect of current age, because this largely comprises the 16–24-year-old age group who have had few years of sexual activity. Nevertheless, changes in sexual behaviour in response to the HIV epidemic must also be considered as part of the explanation.

It is striking that throughout the time period a much higher proportion (consistently greater than 20%) of men than women report more than 10 partners. While this proportion increases over time for both genders, the trend is less marked for men. Some of the possible reasons for gender differences in reported behaviour patterns are discussed in detail below. However, the data may indicate different generational effects in men and women, with multiple partnerships being more widely adopted by men than women earlier in the century. Since it is not possible to account for the point in time that partnerships were formed, the differences may partly relate to the tendency of men to form relationships with younger women (see p. 116), particularly as they become older. These younger women are likely to be those with higher partner numbers, thus diminishing any cohort effect in the data analysed in this way. On the other hand, the social constraints on reporting sexual behaviour may affect women more than men and these may have become weaker over time. The apparent behaviour changes observed are entirely consistent with what is known both of social and technological changes in recent decades which improved women's sexual and reproductive choices, as well as with empirical data on changing sexual behaviour over the period (Klassen *et al.*, 1989; Turner, 1989; Zelnik and Kantner, 1983; Dunnell, 1979).

These trends in behaviour are also reflected in data relating to adverse health effects of changed sexual behaviour. This is, for example, shown by the increased incidence of gonorrhoea and other STDs from the early 1960s onwards (Adler, 1982).

GENDER AND NUMBER OF REPORTED PARTNERS

Consistent with many other surveys of sexual behaviour (Serwadda *et al.*, 1992; ACSF Investigators, 1992; Centers for Disease Control, 1988; Wadsworth and Johnson, 1991; Smith, 1992) men of all ages reported a higher number of sexual partners than women. This holds true whether the mean, median or frequency distribution is considered. Theoretically in a closed population without migration, the average number of heterosexual partners for men and women in a defined time period should be equal. Clearly, these conditions do not hold strictly true. Individuals may have partners outside the sampled population (e.g. abroad) or with partners who may be under-represented in the sample (e.g. prostitutes). Patterns of age mixing (see p. 116) indicate that men tend to have relationships with younger women, who in turn have more partners per unit time than older women (Johnson *et al.*, 1990; Wadsworth, *et al.*, 1993; Smith, 1992). The differences become increasingly marked for increasing time periods. This may in part be a result of the greater variability in the distribution of number of partners with increasing time intervals, but may also reflect the greater difficulties of recall over time. In addition, those with very large numbers of partners have a large effect on summary statistics such as the mean. Consistency between genders would not necessarily be expected when 'lifetime' partners are considered because these involve widely differing time periods for different individuals.

It is unlikely that these explanations can account for all the differences observed and we conclude that a number of social factors may influence reporting in contemporary Britain. British society still condones the behaviour of a man with many partners. This is illustrated by the language used to describe him ('stud', 'a bit of a lad'). On the other hand a woman with many partners may be called a 'slag' or a 'tart' or other pejorative terms, for which no equivalent exists for the male. This double standard remains prevalent in the language, despite the apparent changes in attitudes towards female sexuality promoted by the women's movement and the liberalization of attitudes towards sex outside marriage.

As Weeks has argued, relaxation in sexual mores as expressed in attitudes may not have changed to the extent sometimes implied in the terms 'sexual permissiveness' and 'sexual revolution' (Weeks, 1981) A futher discussion of temporal changes and gender differences in attitudes to sexual behaviour is presented in Chapter 6. Social influences may still lead to reporting bias, characterized by exaggeration of number of partners by men and under-reporting by women, whether this is deliberate, due to memory error, or unconsciously self-censoring.

Smith (1991) has considered the factors that may influence reporting in greater detail than is discussed here, and emphasizes the need for further empirical research in this area. Possible approaches include the exploration of gender differences in mechanisms of recalling numbers of sexual partners; the use of calendar techniques to reconstruct detailed sexual histories and qualitative methods to explore possible variation in definitions of a sexual partner. For example, men might be more likely to include as 'partners' those with whom they had had sexual contact not including intercourse, and women might discount them. In this survey (in contrast to many others) a careful behavioural definition of a sexual partner was given. This may in part account for the smaller gender differences in reporting in the British data than in other surveys (Smith, 1992).

THE INFLUENCE OF MARITAL STATUS

In a society that supports monogamy both socially and legally within marriage, but in which sex among the unmarried has become increasingly accepted as the cultural norm (see Chapter 6), numbers of sexual partnerships might be expected to vary quite markedly by marital status. Table 3.2 shows the proportions of respondents with 2 or more heterosexual partners in the last year by marital status. 4.5% of men and 1.9% of women who are married reported more than

	16–24		25–34		35–44		45–59		all ages	
	%	*base*	%	*base*	%	*base*	%	*base*	%	*base*
					men					
married	3.9	*163*	5.0	*1203*	5.3	*1537*	3.4	*1671*	4.5	*4573*
cohabiting	16.1	*146*	16.2	*239*	13.5	*130*	13.8	*82*	15.3	*597*
widowed/separated/divorced	48.4	*16*	43.0	*105*	36.4	*129*	19.7	*176*	31.6	*426*
single	30.0	*1614*	29.3	*555*	18.3	*178*	7.5	*101*	28.1	*2448*
					women					
married	1.5	*342*	2.2	*1789*	2.4	*1915*	1.1	*1980*	1.9	*6025*
cohabiting	10.3	*303*	6.5	*309*	7.6	*150*	7.1	*58*	8.2	*819*
widowed/separated/divorced	25.9	*36*	18.3	*229*	14.1	*304*	4.5	*450*	11.2	*1019*
single	19.6	*1514*	17.1	*473*	4.7	*113*	0.6	*93*	17.5	*2193*

Table 3.2 Proportion of respondents reporting 2 or more heterosexual partners in the last year by age group and marital status. Source: Booklet Question 7d

1 heterosexual partner in the last year, and a tiny fraction (1.2% of married men and 0.2% of married women) reported more than 2 partners in the last year. Respondents who were neither married nor cohabiting were (not surprisingly) much more likely to have had no partner in the last year. At the same time, they were also much more likely to report multiple partners in the last year. Among single people, more than a quarter of men (28.1%) and close to one-fifth of women (17.5%) reported 2 or more partners in the last year while 13.1% of men and 6.1% of women reported more than 2 partners, a pattern that contrasts strikingly with that of married individuals. Those cohabiting occupy an intermediate position when compared with the married and single. Among these, 15.3% of men and 8.2% of women reported 2 or more partners in the last year.

These bivariate analyses may be confounded by the effects of age, since younger individuals, for example, are both more likely to be single and to report multiple partners. Within all age groups, the married are very much less likely to report multiple partners in the last year than any other group. There is no marked age trend in the probability of reporting 2 or more partners in the last year.

For those cohabiting, as stated, a much higher proportion report 2 or more partners in the last year than married people. This appears not to be an effect of age since the relationship holds true across the age categories with no striking age gradient. This may in turn reflect either the less committed nature of cohabiting relationships or the more liberal attitudes of cohabitees towards non-exclusive relationships. The relationship between attitudes to sexual lifestyle and marital status is discussed more fully in Chapter 6.

Those consistently showing the highest prevalence of multiple partnerships are separated, divorced and widowed people whose levels of activity within each age and sex group exceed those of the single. This is particularly striking for separated, divorced and widowed men aged 25–44, among whom nearly 40% reported 2 or more partners in the last year. It is possible that the breakdown of a stable relationship may lead to a period of relatively rapid partner change before (possibly) adopting a new longer-term partnership. These data suggest that it is not age *per se* that is the dominant influence on frequency of partner change but that the influence of a stable relationship is strong, regardless of the individual's age. There are implications for health education strategies, since attention is primarily focused on the young and single. The data presented here suggest that those who are separated, divorced and widowed may be a group with particularly rapid partner change and may be rather older than the group traditionally targeted for sexual health programmes.

Among single people, the prevalence of multiple partnerships markedly exceeds that of the married in almost all age and sex groups, but, unlike the married and cohabiting, the likelihood of reporting multiple partnerships declines quite markedly with age, although still tending to exceed rates among the married. The interpretation is clearly complex, because the proportion of never-married individuals declines with age. The remaining never-married respondents may include an increasing proportion who are primarily homosexual or who have only limited opportunity for sexual expression. However, data on sexual behaviour patterns among single people clearly indicate the wide acceptance of sex outside marriage. Though hardly startling to an audience in the 1990s, this represents a remarkable shift in social norms from the 1950s (Chesser, 1956).

SEXUAL PARTNERSHIPS AND SOCIAL CLASS

Given the social and cultural influences on patterns of sexual behaviour, social environment and socio-economic status might be expected to have some demonstrable relationship with attitudes and behaviour, though in which direction such influences might operate is not intuitively obvious. Here the relationship between social class and sexual partnerships is examined. Social class was assigned according to the respondent's occupation for those who were single, widowed, separated or divorced, and for those married or cohabiting according to the highest occupational level for the couple.

Social class alone must be recognized as an imperfect indicator of social environment. Social-class distribution is influenced by age, since career paths mean that young people are unlikely to be found in the managerial or professional classes. In addition, and linked to age, those in the higher social classes are more likely to be married (Table 3.3), so that any bivariate relationship between class and lifestyle is confounded by two major influences on sexual behaviour.

Past work examining the relationship between social class and sexual behaviour has been limited, and in some cases conflicting. Dunnell (1979) in her 1976 study found some evidence that women aged 16–24 in manual classes experienced both earlier first intercourse and first pregnancy, basing social-class classification either on the husband's occupation (for married women) or father's occupation (for single women). Class differences in experience of sex before marriage among women aged 20–49 were small, with no obvious social-class trend. In her study of 16–19-year-olds in 1974, Farrell (1978) found some evidence of earlier sexual experience

	social class							
	I, II		III NM		III M		IV, V, other	
	%	*base*	%	*base*	%	*base*	%	*base*
				men				
married	6.1	*1989*	3.6	*1005*	3.3	*1053*	2.2	*526*
cohabiting	16.5	*263*	13.5	*152*	14.9	*102*	14.7	*80*
widowed/separated/ divorced	34.0	*104*	49.4	*37*	31.7	*161*	23.9	*122*
single	26.7	*453*	32.0	*319*	34.2	*600*	24.1	*1072*
				women				
married	2.1	*2680*	2.4	*1209*	1.3	*1367*	1.4	*768*
cohabiting	8.0	*263*	12.6	*206*	4.7	*190*	6.5	*130*
widowed/separated/ divorced	13.2	*193*	11.8	*231*	10.4	*61*	10.2	*532*
single	17.2	*361*	20.1	*652*	14.2	*113*	16.3	*1066*

Table 3.3 Proportion of respondents reporting 2 or more heterosexual partners in the last year by marital status and social class. Source: Booklet Question 7d

NM = non-manual; M = manual

among working-class boys. Gorer (1971) in his 1969 study of English men and women, reported increased premarital intercourse, earlier intercourse and a weak trend towards increasing numbers of partners in manual social classes. However, these analyses did not attempt to control for age or marital status. Chesser's earlier study of women in 1954 suggests a similar class relationship for age at first intercourse and premarital sexual intercourse (Chesser, 1956). Studies of cervical cancer (Brown *et al.*, 1984) have found that the risk of this condition is higher in those in manual social classes. This has been considered as possible evidence of different patterns of sexual behaviour between socio-economic groups. Mant *et al.* (1988) found that women of lower social class attending family planning clinics reported an earlier age of first sexual intercourse, but fewer partners than women of higher social class.

	social class							
	I, II		III NM		III M		IV, V, other	
	%	*base*	%	*base*	%	*base*	%	*base*
				men				
16–24	24.4	*249*	28.8	*313*	34.0	*461*	23.4	*914*
25–34	13.6	*783*	11.7	*437*	14.4	*540*	20.9	*341*
35–44	10.1	*932*	5.3	*365*	11.4	*422*	6.8	*254*
45–59	7.3	*845*	4.1	*398*	4.9	*494*	2.8	*291*
all ages	11.5	*2810*	11.7	*1513*	16.0	*1916*	17.3	*1800*
				women				
16–24	11.4	*279*	19.7	*649*	7.5	*242*	16.0	*1023*
25–34	6.0	*1071*	7.2	*595*	3.7	*564*	9.6	*567*
35–44	4.1	*1143*	6.1	*525*	1.8	*425*	4.4	*386*
45–59	2.2	*1033*	1.9	*529*	0.5	*501*	2.4	*518*
all ages	4.7	*3526*	9.3	*2297*	2.8	*1732*	9.9	*2496*

Table 3.4 Proportion of respondents reporting 2 or more heterosexual partners in the last year by age and social class. Source: Booklet Question 7d

NM = non-manual; M = manual

Examination of the relationship between social class and heterosexual partnerships in the survey data has proved complex. No simple trend in behaviour in relation to social class is seen. However, stratification of the data by marital status and age gives a more complex picture (Tables 3.3 and 3.4) of the likelihood of reporting 2 or more heterosexual partners in the last year. For those who are currently, or have ever been, married, and for cohabitees, there is a trend towards a greater likelihood of reporting multiple partners in the last year with higher social class. This effect is most marked for married men in social classes I and II (6.1% reported 2 or more partners in the last year compared with only 2.2% of men in social classes IV and V). However, for single men and women the class relationships are less clear, with men in social class III manual and non-manual and women in III non-manual being the most likely to report multiple partnerships.

Table 3.4 shows the same variable (2 or more heterosexual partners in the last year) stratified by age group and social class. Men over 45 in social classes I and II were more likely to report multiple partners in the last year than those in social classes IV and V, though for younger age groups and for women there is no obvious trend.

The interpretation of these data must remain speculative, but includes the possibilities of varying attitudes to multiple partnerships in different groups (see Chapter 6) as well as differences in opportunity for sexual partnership formation. There is no obvious class trend and any relationship between social class and sexual behaviour is weak in bivariate analysis compared with that of age and marital status. The relationship is explored further in a multivariate model.

AGE AT FIRST INTERCOURSE

In Chapter 2 variability in age at first intercourse was explored and the relationship with current age and social class discussed. It is reasonable to hypothesize that early sexual experience might influence subsequent sexual lifestyle. To examine this, reporting of first sexual intercourse before the age of 16 has been used as an indicator

	age at first intercourse							
	men				**women**			
	before 16		after 16		before 16		after 16	
	%	*base*	%	*base*	%	*base*	%	*base*
age group								
16–24	42.5	*494*	21.6	*1433*	66.4	*360*	12.1	*1829*
25–34	18.3	*493*	13.5	*1596*	11.3	*261*	6.0	*2525*
35–44	20.3	*319*	6.9	*1639*	17.1	*125*	3.6	*2343*
45–59	10.0	*196*	4.8	*1805*	4.2	*54*	1.8	*2513*
all ages	25.6	*1503*	11.2	*6474*	21.7	*800*	5.4	*9210*

Table 3.5 Proportion of respondents reporting 2 or more heterosexual partners in the last year by age and age at first intercourse. Source: Interview Question 19a; Booklet Question 7d

of early sexual début. Table 3.5 shows the proportion of respondents reporting 2 or more heterosexual partners in the last year by current age and age at first sexual intercourse. For men and women of all age groups, those reporting first intercourse before the age of 16 are consistently more likely to report 2 or more partners in the last year. While the possibility of greater willingness to report and a more permissive attitude to sexual behaviour may be associated with an early sexual début, the data indicate that early sexual experience is associated with higher levels of sexual activity later in life, which persist into the fifth and sixth decades. The relative strength of this effect remains undiminished over time.

MULTIVARIATE ANALYSIS

In order to examine the influence of these different and interdependent factors, a series of logistic regression models were constructed to examine the simultaneous effects of age, marital status, social class

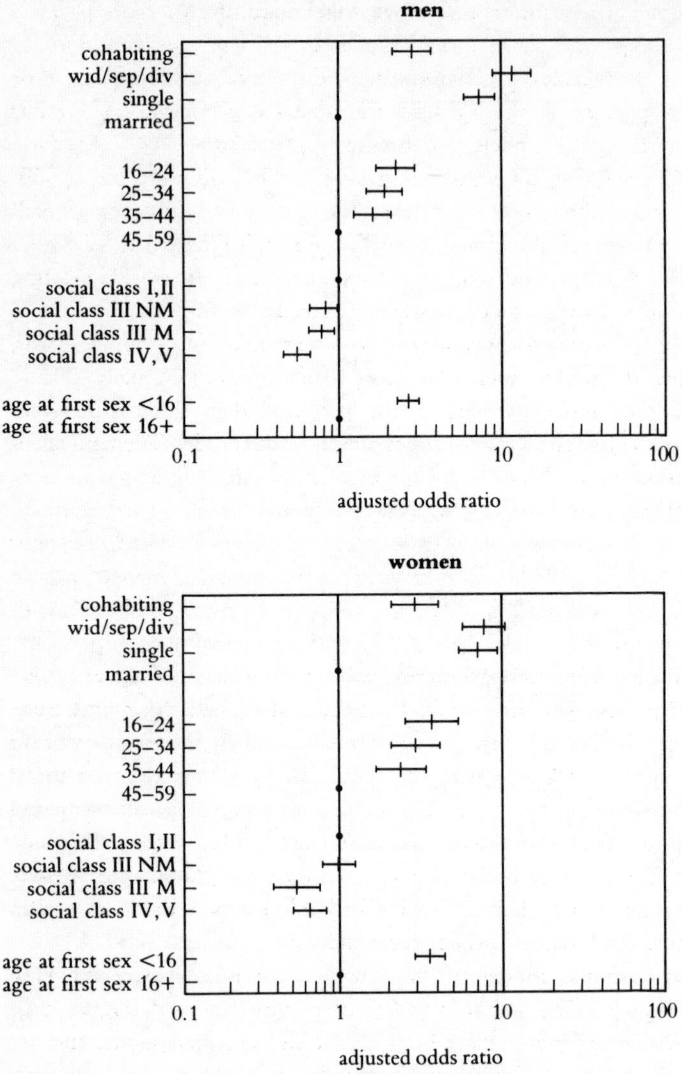

Figure 3.3 Adjusted odds ratios for 2 or more heterosexual partners in the last year. Source: Booklet Question 7d

and age at first intercourse on the likelihood of 2 or more partners in the last year, 5 or more partners in the last 5 years and 10 or more partners ever. The adjusted odds ratios for reporting 2 or more partners in the last year are presented in Figure 3.3. Results from the 5 year models were broadly similar.

The results of the logistic regression models are presented as odds ratios and their 95% confidence intervals after adjustment for all other factors in the model. Influences on multiple partnerships were similar for men and women. The adjusted odds ratio for reporting multiple partners in the last year exceeded 7 for single men and women as compared with those who were married. In other words, single men and women were more than 7 times more likely to have had 2 or more partners in the last year than those who were married after allowing for other factors in the model. The equivalent adjusted odds ratio was 2.8 for men and 3.0 for women who were cohabiting compared with those who were married. The likelihood of reporting 2 or more partners in the last year decreased markedly with age, the effect being strongest for women aged 16–24, with an adjusted odds ratio of 3.8 for multiple partners compared with women over 45.

The inconsistent relationship between social class and sexual behaviour in bivariate analysis was discussed above. In the multivariate model, men and women in the manual social classes were less likely to report 2 or more partners in the last year than those in social classes I and II, but the influence of social class was weak compared with the influence of age and marital status. Men who experienced sexual intercourse before the age of 16 were 2.7 times and women 3.6 times more likely to report multiple partners than those who experienced their first intercourse later.

In a similar model for reporting 10 or more partners over a lifetime (so far), a slightly different picture emerged (Figure 3.4). 'Lifetime' partners reflect both recent and past behaviour, and are influenced by the number of sexually active years. As previously discussed, there is some evidence of a temporal trend of increasing frequency of partner change with successive birth cohorts. The proportion reporting 10 or more partners was higher among those aged 25–44 than among those over 45, though lower among men aged 16–24 who have become sexually active more recently. This

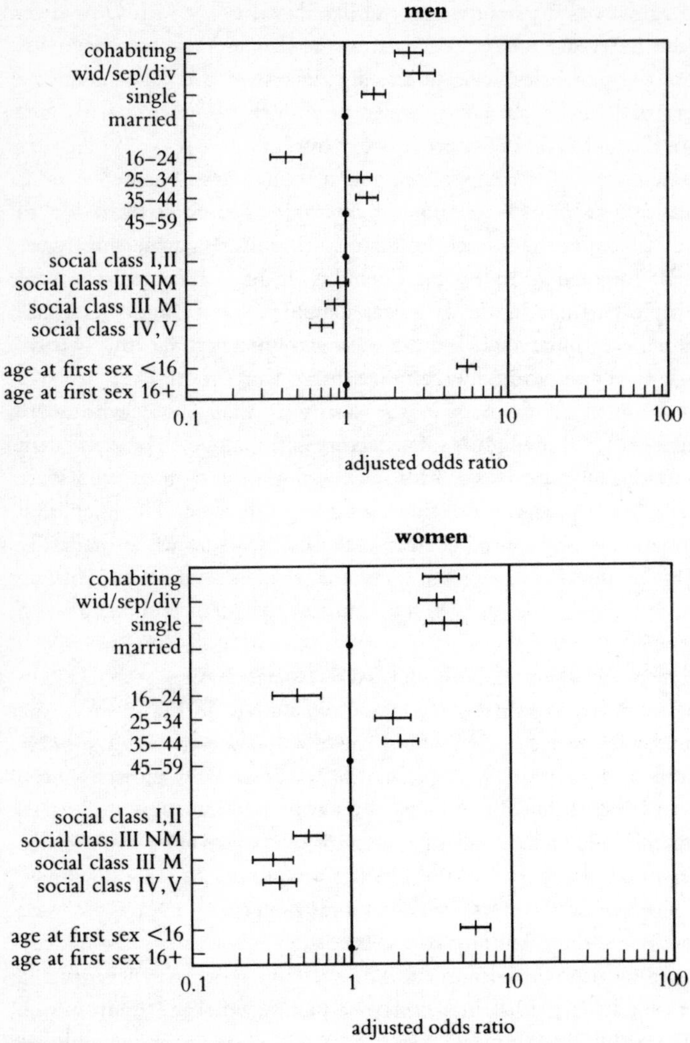

Figure 3.4 Adjusted odds ratios for 10 or more heterosexual partners ever.
Source: Booklet Question 7a

age effect was sustained in the logistic regression model. Unmarried respondents were more likely to report 10 or more partners than were the married, but there was less difference between the marital status categories than there was in models for the shorter time intervals, while the effects of social class and first sexual intercourse under the age of 16 remained similar.

By examining the effects of these demographic and behavioural factors simultaneously, it is possible to characterize those who report more partners in a given time interval. The effects of age were attenuated by inclusion of other factors in the models. While the youngest respondents were the most likely to report more partners in recent time intervals, partner change does not cease in the teens and twenties. The differences in these multivariate models between recent behaviour and lifetime behaviour reflect the influences of both birth cohort and life stages. Attenuation of the effects of age is particularly related to the effects of marital status, confirming the bivariate analysis where those outside married relationships (including to a lesser extent those cohabiting) are much more likely to be forming multiple partnerships at any stage in the life course.

THE PATTERN OF SEXUAL RELATIONSHIPS: MONOGAMY, SERIAL MONOGAMY AND CONCURRENT RELATIONSHIPS

Simple counts of numbers of partners give some indication of the variability in the number of partnerships formed by individuals. They give less indication of the overall pattern of relationships and, in particular, whether they are serially monogamous (one beginning after another has finished) or whether partnerships are concurrent (a new relationship begins before the end of a previous one).

Data of this nature, besides having intrinsic interest for the understanding of human sexual relationships, also have implications for the dynamics of STD transmission. If a sexually acquired infection is introduced into a new relationship with an individual who has other concurrent relationships, a larger number of people will be placed at risk of infection than in a situation of serially monogamous relationships which involve only one effective partnership.

Question 10–12 in the booklet attempted to gather data on partnership patterns for all respondents who reported 2 or more partners in the last 5 years. Questions were limited to the most recent 3 sexual partners but respondents were requested to give considerable detail on the type and duration of partnerships, and the age and gender of each partner.

Not surprisingly, this proved to be one of the most difficult questions for respondents to complete and 9.7% of men and 7.3% of women with 2 or more partners in the last 5 years did not give all details about their 3 most recent partners. Difficulty arose particularly in completion of dates of starting and ending the relationship. Since data were limited to the last 3 partnerships, information is not complete for the total number of partnerships reported in that period. Since respondents were asked to complete questions only about the 3 *most recent* partners, these should represent the partnerships recalled most easily for those with more than 3. Non-response was highest for the youngest responders who also had the highest numbers of partners, due largely to absence of complete dates on which to classify partnerships. These difficulties emphasize the problems of collecting such data over longer time periods and was the basis of the research team's decision not to attempt to collect detailed data over the entire life course.

Figure 3.5 shows the distribution of partnership timing in the last 5 years by age group. This includes both homosexual and heterosexual partnerships. Multiple partnership in the last 5 years was reported by 68% of the sexually active 16–24-year-old men and half of the women, but the prevalence of monogamy increased rapidly with age to nearly 90% of men and 95% of women aged 45–59. Among those with multiple partnerships, serial monogamy dominates the pattern for 16–24-year-olds. For the entire sample, 15.1% of men and 7.6% of women reported concurrent relationships over the last 5 years. With increasing age, concurrent relationships become the dominant pattern among those with multiple partnerships, although the overall proportion of those who are monogamous increases. For example, in men aged 35–44, 13.8% reported

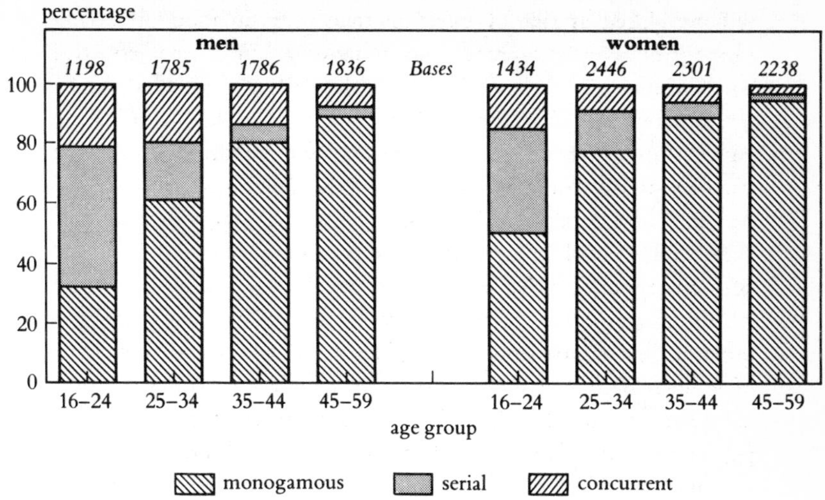

Figure 3.5 Age group by timing of partners in the last 5 years.* Source: Booklet Questions 7b, 10–12

* excludes all those with no sexual partners in the last 5 years

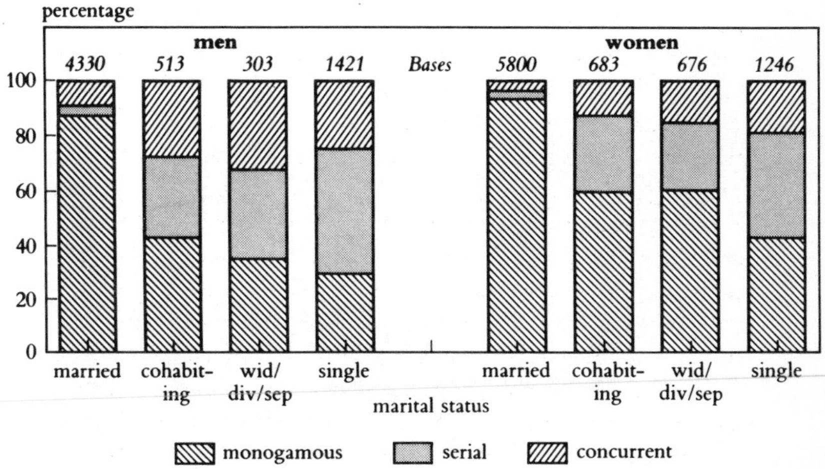

Figure 3.6 Marital status by timing of partners in the last 5 years.* Source: Booklet Questions 7b, 10–12

* excludes all those with no sexual partners in the last 5 years

concurrent partnerships and only 6.3% serial partnerships. This changing pattern over the life course is presumably a reflection of the length and level of commitment to a particular relationship. As the proportion of individuals in married relationships increases with age, so additional relationships become increasingly likely to occur at the same time as, and outside of, a long-term relationship.

Examining the data by marital status (Figure 3.6) indicates that married people are far more likely to be monogamous than any other marital status group. Where multiple relationships occur, not surprisingly these are most likely to be concurrent. The influence of living with a partner as a measure of commitment to a relationship is unclear, since those who are cohabiting show patterns that are more similar to those who are single, divorced, or separated than to those who are married (Figure 3.6). Only 43.1% of cohabiting men and 59.9% of cohabiting women reported monogamy over the last 5 years, with 24.3% of men and 12.7% of women reporting concurrent partnerships. This relationship is likely to be attenuated by the influence of age (cohabitees being younger) and the likelihood that cohabiting relationships may be of shorter duration than 5 years. Nevertheless, it is striking that cohabitation does not appear to exert any strong influence on monogamy. This accords with the data in Table 3.2 and Figure 3.3 which indicate that those cohabiting are more likely to report multiple partnerships independent of age, social class and age at first intercourse.

AGE DIFFERENCE BETWEEN PARTNERS

The age difference between partners is an important component of sexual behaviour. It also has implications for STD transmission, since, for example, men tend to have younger female partners. Women may be put at risk of STD at an earlier age by mixing with more experienced older partners at sexual initiation. This pattern is seen in the HIV epidemic in Africa where women tend to become infected at an earlier age than men (Quinn *et al.*, 1986). The age difference between respondents and their first partner was discussed in Chapter 2 (p. 68).

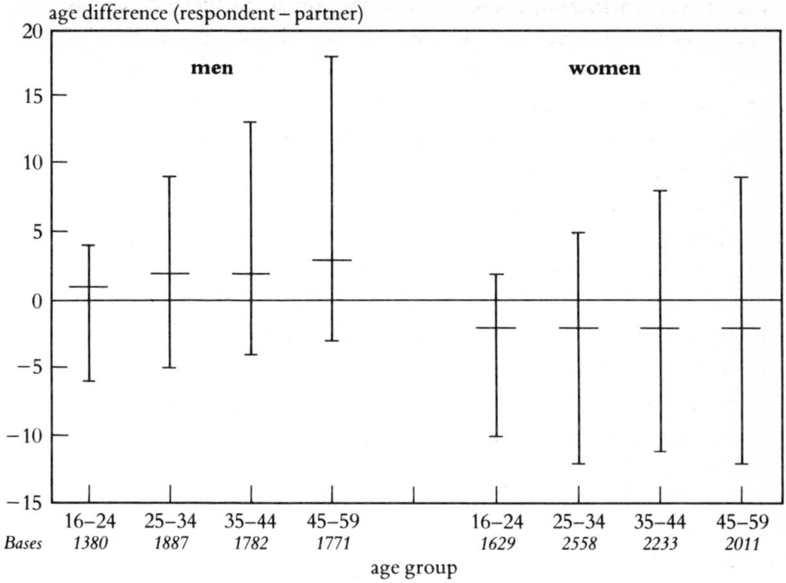

Figure 3.7 Median (95th and 5th centiles) of age difference between heterosexual partners.* Source: Interview Question 1b; Booklet Question 1d

* excludes those whose most recent sexual partnership was more than a year ago

Here, the age difference between respondents who have been sexually active in the last year and their most recent sexual partner is examined, as this gives the most contemporary estimate of age mixing between partners. The age difference is reported in Figure 3.7 as the difference between the age of the respondent and the age of their most recent partner. The median is always greater than zero for men and has a negative value for women indicating, not surprisingly, that men tend to have younger women partners. For men there was an increase in the median age difference from 1 year in the youngest age group to 3 years in those aged 45 or more. For women the median age difference is 2 years for all age groups. The gender difference in age-mixing patterns presumably reflects the tendency for men to select increasingly younger female partners as they grow older, possibly through divorce and remarriage. Nevertheless, heterosexual partnership with an individual within 2 years of

	16–24		25–34		35–44		45–59		all ages	
	%	*base*	%	*base*	%	*base*	%	*base*	%	*base*
men										
partner										
6+ years older	53.8	*63*	25.9	*84*	13.1	*50*	3.7	*26*	28.3	*233*
3–5 years older	51.8	*117*	15.2	*107*	17.3	*91*	3.9	*62*	25.2	*376*
within 2 years	35.2	*962*	12.6	*955*	6.9	*815*	3.7	*688*	15.8	*3420*
3–5 years younger	33.9	*217*	15.2	*496*	4.8	*396*	3.1	*453*	11.7	*1562*
6+ years younger	32.8	*17*★	24.1	*244*	17.3	*428*	11.9	*541*	16.5	*1230*
women										
partner										
6+ years older	23.8	*305*	7.5	*465*	4.6	*393*	2.2	*313*	9.0	*1476*
3–5 years older	20.3	*432*	6.4	*582*	4.5	*496*	1.3	*487*	7.7	*1997*
within 2 years	19.0	*839*	5.5	*1253*	2.5	*1052*	1.6	*965*	6.6	*4110*
3–5 years younger	26.2	*48*	12.1	*166*	13.8	*116*	5.0	*102*	12.4	*432*
6+ years younger	—	*5*★	17.5	*90*	10.8	*174*	8.4	*141*	11.5	*410*

Table 3.6 Proportion of respondents with 2 or more heterosexual partners in the last year by age group and age of most recent partner. Source: Booklet Question 1d, 7d

★ note small base

the age of the respondent is the most frequent combination throughout the life course (Table 3.6).

Table 3.6 reports on the relationship between patterns of age mixing, and the likelihood of reporting 2 or more partners in the last year. For men the pattern is not straightforward. There is a tendency for men with older female partners to be more likely to report multiple partnerships in the last year, but the relationship varies with age. The relationship is strongest for the youngest men (16–24). For those aged 25–44, multiple partnerships were most frequently reported by those with female partners at both extremes of the age difference. For men over 45, those with partners 6 or more years younger than themselves were most likely to report 2 or more partners in the last year. The relationship appears to invert with increasing age. From these data it is not possible to conclude whether this is an age cohort or an ageing effect. However, one explanation might be that younger men with older female partners are more sexually adventurous and may be forming relationships with more sexually experienced women. Conversely, the oldest men with the youngest partners may be those who have recently experienced marital breakdown and adopted new relationships with younger women. The inverse pattern is seen for women, and the probability of reporting 2 or more partners in the last year is highest among women with the youngest male partners. This is consistent across all age groups, with the exception of women aged 16–24, where no clear trend emerges.

Thus, patterns of age mixing and sexual behaviour appear to vary with gender and over the life course. As women become older, they are more likely than men to be without a sexual partner (19.3% of women and 10.8% of men aged 45–59 reported no sexual partners in the last year – Table 3.1), while men become increasingly likely to form relationships with younger women.

MALE EXPERIENCE OF COMMERCIAL SEX

The extent to which men pay money for sex with women is poorly understood. Data in this area are sparse, but are relevant not only to understanding the spectrum of sexual expression but also to the potential spread of HIV and other STDs. The role of prostitute–client contacts in the spread of STDs has through the centuries been a repeated subject for social and moral debate, but seldom the subject of rigorous scientific inquiry before the advent of AIDS (Pankhurst, 1913; Weeks, 1981; Brandt, 1987; Davenport-Hines, 1990). There is some evidence that prostitute–client contacts may have had a significant role in the transmission of gonorrhoea and syphilis in the late nineteenth and early twentieth century, particularly in relation to use of prostitutes by troops during wartime (Adler, 1980).

The role of prostitutes in STD transmission has been reviewed elsewhere (Darrow, 1983). Prostitutes remain at high risk of STD (Ward *et al.*, 1993) but in the late twentieth century the overall contribution of commercial contacts to the burden of STDs is poorly understood. Prostitutes in urban centres in Africa were among the first to suffer a high prevalence of HIV infection, as were their clients (Piot *et al.*, 1987). In societies where there is a high prevalence both of untreated STD and unprotected intercourse with prostitutes commercial sex may have a significant role in HIV transmission. Research in the US and Europe suggests that transmission of HIV through sexual intercourse between female prostitutes and their clients has thus far been limited. Infection among prostitutes has been predominantly associated with injecting drug use and contact with non-paying partners. This may in part be attributed to the high levels of condom use with commercial partners as well as the low prevalence of HIV among clients (Centers for Disease Control, 1987; Day *et al.*, 1988; Padian, 1988).

The prevalence and characteristics of prostitution are poorly understood, due primarily to the clandestine and frequently illegal nature of much activity associated with the sex industry and the formidable methodological problems of realistic estimation of population size.

If little is known about the nature of prostitutes, even less is known about their clients. In particular, there are few estimates of the proportion of men who have experience of paying for sex or the frequency with which such contacts take place. This is a subject that few sexual-behaviour studies have addressed. Time-trend data are virtually non-existent because so much of the research in the last few decades has focused on women.

Among Kinsey's white, college-educated men, about 30% had had contact with a prostitute at least once, but only 4% had had extensive experience (Gebhard and Johnson, 1979). More recent data based on probability samples are not available, although some questions on the subject were asked in the American volunteer sample surveys of the 1960s and 1970s. In his data, Kinsey found some evidence of a temporal decline in use of prostitutes. Men born before 1900 in his sample reported greater frequency of sex with prostitutes than those born later (Kinsey *et al.*, 1948). A few studies have been carried out among clients of prostitutes in recent years, but these suffer from all the problems of volunteer samples and are unable to provide a denominator from which to estimate prevalence of this behaviour among adult males.

Recently published surveys and those still in progress are beginning to provide data from probability sample surveys (ACSF Investigators, 1992; Johnson *et al.*, 1992). This survey included one question (Question 13) in the self-completion booklet which asked men only whether they had ever paid money for sex with a woman; when was the most recent occasion; and how many women the respondent had paid. As with homosexual activity, paying for sex remains a stigmatized behaviour in contemporary British society, and prevalence estimates derived should probably be regarded as minima. Women were not asked a similar question since even such a large sample was inadequate to measure prevalence, which was likely to be exceedingly low. The extreme sensitivity of the inquiry at the time the survey was planned made us reluctant to include a question that might cause undue offence but yield little useful data.

Table 3.7 shows the proportion of men reporting paying for sex with a woman in various time intervals by age, marital status and social class. 6.8% of men reported that they had paid for sex with a woman at some time and 1.8% had done so within the last 5 years (Table 3.7). There is a 5-fold increase in the proportions who had ever paid for sex between the youngest and the oldest age groups (2.1% v. 10.3%). In contrast, recent experience (in the last 5 years) was most common among men aged 25–44. This indicates that, for the older age group, experience of paying for sex was for the majority a past rather than a recent experience. It is difficult to assess whether the decline in lifetime experience of prostitution with younger age is due to a cohort effect or simply due to the fact that younger people have fewer years of sexual experience. Given that recent experience is greatest in those aged 25–44 but 'lifetime' experience less prevalent, this may suggest that there has been a genuine decline in prevalence of experience of commercial sex amongst men. This would be consistent with Kinsey's earlier findings and also with the increasing availability of non-commercial

	in the last 5 years	ever	
	%	%	*base*
age			
16–24	1.7	2.1	*1925*
25–34	2.6	6.3	*2086*
35–44	2.0	8.5	*1942*
45–59	1.0	10.3	*1988*
marital status			
married	1.0	7.2	*4498*
cohabiting	3.9	9.4	*588*
widowed/separated/divorced	4.2	14.2	*424*
single	2.3	4.1	*2431*
social class			
I	2.4	7.2	*554*
II	2.6	9.5	*2226*
III NM	1.3	5.9	*1499*
III M	1.4	6.0	*1888*
IV	1.9	5.7	*852*
V	1.3	4.5	*217*
other	1.2	4.1	*698*
works away from home			
yes	2.4	9.2	*2151*
no	1.6	5.9	*5746*
homosexual partner ever			
yes	7.0	16.3	*312*
no	1.6	6.4	*7626*
all men	1.8	6.8	*7941*

Table 3.7 Proportion of men who have paid a woman for sex by demographic characteristics. Source: Booklet Question 13

partners suggested by the rising proportion of women with 10 or more partners in their lifetime (Figure 3.1).

Single men are the least likely ever to have paid money for sex (4.1%), though, in the last 5 years, married men are the least likely to have done so. Widowed, separated and divorced men are the most likely to have paid for sex ever or in the last 5 years (4.2%), a finding that is consistent with the relatively high frequency of partner change in this group discussed earlier. There is no clear social-class gradient for ever paying for sex, although in the last 5 years those in social classes I and II are more likely to have paid for sex than those in other social classes. This may be linked with the finding that those whose work takes them away from home are more likely to have paid money for sex than those who do not stay away from home for work (Table 3.7).

A 2.5-fold increase in the proportions ever paying for sex was found among men who have ever had a male partner. This excess remains when payment for sex in the last 5 years is considered. Among men who reported ever paying for sex, 38.5% had 1 paid partner, 50.5% had 2–9 paid partners and 10.9% reported paying for sex with 10 or more women. The proportions of men reporting ever paying for sex increases with number of female partners ever

	all partners		all unpaid partners†	
	%	*base*	%	*base*
number of partners				
			100.0	*13**
0	0.1	*527*	1.6	*535*
1	0.2	*1617*	1.6	*1640*
2	1.7	*829*	3.8	*847*
3–4	4.7	*1445*	4.8	*1446*
5–9	7.9	*1539*	7.4	*1532*
10+	17.0	*1941*	11.7	*1824*

Table 3.8 Proportions of men who have paid money for sex with a woman by number of heterosexual partners ever. Source: Booklet, Questions 7a, 13

* fewer partners in total than paid partners

† difference between total partners and paid partners

(Table 3.8) rising from 1.7% of men with 2 lifetime partners to 17.0% of men with 10 or more lifetime partners. By subtracting the number of partners who have been paid for sex from the total number of female partners reported, an estimate of the number of unpaid female partners can be derived. This calculation yields at first sight a somewhat unexpected distribution. It suggests that some men did not count their prostitute partners among their total partners since they reported greater numbers of paid partners than total partners. The size of this discrepancy is likely to be small since only 2.7% of those who reported any paid partners reported fewer total partners than paid partners. The discrepancy may not necessarily be illogical since men may have paid for sexual experiences such as non-penetrative sex with women who would not be included in the definition of a sexual partner in Question 7. The relationship between total number of partners and experience of paying for sex is not simply a function of additional commercial partners, since the proportion of men who have ever paid for sex also increases with the numbers of unpaid partners (Table 3.8) to 11.7% of those with 10 or more unpaid partners.

The factors associated with ever paying for sex in bivariate analysis were examined in a logistic regression model that includes age, marital status, social class, work away from home and a homosexual partner ever. The results (expressed as adjusted odds ratios with their 95% confidence limits) are shown in Figure 3.8 after controlling for other variables in the model. Age and marital status exerted the dominant effects in the model with the odds ratio for commercial sex increasing rapidly with age. Men who were cohabitees or widowed, separated and divorced were significantly more likely than married men to report contact with prostitutes. After controlling for other variables in the model, single men did not differ significantly from married men in the odds of reporting experience of commercial sex. This contrasts with the bivariate models, which suggest a lower prevalence among single men. The difference in effect is due to confounding by other variables in the model, particularly age. Working away from home was sustained as an independent effect in the model. A history of a homosexual partner ever was associated with significantly raised odds of commercial sex contact. The implication of this finding is

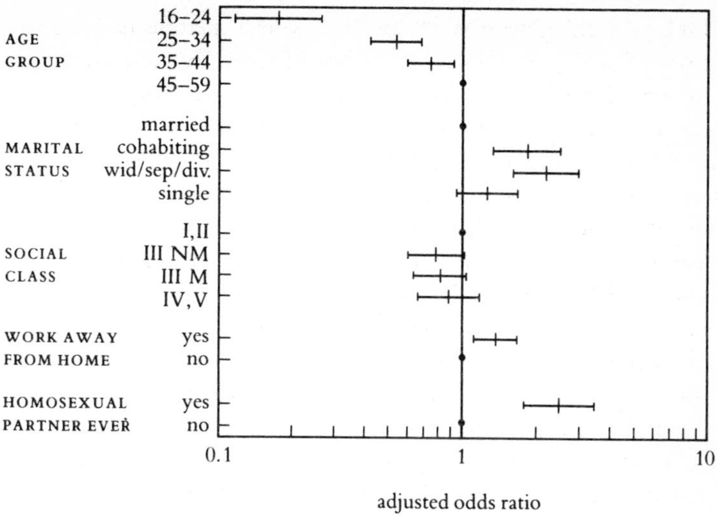

Figure 3.8 Adjusted odds ratios for ever paying for sex with a woman. Source: Booklet Question 13

that women in the sex industry may encounter a disproportionate number of bisexual men as clients (Day *et al.*, 1993). Such a finding is not novel, and Bell and Weinberg (1978) found that 13% of homosexual men interviewed by them had paid for sex with a woman at least once (re-analysis of data in Reinisch *et al.*, 1990).

TRAVEL AND SEXUAL PARTNERSHIP

Increasing attention has been paid to the potential role of sex tourism, and the adoption of new sexual partners while travelling, as a source of both STDs and HIV infection. All respondents were asked whether their work ever took them away from home overnight. This was used as a proxy indicator for travel, which might provide opportunities for forming new sexual partnerships. Table 3.9 shows the distribution of number of sexual partners for those who gave a history of travelling away from home for work, as

	men		women	
	work away from home %	no work away from home %	work away from home %	no work away from home %
Number of heterosexual partners in the last 5 years				
0	2.9	10.9	6.0	9.4
1	60.6	54.9	56.6	68.3
2	11.1	9.6	16.4	10.6
3–4	12.4	11.9	14.1	7.5
5–9	8.1	7.9	5.0	3.5
10+	4.9	4.8	2.0	0.7
base	*2175*	*5826*	*779*	*9230*

Table 3.9 Distribution of number of heterosexual partners in the last 5 years by experience of work away from home. Source: Interview Classification Section, Question 9c; Booklet Question 7b

compared with those who did not. For men there is very little difference in the overall frequency distribution between those who do and do not work away, apart from the higher proportion of those with no partners among those who do not travel for work.

For women, there are quite marked differences in the distribution of partners between the groups, although the proportion of women working away from home is very much smaller than for men. The causal chain in this relationship for women is unclear. As well as the many influences that determine whether a woman is able to work away from home, travel away from home may afford opportunities for new sexual relationships.

This has been explored further in Table 3.10, which examines the relationship between types of sexual partnership and work away from home. For men, those with concurrent partnerships were more likely to work away from home than those who reported one partner or serial relationships. The effects are different for women, indicating, as in Table 3.9, that women with multiple partners of

	men		women	
	work away from home %	*base*	work away from home %	*base*
monogamous	26.4	*5144*	6.3	*7636*
serial partners	26.8	*1079*	13.5	*1005*
concurrent partners	36.3	*996*	16.3	*636*
all	27.8	*7219*	7.8	*9277*

Table 3.10 Proportion of respondents whose work takes them away from home by types of sexual partnerships in the last 5 years. Source: Interview Section, Question 9c; Booklet Questions 10–12

any type are more likely than those with one partner to report working away from home.

Any interpretation is complex, but the findings may reflect the marked difference in mobility between men and women. It appears that social constraints may have a greater effect on women than on men. Causality cannot be attributed, because age, marital status, domestic responsibility, and work opportunities are likely to confound the relationship.

SUMMARY

This chapter has focused on the distribution of numbers and types of heterosexual partnerships and their associations with demographic characteristics. The difficulties of obtaining accurate data over long time periods have been emphasized. The data confirm the extreme variability in numbers of partners in different time intervals.

The dominant effects on multiple partnerships in multivariate analysis were those of age and marital status. The young and those who are previously married or single (including cohabitees) were those most likely to report high partner numbers. The effects of social class were small in comparison with those of age and marital status, but there was a significant trend of increasing partner change with higher social class.

First intercourse before the age of 16 was associated with multiple partnerships, in all age groups and later in life.

The data show evidence of changing patterns of sexual behaviour over historical time characterized by increasing numbers of partners. This effect may be exaggerated by greater willingness to report or greater ease of recall of partnerships among younger respondents, but the findings are consistent with other data sources and with other findings from the survey.

Patterns of partnership formation varied with age and marital status. The proportion of individuals reporting multiple partnerships in the last 5 years declined with increasing age. Among those with 2 or more partners, serial monogamy was the dominant pattern for those aged 16–24, while for those over 35 concurrent partnerships became a greater fraction of multiple partnerships, reflecting the higher proportion of individuals in regular, married or cohabiting relationships with age.

Age mixing was explored and demonstrated the tendency for men to form sexual partnerships with younger women. Although for men the age differences between them and their female partners increased with age, nevertheless close to half the sample reported that their current partner's age was within two years of their own.

Experience of ever paying for sex with a woman was relatively infrequent among men. Experience in the last 5 years was most common among men aged 25–34. In multivariate analysis, raised odds of ever paying for sex were associated with age, previous marriage or current cohabitation, with a history of working away from home and with a history of ever having a homosexual partner.

REFERENCES

ACSF Investigators (1992). 'AIDS and Sexual Behaviour in France', *Nature*, *360*, 407–9

Adler, M. W. (1980). 'The Terrible Peril: A Historical Perspective on the Venereal Diseases', *British Medical Journal*, *281*, 206–11

Adler, M. W. (1982). 'Sexually Transmitted Disease', in D. L.

Miller and R. D. T. Farmer (eds), *Epidemiology of Diseases*. Oxford: Blackwell Scientific Publications

Anderson, R. M., and A. M. Johnson (1990). 'Rates of Sexual Partner Change in Homosexual and Heterosexual Populations in the United Kingdom', in B. Voeller, J. M. Reinisch, and M. Gottlieb (eds), *AIDS and Sex: An Integrated Biomedical and Biobehavioural Approach*. Oxford: Oxford University Press

Bell, A. P., and M. S. Weinberg (1978). *Homosexualities: A Study of Diversity among Men and Women*. New York: Simon and Schuster

Brandt, A. (1987). *No Magic Bullet: A Social History of Venereal Disease in the United States since 1880*. New York: Oxford University Press

Brown, S., M. Vessey, and R. Harris (1984). 'Social Class, Sexual Habits and Cancer of the Cervix', *Community Medicine*, *6*, 281–6

Centers for Disease Control (1987). 'Antibody to Human Immunodeficiency Virus in Female Prostitutes', *MMWR*, *36*, 157–61

Centers for Disease Control (1988). 'Number of Sex Partners and Potential Risk of Exposure to Human Immunodeficiency Virus', *MMWR*, *37*, 565–8

Chesser, E. (1956). *The Sexual, Marital and Family Relationships of the English Woman*. London: Hutchinson's Medical Press

Darrow, W. W. (1983). 'Prostitution and Sexually Transmitted Diseases', in K. K. Holmes *et al.* (eds), *Sexually Transmitted Diseases*. New York: McGraw Hill

Davenport-Hines, R. (1990). *Sex, Death and Punishment*. London: Collins

Day, S., H. Ward, and J. W. R. Harris (1988). 'Prostitute Women and Public Health', *British Medical Journal*, *297*, 1585

Day, S., H. Ward, and L. Perrotta (1993). 'Prostitution and Risk of HIV: Male Partners of Female Prostitutes', *British Medical Journal*, 307, ii, 359–61

Dunnell, K. (1979). *Family Formation 1976*. London: HMSO

Farrell, C. (1978). *My Mother Said . . . The Way Young People Learned about Sex and Birth Control*. London: Routledge and Kegan Paul

Gebhard, P. H., and A. B. Johnson (1979). *The Kinsey Data:*

Marginal Tabulations of the 1938–1963 Interviews Conducted by the Institute of Sex Research. Philadelphia: W. B. Saunders

Gorer, G. (1971). *Sex and Marriage in England Today*. London: Nelson

Hethcote, H. W., and J. A. Yorke (1984). 'Gonorrhoea: Transmission Dynamics and Control. Lecture Notes', *Biomathematics*, *56*, 1–105

Holmes, K. K., and S. O. Aral (1991). 'Behavioural Interventions in Developing Countries', in J. N. Wasserheit, S. O. Aral, and K. K. Holmes (eds), *Research Issues in Human Behaviour and Sexually Transmitted Diseases in the AIDS Era* (pp. 318–44). Washington DC: American Society for Microbiology

Hunt, A. J., P. M. Davies, P. Weatherburn, A. P. Coxon, and T. J. McManus (1991). 'Sexual Partners, Penetrative Sexual Partners and HIV Risk', *AIDS*, *5*, 723–8

Johnson, A. M., J. Wadsworth, P. Elliott, *et al.* (1989). 'A Pilot Study of Sexual Lifestyle in a Random Sample of the Population of Great Britain', *AIDS*, *3*, 135–41

Johnson, A. M., J. Wadsworth, J. Field, K. Wellings, and R. M. Anderson (1990). 'Surveying Sexual Lifestyles' (letter), *Nature*, *343*, 109

Johnson, A. M., J. Wadsworth, K. Wellings, S. Bradshaw, and J. Field (1992). 'Sexual Behaviour and HIV Risk', *Nature*, *360*, 410–12

Kinsey, A. C., W. B. Pomeroy, and C. E. Martin (1948). *Sexual Behaviour in the Human Male*. Philadelphia: W. B. Saunders

Klassen, A. D., C. J. Williams, E. E. Levitt, L. Rudkin-Mincot, H. G. Miller, and S. Gunjel (1989). 'Trends in Premarital Sexual Behaviour', in C. F. Turner, H. G. Miller and L. E. Moses (eds), *Sexual Behaviour and AIDS* (pp. 548–67). Washington DC: National Academy Press

Mant, D., M. Vessey, and N. Loudon (1988). 'Social Class Differences in Sexual Behaviour and Cervical Cancer', *Community Medicine*, *10*, 52–6

May, R. M., and R. M. Anderson (1987). 'Transmission Dynamics of HIV Infection', *Nature*, *326*, 137–42

Padian, N. S. (1988). 'Prostitute Women and AIDS: Epidemiology', *AIDS*, *2*, 413–19

Pankhurst, C. (1913). *The Great Scourge: E. Pankhurst*. London.

PHLS (1992). 'Sexually Transmitted Diseases in England and Wales: 1981–1990', *Communicable Diseases Report*, *2*, R1–12

Piot, P., F. A. Plummer, M. A. Rey, *et al.* (1987). 'Retrospective Seroepidemiology of AIDS Virus Infection in Nairobi Prostitutes', *Journal of Infectious Diseases*, *155*, 1108–12

Potts, M., R. Anderson, and M.-C. Boily (1991). 'Slowing the Spread of Human Immunodeficiency Virus in Developing Countries', *Lancet*, *338*, 608–12

Quinn, T. C., J. M. Mann, J. W. Curran, and P. Piot (1986). 'AIDS in Africa: An Epidemiologic Paradigm', *Science*, *234*, 955–63

Reinisch, J. M., M. Ziemba-Davis, and S. A. Sanders (1990). 'Sexual Behaviour and AIDS: Lessons from Art and Sex Research', in B. Voeller, J. M. Reinisch, and M. Gottlieb (eds), *AIDS and Sex: An Integrated Biomedical and Biobehavioural Approach* (pp. 37–80). Oxford: Oxford University Press

Serwadda, D., M. J. Wawer, S. D. Musgrave, N. K. Sewankambo, J. E. Kaplan, and R. H. Gray (1992). 'HIV Risk Factors in Three Geographic Strata of Rural Rakai District, Uganda', *AIDS*, *6*, 983–9

Smith, T. W. (1991). 'Adult Sexual Behaviour in 1989: Number of Partners, frequency of Intercourse and Risk of AIDS', *Family Planning Perspectives*, *23*, 102–7

Smith, T. W. (1992). 'A Methodological Analysis of the Sexual Behaviour Questions on the General Social Surveys', *Journal of Official Statistics*, *8*, 309–25

Spencer, L., A. Faulkner, and J. Keegan (1988). *Talking about Sex*. London: Social and Community Planning Research

Turner, C. F. (1989). 'Research on Sexual Behaviors that Transmit HIV: Progress and Problems', *AIDS*, *3*, S63–9

Wadsworth, J., and A. M. Johnson (1991). 'Measuring Sexual Behaviour', *Journal of the Royal Statistical Society*, series A, *154*, 367–70

Wadsworth, J., K. Wellings, A. M. Johnson, and J. Field (1993). 'Sexual Behaviour', *British Medical Journal*, *306*, 582–3

Ward, H., S. Day, and J. Mezzone *et al.* (1993). 'Prostitution and Risk of HIV: Female Prostitutes in London', *British Medical Journal*, 307, ii, 356–8

Weeks, J. (1981). *Sex, Politics and Society: The Regulation of Sexuality since 1800*. New York: Longman

Zelnik, M., and J. F. Kantner (1983). 'First Intercourse among Young Americans', *Family Planning Perspectives*, 15, 64–70

CHAPTER 4

Heterosexual Practices

INTRODUCTION

Heterosexual relationships include a range of practices which are a source of sexual pleasure. In addition to penile-vaginal intercourse, practices such as oro-genital contact, anal intercourse and manual genital stimulation have been part of the repertoire of human sexual behaviour throughout history. These practices may be a prelude to, in addition to, or an alternative to coitus. Little is known about the pattern, frequency or variability of this repertoire in contemporary British society.

Different sexual activities were frequently depicted in the erotic art of antiquity. Reinisch documents the practice of oro-genital and anal intercourse in the art and literature of ancient Greek and Roman cultures (Reinisch *et al.*, 1990). Similar material survives from prehistoric Peru (Gebhard, 1970) and later material abounds from China, Japan, Africa and Europe. Reinisch (1990) and others have argued that Christianity severely curtailed the acceptance of sexual pleasure and its expression in art. Sex became increasingly dominated by its procreative function while the expression of sexual pleasure became associated with lust and immorality (Wilson, 1973).

In the twentieth century, sexual expression has become increasingly separated from its reproductive function by the availability of effective contraception and treatment for sexually acquired infections. At the same time, sex research has focused on the pleasurable nature of the human sexual response (Masters and Johnson, 1966).

While art and literature provide evidence of the occurrence of a wide range of sexual practices in many human populations, the frequency and extent of these practices is not known. The prevalence, or at least the acceptability, of practices has been influenced by differing cultural norms between societies and throughout history (Weeks, 1981).

The Kinsey studies (Kinsey *et al.*, 1948; Kinsey *et al.*, 1953) provide detailed accounts of the variety of human sexual practices but, because of the lack of population representativeness of the samples (see Chapter 1), are not suitable for comparison with the prevalence of different activities reported from this survey. Gorer (1971) provided some indication of the frequency of intercourse within and outside marriage in his 1969 random sample survey of nearly 2000 English men and women, but did not report on specific sexual practices. Little is known about sexual practices other than intercourse from probability samples although some inconclusive data can be obtained from studies carried out in clinic, quota and magazine surveys (Gorer, 1971; Simon *et al.*, 1990; Voeller, 1990).

The potential range of questions that might be asked in this context is wide, but the objectives of the study served to focus the inquiry on practices of particular relevance to contemporary concerns. An understanding of the range and prevalence of experience was required for the design of sexual health promotion programmes. The practices selected were those that are particularly relevant to the transmission of sexually acquired organisms (such as vaginal and anal intercourse) and to the occurrence of unwanted pregnancy. Also included were those forms of sexual expression that have a very low risk in this context, such as mutual masturbation and oro-genital contact, and which, in the absence of penetrative sex, may be regarded as safer sexual practices. Ironically, the behaviour that received the greatest approval in Christian teaching, unprotected vaginal intercourse, has come to be seen as one of the most problematic in terms of potential health risk, for both unwanted pregnancy and STD.

Reluctantly, questions on masturbation were excluded from the survey, because discussion of this practice had met both with distaste and embarrassment from respondents involved in the qualitative work on question design (Spencer *et al.*, 1988). It appeared unwise to prejudice response to questions of greater relevance to public health policy in order to obtain data on this undoubtedly important area of sexual expression.

As with other aspects of behaviour, the questions on sexual practices were designed to assess whether behaviour patterns are associated with particular demographic or social characteristics of respondents, how prevalent the behaviours are, and to what extent these may have varied over time.

QUESTION FORMAT

All questions on frequency and type of sexual practice were asked in the self-completion booklet. This chapter focuses on heterosexual practices reported in Questions 1, 2 and 3 of the booklet. These covered the frequency of heterosexual sex in the last 4 weeks and the last 7 days; the most recent occasion of vaginal intercourse; active (by the respondent to a partner) and passive (by a partner to the respondent) oral sex; anal sex, and non-penetrative sex. All the terms used were defined in a glossary at the beginning of the questionnaire, as well as in the questions themselves.

The preference for more formal terms describing sexual practices which emerged from the qualitative research guided the decision to use precise and neutral language (Spencer *et al.*, 1988). While using formal language rather than the vernacular, higly technical scientific language which might be misunderstood was avoided. The questionnaire contained relatively simple descriptions of the behaviours of interest. In presenting the data, more technical language is used in order to simplify data presentation without repetition of cumbersome terms.

RESPONSE ASSUMPTIONS

In calculating prevalence estimates for different behaviours, strict assumptions were made about the experience of those who did not complete the booklet. Those who reported never having experienced heterosexual intercourse; those reporting no sexual experience and who gave no age at first intercourse after the age of 13 were counted as never having had vaginal, oral or anal sex. The assumption that the respondent had no experience of genital contact which had not led to intercourse (non-penetrative sex), could be made only for those who reported in face-to-face interview that they had no heterosexual experience at all (Interview Question 31d).

The self-completion questionnaire included a number of 'skips', where subsequent questions were asked only when an affirmative answer was given to a stem question. For example, those who reported (Booklet Question 1a) that they had never had vaginal, oral or anal sex with an opposite-sex partner (213 men, 208 women) skipped subsequent questions on practices and frequency. For prevalence estimates of vaginal, oral and anal sex (Booklet Questions 3a–d), these respondents were assumed never to have experienced these practices. No assumptions could be made about non-penetrative sex for this group of respondents.

Item non-response on frequency and type of sexual practice varied from question to question depending on the content and complexity of the inquiry. Overall item non-response for sexual practices was approximately 6–7% of the total sample for most questions. This is made up of those who declined to complete the booklet (3.7% of men and 4.0% of women) as well as those who for whatever reason failed to complete a particular question, whether due to refusal, inability to understand the question, or inadvertently skipping questions.

THE FREQUENCY OF HETEROSEXUAL SEX

The frequency of sexual contact may be influenced by a number of factors. Apart from the many emotional, psychological and physical factors that may determine frequency, other influences include the availability of partners, the stability of the sexual relationship, whether the partners live together, and the age of the partners. Rates might also be expected to vary with the length of the relationship and with the number of recent sexual partners reported. All these factors were explored from the responses to the question on frequency of heterosexual intercourse (Booklet Question 2a):

On how many occasions in the last four weeks have you had sex with a man (woman)?

'Sex' was defined as vaginal intercourse, oral sex or anal sex. In addition, a question was asked about frequency of sex in the last seven days (Booklet Question 2e). The analysis here focuses on frequency in the last 4 weeks, since the longer time scale more readily captures the considerable variability in activity. Although the 4-week time scale may be affected by greater difficulties of recall, it provides a more realistic period for behavioural estimates. Frequency measured over only 7 days may be influenced by factors such as temporary absence of a partner or menstruation.

The overall distribution of reported frequency of heterosexual sex by age is shown in Figure 4.1 expressed as centiles by age for men and women. In contrast to gender differences in reporting numbers of partners (Chapter 3), men and women show high levels of consistency in the overall pattern of reported frequency of heterosexual sex. The distribution is highly skewed, indicating considerable variability in frequency of occasions. The median of the distribution never exceeds 5 acts of heterosexual sex in the last month at any age while the 95th centile for women reaches 25 acts in the last 4 weeks. Above this a small proportion of respondents reported very high frequencies, up to a maximum of 130 occasions in the last 4 weeks.

AGE AND FREQUENCY OF HETEROSEXUAL SEX

The frequency of sex varies substantially with age for both men and women (Figure 4.1). The reported median rises to a maximum of 5 times per month for women aged 20–29 and for men aged 25–34, thereafter declining to median of 2 for men aged 55–59, with more than 50% of women in this age group reporting no sex in the last month. In general men and women were very consistent in reporting, but where gender differences occur in frequency of sex this is most striking at the extremes of the age distribution. Women aged 16–24 reported higher frequencies than men of the same age but after the age of 50 the median frequency is lower for woman than for men.

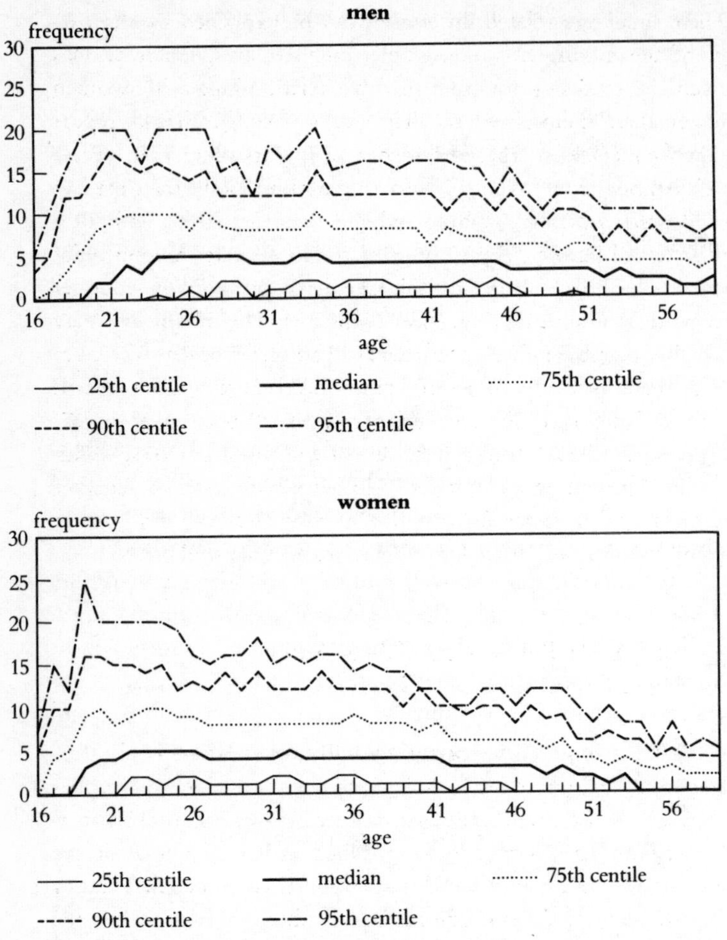

Note: Each centile gives the proportion of respondents reporting frequency of intercourse at or below the level indicated; e.g. the bottom line (25th centile) indicates that 25% of respondents report frequency of intercourse at or below this level for each age

Figure 4.1 Frequency of heterosexual sex in the last 4 weeks: centiles by age. Source: Booklet Question 2

These small age-related differences can be explained by the patterns of age mixing between couples discussed in Chapter 3. This showed the tendency for men to form relationships with women younger than themselves, so that young women should report similar frequencies to those of men a few years older than themselves. Among those over 50, women are more likely than men to be widowed, separated or divorced and therefore to be without a regular sexual partner, accounting for the lower rates among older women. Conversely, men of this age have on average younger partners than at an earlier age (see Chapter 3). The menopause may be another possible influence, particularly among women over 50 in whom there is evidence from community surveys of increased sexual dysfunction (Starr and Weiner, 1981; Osborn *et al.*, 1988; Bungay *et al.*, 1980). Whether the decrease in frequency of sex with increasing age can be attributed to biological influences or whether it is the result of other factors such as marital status and partner availability can be elucidated only by more detailed studies.

MARITAL STATUS AND FREQUENCY OF SEX

Marital status might be expected to influence profoundly the frequency of sexual intercourse, since marriage or cohabitation implies the availability of a regular sexual partner. In turn, marital status is influenced by age, with a predominance of single people in the youngest age groups and the highest proportions of married and of widowed, separated and divorced individuals in the older age categories. Table 4.1 shows the reported frequency of heterosexual sex in the last 4 weeks stratified by age and marital status. The marital status categories used are not simply those of civil status but take account of all those who live with but are not married to a sexual partner. Those who were married or cohabiting reported very much higher frequency of sex than respondents not currently living with a sexual partner. Cohabiting respondents reported slightly higher frequency of heterosexual sex than the married respondents. More than half of single respondents and more than three-quarters of those who were widowed reported no acts of

	centiles							
	25th	50th median	75th	*base*	25th	50th median	75th	*base*
age								
single	**women**				**men**			
16–24	0	0	6	*1475*	0	0	4	*1588*
25–34	0	0	5	*460*	0	0	5	*533*
35–44	0	0	1	*108*	0	0	1	*170*
45–59	0	0	0	*91*	0	0	0	*99*
all	0	0	5	*2134*	0	0	4	*2390*
separated/divorced								
16–24	0	2.5	8	*33*	0	3	15	*16**
25–34	0	2	8	*222*	0	2.5	8	*101*
35–44	0	0	4	*273*	0	2	6	*119*
45–59	0	0	1	*283*	0	0	5	*133*
all	0	0	4	*810*	0	1	6	*369*
widowed								
16–24	—	—	—	*1**	—	—	—	*0*
25–34	—	—	—	*3**	—	—	—	*0*
35–44	0	0	0	*26*	0	0	2	*6**
45–59	0	0	0	*161*	0	0	0	*40*
all	0	0	0	*191*	0	0	0	*46*
married								
16–24	4	6	10	*319*	4	7	10	*155*
24–34	3	5	8	*1716*	3	6	10	*1166*
35–44	2	5	8	*1832*	3	5	8	*1475*
45–59	1	2	4	*1858*	1	3	6	*1591*
all	2	4	8	*5724*	2	4	8	*4387*
cohabiting								
16–24	3	7	12	*297*	5	8	15	*144*
25–34	3	6	10	*301*	4	6	12	*241*
35–44	2	5	10	*141*	3	6	10	*132*
45–59	0	4	6.5	*57*	2	3	8	*82*
all	3	6	10	*797*	3	6	12	*599*

Table 4.1 Frequency of heterosexual sex in the last 4 weeks by age and marital status. Source: Booklet Question 2

* small base

heterosexual sex in the last 4 weeks. The separated and divorced reported higher rates of contact than the single or widowed. These findings on lower frequency of contact contrast with the greater numbers of partners reported by respondents not living with a partner (Chapter 3) and indicate the importance of availability of a regular partner for frequency of contact.

Within marital status categories, there is a consistent trend of falling frequency of heterosexual sex with increasing age (Table 4.1). For example, the median frequency of heterosexual sex reported by married women aged 16–24 was 6 times in the last 4 weeks, falling to twice in 4 weeks among those aged 45–59. Similarly, for separated and divorced men, median frequency falls from 3 times a month in the youngest age group to less than once a month in the oldest age group (45–59). The apparently lower frequency of sexual contact among men aged 16–24 overall is a function of the preponderance of single men in this age group who do not yet have a regular relationship. Stratifying the data by marital status, thus in part taking account of partner availability, clearly demonstrates the declining frequency of contact with increasing age.

SOCIAL CLASS AND FREQUENCY OF SEX

The relationship between social class and reported frequency of sex is shown in Table 4.2, stratified by age. There are no obvious reasons why there might be social-class differences in the frequency of sexual intercourse. Other aspects of behaviour, such as eating, drinking and smoking, show marked differences in relation to social class, but all these are means related while sexual practice may be both culturally and biologically determined (Cox *et al.*, 1987). Perhaps the most striking feature about the data presented in Table 4.2 is the absence of any strong trend in the reported frequency of sex between the different class groups.

There is a weak trend for those in social classes IV and V to report a lower frequency of sex in the last 4 weeks than those in Social classes I, II and III, but this may in turn be influenced by

	16–24				25–34				35–44				45–59				all ages			
centiles	25th	50th	75th	*base*	25th	50th	75th	*base*	25th	50th	75th	*base*	25th	50th	75th	*base*	25th	50th	75th	*base*
social class																				
men																				
I	0	1.5	8	*34*	0	3	6	*203*	2	4	8	*165*	0	3	6	*159*	1	4	6	*561*
II	0	4	10	*172*	2	5	8	*646*	2	4	8	*767*	1	3	6	*613*	1	4	8	*2198*
III NM	0	3	10	*239*	2	5	8	*455*	2	4	8	*359*	1	3	6	*351*	1	4	8	*1404*
III M	0	2	7	*345*	1	5	9	*574*	1	4	8	*422*	0	2	4.5	*460*	0	3	7	*1801*
IV	0	2	8	*224*	0	4	9	*211*	0	4	8	*183*	0	2	4	*204*	0	3	7	*822*
V	0	1	4	*49*	0	2	8	*70*	0	3	6	*51*	0	0	3	*44*	0	1	6	*214*
other	0	0	2	*358*	0	1	6	*75*	0	0	5	*49*	0	0	2	*69*	0	0	2	*551*
women																				
I	3	6	10	*26*	2	4	8	*203*	2	4	8	*189*	1	3	6	*156*	2	4	8	*574*
II	2	5	10	*215*	2	4	8	*903*	2	4	8	*910*	0	2	4	*851*	1	4	7	*2879*
III NM	0	4	8	*507*	1	5	8	*655*	1	3	7	*525*	0	2	4	*556*	0	3	7	*2243*
III M	1.5	5	9	*212*	3	6	9	*577*	2	5	8	*374*	0	2	4	*475*	1	4	8	*1638*
IV	0	3.5	8	*284*	0	3	8	*296*	1	3	7	*172*	0	0	3	*285*	0	3	6	*1037*
V	2	6	10	*27*	0	5	9	*67*	0	4	6	*53*	0	0	2	*71*	0	3	7	*218*
other	0	0	5	*514*	0	2	8	*356*	0	0	4	*197*	0	0	0	*277*	0	0	4	*1344*

Table 4.2 Frequency of heterosexual sex in the last 4 weeks by age and social class. Source: Booklet Question 2

marital status and age within class groups. The finding is similar to that in Chapter 3 where the relationship between social class was weak in comparison with the strong relationships between age, marital status and numbers of partners. The independent influence of social class is examined in a multivariate model later in this chapter.

One possible influence on this relationship may be the nature of work itself, with those in manual occupations being more likely to do shift work, overtime and to work unsocial hours, as well as doing physically demanding work. All these might be expected to influence coital frequency.

LENGTH OF RELATIONSHIP AND FREQUENCY OF SEX

In addition to the influence of age, and the availability of a regular partner, the frequency of sex may be influenced by the length of a relationship. This factor was examined for those who were currently married or cohabiting with a heterosexual partner. In this group, the data are not confounded by the variability introduced by absence of a regular and available partner. Data on length of relationship were derived from Question 1 (classification section) which records the length of marriage or cohabitation (although not necessarily the time from first intercourse in that relationship).

Table 4.3 shows the relationship between length of marriage or cohabitation and the reported frequency of sex in the last 4 weeks stratified by age group. For all age groups, and for men and women, there is a clear trend of reducing frequency of sexual intercourse with increasing length of relationship. When account is taken of the length of relationship, the age effects are less marked than those apparent in Table 4.1. For those who have been married or cohabiting for less than 2 years and are under the age of 45, no age-related trend is discernible. For those in longer-established relationships (6 or more years), age effects are relatively small below the age of 45.

Length of relationship appears to be closely associated with the

age and length of marriage or cohabitation	centiles 25th	50th median	75th	*base*
		men		
16–24				
<2 years	5	10	14	*166*
2–5 years	3	6	10	*126*
6+ years	—	—	—	5†
25–34				
<2 years	4	8	12	*217*
2–5 years	3	6	10	*563*
6+ years	3	6	9	*602*
35–44				
<2 years	4	9	15	*68*
2–5 years	3	6	10	*162*
6+ years	3	5	8	*1353*
45–59				
<2 years	4	7.5	12	*34*
2–5 years	2	4	7	*73*
6+ years	1	3	5	*1552*
		women		
16–24				
<2 years	4	8	12	*274*
2–5 years	3	6	10	*309*
6+ years	3	5	8	*26*
25–34				
<2 years	4	8	12	*220*
2 2–5 years	3	5	8	*631*
6+ years	3	5	8	*1147*
35–44				
<2 years	6	10	14	*51*
2–5 years	3	6	10	*180*
6+ years	2	4	8	*1721*
45–59				
<2 years	3	6	8	*24*
2–5 years	2	4	7.5	*59*
6+ years	0	2	4	*1808*

frequency of sex and partly accounts for the observed association between age and frequency, suggesting that the notion of declining sexual activity or appetite with age is too simple an explanation for the observed decline in frequency of sexual activity with advancing years. The excitement of a relatively new partnership presumably has a role to play in the increased frequency of activity in the early years of a relationship. As relationships mature, other responsibilities, such as child care, work, and familiarity may influence the frequency of sexual contact.

NUMBER OF PARTNERS AND FREQUENCY OF HETEROSEXUAL SEX

Since frequency of sex is influenced by the availability of a regular partner, it may also be influenced by the number of partners with whom sexual intercourse occurs. The net result of these two influences is by no means obvious. Those with many partners may engage in frequent short-term serial relationships and in the absence of a regular partner experience relatively low rates of intercourse. This possibility must be balanced against the observed higher rates of intercourse apparent in new relationships, the higher rates of intercourse and the greater numbers of partners reported by younger age groups, and the greater opportunities offered by concurrent relationships with more than one partner.

Table 4.4 shows the relationship between the number of heterosexual partners reported in the last 5 years and the reported frequency of intercourse, separating those who are married and cohabiting from those who are not. Once the data are stratified in this way, the frequency of intercourse for men and women increases with increasing numbers of sexual partners, although this effect is least evident in women who are not married or cohabiting. The relation-

Table 4.3 (*opposite*) Frequency of heterosexual sex in the last 4 weeks by age and length of marriage or cohabitation.* Source: Booklet Question 2
* analysis restricted to those currently married or cohabiting with an opposite-sex partner
† note small base

	men				women			
centiles	25th	50th median	75th	*base*	25th	50th median	75th	*base*
married or cohabiting								
number of partners								
0	0	0	0	*32*	0	0	0	*64*
1	2	4	8	*3838*	2	4	8	*5513*
2	3	5	10	*418*	3	6	10	*524*
3–4	4	6	12	*380*	4	7	12	*283*
5–9	4	8	12	*188*	3.5	8	12	*103*
10+	6	9	15	*105*	8	17	25	*21*
not married or cohabiting								
number of partners								
0	0	0	0	*669*	0	0	0	*850*
1	0	0	3	*528*	0	0	3	*921*
2	0	0	4	*368*	0	3	7	*552*
3–4	0	2	6	*553*	0	3	8	*497*
5–9	0	2	7	*431*	0	2	8	*253*
10+	2	5	12	*267*	0	2.5	10	*61*

Table 4.4 Frequency of heterosexual sex in the last 4 weeks by numbers of sexual partners in the last 5 years. Source: Booklet Questions 2, 7b

ship is consistent for those who are married or cohabiting and those who are not, although overall rates are much higher in the former group. It is important to appreciate in this analysis that current sexual activity (in the last 4 weeks) has been analysed in relation to numbers of partners over the longer time period of 5 years. To this extent the observed relationship is simply an indicator of levels of sexual activity in relation to partner numbers.

Although a relationship between frequency and numbers of partners can be demonstrated, it is noteworthy that among those who are not married or cohabiting, current levels of activity are only at a similar level to that of married or cohabiting individuals even for those who have 10 or more partners in the last 5 years. Availability of a regular partner in this analysis continues to be a dominating influence on coital frequency.

As the data presented in Chapter 3 indicate, many of the demographic characteristics associated with numbers of partners are also associated with frequency of heterosexual sex although the effects are not necessarily in the same direction. The single, for example, have more sexual partners but lower sexual frequency. In order to assess fully the relationship between numbers of partners and frequency of intercourse, multivariate models are required to take account of the various possible influences on frequency of heterosexual activity.

MULTIVARIATE ANALYSIS OF FREQUENCY OF HETEROSEXUAL SEX

In order to examine the independent influence of the factors identified as being associated with the reported frequency of heterosexual sex in the last 4 weeks in bivariate analysis, a simple linear model was developed. Gender, age, marital status, social class and number of heterosexual partners in the last 5 years were entered into the model. All these factors, with the exception of gender, contributed significantly to the reported frequency of sexual intercourse in the last 4 weeks. Frequency of intercourse was significantly lower in those in social class IV and V and significantly higher with increasing number of partners after controlling for other variables in the model. The lack of influence of gender on reported frequency confirms the consistency between men and women in reporting frequency of sexual contact.

Since partner's age might influence the frequency of intercourse a further model was developed including age of partner and restricting the analysis to those who have been sexually active in the last year. In this model social class no longer exerted a significant effect, while partner's age was significantly associated with frequency of intercourse, confirming the influence of both partners on recent frequency of contact.

By confining the model to those who were married or cohabiting, the length of the current relationship and the age of the partner could be included in the analysis. On this reduced sample, the model was broadly similar. The influence of age of spouse or cohabitee and length of relationship was significant, but there was no significant contribution from gender or social class. This multivariate model confirms the initial bivariate findings, and underlines the remarkably similar patterns of reporting between men and women.

Age and marital status are thus confirmed as significantly related to frequency of contact, but unlike the data on number of partners (Chapter 3), frequency of activity is greater among the married and cohabiting. As with partner numbers, associations with social class are weak. Within the model, a significant association with numbers of partners is found but the practical importance of this effect must be interpreted with care, in view of the overwhelming influence of partner availability as measured by marital status.

THE REPERTOIRE OF HETEROSEXUAL PRACTICES

In addition to the frequency of sex, the inquiry focused attention on the repertoire of heterosexual practices of particular interest to sexual health issues. The range of experience was explored in a series of questions that invited the respondent to report the last time that s/he experienced different sexual practices (if ever) (Booklet Question 3). Six possible options were offered for the most recent occasion ranging from 'in the last 7 days' to 'more than 5 years ago' and 'never'.

The inquiry encompassed a number of practices (Questions 3a–e). Vaginal sexual intercourse was defined as a man's penis entering a woman's vagina. Oral sex (oral sexual intercourse) was defined as a man's or woman's mouth on a partner's genital area. Respondents were asked to discriminate between active ('by you to a partner') and passive ('by a partner to you') oral sex. For the purposes of analysis, these have been termed cunnilingus (oral stimulation of the female genitals) and fellatio (oral stimulation of the male genitals). Anal sex (anal sexual intercourse) was defined to respondents as a man's penis entering a partner's anus (rectum or back passage).

A measure of the practice of sexual stimulation without intercourse (non-penetrative sex) between couples was included because of its potential importance as a means of sexual expression avoiding pregnancy and the risk of STD. The qualitative work for the survey revealed a poor understanding of the terms 'non-penetrative sex' and 'mutual masturbation' as well as a distaste for the latter term (Spencer *et al.*, 1988). The question was one of the most difficult to design. The form of words finally chosen was 'genital contact with a man (woman) *NOT* involving intercourse (for example, stimulating sex organs by hand but not leading to vaginal, oral or anal intercourse)'. Despite this long-winded terminology, the description appeared to be well understood by respondents, particularly after the explanation in parenthesis was added to the question.

Figure 4.2 shows the overall proportions of the population reporting different sexual activities in different time periods, presented as cumulative percentages. Women and men reported broadly similar patterns. There were however marked differences in the proportions of the population who reported experience of different practices.

All but 6.3% of women and 7.3% of men reported experience of vaginal intercourse at some time in their life so far, with 56.2% of men and 56.6% of women reporting this activity in the last week. After vaginal intercourse, non-penetrative sex was the most frequently reported activity. 75% of women and 82% of men had experience of genital stimulation which did not result in intercourse (non-penetrative sex) at some time, and one in four had experienced this in the last 7 days.

Cunnilingus and fellatio were common experiences although both genders reported slightly greater experience of cunnilingus than fellatio (72.9% v. 69.4% for men, 66.2% v. 64.0% for women). Some experience of either cunnilingus or fellatio was reported by 75.2% of men and 69.2% of women, while 24.5% of men and 19.9% of women reported cunnilingus or fellatio in the last week (Figure 4.2).

A lower proportion of respondents reported oral sex than reported vaginal intercourse in the last week, despite the fact that a high proportion of individuals have some experience of the practice. This indicates that oral sex is a rather less frequent practice than vaginal intercourse. There was a strong association between practising cunnilingus and fellatio (Table 4.5). Among all those reporting either

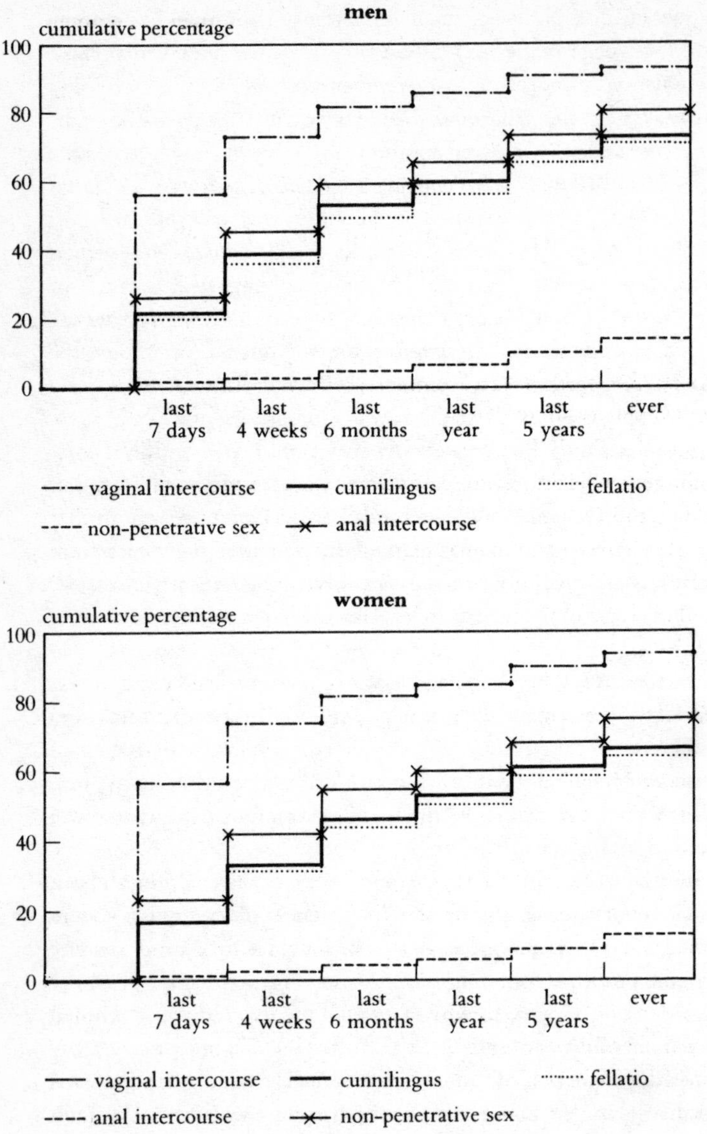

Figure 4.2. Last occasion of different practices: cumulative percentages.
Source: Booklet Questions 3a–e

	men %	**women** %
cunnilingus only	6.4	5.5
fellatio only	2.7	3.3
both cunnilingus and fellatio	46.5	40.7
any oro-genital contact	55.6	49.5
no oro-genital contact	44.4	50.5
base	*7747*	*9434*

Table 4.5 Oro-genital sexual contact reported in the last year. Source: Booklet Questions 3b, 3c

cunnilingus or fellatio in the last year (55.6% of men and 49.5% of women), more than four-fifths reported both practices in the last year. Thus fellatio and cunnilingus appear to be reciprocal activities in relationships. Although a slightly lower proportion of women than men reported oral sex in the last year, the differences were small.

In contrast to other heterosexual practices, anal intercourse was infrequently reported. 13.9% of men and 12.9% of women reported ever having experienced anal intercourse, while less than 7% of men and women reported this practice in the last year (Figure 4.2). Anal intercourse is therefore the least common component of the sexual repertoire when compared with other practices. Nevertheless, it is worth bearing in mind that legal and moral sanctions against anal intercourse could mean that it is more likely to be under-reported than practices that may be regarded as more socially acceptable (Voeller, 1990).

In order to give a picture of the sexual repertoire, over a defined time period, Figure 4.3 shows the pattern of sexual practice over the last month for the 3 most common practices, vaginal, oral and non-penetrative sex. Vaginal sex predominates with only 2.4% of men and 3.5% of women reporting oral or non-penetrative sex in the absence of vaginal intercourse. The majority of men and women reported a variety of sexual practices. Figure 4.4 shows oral, anal and non-penetrative sex among those who reported vaginal inter-

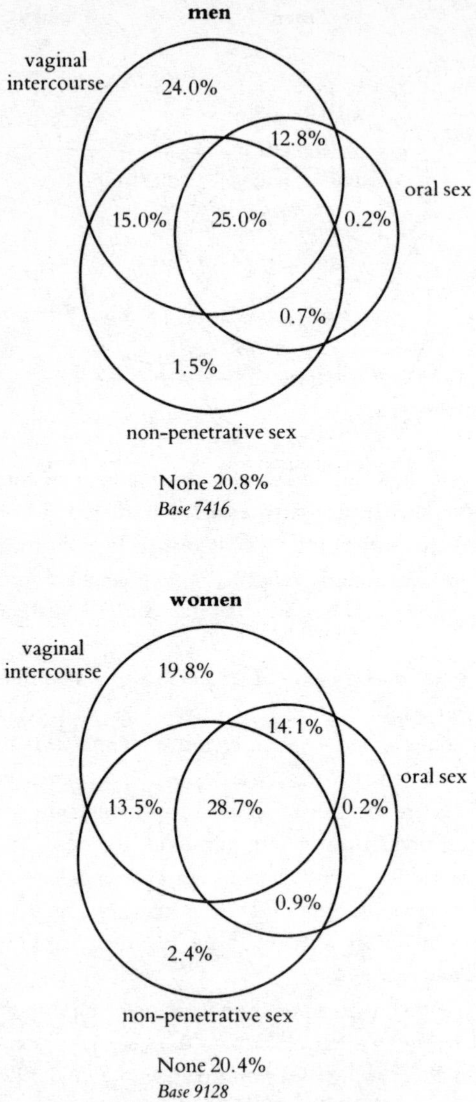

Figure 4.3 Repertoire of sexual practices in the last month. Source: Booklet Questions 3a–c, 3e

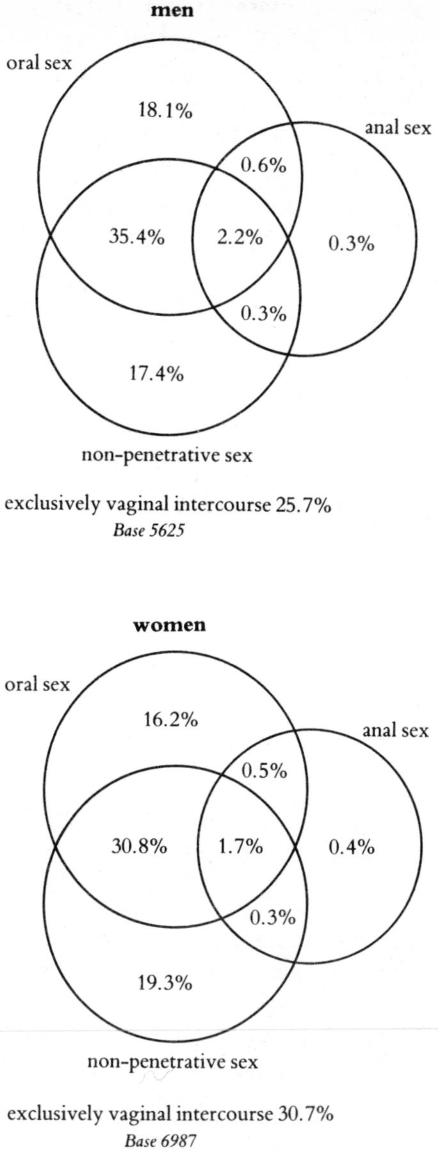

Figure 4.4 Repertoire of sexual practices in addition to vaginal intercourse in the last month. Source: Booklet Questions 3b–e

course in the last month. 25.7% of men and 30.7% of women reported exclusively vaginal intercourse. However, 35.4% of men and 30.8% of women reported experience of vaginal, oral *and* non-penetrative sex. Anal sex, as discussed, was a minority activity (3.4% of men and 2.9% of women) but the majority of these reported all other practices as well. Taken together, these data indicate that a variety of sexual activities are commonly practised by the majority of those who are sexually active, though vaginal intercourse continues to predominate as the most frequent form of sexual activity. Anal intercourse remains an infrequent activity, while those with recent experience of it have also engaged in vaginal intercourse and other practices over the same period.

FACTORS INFLUENCING THE REPERTOIRE OF HETEROSEXUAL PRACTICES

As with the frequency of sexual contact, the repertoire of sexual practices may be influenced by a number of factors. These include life stage and generational effects, previous experience (as measured by number of partners), and familiarity with partner (measured by length of relationship), as well as cultural influences in different societies at different times.

AGE AND SEXUAL PRACTICES

Both frequency of sex and numbers of partners have been shown to be related to current age and here the relationship between age and sexual practices is examined. The data for the last year and ever are shown in Table 4.6. While experience of vaginal intercourse is a near universal experience for men and women by the age of 25, there are marked age differences in other practices, most notably for oral sex (either cunnilingus or fellatio) (Table 4.6). While more than 60% of men and women aged 18–44 reported oral sex in the last year, this declined to less than 30% of women and 42% of men aged 45–59. While this might be explained partly by diminishing

	vaginal intercourse			oral sex*			anal sex			non-penetrative sex		
	last year	ever	*base*	last year	ever	*base*	last year	ever	*base*	last year	ever	*base*
							men					
16–17	40.1	42.5	*361*	30.5	32.0	*360*	7.4	7.7	*363*	57.1	61.5	*210*
18–24	78.7	86.9	*1540*	69.6	76.7	*1533*	8.1	11.0	*1542*	75.7	85.3	*1427*
25–34	90.8	96.6	*2069*	77.0	87.8	*2058*	6.6	16.1	*2053*	75.3	86.4	*2015*
35–44	91.4	97.6	*1934*	68.1	82.5	*1912*	6.2	16.5	*1913*	66.6	83.7	*1896*
45–59	87.9	97.5	*1969*	41.7	61.8	*1951*	5.1	12.3	*1958*	47.7	68.3	*1942*
all ages	85.5	92.7	*7870*	62.4	75.2	*7814*	6.5	13.9	*7828*	65.5	80.1	*7490*
							women					
16–17	38.0	39.4	*442*	32.1	32.8	*442*	5.4	5.6	*446*	65.4	66.7	*236*
18–24	84.4	88.6	*1712*	69.8	75.8	*1706*	8.6	13.9	*1709*	78.2	84.8	*1570*
25–34	92.2	97.5	*2747*	73.3	83.2	*2706*	6.6	14.4	*2726*	68.1	81.1	*2666*
35–44	91.5	100.0	*2411*	59.0	74.6	*2374*	4.8	13.1	*2390*	60.6	76.7	*2368*
45–59	78.4	97.5	*2476*	29.8	50.2	*2426*	4.3	11.6	*2450*	39.0	61.2	*2417*
all ages	84.7	95.7	*9789*	56.3	69.2	*9654*	5.9	12.9	*9721*	60.2	75.0	*9257*

Table 4.6 Prevalence (percentage) of different sexual practices in the last year and ever by sex and age group.
Source: Booklet Question 3
* either cunnilingus or fellatio

availability of partners in the older age group, the relationship is sustained for experience of oral sex ever. Half the women and nearly two-thirds of the men over the age of 45 reported ever having oral sex as compared with over four-fifths of those aged 25–34. The last in turn exceed the older cohort aged 35–44 in their experience of oral sex. Even among the group aged 18–24, who have relatively few years of sexual experience, women and men exceed those older than 45 in the proportion reporting any experience of oral sex. In the age group 16–24, among those who had *ever* had vaginal intercourse, 79% reported oral sex in the last year and 85% ever, suggesting that this practice may be becoming particularly prevalent among those embarking on their sexual careers.

The data indicate that there are generational changes in the practice of oral sex and that this has become an increasingly common practice in recent decades. Gagnon and Simon (1987) provide supporting evidence for this view from the Kinsey data and from a subsequent survey of young college-educated men and women in the 1960s. While difficult to compare directly, because of the lack of sample representativeness, there is evidence of increasing experience of oro-genital contact among American men and women born in the first 30 years of the twentieth century in the early Kinsey data. Gagnon and Simon also conclude that 'in the 1967 cohort about 80% of both men and women with frequent coitus had oral sex, a substantial increase from the 45% amongst comparably coitally experienced women in the Kinsey *et al.* studies'. They also argue that in 1967 oro-genital contact was still practised largely by those who had already experienced coitus.

More recent data, however, suggest that in a proportion of young people experience of oral sex may precede coitus (Coles and Stokes, 1985). Newcomer and Udry (1985), in a survey of American teenagers from a Southern US city, found that 25% of virgin boys and 15% of virgin girls had given or received oro-genital stimulation. Cunnilingus was more frequently reported than fellatio. In our data, among those over 18 who had not yet experienced vaginal intercourse, but reported that they had had some sexual experience, 6.3% of men and 3.4% of women reported experience of fellatio and 5.2% of men and 4.4% of women reported experience of cunnilingus.

The data from the survey, together with that from other sources, support the view that oro-genital contact, though a well-recognized form of sexual expression throughout history, has become more widely practised through the twentieth century. Earlier in this chapter, attention was drawn to the Christian focus on sex only for procreation as an influence that may in the past have decreased the prevalence of other forms of sexual expression, or at least the reporting of them. Simon and others (1990) have argued that the practice may have become more common as sexual activity in the twentieth century became viewed as 'a positive experience, rather than as a matter of obligation or reproductive responsibility'. Improved hygiene may also have had a role to play.

Evidence is emerging that oro-genital contact may be experienced by increasing proportions of those who have not yet had vaginal intercourse. This behaviour may be becoming more publicly acceptable in the recent era which has focused on risk-reduction strategies in the face of AIDS. Behaviours that in previous centuries might have been regarded as socially unacceptable may be increasingly encouraged as alternatives to sexual practices that are riskier in terms of unwanted pregnancy, STD and HIV.

To study this further, the data were examined for evidence of individuals (and particularly young people) practising oral and non-penetrative sex as an alternative to vaginal intercourse. Table 4.7 shows that a small proportion of respondents reported exclusively oral or non-penetrative sex in the last year, and that this was more common among men than women. The practice was most frequent among men in the age group 18–24. In this group, 1 in 4 of those who reported no vaginal or anal intercourse in the last year reported oral or non-penetrative sex in the same time period. Across the age groups, such experience seems to be an infrequent alternative to penetrative sex. Nevertheless, there may be some under-estimation of non-penetrative sex among those who have never had oral, anal or vaginal sex, since the question was not asked of this last group (see methods section, p. 92).

In contrast to the high prevalence of oro-genital contact, anal sex was reported relatively infrequently in all age groups (Table 4.6). Nevertheless, some evidence of a weak age trend is apparent. Experience of anal sex in the last year was most common among

	oral or non-penetrative sex only %	other %	no sex %	*base*
		men		
16–17*	1.2	69.7	29.1	*215*
18–24	4.5	85.3	10.1	*1434*
25–34	1.2	92.7	6.2	*2035*
35–44	0.8	93.3	5.9	*1913*
45–59	1.4	89.1	9.6	*1976*
all ages	1.8	89.8	8.4	*7572*
		women		
16–17*	0.7	73.0	26.4	*238*
18–24	1.7	91.9	6.4	*1582*
25–34	0.9	93.6	5.6	*2719*
35–44	0.9	92.1	7.0	*2416*
45–59	1.8	80.0	18.2	*2480*
all ages	1.3	88.8	9.9	*9434*

Table 4.7 Proportions reporting oral and non-penetrative sex in the last year. Source: Booklet Questions 3a–e

* respondents aged 16–17 without experience of sexual intercourse were not asked to complete the booklet.

those aged 18–24 (women 8.6%, men 8.1%) and reporting becomes less frequent with increasing age. Similarly for lifetime experience, a higher proportion of those aged 25–44 have experience of anal sex than those over 45, but these age differences are small compared with those for oral sex. Those aged 18–24 report similar or greater levels of experience of anal intercourse ever as those aged 45–59, despite being sexually active for a shorter period.

Historical data with which to compare the results are hard to find. Kinsey and others (1948; 1953) paid scant attention to the practice of anal intercourse in their original books. Gebhard and Johnson (1979) have reported data from Kinsey's work more recently and in these 11% of married white men and women with some college education reported attempting anal intercourse with their spouse.

Voeller (1990) has reviewed studies of heterosexual anal intercourse and concluded that 'at least 10% seems an appropriate lower limit for the number of sexually active American women who engage in heterosexual anal intercourse with some regularity'. However, many of the studies cited by Voeller are based on clinical, volunteer or magazine samples which cannot be regarded as representative of the general population. A further problem discussed in his article is the problem of comparability in question wording, mode of data collection and precision of the terms used. In some studies it is not clear whether the inquiry sought information on anal stimulation, anal penetration or specifically penile-anal penetration.

The wording used in our study was precise and anal sex (anal sexual intercourse) was defined as 'a man's penis entering a partner's anus/rectum or back passage'. Great care was used in employing this particular definition because of the importance of anal intercourse in the transmission of HIV. In homosexual men, unprotected receptive anal intercourse has been repeatedly shown to be the sexual activity associated with the greatest risk of transmission (Johnson, 1988). Heterosexual partners studies have also shown that women who engage in both vaginal and anal intercourse with their HIV positive male partners are more likely to become infected than those who practise vaginal intercourse alone (Padian *et al.*, 1987; European Study Group, 1989). However, anal intercourse is not necessary for HIV transmission. The prevalence of anal intercourse in the heterosexual population is therefore relevant in assessing the population attributable risk of HIV infection through anal intercourse. In societies where anal intercourse is rarely practised (and our data would suggest that in British society this is a relatively infrequent practice compared with vaginal intercourse) the overall contribution of anal intercourse to the heterosexual spread of HIV is likely to be small and the majority of viral spread is likely to occur through vaginal intercourse. This has important policy implications, since undue emphasis on the risks of heterosexual anal intercourse may detract from the importance of vaginal intercourse as a means of transmission.

In considering education strategies, it is of concern that the highest prevalence of recent anal intercourse (in the last year) is occurring among those aged 16–24 who have experience of vaginal intercourse. This is also the group experiencing the highest rate of partner change and who are passing through a sexually experimental phase of their lives (see Chapter 3). However, in interpreting data on the influence of age on sexual practices, account must also be taken of sexual careers. Older people may have practised anal intercourse at an earlier time in their lives, but no longer include it in their current sexual repertoire. Nevertheless, as Figure 4.2 indicates, the majority of those who have ever had anal intercourse have experience of this in the last 5 years.

Analysis of reporting non-penetrative sex by age group also showed age differences in behaviour (Table 4.6). For both men and women aged 18–59, the proportion reporting non-penetrative sex in the last year and ever declined with increasing age. Over 75% of men and women aged 18–24 reported this activity in the last year, but this proportion fell to 47.7% of men and 39% of women among the over-45s. Nevertheless, this was a common activity in all age groups. The data suggest that such activity may also have increased with successive generations since 68.3% of men and 61.2% of women over 45 reported ever having experience of non-penetrative sex not leading to intercourse, as compared with 85.3% of men and 84.8% of women in the youngest age group (18–24). At first sight, these findings may appear surprising, since those aged 45–59 are the group who became sexually active in the era before the availability of reliable contraception. They might be expected to have relied to a greater extent on non-penetrative sex as a means of sexual expression in order to avoid unwanted pregnancy. Balanced against this is the greater discussion, education and openness in sexual matters in later generations which may have led to greater knowledge and practice of a wider sexual repertoire. There remains the possibility that the question on non-penetrative sex was less well understood by older respondents than younger respondents, leading to under-reporting, but this in turn would lend support to an explanation involving generational changes in knowledge of possible modes of sexual expression.

Age differences in the overall pattern of behaviour are shown in Figure 4.5 for the last year and ever. It is evident that the proportion

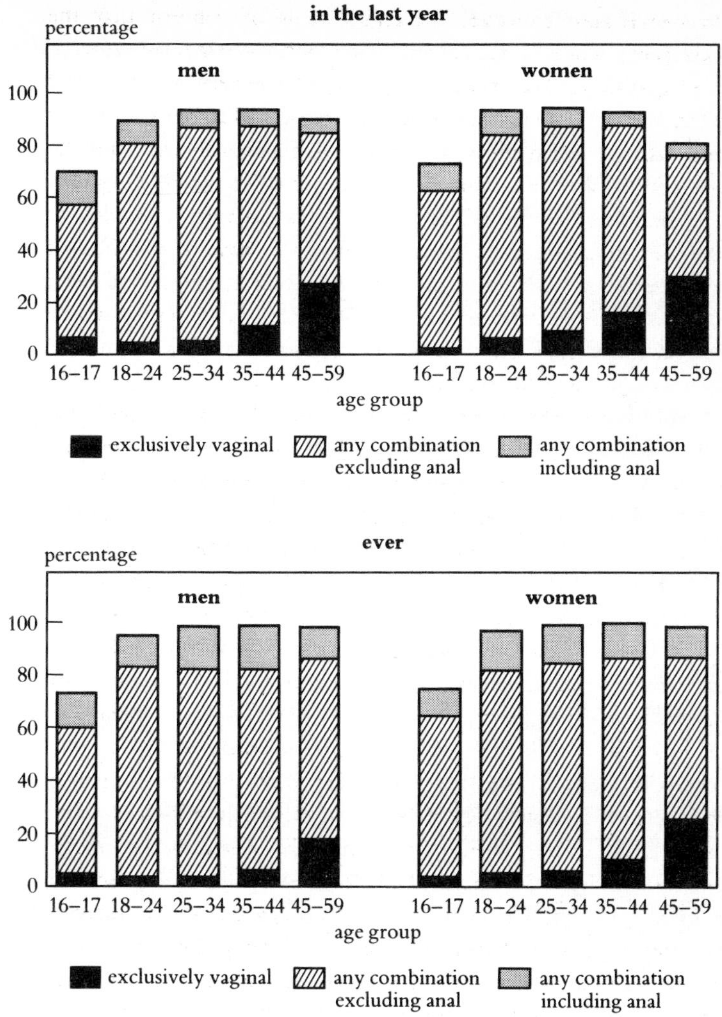

Figure 4.5 Patterns of sexual practices by age group. Source: Booklet Questions 3a–e

reporting only vaginal intercourse in the last year increases with age. These age effects are less marked in the data for patterns of sexual practices ever, the most marked pattern being the large increase in those over 45 reporting only vaginal intercourse in their lifetime. This suggests an effect of both ageing and age-cohort effects in the data. Both these effects are, however, less evident for the practice of anal intercourse.

SECULAR TRENDS IN SEXUAL PRACTICES

The foregoing discussion has commented in some detail on the age effects on both recent and lifetime experience of sexual practices. It is evident from this that, in addition to possible ageing effects in the frequency and variety of sexual practices, there have also been marked secular trends in patterns of behaviour. These are summarized in Figure 4.6, where reporting of sexual practices ever and in the last year are presented by year of first intercourse. For both men and women experience of oral and non-penetrative sex appears to have increased through the decades of the 1950s and 1960s, reaching a steady level of more than 80% of those who experienced their first sexual intercourse in the 1970s onwards.

By contrast, there is very little in the way of a secular trend in reporting of anal intercourse other than a slight tendency for the most recently sexually active to report this in the last year. This may reflect a more sexually adventurous phase in their careers than their older counterparts, rather than a true trend representing increased frequency of anal intercourse over the generations.

MARITAL STATUS AND SEXUAL PRACTICES

As for frequency of sex, the married state implies the availability of a regular partner, as well as familiarity with the partner, which in turn may influence the range of sexual practices.

Table 4.8 indicates that a much higher proportion of those who were married or cohabiting reported vaginal intercourse in the last year than their counterparts who are single, widowed, separated or divorced. Nevertheless 3% of married men and 3.7% of married women overall reported no vaginal intercourse in the last year. This rose to 9% of married women and 5.8% of married men over the age of 45.

In contrast, more than one-third of single people of all ages reported no vaginal intercourse in the last year. Similar trends are seen for oral sex, with lower rates of reporting among those outside married or cohabiting relationships.

For the practice of anal sex, perhaps surprisingly, consistently higher rates are observed among the cohabiting men and women and widowed, divorced and separated men than among married respondents, a point discussed later in relation to number of sexual partners.

Among single people, the proportion reporting anal intercourse is similar to the married, despite the fact that a high proportion do not report vaginal intercourse in the last year. While higher proportions of those in married or cohabiting relationships report non-penetrative sex in the last year than those without such partnerships, this remains a common practice regardless of marital status.

As with the data accounting for age alone (Table 4.6), the age effects on sexual practices persist within marital-status categories and there is a consistent decrease in the proportion of respondents reporting different practices in the last year with increasing age.

In order to overcome the problems of comparisons between groups with and without an available partner, reporting of practices was analysed only for respondents who had had vaginal intercourse in the last year. The data are shown stratified by marital status in Table 4.9. In this analysis, women and men who are not currently married show consistently higher rates of oral, anal and non-penetrative sex in the last year than the married. This relationship also generally holds true within age categories. This suggests that the apparently lower rates of reporting among *all* those who are not married or cohabiting (Table 4.8) are primarily a function of lack of partner availability rather than a reflection of a more limited sexual

IN THE LAST YEAR

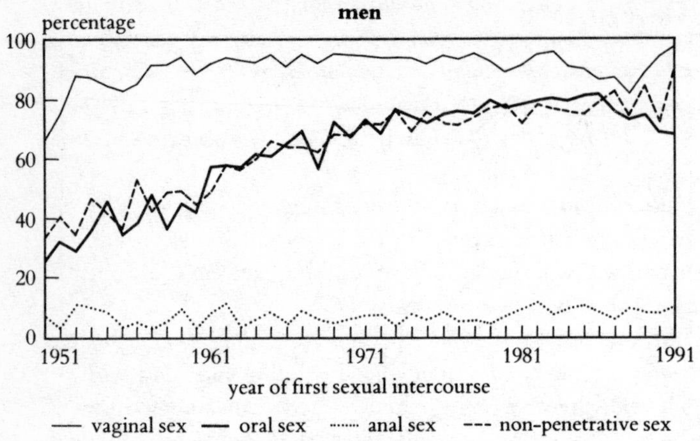

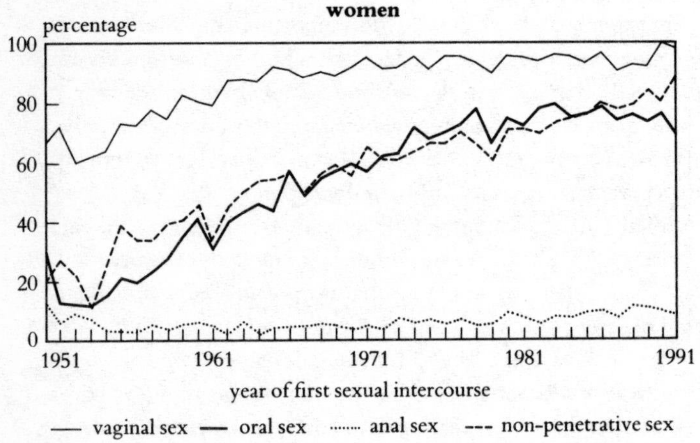

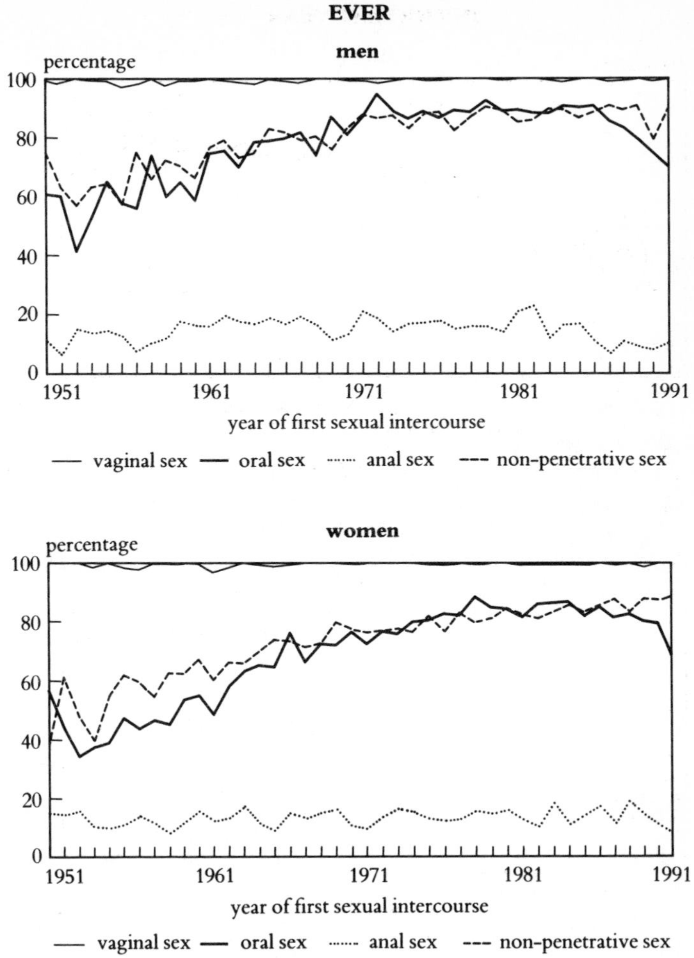

Figure 4.6 Sexual practices by year of first sexual intercourse. Source: Booklet Questions 3a–e

	vaginal intercourse		oral sex		anal sex		non-penetrative	
	%	*base*	%	*base*	%	*base*	%	*base*
				men				
married	97.0	*4467*	63.7	*4433*	5.5	*4425*	65.0	*4419*
cohabiting	98.2	*588*	87.9	*585*	9.9	*585*	80.5	*584*
widowed/separated/divorced	71.6	*410*	60.2	*403*	11.3	*415*	52.7	*413*
single	63.6	*2402*	54.2	*2385*	6.7	*2401*	64.8	*2073*
				women				
married	96.3	*5832*	58.0	*5728*	5.4	*5764*	60.9	*5725*
cohabiting	98.6	*802*	78.7	*794*	9.9	*798*	76.8	*787*
widowed/separated/divorced	55.6	*995*	39.6	*983*	5.1	*990*	36.6	*988*
single	61.8	*2158*	51.4	*2147*	6.0	*2167*	64.1	*1755*

Table 4.8 Prevalence (percentage) of different sexual practices in the last year by marital status. Source: Booklet Questions 3a–e

	oral sex		anal sex		non-penetrative	
	%	*base*	%	*base*	%	*base*
			men			
married	65.2	*4293*	5.4	*4280*	66.3	*4274*
cohabiting	88.7	*574*	9.8	*574*	80.9	*573*
widowed/separated/divorced	81.8	*294*	14.9	*293*	70.1	*293*
single	83.3	*1514*	10.3	*1510*	82.8	*1515*
			women			
married	60.0	*5495*	5.4	*5520*	62.4	*5485*
cohabiting	79.6	*782*	10.1	*785*	77.3	*776*
widowed/separated/divorced	70.0	*545*	9.1	*546*	64.3	*545*
single	80.9	*1322*	9.6	*1328*	80.7	*1322*

Table 4.9 Sexual practices in the last year reported by respondents who have had vaginal intercourse in the last year by marital status. Source: Booklet Questions 3a–e

repertoire among the single, separated, widowed and divorced. Those who have had a partner in the last year may however differ from those who have not with respect to other characteristics and past sexual experience.

SEXUAL PRACTICES AND SOCIAL CLASS

The relatively weak relationship between social class and numbers of heterosexual partners has been discussed elsewhere (Chapter 3). Here the relationship between social class and sexual practices is shown (Table 4.10). Overall trends indicate that for both men and women the proportion reporting vaginal, oral and non-penetrative sex increases with higher social class. These differences persist after controlling for age.

	vaginal intercourse			oral sex			anal sex			non-penetrative		
social class	last year	ever	*base*	last year	ever	*base*	last year	ever	*base*	last year	ever	*base*
						men						
I, II	91.5	97.7	*2757*	67.9	84.3	*2748*	4.6	14.2	*2751*	67.8	86.3	*2710*
III NM	90.3	95.5	*1486*	67.9	78.2	*1475*	6.6	13.7	*1472*	67.7	79.6	*1446*
III M	86.1	95.2	*2077*	60.4	72.8	*2058*	8.3	15.3	*2067*	64.5	77.2	*2011*
IV, V	83.3	91.0	*849*	57.6	67.3	*840*	10.0	15.3	*840*	60.8	72.5	*803*
other	52.9	61.6	*693*	40.8	50.0	*686*	4.4	6.9	*692*	59.0	72.0	*513*
						women						
I, II	91.8	98.2	*3460*	61.0	76.2	*3413*	4.9	12.9	*3445*	63.7	79.7	*3380*
III NM	85.9	94.3	*2248*	60.3	71.5	*2216*	6.0	13.5	*2234*	63.8	76.8	*2135*
III M	90.1	97.2	*1857*	54.5	65.5	*1826*	7.0	13.0	*1834*	55.0	67.7	*1803*
IV, V	81.9	93.6	*1007*	52.4	64.3	*992*	8.0	13.0	*989*	57.3	71.8	*952*
other	56.7	74.5	*1212*	41.9	54.7	*1200*	5.1	11.6	*1213*	53.4	72.1	*981*

Table 4.10 Prevalence (percentage) of different sexual practices in the last year and ever by social class. Source: Booklet Question 3a–e

For anal intercourse, the differential reporting between social classes is less clear. Overall there is no class trend in reporting of anal intercourse at any time, although reporting over the last year shows an increased proportion reporting anal intercourse among those in lower social classes.

Perhaps the most remarkable finding is in the similarities rather than the dissimilarities across the groups. Given the strong age effects that have been observed in sexual practices, which suggest that there have been rapidly changing fashions in sexual behaviour over the last few decades, our evidence suggests that these have been widely adopted throughout different social groups. In view of the relationships between age, marital status and social class, these bivariate relationships are examined further in a multivariate model.

NUMBERS OF PARTNERS AND SEXUAL PRACTICES

The sexual repertoire may be influenced by previous sexual experience as well as by other identified variables such as age and marital status. Table 4.11 shows the relationship between numbers of partners in the last 5 years and sexual practices over the same time period. There is a clear trend of increasing proportions reporting oral, anal and non-penetrative sex with increasing numbers of partners. While this relationship may be confounded by age (which is associated both with types of sexual practice and with numbers of partners), the trend holds true within age groups for both men and women. Those with greater numbers of partners may have a greater repertoire of practices. This may result either from greater experience of learning different techniques from different partners or because preference for sexual variety provides motivation to seek larger numbers of partners.

This finding may help to explain the data in Table 4.9 demonstrating the greater range of sexual practices among those who are sexually active but not currently married, since these respondents are among those known to report greater numbers of partners (Chapter 3).

number of partners	0		1		2		3–4		5–9		10+	
	%	*base*	%	*base*	%	*base*	%	*base*	%	*base*	%	*base*
					vaginal intercourse							
men	1.1*	*693*	98.9	*4425*	98.7	*791*	98.9	*943*	99.5	*625*	98.6	*378*
women	1.3*	*904*	99.0	*6546*	98.8	*1094*	99.8	*792*	100.0	*358*	99.4	*82*
					oral sex							
men	1.3*	*688*	69.1	*4390*	82.1	*788*	91.6	*937*	93.7	*622*	96.4	*377*
women	1.3*	*900*	63.6	*6430*	85.0	*1084*	90.7	*784*	96.9	*360*	98.8	*82*
					anal sex							
men	0.1*	*692*	7.1	*4394*	12.7	*793*	14.9	*939*	15.7	*622*	31.9	*377*
women	0.1*	*903*	7.6	*6477*	13.3	*1089*	17.6	*794*	19.6	*361*	27.0	*82*
					non-penetrative sex							
men	6.7	*362*	70.5	*4385*	82.9	*792*	85.7	*939*	90.4	*624*	87.7	*377*
women	5.3	*496*	67.2	*6437*	81.8	*1081*	85.0	*786*	89.2	*361*	94.6	*82*

Table 4.11 Proportion of respondents (percentage) reporting different sexual practices in the last 5 years by number of heterosexual partners in the last 5 years. Source: Booklet Questions 3a–e, 7b

* these responses are theoretically inconsistent but may arise from differential recall in different sections of the questionnaire

MULTIVARIATE ANALYSIS

In order to examine the interactions between the various factors shown to be associated with different sexual practices in the last year, a series of logistic models was constructed. Variables included in the models were age group, marital status, social class and number of partners in the last year.

The results of the models are presented as adjusted odds ratios with 95% confidence intervals in Figure 4.7. All respondents were included in the models. Oral and non-penetrative sex remained strongly related to age, marital status, and numbers of partners in the last year. Social class exerted a relatively weak effect, with those

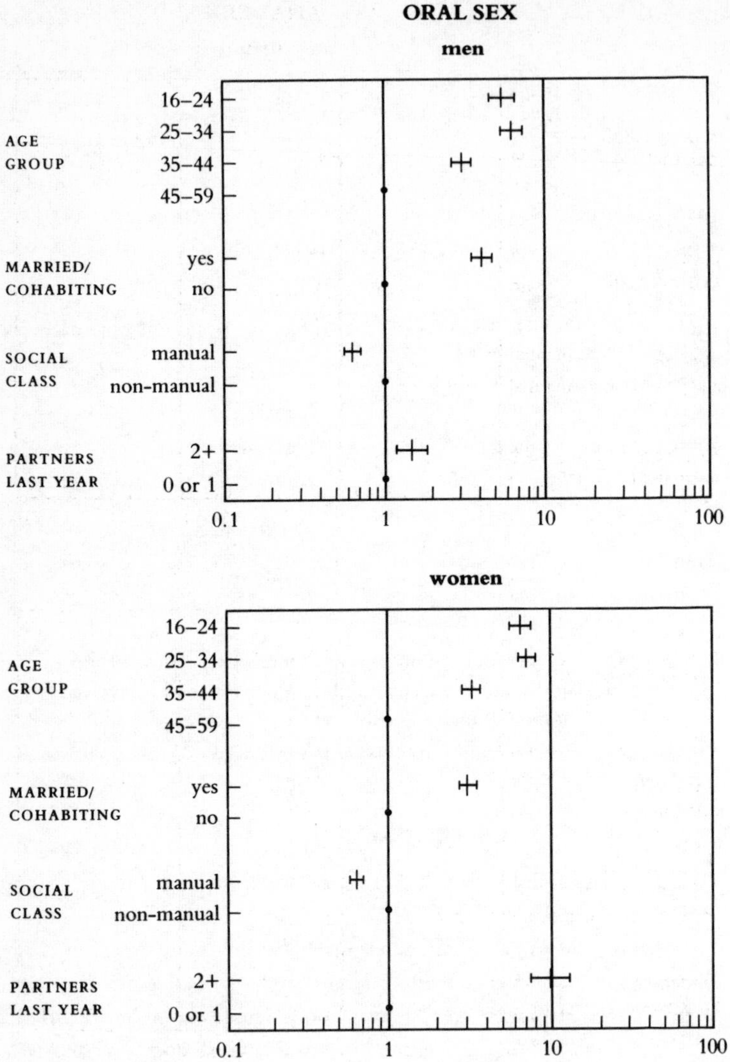
ORAL SEX
men
AGE GROUP
16–24
25–34
35–44
45–59
MARRIED/ COHABITING
yes
no
SOCIAL CLASS
manual
non-manual
PARTNERS LAST YEAR
2+
0 or 1
0.1
1
10
100
women
AGE GROUP
16–24
25–34
35–44
45–59
MARRIED/ COHABITING
yes
no
SOCIAL CLASS
manual
non-manual
PARTNERS LAST YEAR
2+
0 or 1
0.1
1
10
100

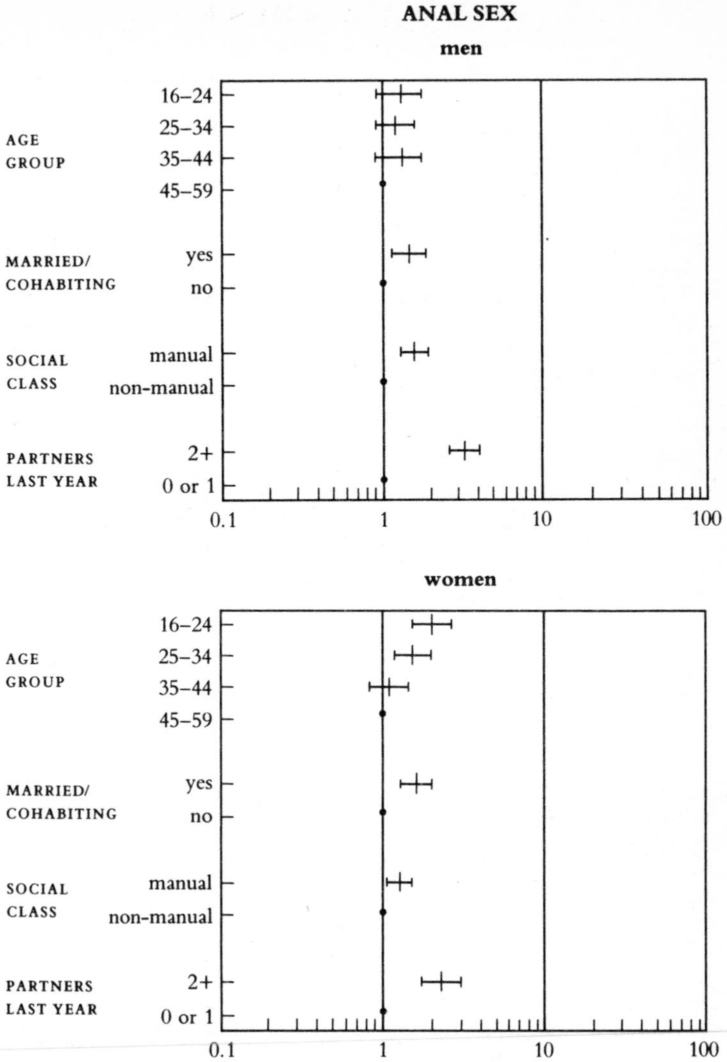

Figure 4.7 *continued overleaf*

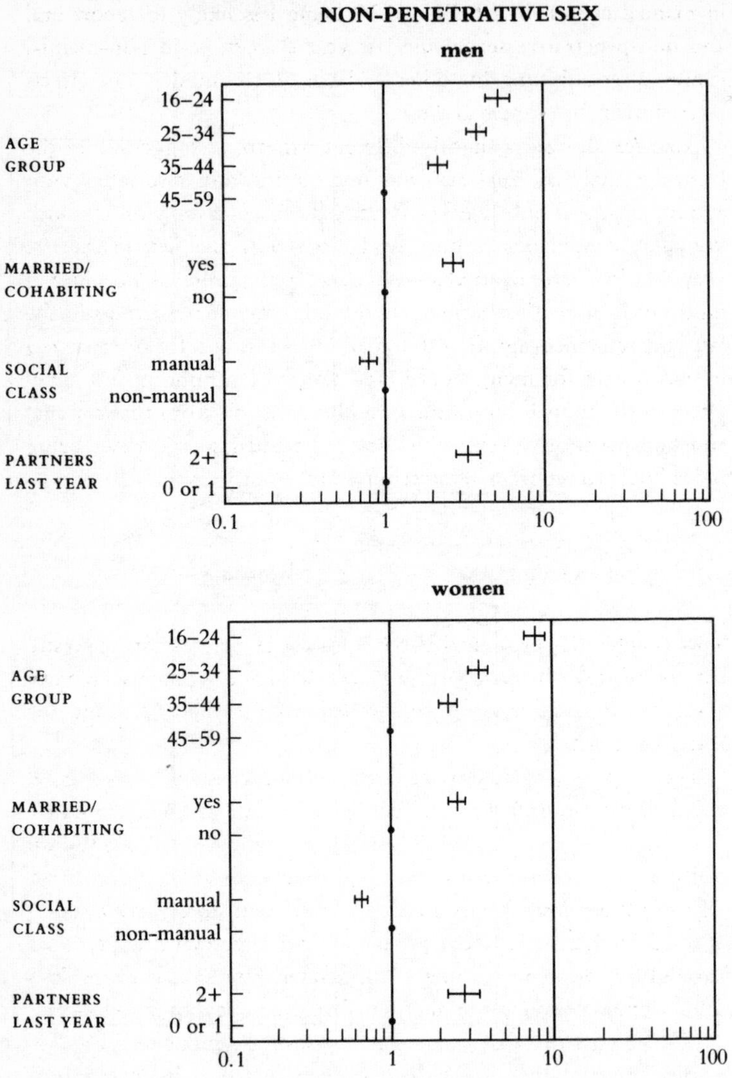

Figure 4.7 Adjusted odds ratios with 95% confidence intervals for different sexual practices in the last year. Source: Booklet Questions 3b–e

in manual classes (III M, IV and V) being less likely to report oral and non-penetrative sex in the last year than those in non-manual classes, after adjusting for other variables in the model. The effects were similar for women and men.

Anal sex showed a slightly different pattern, as suggested by the bivariate analysis. Anal sex was not significantly associated with age for men and only weakly associated with age for women, with younger women being more likely to report anal sex in the last year. Marital status exerted a weak effect in the model. The adjusted odds ratio for anal sex among those with 2 or more partners in the last year remained significantly raised (in excess of 2 for women and in excess of 3 for men). Social class exerted a significant but small effect in the model, but in the opposite direction from that for oral and non-penetrative sex, with those in manual social classes being more likely to report anal intercourse in the last year.

SUMMARY

This chapter has examined the frequency of heterosexual sex and the repertoire of heterosexual practices. Men and women were very consistent in their reporting of both the frequency of sex and the pattern of practices.

The frequency of heterosexual sex (defined as acts of oral, vaginal and anal intercourse) showed very wide variability as measured by the number of occasions in the last 4 weeks with a small proportion of the population reporting very high frequency of sexual contact. Age was closely related to number of acts, with frequency peaking in the mid-twenties and thereafter showing a gradual decline, more marked for women than men. This gender difference is probably a result of men adopting younger female partners as they grow older.

Not surprisingly partner availability strongly influenced the frequency of sex, which was highest in the married and cohabiting of all ages. There was only a very weak relationship between social class and frequency of sex.

There was a strong association in all age groups between length of relationship and frequency of sex, with the number of occasions in the last 4 weeks being much lower in longer relationships. It appears that the lower frequency of sex among older respondents is partly related to their longer relationships.

Within marital-status categories, frequency of sex in the last 4 weeks increased with increasing numbers of partners in the last 5 years. However, among those outside married or cohabiting relationships, even those with high numbers of partners only achieved rates of heterosexual intercourse similar to those of the married. The bivariate findings in relation to frequency of sex were largely confirmed in multivariate analysis.

Respondents reported a varied repertoire of sexual practices. While vaginal intercourse predominated as the most prevalent practice, more than three-quarters of the sample had experience of non-penetrative sex not leading to intercourse and 70% had some experience of either cunnilingus or fellatio. In contrast, any experience of anal intercourse was reported by only 13.9% men and 12.9% of women.

A number of factors are identified as influencing the repertoire of sexual practices. Recent and lifetime experience of oral and non-penetrative sex increased with decreasing age, indicating evidence of both age and age cohort effects. The data are consistent with other sources indicating a considerable increase in popularity of oro-genital contact. There was evidence of oro-genital contact occurring as a prelude to first intercourse in a minority of respondents. Oral and non-penetrative sex in the absence of vaginal intercourse appeared to be unusual, although reported most frequently in those aged 18–24. There was, however, little evidence of widespread adoption of these activities as alternatives to vaginal intercourse in order to reduce risk of unwanted pregnancy or STD. In contrast to oral and non-penetrative sex, there was little evidence of an increase in the practice of anal sex over recent decades. However, recent experience of anal intercourse was most frequent among young respondents and those with multiple partners.

Among those who were not married, and who had had vaginal intercourse in the last year, oral, anal and non-penetrative sex were reported at consistently higher rates than among the married, indicating that this group may have a wider repertoire than those in more stable relationships.

This effect appears to be related to the relationship between number of partners and practices. The prevalence of oral, anal and non-penetrative sex all increased with numbers of partners.

As with other areas of behaviour, social class had only a weak relationship with reported patterns of behaviour. In a multivariate analysis which controlled for the factors evident in bivariate analysis, those in non-manual classes were more likely to report oral and non-penetrative sex while those in manual classes were more likely to report anal sex. These effects were weak compared with the influences of age, marital status and number of partners.

As with number of partners, there is wide variability in frequency of sex and patterns of sexual practices. Those outside married or cohabiting relationships may overall experience less frequent sex, but they are more likely to have multiple partners, to experience a wider range of practices and to have recent experience of more risky practices, such as anal intercourse. At the same time, this is a group who also have a wider experience of non-penetrative and oral sex, implying skills for adoption of lower-risk sexual practices and for expressing sexual pleasure through a range of different activities.

REFERENCES

Bungay, G. T., M. P. Vessey, and K. McPherson (1980). 'Study of Symptoms in Middle Life with Special Reference to the Menopause', *British Medical Journal*, 281, 181–3

Coles, R., and G. Stokes (1985). *Sex and the American Teenager.* New York: Harper and Row

Cox, B. D., M. Blaxter, A. L. J. Buckle, N. P. Fenner, J. P. Golding, M. Gore, *et al.* (1987). *The Health and Lifestyle Survey.* London: Health Promotion Research Trust

European Study Group (1989). 'Risk Factors for Male-to-Female Transmission of HIV', *British Medical Journal*, 298, 411–15

Gagnon, J. H., and W. Simon (1987). 'The Sexual Sampling of Oro-genital Contacts', *Archives of Sexual Behaviour*, 16, 1–25

Gebhard, P. H. (1970). 'Sexual Motifs in Prehistoric Peruvian Ceramics', in T. Bowie and C. V. Christiansen (eds), *Studies in Erotic Art* (pp. 109–44). New York: Basic Books Inc.

Gebhard P. H., and A. B. Johnson (1979). *The Kinsey Data: Marginal Tabulations of the 1938–1963 Interviews Conducted by the Institute of Sex Research*. Philadelphia: W. B. Saunders

Gorer, G. (1971). *Sex and Marriage in England Today*. London: Nelson

Johnson, A. M. (1988). 'Social and Behavioural Aspects of the HIV Epidemic – A Review', *Journal of Royal Statistical Society*, series A, 151, 99–114

Kinsey, A. C., W. B. Pomeroy, and C. E. Martin (1948). *Sexual Behavior in the Human Male*. Philadelphia: W. B. Saunders

Kinsey, A. C., W. B. Pomeroy, C. E. Martin, and P. H. Gebhard (1953). *Sexual Behavior in the Human Female*. Philadelphia: W. B. Saunders

Masters, W., and V. Johnson (1966). *Human Sexual Response*. London: Churchill

Newcomer, S. F., and J. R. Udry (1985). 'Oral Sex in an Adolescent Population', *Archives of Sexual Behaviour*, 41–6

Osborn, M., K. Hawton, and D. Gath (1988). 'Sexual Dysfunction among Middle-aged Women in the Community', *British Medical Journal*, 296, 959–62

Padian, N., L. Marquis, D. P. Francis, R. E. Anderson, G. W. Rutherford, P. M. O'Malley, *et al.* (1987). 'Male-to-Female Transmission of Human Immunodeficiency Virus', *Journal of American AIDS*, 258, 788–90

Reinisch, J. M., M. Ziemba-Davis, and S. A. Sanders (1990). 'Sexual Behaviour and AIDS: Lessons from Art and Sex Research', in B. Voeller, J. M. Reinisch, and M. Gottlieb (eds), *AIDS and Sex: An Integrated Biomedical and Biobehavioural Approach* (pp. 37–80). Oxford: Oxford University Press

Simon, W., D. M. Kraft, and H. B. Kaplan (1990). 'Oral Sex: A Critical Overview', in B. Voeller, J. M. Reinisch, and M. Gottlieb (eds), *AIDS and Sex: An Integrated Biomedical and Biobehavioural Approach* (pp. 257–75). Oxford: Oxford University Press

Spencer, L., A. Faulkner, and J. Keegan (1988). *Talking about Sex*. London: Social and Community Planning Research

Starr, B. D., and M. B. Weiner (1981). *The Starr–Weiner Report on Sex and Sexuality in the Mature Years*. New York: McGraw-Hill

Voeller, B. (1990). 'Heterosexual Anal Intercourse: An AIDS Risk Factor', in B. Voeller, J. M. Reinisch, and M. Gottlieb (eds), *AIDS and Sex: An Integrated Biomedical and Biobehavioural Approach* (pp. 276–310). Oxford: Oxford University Press

Weeks, J. (1981). *Sex, Politics and Society: The Regulation of Sexuality since 1800*. New York: Longman

Wilson, S. (1973). 'Short History of Western Erotic Art', in R. Melville (ed.), *Erotic Art of the West* (pp. 11–31). New York: G. P. Putnam and Sons

CHAPTER 5

Sexual Diversity and Homosexual Behaviour

INTRODUCTION

The aim of this chapter is to map the extent and range of patterns of sexual diversity. A major problem for scientific investigation in this area is that the choice of gender of sexual partner is not neutral; different social and moral values are attached to particular preferences. Diversity of sexual orientation may be universal in human societies (Ford and Beach, 1952), but the level of approval varies markedly and in most Western societies homosexual preference is tolerated but stigmatized.

Only in very recent times has there been a shift away from the treatment of homosexuality as sickness or sin. Until 1967 male homosexuality was a criminal offence in Britain and only in 1974 was it removed from the list of psychiatric disorders by the American Psychiatric Association (to be replaced by the diagnosis 'sexual orientation disturbance' (Bayer, 1981)). Only comparatively recently, too, have social scientists come to view homosexuality as other than clinical or social deviance (Weeks, 1986).

The emerging perspective in the latter part of the twentieth century is that homosexuality is part of a broad spectrum of sexual expression. The origins of this view are to be found partly in Freud's concept of the 'polymorphous perverse' sexuality of infancy, (though Freud was inclined to see this more as an innate capacity than as a social or psychological norm (Freud, 1953)). Empirically, the perspective owes much to the work of Kinsey, who for the first time designed a research instrument to represent sexual orientation as a continuum rather than two fixed and dichotomous points (Kinsey *et al.*, 1948).

If the scientific community has been slow to accept sexual diversity, the general public has shown even greater resistance. Public attitudes to homosexuality are still characterized by a deep ambivalence (see Chapter 6). The growing acceptance of same-gender sexual relations in the 1970s suffered a setback in the 1980s with the emergence of AIDS, which seemed to precipitate a resurgence of anti-gay sentiment (Wellings and Wadsworth, 1990). Socially acceptable sexual behaviour is still predominantly heterosexual. We have not yet moved into a culture that tolerates sexual variety.

Implications for Research

Public and professional attitudes to homosexuality are not merely of academic or sociological interest but of direct *practical* relevance to the conduct of research. Researchers cannot escape locating themselves within a particular paradigm, which is reflected in the research instrument. It is perhaps worth stating at the outset the assumptions that guided construction of the questions relating to sexual orientation in this survey:

1. The polarity 'homosexual–heterosexual' is an inadequate categorization of the population; same- and opposite-gender sexual expression are better represented as a continuum. The Kinsey scale – rating same- and opposite-gender sexual attraction and experience on a 7-point rating scale – has been adapted for this survey as a 5-point scale (see below).
2. The terms heterosexual and homosexual were not used within the research instrument for the following reasons:
   a) The use of the term 'homosexual' might invite a low rate of reporting, on the assumption that a respondent is less likely to ascribe to him- or herself a stigmatizing identity than to report a particular practice.
   b) The use of terms denoting sexual identities is irrelevant in the context of HIV and STD since it is sexual practice and not identity that is relevant to understanding the dynamics of transmission.

c) Development work for the survey revealed some lack of understanding of the term 'homosexual' (Spencer *et al.*, 1988), which was confirmed in the *British Social Attitudes* survey (Wellings and Wadsworth, 1990). Possibly because of a misunderstanding over the Greek root *homo* meaning 'same', a sizeable minority believed homosexuality to refer to sex between two men, and not to refer also to sex between two women.

Thus, although the terms homosexual and heterosexual are used throughout this chapter to describe sexual activity with same- and opposite-gender partners respectively, these terms did not feature in the questionnaire. Respondents were simply asked to report attraction and experience, with men and with women (see below).

How homosexual behaviour is viewed socially influences not only the kinds of questions asked and the way in which they are phrased, but also responses to them and even the uses to which the data might be put. An important caveat here is that since homosexual sex is stigmatized in Britain, it can be expected to be under- rather than over-reported. For the same reason it is possible that some people who had experienced homosexual sex would be less willing to participate in the survey. Because of possible reporting and response bias all prevalence figures relating to homosexual activity should be regarded as minimum estimates.

In terms of the use of the data, the prevalence of same-gender sexual practice is clearly of central significance as a public health question in the AIDS era. Where transmission of a virus is linked with particular sexual practices it is important to estimate their prevalence. At the same time, political use of these data cannot be ignored. According to some observers, one of the most important contributions a survey of sexual behaviour can make is to provide the empirical framework for a recognition of sexual diversity (Gagnon and Simon, 1973). Statistical and moral deviance tend to be equated in this context. While deviation from a statistical norm might properly be termed *diversity*, relating to a continuum of behaviours in which no more value is attached to one point than another, deviation from a moral norm denotes *perversion* – a term heavily laden with opprobrium. Statistics have political significance in so far as they have the potential to normalize particular practices.

For this reason Kinsey's findings (Kinsey *et al.*, 1948; Kinsey *et al.*, 1953), indicating a larger than expected prevalence of same-gender sexual practice, were greeted enthusiastically by the gay community.

Question Formulation

Two questions relating to sexual orientation were asked in the face-to-face interview and the self-completion booklet contained questions on homosexual behaviour. The first of these (Question 31), in the face-to-face part of the schedule, requested respondents to locate themselves, in terms of both sexual attraction and experience, on a 5-point rating scale. At this point, sexual experience was self-defined (see below). Show-cards were used enabling respondents to read the statements themselves and to respond using only a letter of the alphabet. The questions were worded as follows for men; for women the terms male and female were transposed.

CARD K

I have felt *sexually attracted* . . .

. . . only to females, never to males	(K)
. . . more often to females, and at least once to a male	(C)
. . . about equally often to females and to males	(F)
. . . more often to males, and at least once to a female	(L)
. . . only ever to males, never to females	(D)
I have never felt sexually attracted to anyone at all	(N)

CARD L

Sexual experience is any kind of contact with another person that you felt was sexual (it could be just kissing or touching, or intercourse or any other form of sex).

I have had some *sexual experience* . . .

. . . only with females (or with a female), never with a male	(R)
. . . more often with females, and at least once with a male	(Q)
. . . about equally often with females and with males	(T)
. . . more often with males, and at least once with a female	(O)
. . . only with males (or a male), never with a female	(Z)
I have never had sexual experience with anyone at all	(W)

Within the booklet the first two questions on homosexual behaviour addressed to men are:

4a) Have you ever had ANY kind of sexual experience or sexual contact with a male?

A further question asks for reports of genital contact:

4c) Have you ever had sex with a man involving genital area/penis contact?

Subsequent questions asked about time intervals of decreasing recency, i.e. from the last 7 days to longer than 5 years ago. The somewhat biological term *male* was used to obviate the need to use the terms *man* (which might prompt respondents to exclude experience with youths) and *boy* (with possible unwanted connotations in terms of sex with a minor). Women were asked these same questions with the term *female* substituted for *male*.

Further questions in the booklet (Questions 5 and 8) asked about frequency of same-gender sex and numbers of same-gender sexual partners:

Altogether, in your life so far, with how many men have you had sex (that is, oral, anal or genital contact)?

Again *women* was substituted for *men* for female respondents, and a female partner as someone with whom the respondent had had oral sex or other forms of genital contact. Thereafter the numbers of partners in different time periods were reported by the respondent.

ATTRACTION AND EXPERIENCE

As shown in Table 5.1, over 93% of respondents were attracted exclusively to people of the opposite sex. Similar proportions (92.3%, of men and 95.1% of women) reported exclusively heterosexual experience.

The degree of congruence between sexual attraction and sexual experience in terms of gender preference is clearly of interest in the context of social and cultural influences on sexual orientation. The suggestion has been made that since homosexual activity is stigma-

	attraction		experience	
	men %	**women** %	**men** %	**women** %
only heterosexual	93.3	93.6	92.3	95.1
mostly heterosexual	4.0	3.8	3.9	2.2
both hetero- and homosexual	0.5	0.2	0.3	0.1
mostly homosexual	0.5	0.2	0.6	0.2
only homosexual	0.5	0.3	0.4	0.1
none	0.8	1.2	2.0	1.6
refused	0.5	0.7	0.6	0.7
base	*8384*	*10492*	*8384*	*10492*

Table 5.1 Reported homosexual and heterosexual attraction and experience. Source: Interview Questions 31a, 31b

tized, the proportion of people who feel sexually inclined to others of the same gender may be higher than the number acting out that inclination (Davies, 1988). In so far as sexual attraction can be taken as an indicator of prior inclination, and experience as its lived-out reality, the proportion of people reporting same-gender sexual *attraction* might be expected to be higher than that reporting same-gender *experience*.

As Tables 5.2 and 5.3 show, by far the largest proportion of people (90.2% of men and 92.4% of women) report exclusively heterosexual experience and attraction. If this definition is widened to include mostly heterosexual attraction and experience, the proportions increase to 96.0% and 97.0% respectively. Those who, at this point in the interview schedule, describe their sexual experience as *mostly* or *exclusively* with others of the same gender is small, making up barely 1% of the total sample of men, and less than 0.25% of women. 0.4% of men and 0.5% of women report no sexual attraction or experience of any kind, and 0.4% of men and 0.7% of women report only heterosexual contact with no sexual attraction.

The remaining respondents align themselves predominantly along the axis of congruence in terms of sexual attraction and experience.

	attraction					
experience	only to women	mostly to women	equally to women and men	mostly to men	only to men	no attraction
only with women	90.19	2.01	0.15	0.02	0.03	0.37
mostly with women	1.96	1.82	0.09	0.04	0.04	0.00
equally with women and men	0.00	0.08	0.20	0.02	0.02	0.00
mostly with men	0.08	0.01	0.02	0.35	0.10	0.00
only with men	0.02	0.01	0.00	0.10	0.26	0.00
no experience	1.56	0.05	0.02	0.02	0.01	0.37
base = 8335						

Table 5.2 Orientation (percentage) of sexual experience and attraction: men. Source: Interview Questions 31a, 31b

	attraction					
experience	only to men	mostly to men	equally to women and men	mostly to women	only to women	no attraction
only with men	92.42	2.44	0.08	0.02	0.07	0.74
mostly with men	0.78	1.38	0.02	0.05	0.03	0.00
equally with women and men	0.03	0.01	0.04	0.02	0.03	0.00
mostly with women	0.02	0.00	0.01	0.10	0.03	0.00
only with women	0.01	0.00	0.00	0.01	0.10	0.00
no experience	1.02	0.01	0.01	0.00	0.03	0.50
base = 10412						

Table 5.3 Orientation (percentage) of sexual experience and attraction: women. Source: Interview Questions 31a, 31b

The data provide no evidence of major discordance between preference and practice and seem to offer little support for the theory that large proportions of the population harbour unrealized fantasies about same-gender sex. 2.2% of men report having felt attracted to, but having no experience with, someone of their own gender and for women the comparable figure is 2.6%. Conversely, 2.1% of men and 0.8% of women report homosexual experience but exclusively heterosexual attraction.

PREVALENCE OF HOMOSEXUAL EXPERIENCE

The answer to the question 'What is a reasonable estimate of the prevalence of homosexual experience among British men and women?' depends largely on the context in which the question is posed and the purposes for which the data are collected. As stated above, it is both possible and desirable to produce several estimates of prevalence depending on the criteria used to define homosexual activity (Figure 5.1 and Table 5.4). In the context of the HIV/AIDS epidemic, a definition that includes genital contact will clearly be important since this describes the practices that could lead to the exchange of body fluids. If we are concerned with *currently practising* homosexuals then a definition must incorporate some measure of recency.

Responses to all questions relating to same-gender sexual contact were used to provide prevalence estimates for several same-gender experiences which are summarized in Table 5.4. It should be emphasized that no one of these individually can be taken as a single prevalence estimate of homosexual orientation.

It will be recalled that the first question asking about same-gender experience was asked in the face-to-face interview, while all others relating to sexual orientation were contained within the self-completion booklet. The use of show-cards and letters of the alphabet indicating particular responses, allowed respondents to avoid audibly disclosing personal information. Even so respondents might still have felt more at ease reporting under conditions of greater privacy provided by the self-completion booklet. Higher

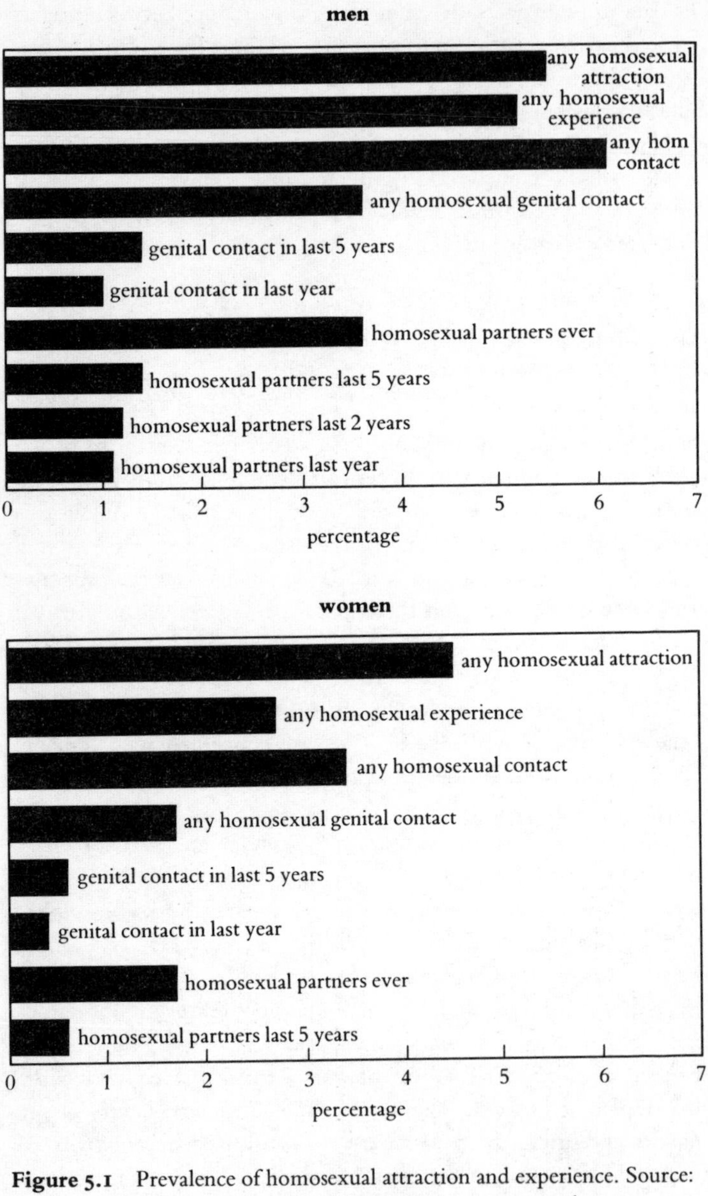

Figure 5.1 Prevalence of homosexual attraction and experience. Source: Interview Questions 31a, 31b; Booklet Questions 4a, 4c, 8a–d

	16–24		25–34		35–44		45–59		total	
	men %	**women** %	**men** %	**women** %	**men** %	**women** %	**men** %	**women** %	**men** %	**women** %
face-to-face interview										
any homosexual attraction	6.6	5.1	5.3	5.7	5.9	5.0	4.1	2.3	5.5	4.5
any homosexual experience	4.6	2.4	4.9	3.2	7.1	3.1	4.2	1.9	5.2	2.7
self-completion booklet										
any homosexual experience	4.3	3.0	5.9	4.0	8.5	4.2	5.7	2.6	6.1	3.4
any genital contact	2.4	1.4	3.8	1.9	5.1	2.1	3.1	1.3	3.6	1.7
at least 1 homosexual partner ever	2.6	1.4	3.6	2.0	4.8	2.1	3.2	1.3	3.5	1.7
at least 1 homosexual partner in last 5 years	1.7	1.2	1.9	0.8	1.0	0.5	0.9	0.1	1.4	0.6
at least 1 homosexual partner in last 2 years	1.3	0.8	1.5	0.6	0.9	0.3	0.8	0.1	1.1	0.4
at least 1 homosexual partner in the last year	1.2	0.6	1.5	0.6	0.8	0.2	0.7	0.1	1.1	0.4
range of bases	*1977–1978*	*2230–2234*	*2154–2158*	*2879–2881*	*2033–2039*	*2558–2559*	*2159–2165*	*2742–2750*	*8329–8340*	*10411–10420*

Table 5.4 Prevalence of homosexual attraction and experience by age group. Source: Interview Questions 31a, 31b; Booklet Questions 4a, 4c, 8a–d

levels of reporting of homosexual activity could be expected within the booklet than in the questionnaire.

The repetition of the question asking about any homosexual contact within the booklet (Question 4a) allowed respondents a further opportunity to report such experience and also permitted direct comparisons to be made between responses to the two. Since the main difference between these questions lies in the manner of data collection (face-to-face in the case of the one, self-recorded in the other) any reporting variation might be attributed to this difference. In fact, as Figure 5.2 shows, for women of all ages, and for men older than 19, the proportion reporting same-gender sexual contact in the booklet was higher than in the face-to-face interview. Among men (though not so notably among women) the disparity between face-to-face and booklet responses increased with age, so that for those aged 40 and over, it is greater than for younger men.

As Table 5.4 shows, 6.1% of men reported some kind of homosexual experience, 3.6% genital contact with a man and 1.4% having had a male sexual partner within the last 2 years. The equivalent figures for women are 3.4%, 1.7% and 0.6%. Comparisons with other surveys are limited by variation in question wording and by differences in the age range of the sample, timing of fieldwork, etc., but selecting the appropriate definition from the questionnaire allows some comparisons to be made. The figure of 3.6% for male homosexual genital contact is higher than that found in other British surveys. Forman and Chilvers (1989), for example, found that 1.7% of the sample of 480 white British males aged 15–49 gave a positive answer to the question 'Have you ever had homosexual intercourse?', though admittedly the question wording in that case was ambiguous. McQueen and others (1991) asked a general population sample aged 18–60 from Scotland and London, 'Do you or have you engaged in any sexual activities with a person of your own sex?', to which 2.3% of men reported having done so ever, and 0.9% in the past 5 years. The question was not asked of women.

Results from this survey are, however, remarkably consistent with those of other, non-British surveys, though the comparisons are in most cases possible only for men. Rogers and Turner (1991), in a comparison of three contemporary national surveys in the US,

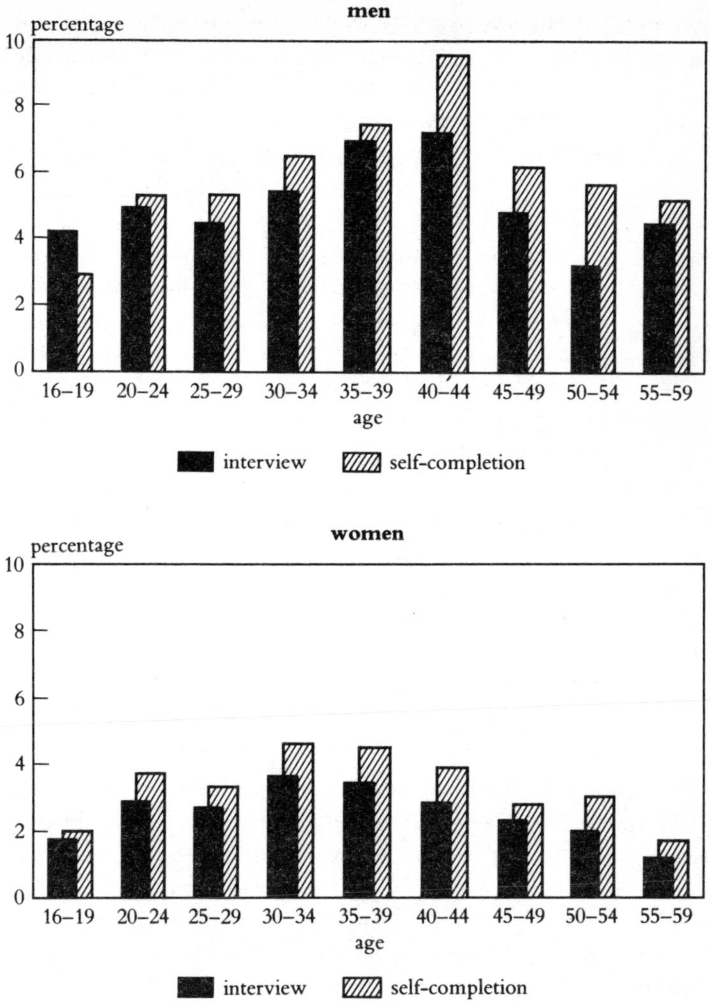

Figure 5.2 Homosexual experience reported at interview and self-completion by age group. Source: Interview Question 31b; Booklet Question 4a

derive lifetime prevalence estimates of male–male experience within the range 4.8% and 4.9%. Prevalence estimates for male–male contact within the last year lie within the range 1.2% to 2.4%.

The French national survey of sexual lifestyles found that 4.1% of men report at least one occurrence of intercourse with a person of the same sex during their lifetime (ACSF Investigators, 1992). Sundet and others (1988), from a random sample survey of the Norwegian population aged 18–60, report that 3.5% of men and 3.0% of women claim to have had at least one same-gender sexual partner, which again is consistent with the British data for men. The Norwegian survey also asked about same-sex partners in the last 3 years, a time period that is not directly comparable with the time periods of 2 and 5 years in this survey, but provides a figure of 0.9% for men and 0.9% for women.

The aggregate figures show a marked difference in the prevalence of same-sex experience between men and women. While 6.1% of men have had some kind of homosexual experience, only 3.4% of women have done so, and this ratio of roughly 2:1 is consistent across all definitions despite the similarity in prevalence of same-sex attraction. This is in contrast to the Norwegian data in which no difference was found between men and women (Sundet *et al.*, 1988).

Analysis by age does, however, show signs of some convergence between the sexes in terms of reporting same-gender experience. The ratio of men to women reporting at least one lifetime homosexual partner is 1.9:1, 1.8:1, 2.3:1, and 2.5:1 for the four successive age bands 16–24, 25–34, 35–44 and 45–59. It may be that social pressures on women which contribute to the greater difference between attraction and experience are weakening with successive generations.

SOCIO-DEMOGRAPHIC VARIATION IN PREVALENCE

To date it has been difficult to draw generalizable conclusions from research on homosexuality because of non-random sampling procedures and the problems involved in finding representative samples of those who have same-gender sex. Most recent studies have tended to use volunteer samples, obtaining respondents through gay and lesbian bars, social and friendship networks, organizations and clubs.

While these samples are essential to an understanding of homosexual behaviour and relationships, they do not constitute representative samples of men with same-sex experience. Gay-bar samples draw heavily on individuals in particular social environments, and are skewed towards urban, young, self-identified homosexuals, and those seeking partners. Homosexual organizations are likely to attract those who feel able to be more open about their sexual orientation.

Focused or purposive samples of homosexual men have tended to be middle class and urban. They are also biased towards younger and more highly educated men who are in employment (Hunt *et al.*, 1991). This survey provides an opportunity to explore to what extent some of these attributes are inherent characteristics of people who have same-gender sex. Since the sample is randomly selected it can be expected to contain more of those who do not self-identify as gay than purposive samples.

The extent to which the population with homosexual experience differs from that of the British population as a whole is of interest not only for the purposes of assessing the reliability of other studies, but also in the context of HIV/AIDS since unprotected sex between men is a major risk factor for acquiring the virus. The socio-demographic characteristics of those at higher risk is important in the context of both prevention and treatment of the disease.

Social diversity among homosexual men (there is less empirical work on women) is well documented (e.g. Bell *et al.,* 1981). Paul and Weinrich (1982) have described homosexuals as 'unsurprising members of the greater community'. An examination of differences in the backgrounds of US men who do and do not report having had same-gender contacts found that generally the homosexual population seemed to differ little from the US population as a whole, except that its members tend to be disproportionately unmarried and childless (Rogers and Turner, 1991). Their conclusion, that 'homosexual behaviour remains remarkably uncorrelated with most of the major groups into which social science groups its subjects', is echoed in the reports from the British Project Sigma: '. . . all recent sociological studies emphasize the multiplicity and heterogeneity of styles of homosexual living, which are at least as many and as varied as the available styles of heterosexual life' (Coxon, 1985).

Social Class

Men and women in social classes I and II are more likely than those in lower social-class groups to report any same-gender sexual contact and experience (Table 5.5) by a factor of 2 for women and 1.5 for men. However, for partnerships in the last 5 years there are no clear social-class differences. It is not clear what mechanism might explain this, but it is important to bear in mind that social class varies with age, so that the relationship between the reporting of homosexual

	I, II		III NM		III M		IV, V, other	
	%	*base*	%	*base*	%	*base*	%	*base*
men								
any homosexual contact	9.5	*2898*	5.2	*1551*	3.2	*2002*	4.7	*1873*
genital contact	5.8	*2895*	3.3	*1551*	1.6	*2000*	2.7	*1871*
1 + homosexual partner								
ever	5.8	*2891*	3.1	*1547*	1.7	*2000*	2.8	*1870*
last 5 years	1.8	*2893*	1.4	*1547*	0.7	*2000*	1.6	*1869*
women								
any homosexual contact	5.0	*3619*	3.0	*2371*	1.3	*1829*	3.2	*2587*
genital contact	2.4	*3616*	1.4	*2370*	0.7	*1827*	1.6	*2583*
1 + homosexual partner								
ever	2.5	*3617*	1.4	*2370*	0.8	*1828*	1.6	*2581*
last 5 years	0.5	*3617*	0.8	*2370*	0.2	*1828*	0.9	*2582*

Table 5.5 Social class and homosexual experience. Source: Booklet Questions 4a, 4c, 8a, 8b

experience and social class may be confounded by age. This is explored in the multivariate model (see pp. 206–9).

A further possibility is that tolerance and acceptance increase with social status (Wellings and Wadsworth, 1990). If this were the case, then we might also expect to see a reporting bias in the same direction here, since greater tolerance would be likely to influence not only the respondent's behaviour, but also his or her willingness to report that behaviour. Equally, it could be the case that some characteristic of homosexually inclined men and women is associated with upward mobility (since social-class categories are defined in terms of current employment status of the respondent).

Region

Variation in terms of current residence is very marked, particularly for men. There is a large difference, as Figure 5.3 shows, between different regions of Britain in terms of the prevalence of homosexual orientation. Multivariate analysis shows that lifetime experience is strongly associated with social class, but, in the case of men, recent experience is strongly associated with region. Most striking is the concentration of those reporting homosexual experience in the capital (Figure 5.3). Greater London seems to be home to more than twice the proportion of men reporting both a history of same-gender experience and current practice than anywhere else in Britain. The concentration in the capital is no doubt attributable to its attractions in terms of providing a hospitable environment, as suggested elsewhere. 'Many gay people gravitate to the town. Life here can be more anonymous, immediate family can be avoided or contained, and "gay ghettos" can provide a welcome relief from a hostile environment' (Coxon, 1985). Table 5.6 shows that men and women who report a homosexual partner in the past 5 years are far more likely to report having moved to live in London than are those who do not, and this difference is not apparent for migration elsewhere in Britain.

Again, the possibility of a reporting bias operating here cannot be ruled out since the more hospitable environment which attracts men who have sex with men to London might also make it easier to report such relationships. Our data suggest that the advantages of

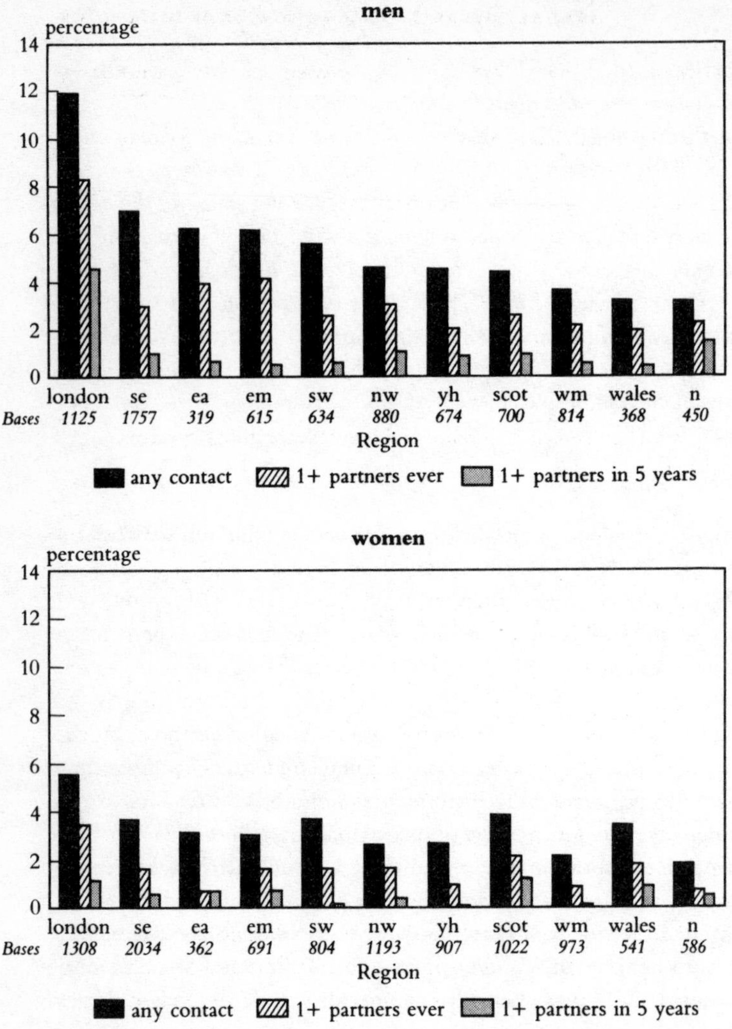

Figure 5.3 Homosexual contact and experience by region. Source: Booklet Questions 4a, 8a, 8b

london = Greater London	sw = South-West	scot = Scotland
se = South-East	nw = North-West	wm = West Midland
ea = East Anglia	yh = Yorkshire	wales = Wales
em = East Midlands	and Humberside	n = North

	men		women	
homosexual partner in last 5 years	yes %	no %	yes %	no %
London always	8.3	2.6	1.8	2.1
moved to London	35.2	10.4	22.2	10.4
moved (not to London)	48.7	64.4	54.4	64.7
didn't move (not in London)	7.8	22.6	21.7	22.8
base	*118*	*8189*	*65*	*10333*

Table 5.6 Residence and mobility by homosexual activity. Source: Booklet 8b

living in the capital in terms of acceptance and anonymity may be more real for men than for women, for whom the regional variation is less marked (Figure 5.3).

Age-related Variations in Same-gender Sexual Experience

Clear age-related patterns emerge from the data on sexual orientation. In response to the question about same-gender attraction, the youngest age group of male respondents, aged 16–24 (though not female respondents in this age group), are more likely to report having been attracted to someone of the same gender compared with other age groups (Table 5.4). In terms of lifetime experience, the age-related pattern differs markedly for men and women. The proportion of male respondents who report ever having had same-gender sexual experience peaks for the 35–44 year age group (Figure 5.4, Table 5.4). For women no such peak occurs among 35–44-year-olds, and prevalence is lowest for women aged 45 and over. This is a consistent result across responses relating to lifetime experience of any form of sexual contact but it does not apply to more recent practice – see below.

The atypical position of 35–44-year-old men is particularly clear in Figure 5.5, cumulative percentages for age at first homosexual experience for men and women by age group. (The booklet asked

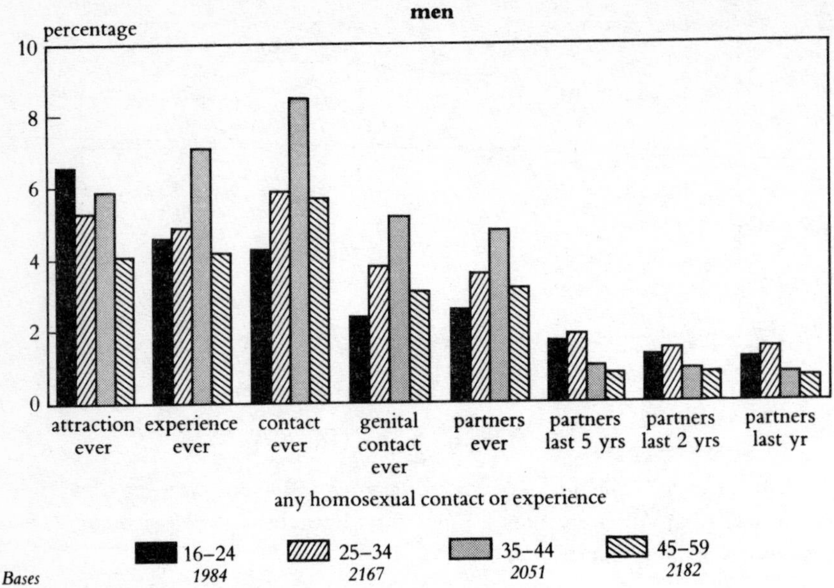
men
percentage
10
8
6
4
2
0
attraction ever
experience ever
contact ever
genital contact ever
partners ever
partners last 5 yrs
partners last 2 yrs
partners last yr
any homosexual contact or experience
16–24
25–34
35–44
45–59
Bases
1984
2167
2051
2182

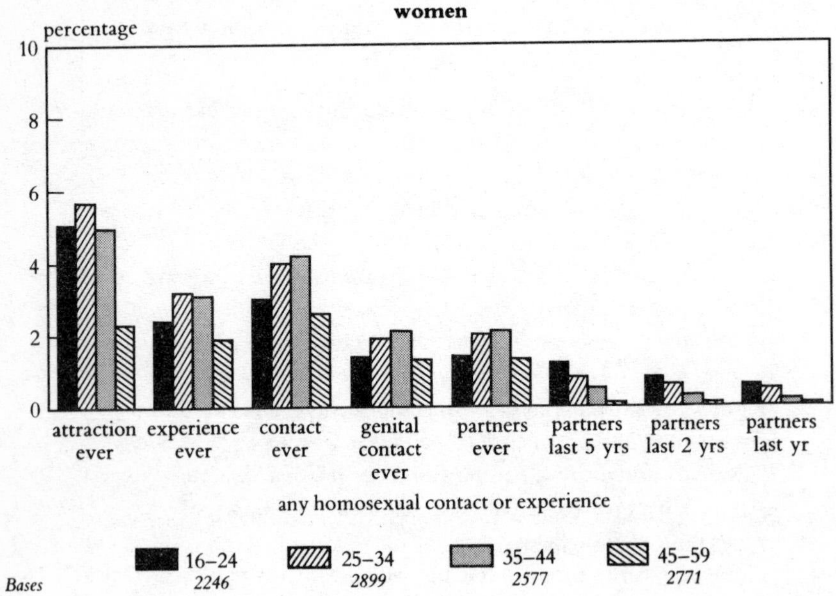
women
percentage
10
8
6
4
2
0
attraction ever
experience ever
contact ever
genital contact ever
partners ever
partners last 5 yrs
partners last 2 yrs
partners last yr
any homosexual contact or experience
16–24
25–34
35–44
45–59
Bases
2246
2899
2577
2771

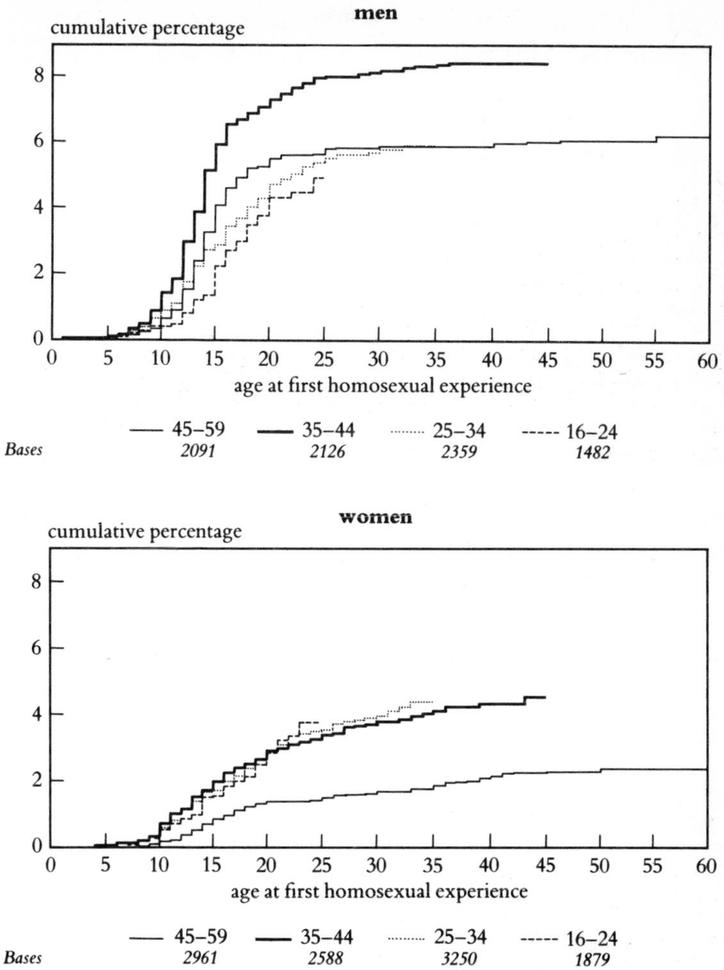

Figure 5.5 Age at first homosexual experience by age group. Source: Booklet Question 4b

Figure 5.4 (*opposite*) Summary of homosexual attraction and experience by age group. Source: Interview Questions 31a, 31b; Booklet Questions 4a, 4c, 8a–d

those who reported ever having any kind of sexual experience or sexual contact with someone of the same gender as themselves, 'How old were you the first time that ever happened?') Again, men aged 35–44 are distinct from all other age groups. They are more likely to report homosexual experience at some time in their lives, compared with those younger and older than themselves, and more than twice as likely to report having a homosexual experience before the age of 16 as those 20 years younger than themselves (Table 5.7, Figure 5.5).

This pattern is not the same for women. One of the noticeable features of Figure 5.5 is the difference between the shape of the curves for men and women. For women, the chances of making a homosexual début at any age are remarkably constant, up to the fifth decade. For men, the curve rises steeply during the early teens but thereafter shows a more gradual rise until the late twenties and early thirties, when the probability of a homosexual experience occurring for the first time diminishes. Lifetable analysis of age at first homosexual experience shows a significant difference between age groups for men and women.

Further, for women, all age groups except the oldest are remarkably homogeneous in terms of age at first homosexual experience. Only the experience of women aged 45–59 diverges appreciably from that for other age groups. Women of this age were less likely to have had a homosexual experience, and the proportions doing so

	men		**women**	
	%	*base*	%	*base*
age group				
16–24	2.47	*1975*	1.56	*2232*
25–34	3.25	*2156*	1.83	*2878*
35–44	5.92	*2036*	1.94	*2557*
45–59	3.77	*2159*	1.03	*2742*
all ages	3.85	*8326*	1.59	*10408*

Table 5.7 Proportions of respondents who reported some homosexual experience before the age of 16. Source: Booklet Question 4b

for the first time after the age of 20 is markedly lower than for women aged 25–44. This subgroup of women had completed the years of their teens and early twenties before the beginning of the 1960s.

Comparing trends in age at first homosexual and heterosexual experience, the atypical pattern for the 35–44 age group of men is not found in the data for heterosexual experience (Figures 5.6a and 5.6b). The comparison here is with first heterosexual experience rather than intercourse – which like first homosexual experience was self-defined. First homosexual and heterosexual experience in different age groups is shown by the year in which it occurred. These two graphs show substantially different patterns.

Data on first, and to some extent lifetime, homosexual experience can be interpreted in the context of secular changes – in particular, the changing cultural climate relating to sexual expression. Men aged 35–44 at interview were born between 1946 and 1955 and were between the ages of 12 and 21 in 1967 – the year in which homosexual acts became legal between consenting male adults over the age of 21 in England and Wales. These data may suggest some relationship between expressed homosexuality and legal and social reform. This interpretation is lent support by the fact that the configuration by age for men is not apparent for women. Women between the mid-twenties to mid-forties are more likely than those either younger or older than this to report ever having had homosexual experience.

The age pattern, however, seems more to reflect a general liberalizing effect of the early 1960s following the deliberations of the Wolfenden Committee's Report on Homosexuality (1957) which culminated in the 1967 Act, than of the Act itself. There is little evidence that the 1967 legislation *per se* had any major impact on behaviour. There is no marked increase in the proportions reporting homosexual experience after the age of 21, the age at which homosexual relations became legal between consenting men, and the slope of the curve for 35–44-year-old men shows no obvious change immediately before or after 1967 (Figure 5.6a).

The year in which laws are actually enacted is relatively arbitrary. Legal reform both responds to and accelerates the process of social change, and it is the underlying social trends that are probably more

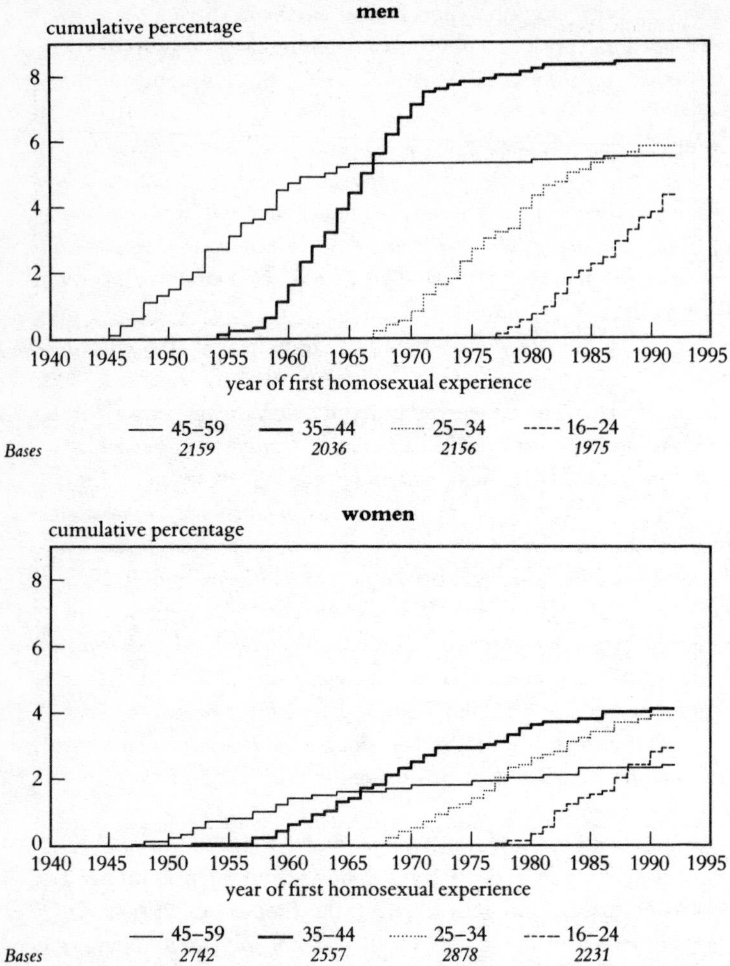

Figure 5.6a Year of first homosexual experience by age group. Source: Booklet Question 4b

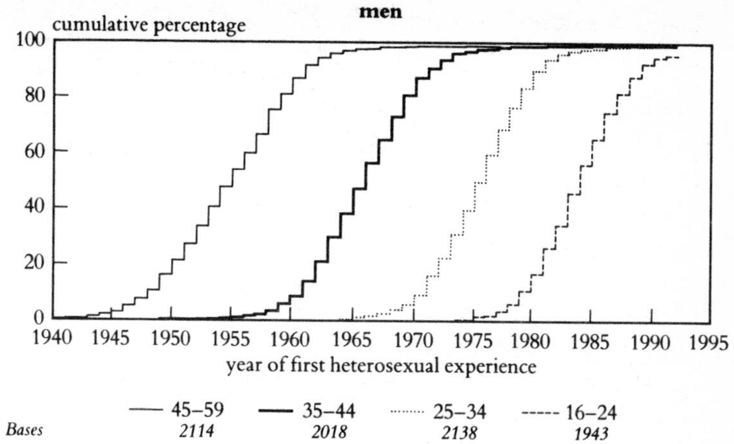

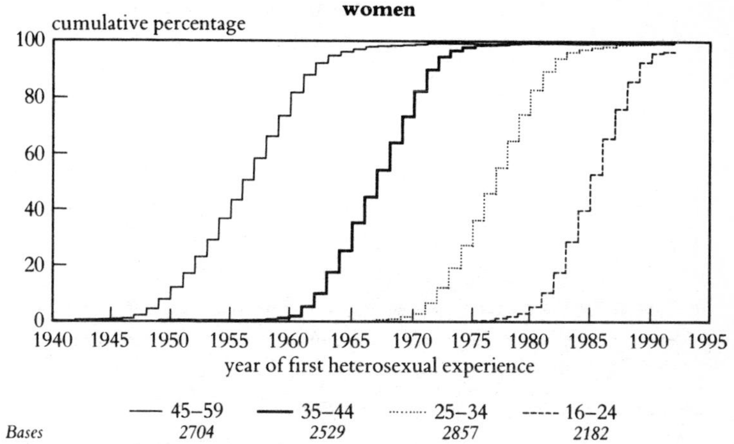

Figure 5.6b Year of first heterosexual experience by age group. Source: Interview Question 19a

important in explaining behaviour. Shortly after the Wolfenden Committee, a contemporary poll showed nearly a quarter of British people to be in favour of a change in the law; 8 years later the proportion had increased to nearly two-thirds (Bancroft, 1989). The 1967 Act both reflected and furthered a social climate in which the gay population was able to be less covert but it seems likely that it was this social climate rather than the specific legislation that had a major impact on behaviour.

If this hypothesis provides the explanation for the different pattern in those aged 35–44, it is at first sight curious that the trend does not seem to have been sustained in the younger age groups. The pattern for first homosexual experience among men younger than 35 follows that of men aged 45–59 rather than those aged 35–44. There seems no reason to suppose that the trend initiated in the 1970s should not have continued, had it not been halted by other circumstances. One explanation might be that the upward trend in homosexual activity with successive age groups was reversed by the AIDS epidemic. Those in the 25–34 age group would have been between the ages of 16 and 25 in 1981 when the first case of AIDS was recorded in the UK, and those aged 16–24, 15 or younger.

The age-related pattern for lifetime experience described above does not apply to accounts of more recent practice (Table 5.4, Figure 5.4). Reports of same-gender partners in the most recent periods: 5 years, 2 years and 12 months, decrease with increasing age for all but the youngest age group. For women, the likelihood of having had a female sexual partner in the recent past decreases steadily with current age. In general, the older the respondent, the less likely it is that recent same-gender partners will be reported, and this age profile is consistent for all but the youngest age group of men.

It is not clear what might account for the slight reduction in recent experience among 16–24-year-old men. In the case of recent practice, age-related trends must clearly be interpreted in the context of life-course factors and secular change, though there will be interplay between the two. Some men in this age group may have yet to experience same-gender sex. A further explanatory factor might be that since the age of homosexual consent is 21, young men under that age reporting homosexual experience may be doing so in the knowledge that they are acting unlawfully, which may result in under-reporting.

The apparent restraint among younger men might also reflect concerns brought about by the AIDS epidemic or, indirectly, AIDS-related changes in the social climate surrounding male homosexuality – particularly since it does not feature in the data for women. The exact balance of these different factors in terms of their influence on behaviour remains a matter for conjecture.

STABILITY OF ORIENTATION

The extent to which the recording procedures used in the questionnaire can be used to measure change in sexual orientation over time is limited. The fact that reports of lifetime same-gender experience are cumulative rather than relating to discrete time periods in the past, restricts analysis in terms of life history. There is no opportunity for measuring the duration of relationships (except those involving a same-gender partner in the last 5 years) or the point in people's lives at which they occurred.

The difference in prevalence between lifetime and current homosexual experience points to the likelihood that homosexual experience is often a relatively isolated or passing event. Almost certainly, respondents who report having had some homosexual experience but no genital contact (2.4% of men and 1.7% of women) are predominantly those for whom the same-gender experience was a transient part of their sexual development. For the majority of respondents reporting same-gender genital contact, the event took place more than 5 years ago.

The proportion of respondents reporting *ever* having a same-gender sexual partner is higher than in more recent time periods, for both men and women. 3.5% of men report having ever had a male sexual partner, 1.4% in the last 5 years and 1.1% in the last year. For women, the comparable figures are 1.7%, 0.6% and 0.4% respectively (Table 5.4). This 'seemingly episodic character' of same-gender sexual contacts is noted by Rogers and Turner (1991) for men, and our data seem to confirm this for women too.

Some observations can be made on the life course of homosexual behaviour from the relationship between the time of first homosexual experience and subsequent experience. Fewer questions were asked about first homosexual experience compared with first heterosexual experience, and they were asked within the self-completion component of the questionnaire rather than face to face. Homosexual experience occurring for the first time in the early teens is unlikely to lead on to more consistent homosexual behaviour. Men and women whose first experience of same-gender sex occurred before the age of 16 were less likely to have had genital contact, and less likely to report having had a same-gender sexual partner within the last 5 years (Figure 5.7) than those for whom this experience occurred at the age of 16 or later. Other sources suggest that later homosexual experiences are more important in predicting more persistent homosexual orientation (Dank, 1971).

These findings at least support the view that, for some, sexual development is characterized by a labile stage of orientation preceding a later stage of greater stability. A form of bisexuality prevalent in early adulthood may represent a transitional phase in which preferences are tested through experimentation with different lifestyles and relationships. Kinsey *et al.* (1948) interpreted their data as showing that homosexual activity peaks in the early teens and declines slowly with increasing age. Using data from the 1970 Kinsey Institute survey, Rogers and Turner (1991) estimate that of more than 20% of US men who reported sexual contact to orgasm with another man at some time in their life, only a third reported such contact occurring after the age of 20.

It has been observed that homosexual acts may occur in situations where the sexes are segregated – in prisons, for example, and in the armed forces – where same-gender contact might be exploited in the absence of opportunities for contact with members of the opposite sex (Bancroft, 1989). Implicit in this is the notion of a so-called 'facultative' homosexuality, according to which homosexual expression borne out of co-existence with people of the same gender is more likely to be opportunistic.

Our data afford an opportunity for investigating this phenomenon, in the context of single-sex boarding schools. The data have been analysed by attendance at such schools for men and women. If 'facultative' homosexual expression occurred more frequently in a

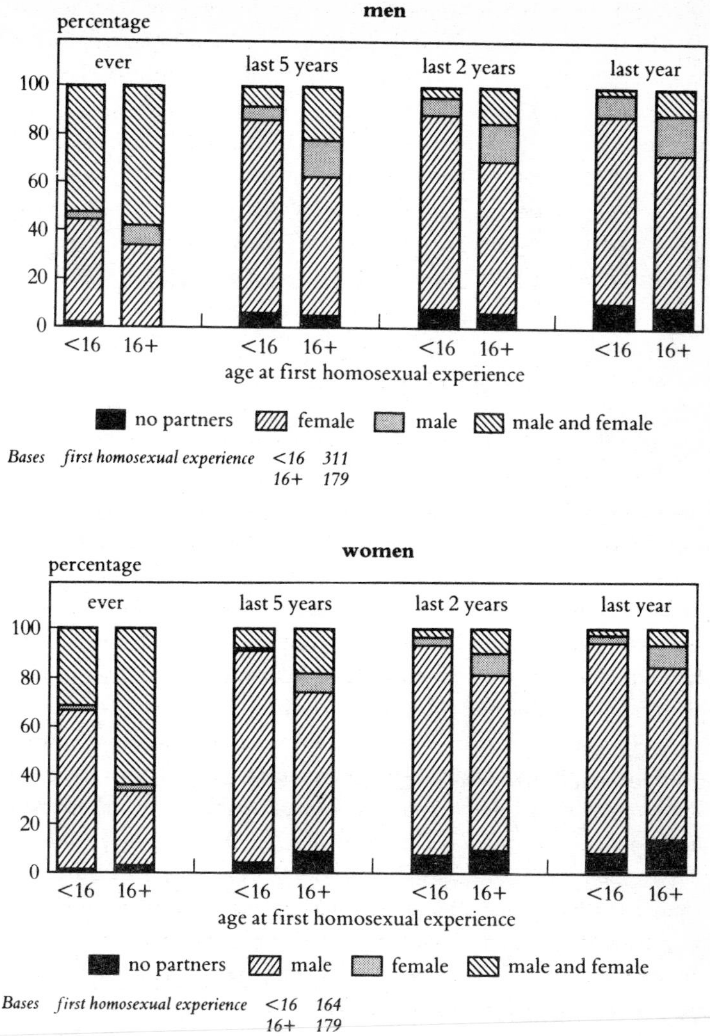

Figure 5.7 Gender of partners in different time intervals by age at first homosexual experience. Source: Booklet Questions 4b, 7a–d, 8a–d

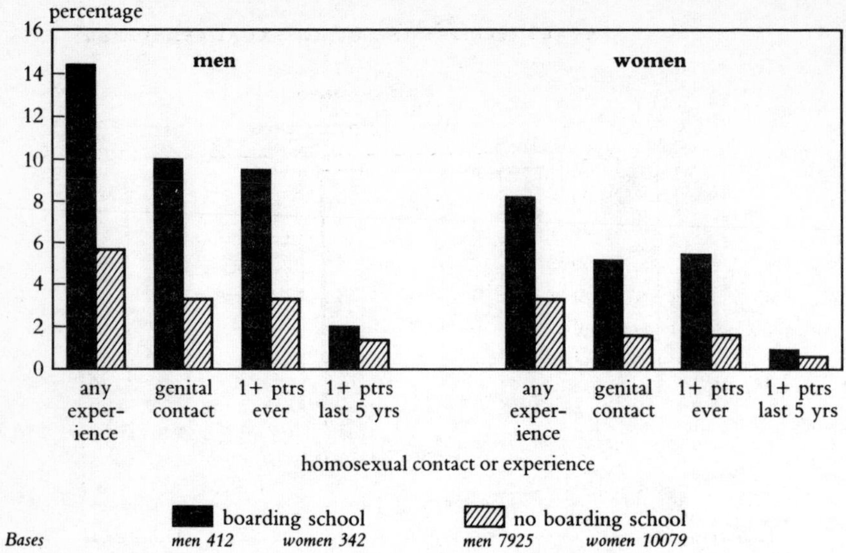

Figure 5.8 Percentage of respondents reporting homosexual experience by boarding-school attendance. Source: Booklet Questions 4a, 4c, 8a, 8b

single-sex environment, a higher proportion of those who attended boarding school might be expected to report homosexual experience *ever* compared with those who did not, but the effect of institution would not be expected to be sustained up to the most recent period of reporting. As Figure 5.8 shows, the data are entirely consistent with this hypothesis. For the questions asking about any same-gender sexual contact, genital contact and sexual partnerships, those who had boarding-school education are more likely than those who did not to have had homosexual experience. The findings are broadly similar for both men and women. In the more recent time period, however, there is little difference between the two groups. Thus, although boarding-school education seems to provide greater opportunities for same-gender experience, it seems to have little or no effect on homosexual practice later in life.

Multivariate Analysis

Drawing age, schooling, social class and region together in logistic regression models (Figures 5.9 and 5.10), there are clearly different associations for men and women and for experience ever and in the

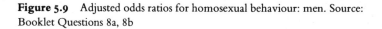

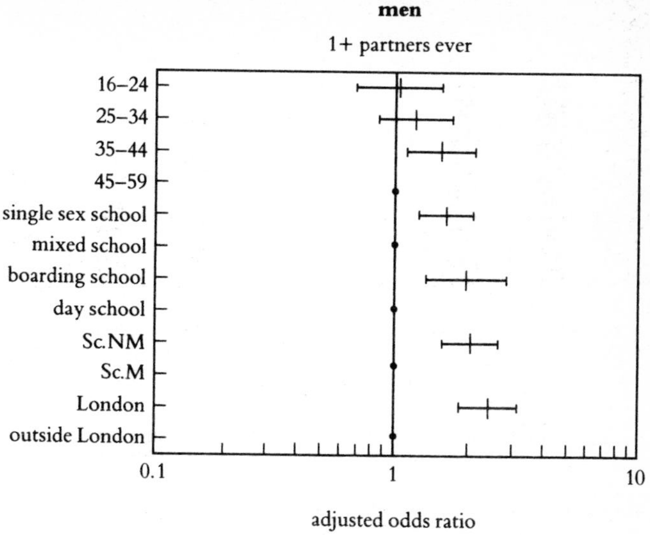

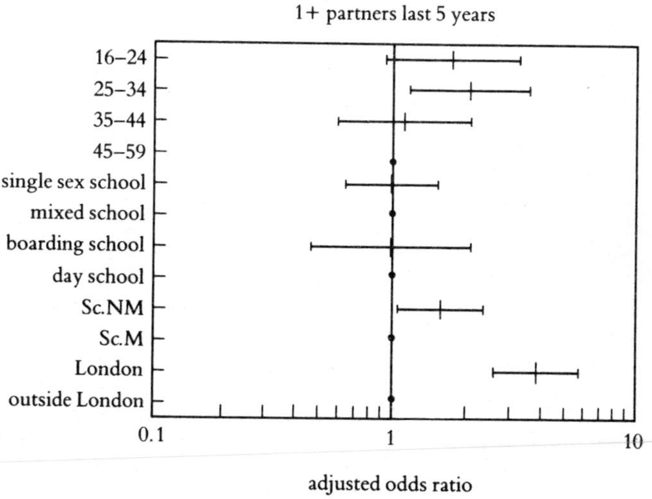

Figure 5.9 Adjusted odds ratios for homosexual behaviour: men. Source: Booklet Questions 8a, 8b

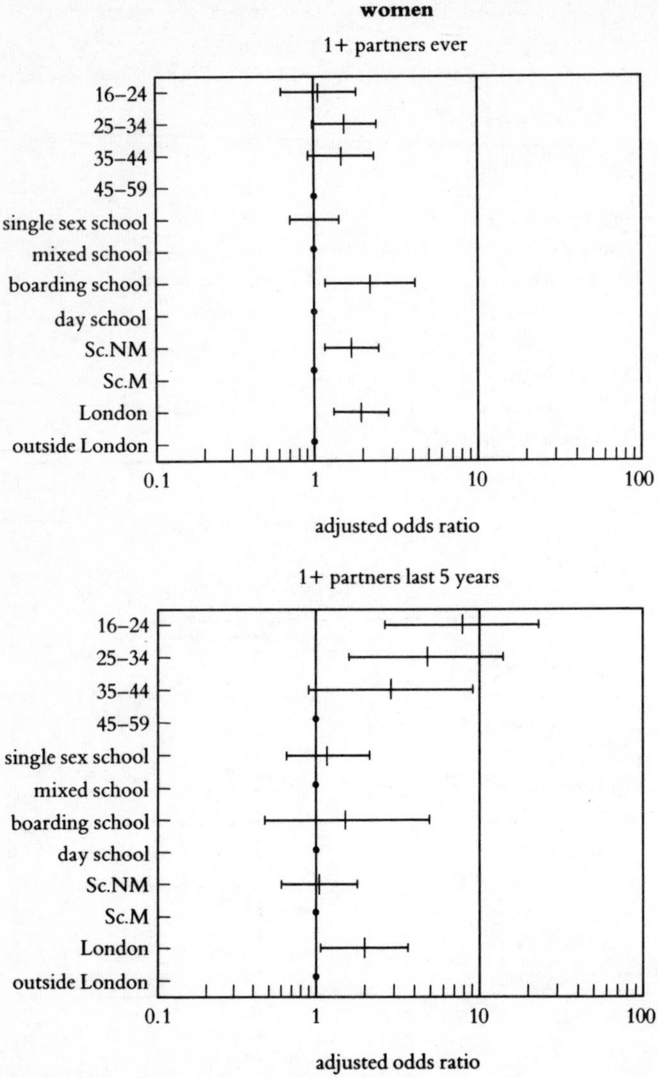

Figure 5.10 Adjusted odds ratios for homosexual behaviour: women. Source: Booklet Questions 8a, 8b

Table 5.8 (*opposite*) Gender of partners in different time intervals. Source: Booklet Questions 7a–d, 8a–d

last 5 years, but these influences are not necessarily mutually independent. Schooling has an important influence on whether someone has ever had a homosexual partner but no significant impact on homosexual partnerships in the last 5 years. Social class also shows a stronger effect on partners ever than partners in the last 5 five years. In contrast, for men the effect of region increases as the time interval decreases. This is consistent with the concept of migration to London to seek a more favourable environment for a homosexual lifestyle. The effect of age is not clear cut and exerts a stronger influence on the behaviour of women than of men.

EXCLUSIVENESS OF SAME-SEX EXPERIENCE

Exclusively homosexual behaviour appears to be rare. Table 5.8, and Figures 5.11 and 5.12, illustrate the mixing of male–male, female–female and male–female sex reported by British men and women. It can be seen that very substantial proportions of those

	Time periods for sexual partner reporting			
	ever %	in last 5 years %	in last 2 years %	in last year %
			men	
exclusively female	90.1	90.5	88.8	86.5
exclusively male	0.3	0.6	0.6	0.7
male and female	3.4	0.8	0.5	0.4
no partners	6.2	8.1	10.1	12.4
base	*8009*	*8044*	*8039*	*8047*
			women	
exclusively male	92.7	90.4	88.1	86.0
exclusively female	0.1	0.2	0.2	0.2
male and female	1.7	0.5	0.2	0.2
no partners	5.6	9.0	11.4	13.6
base	*10040*	*10055*	*10048*	*10057*

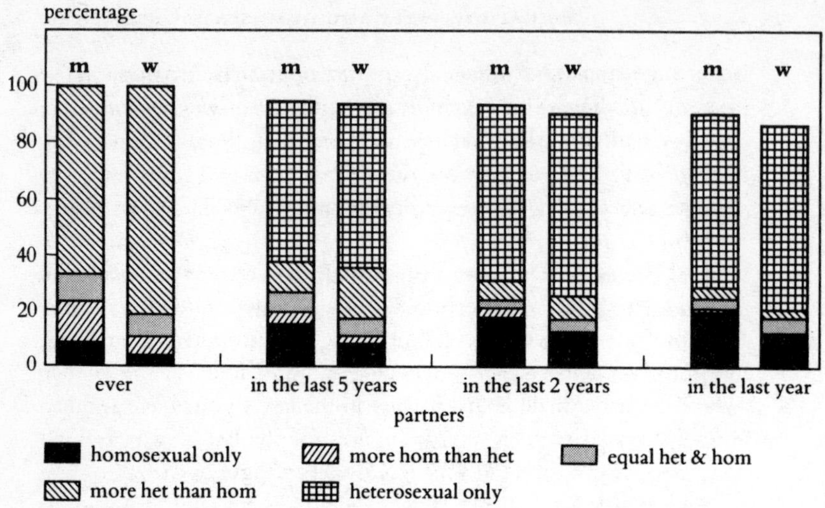

Base = Those with same gender genital contact men 290
women 174

Figure 5.11 Sex mixing of partners in different time intervals. Source: Booklet Questions 4c, 7a–d, 8a–d

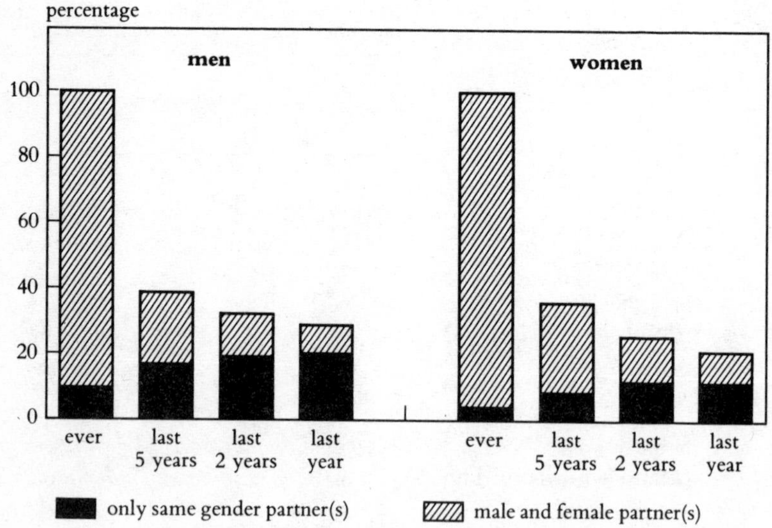

Base = Respondents with same gender genital contact men 290
women 174

Figure 5.12 Gender of sexual partners in different time intervals. Source: Booklet Questions 4c, 8a–d

reporting same-sex partners also report opposite-sex partners. The majority of those who have had some homosexual experience have had sex with both men and women. Of men who report having ever had a male sexual partner in their lifetime, 90.3% have also had a female sexual partner, and for women the equivalent proportion is 95.8%.

As Table 5.8 shows, the proportions of men and women who have had sex with both men and women is smaller for recent time periods but is nevertheless similar to the proportion reporting exclusively homosexual partners in all time periods. 58.4% of men who have had a male sexual partner in the last 5 years have also had a female sexual partner, and the figures for the last 2 years and last year are 42.0% and 29.9% respectively (Figure 5.12). Among women reporting having had female partners, the proportions reporting also having had male partners is even higher: 75.8% in the past 5 years, 53.6% in the last 2 years and 44.6% in the last year.

Predictably, as Table 5.9 shows, the great majority of currently or ever married men and women have had no same-gender partners during their lifetime or in recent time periods. A small but important group is the 1.3 per cent of currently married men reporting at least one male sexual partner in the past 5 years (Table 5.9). Only a very small proportion of married women, 0.2%, have had a female sexual partner in the past 5 years.

The high prevalence of bisexual behaviour is well documented in surveys of homosexual behaviour. Weinberg and Williams (1974) found that 36–59% (depending on the country) of predominantly homosexual individuals studied had also had heterosexual intercourse. Contemporary British surveys show the proportion of homosexual men reporting both male and female partners in a lifetime to be between 58% and 61% (Boulton and Weatherburn, 1990), and in the past year between 10% and 12% respectively. Weatherburn and others (1990) report 60.6% of their cohort of homosexual men having had at least one female partner in their lifetime, 29.7% in the past 5 years and 11.7% in the year before interview. The proportions of men with recent homosexual activity who report that they have also had sex with women are clearly considerably higher in this survey using a national probability sample than in surveys using purposive or focused samples.

	ever				last 5 years				last year	
	0	1	2+		0	1	2+		1+	
	%	%	%	*base*	%	%	%	*base*	%	*base*
					men					
married	97.5	1.5	1.0	*4760*	99.6	0.3	1.0	*4760*	0.2	*4760*
cohabiting opposite sex	96.0	2.6	1.5	*606*	100.0	0.0	0.0	*606*	0.0	*606*
same sex	0.0	5.1	94.9	*19**	0.0	29.7	70.3	*20*	95.0	*20*
widowed	97.1	0.0	2.9	*49*	100.0	0.0	0.0	*49*	0.0	*49*
divorced/ separated	95.5	3.5	1.0	*391*	99.0	0.5	0.5	*392*	0.8	*392*
single	95.2	1.9	3.0	*2491*	96.9	1.2	1.9	*2492*	2.3	*2491*
					women					
married	98.8	0.9	0.3	*6294*	99.8	0.1	0.1	*6296*	0.1	*6296*
cohabiting opposite sex	97.6	1.5	0.9	*829*	99.2	0.7	0.1	*829*	0.2	*829*
same sex	13.6	10.8	75.6	*11**	13.6	19.9	66.5	*11**	86.4	*11**
widowed	99.1	0.2	0.7	*200*	100.0	0.0	0.0	*200*	0.0	*200*
divorced/ separated	97.1	2.4	0.5	*854*	99.4	0.5	0.1	*854*	0.2	*854*
single	97.8	1.3	0.9	*2217*	98.5	0.9	0.6	*2217*	1.0	*2217*

Table 5.9 Numbers of homosexual partners by marital status. Source: Booklet Questions 8a, 8b, 8d

* note small base

This suggests that non-random samples of homosexual men may be biased towards those who self-identify as 'gay', while the national sample may also have recruited those who are more covert and closeted. Prevalence estimates from other general population surveys using probability samples quite closely resemble those from this British survey. For example, Rogers and Turner in their review of the US data (1991) demonstrate that 'very substantial proportions of men who report male–male sexual contacts in adulthood also report male–female sexual contacts'. 92.3% of men who reported having had one male sexual partner in adulthood, and 86.4% of those who reported more than one male sexual partner, had had at least one female sexual partner (Rogers and Turner, 1991). Data from the French survey of sexual lifestyles show that 82% of men and 78% of women who had had homosexual intercourse at least once had also had heterosexual intercourse (ACSF Investigators, 1992). From the Norwegian national survey, Sundet and others (1988) report that of men and women reporting same-gender practice, 83% and 75% respectively also reported opposite-gender practices.

These findings have important implications for HIV-preventive strategies, since they suggest that the proportion of men who have sex with both men and women may be larger than indicated in surveys using purposive samples. If the hypothesis is correct, these men may be covert in their homosexual practice, and may represent a hard-to-reach population in terms of health education and prevention.

NUMBER OF PARTNERS

There is a prevailing view that men who have sex with men have far larger numbers of sexual partners than those who have sex with women (Bancroft, 1989). As far as women are concerned, little seems to be known or surmised, but what empirical work there is points to a tendency of lesbian women to experience relatively stable, long-term relationships (Bell and Weinberg, 1978). Of interest in these data is the extent to which they support this stereotypical image.

Looking at the aggregate data for responses to the question asking about numbers of same-gender partners (Table 5.10), roughly half of all men and two-thirds of women who report having had a same-gender partner in their lifetime have had only one. At the opposite end of the spectrum, 11.4% of men had 20 or more male sexual partners and 3.9% had 100 or more. No woman had more than 20 female partners.

(A male sexual partner, it will be recalled, was defined as someone with whom a man has had oral sex or anal intercourse, or with

	men		women	
	homosexual %	heterosexual %	homosexual %	heterosexual %
partners ever				
1	50.4	22.0	67.4	41.7
2–9	32.6	51.9	30.6	51.1
10–19	5.6	14.5	2.0	5.3
20–99	7.5	10.8	0.0	1.8
100+	3.9	0.8	0.0	0.1
base	*286**	*7489†*	*174**	*9471†*
partners in the last 5 years				
0	61.8	2.3	64.1	3.6
1	16.3	60.5	22.4	71.4
2–9	12.8	32.0	13.0	24.0
10–19	4.9	3.5	0.5	0.7
20–99	3.2	1.7	0.0	0.2
100+	1.0	0.01	0.0	0.01
base	*290**	*7484†*	*175**	*9459†*

Table 5.10 Heterosexual and homosexual partners ever and in the last 5 years. Source: Booklet Questions 4c, 7a, 7b, 8a, 8b

* any same-gender sexual contact

† any opposite-gender partner

whom other forms of genital contact have taken place, and a female partner one with whom a woman has had oral sex or other forms of genital contact. This differs from the definition of a heterosexual partner which includes vaginal intercourse, oral or anal sex and does not include non-penetrative sex.)

It would be misleading to base any assumptions about homosexual behaviour in general on these figures, since the proportion reporting a same-sex partner includes a large number of respondents for whom the experience was a single, possibly youthful and experimental, occurrence and for whom homosexual inclination was not a lasting orientation. Figure 5.13 shows that the likelihood of having a recent partner of the same gender decreases markedly with age. Yet looking at the more recent time period of 5 years, 61.8% of

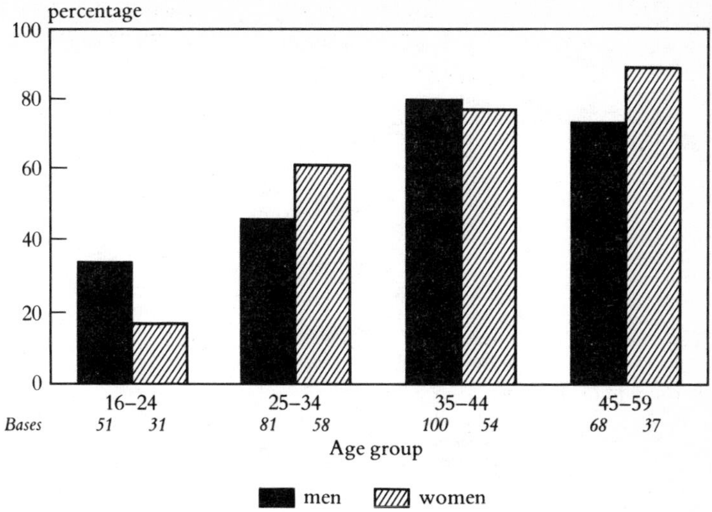

Figure 5.13 Proportion of respondents reporting some homosexual genital contact ever but no homosexual partners in the last 5 years. Source: Booklet Questions 4c, 8a, 8b

men and 64.1% of women who ever had genital contact with someone of the same gender had no partner in the last 5 years. In contrast, 2.3% of men and 3.6% of women had no heterosexual partner in the last 5 years (Table 5.10).

Marked differences can be seen in the pattern of numbers of same-gender compared with opposite-gender partners (Figure 5.14). Broadly speaking, the proportion reporting large numbers of sexual partners in the last 5 years is higher for men reporting homosexual partners than it is for men reporting heterosexual partners. Though, as Hunt and others (1991) argue, the proper comparison is to be made between the median number of lifetime *penetrative* homosexual partners (in the Project Sigma study this was 7) and the median number of female partners for heterosexual men.

As with heterosexual partners, the pattern of influence on numbers of partners is complex. Increasing age will lengthen the time period during which partners can be accumulated and serves to increase the total number of lifetime partners. For the more recent past, this

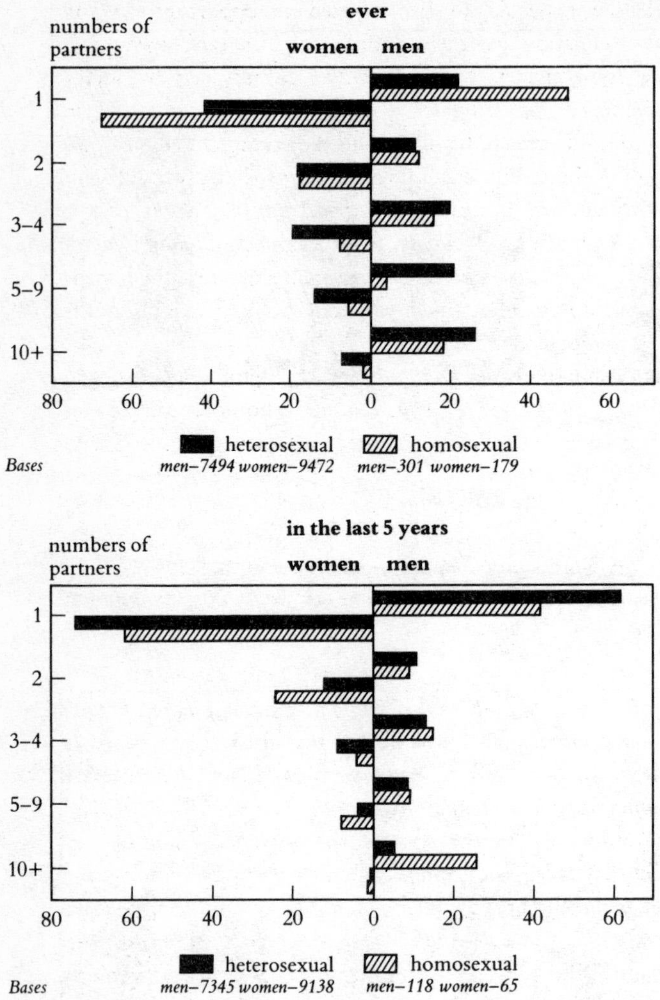

Note: excludes those with no partners

Figure 5.14 Comparison of number of heterosexual and homosexual partners. Source: Booklet Questions 4c, 7a, 7b, 8a, 8b

effect might be expected to be reversed as opportunities, and perhaps the inclination, to meet people decrease with advancing years. These life-course factors are further complicated by socio-historical influences on behaviour which will be manifested in further differences between the oldest and the youngest age groups.

Disentangling these different influences retrospectively is difficult and hazardous and any attempt at interpretation belongs at least as much to the realms of conjecture as to empiricism. But by any reckoning, the general picture that emerges is not one of a homosexual appetite for large numbers of partners, though this is undoubtedly the lifestyle chosen by a few.

The relationship between the number of lifetime heterosexual partners and the likelihood of ever having a homosexual partner differs between men and women (Figure 5.15). Generally, men who have had a male sexual partner are marginally less likely than those who have not to report having had a female sexual partner (3.6% cf. 4.7%). For women, there is very little difference (1.8% cf. 1.5%). Similarly, both men and women with only one opposite-sex

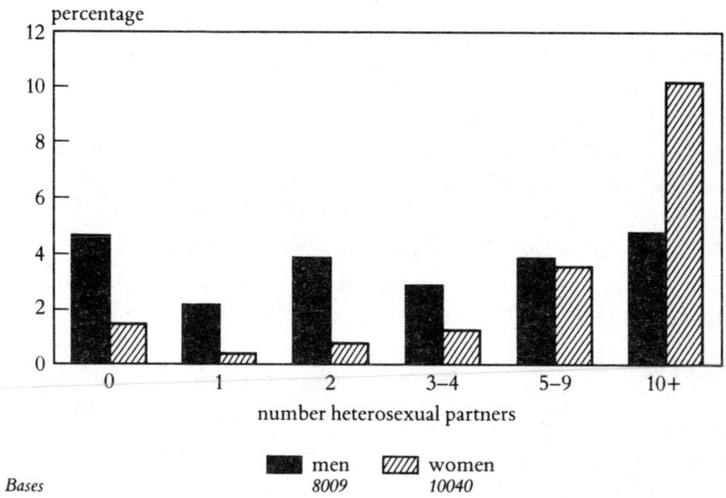

Figure 5.15 Proportions of men and women reporting ever having had a homosexual partner by number of heterosexual partners. Source: Booklet Questions 7a, 8a

partner are rather less likely to report having had a same-gender partner than are those with none.

Where major differences emerge between men and women is in the subgroup of those with larger numbers of heterosexual partners. Men with 10 or more female partners are more likely to have had a male sexual partner than are those with one (4.8% cf. 2.2%), but women with this number of male partners are considerably more likely to have had a female partner than are those with only one male partner (10.2% cf. 0.4%). 39% of women who have had sex with a woman are in the subgroup of those with 10 or more opposite-gender partners. There may be grounds for suggesting a consistent profile of experience-seeking among a small minority of women, such that those who seek diversity in terms of *numbers* of partners do so also in terms of the gender of those partners.

HOMOSEXUAL PRACTICES

Questions were asked about sexual practices relating to same-gender partners in particular periods. Thus, male respondents were asked to provide information on whether or not they had experienced oral and anal sex, and genital stimulation with a man, and female respondents on whether they had experienced oral sex and genital stimulation with a woman.

There is marked evidence of a broad repertoire of sexual acts among those with same-gender partners. There is certainly less emphasis on penetrative intercourse (anal in this case) among those with homosexual experience compared with those with heterosexual experience. This is of particular interest in the context of HIV, since homosexual anal sex has been so heavily implicated in transmission of the virus, and safer-sex strategies directed towards male homosexuals constantly stress the wisdom of adopting alternative forms of sexual expression. As Table 5.11 and Figures 5.16 and 5.17 show, oral sex and non-penetrative sex are more commonly reported by men with recent homosexual contact than are receptive and insertive anal sex. Only 10.5% of men with some same-gender genital contact report never having experienced non-penetrative sex, compared with 66.3% who report no insertive anal sex, and 64.6% no receptive anal sex.

	< 1 year %	1–5 years %	5+ years %	never %
		16–24 (*base** = 48)		
receptive anal	21.0	3.6	12.6	62.8
insertive anal	25.1	6.6	3.2	65.1
receptive oral	34.1	16.0	17.9	32.0
insertive oral	37.7	11.4	14.5	36.4
non-penetrative	33.8	27.2	33.0	6.1
		25–34 (*base** = 80)		
receptive anal	16.3	14.4	17.4	51.9
insertive anal	24.8	11.6	9.5	54.1
receptive oral	35.0	12.1	24.9	28.1
insertive oral	35.4	11.5	18.9	34.2
non-penetrative	33.9	10.1	43.4	12.6
		35–44 (*base** = 105)		
receptive anal	9.7	1.8	15.2	73.3
insertive anal	8.7	2.3	17.3	71.6
receptive oral	9.5	6.3	29.1	55.1
insertive oral	12.4	5.1	21.5	61.0
non-penetrative	16.5	4.1	68.8	10.6
		45–59 (*base** = 67)		
receptive anal	10.0	1.4	21.4	67.2
insertive anal	8.8	2.3	15.6	73.3
receptive oral	16.6	4.5	27.9	51.0
insertive oral	15.1	1.6	27.8	55.4
non-penetrative	16.3	6.2	66.5	11.0

Table 5.11 Reporting of same-gender sexual practices in different time intervals: men. Source: Booklet Questions 4c, 6a–e

* men reporting same gender genital contact

insertive oral sex

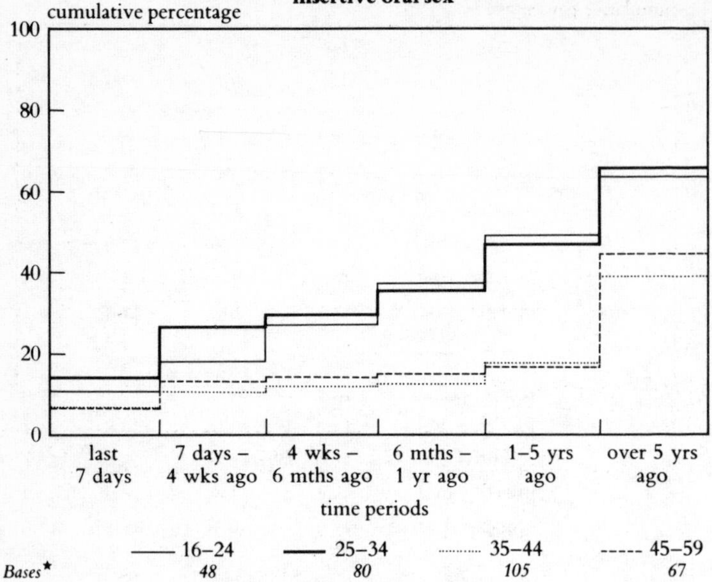

receptive oral sex

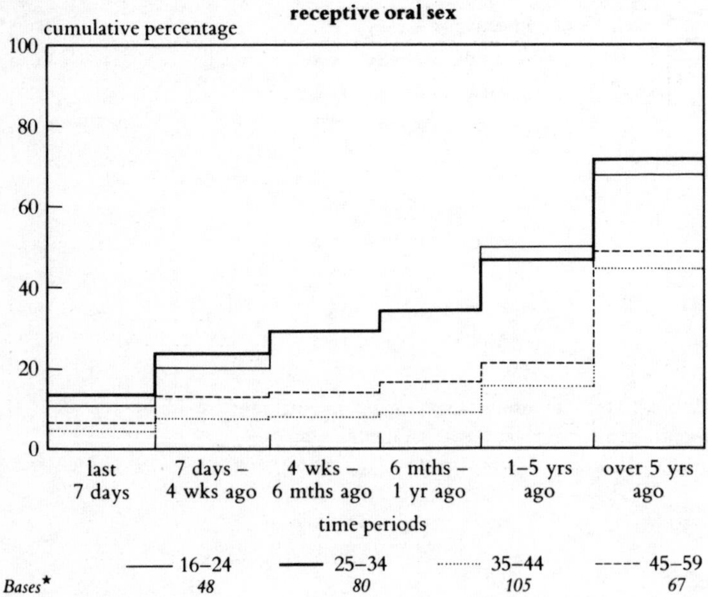

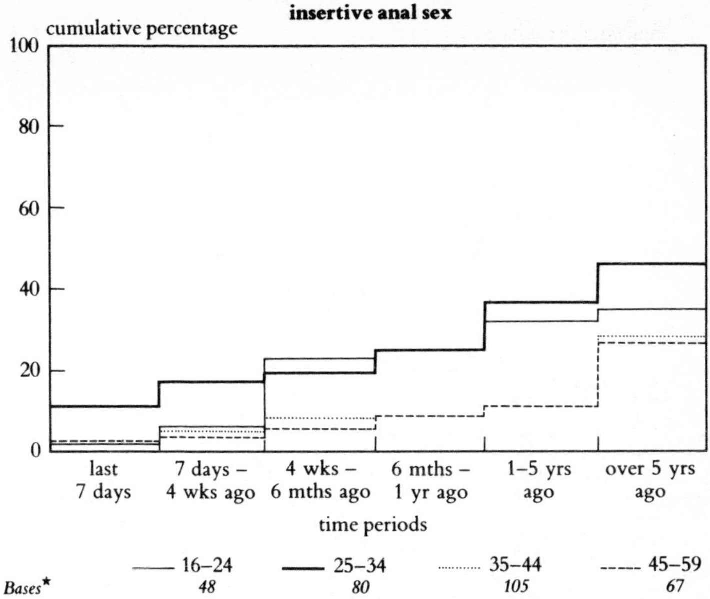

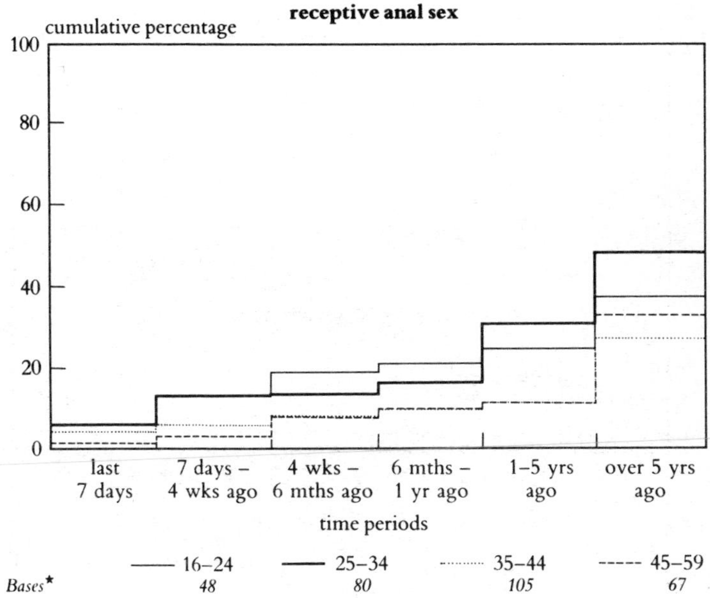

Figure 5.16 Timing of homosexual practices: men. Source: Booklet Questions 4c, 6a–d

* those reporting homosexual genital contact

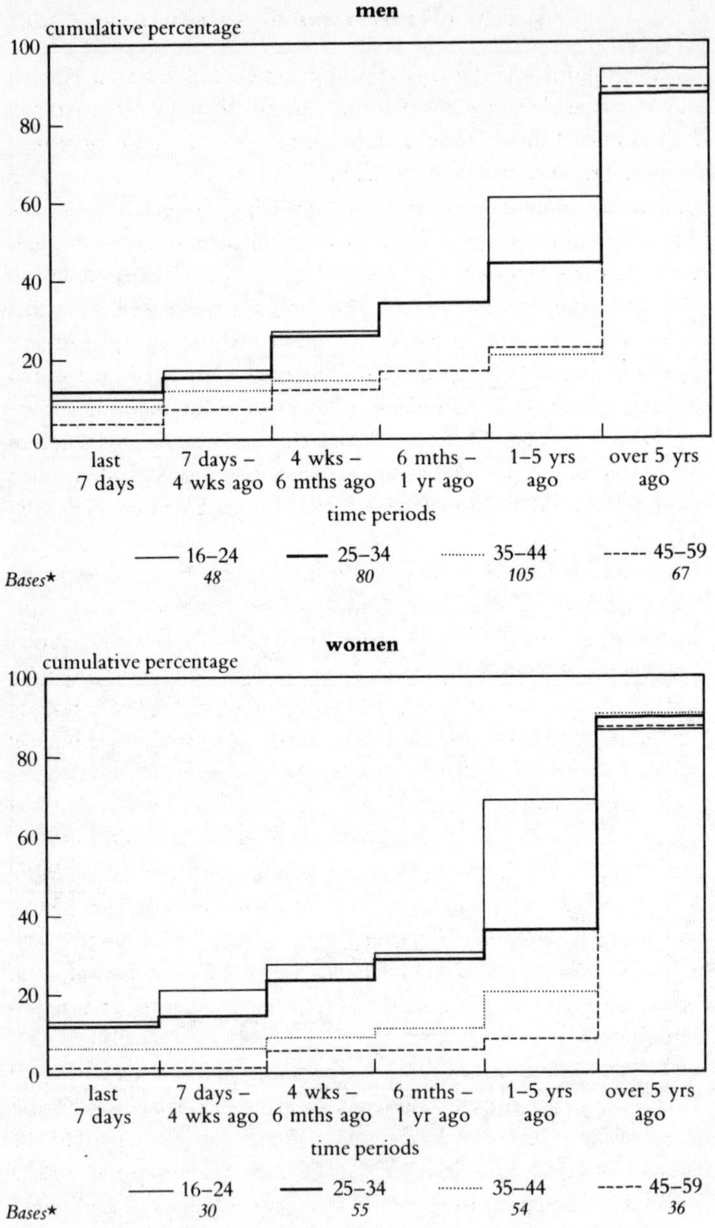

Figure 5.17 Timing of homosexual practices: non-penetrative sex. Source: Booklet Questions 4c, 6e

* those reporting homosexual genital contact

The proportions of men reporting same-gender sexual contact who report anal sex are lower for our sample than for other samples of homosexual men. Surveys based on focused samples of gay men show that the prevalence of penetrative sex is lower in homosexual than in heterosexual relationships. Reporting Project Sigma data, Hunt and others (1991), show that the median number of male sexual partners reported is 4 times as large as the median number of penetrative partners in the past year, and Davies *et al.* (1992) that fewer than half (46%) of gay men interviewed had engaged in anal sex in the month before interview. The survey reported here shows the proportions to be considerably lower even for the longer time period of one year (Table 5.11) and this adds to the evidence of differences in composition of this randomly selected sample of men with some homosexual experience, and samples based on men who self-identify as gay.

A common belief relating to homosexual relationships is that they mimic heterosexual patterns of sexual activity, adopting complementary masculine and feminine roles (Larson, 1982). Despite the popular stereotype, data from purposive samples indicate that most gay men experience both insertive and receptive intercourse. The evidence (Saghir and Robins, 1973; Harry and DeVall, 1978; Weatherburn *et al.*, 1992) is that, for all age groups, the majority of homosexuals tend to interchange insertive and receptive roles. Project Sigma data, for example, show that of homosexual men who had anal intercourse in the last year, 22.5% were exclusively the insertive partner, 16.9% were exclusively the receptive partner and 60.6% interchanged modes (Weatherburn *et al.*, 1992). This is also shown to be the case in our data, as shown in Figure 5.18. Fewer men experience exclusively insertive or receptive intercourse than experience both.

The proportion reporting exclusively insertive anal sex is higher than the proportion reporting exclusively receptive anal sex for all time periods except the most distant. Coxon (1985) notes that the reported insertive rate is often higher than the receptive rate, a predictable finding on the grounds of its lower risk, and the 'higher prestige assigned to it in the gay community' (p. 36). This differential might also be a function of age mixing (Coxon, 1985).

For the sample of women who have had same-gender sexual

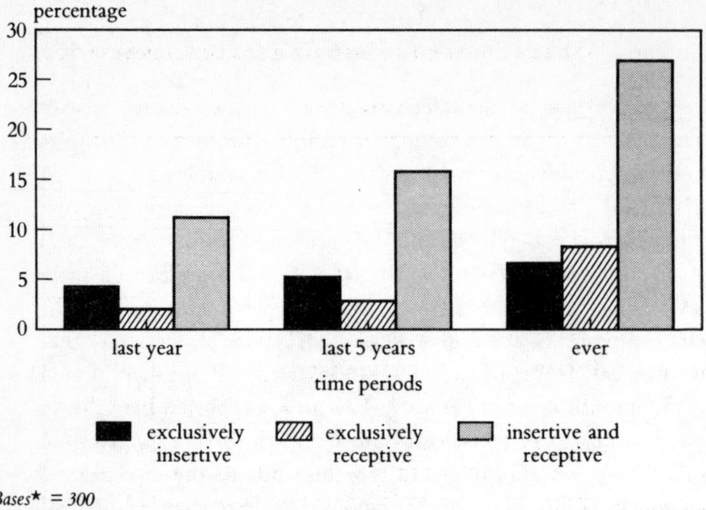

Figure 5.18 Modality of anal sex: men reporting homosexual genital contact. Source: Booklet Questions 4c, 6c, 6d

* those reporting homosexual genital contact

	< 1 year %	1–5 years %	5+ years %	never %
		16–24 (*base** = 30)		
passive oral	42.3	25.7	12.1	19.9
active oral	30.0	28.6	9.1	32.2
non-penetrative	30.6	38.2	17.5	13.7
		25–34 (*base** = 54)		
passive oral	20.3	7.8	31.9	40.0
active oral	23.4	8.7	25.6	42.3
non-penetrative	28.8	7.4	53.3	10.5
		35–44 (*base** = 53)		
passive oral	9.0	2.7	40.1	48.2
active oral	9.0	4.2	40.4	46.3
non-penetrative	11.3	9.1	70.0	9.6
		45–59 (*base** = 36)		
passive oral	3.0	3.9	30.5	62.7
active oral	3.0	2.5	29.2	65.3
non-penetrative	5.6	2.7	78.6	13.1

Table 5.12 Reporting of same-gender sexual practices in different time intervals: women. Source: Booklet Questions 4c, 6a, 6b, 6e

* women reporting genital contact

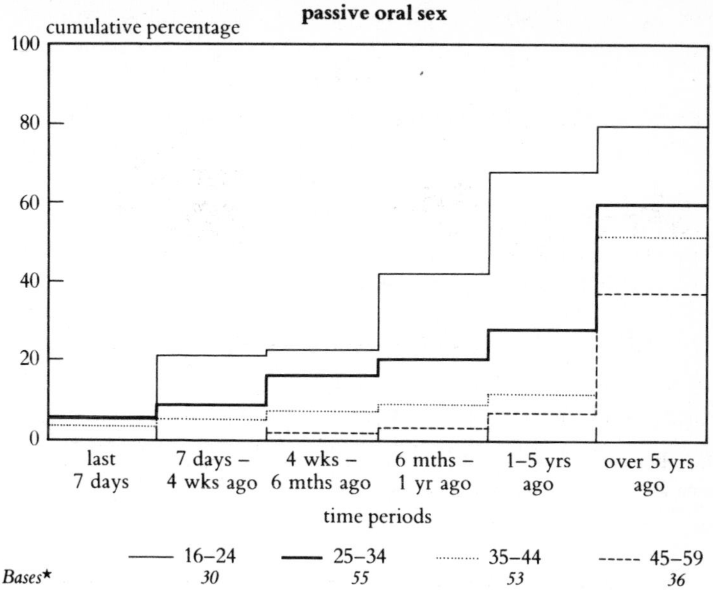

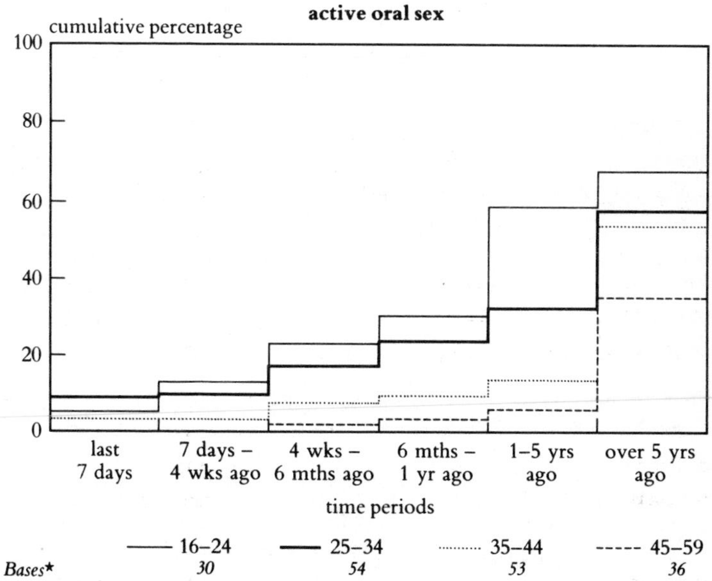

Figure 5.19 Timing of homosexual practices: women. Source: Booklet Questions 4c, 6a, 6b

* those reporting homosexual genital contact

contact, activities investigated included passive and active oral sex, and mutual masturbation (Table 5.12, Figures 5.17, 5.19). Using differences between age groups to detect trends over time, the practice of oral sex can be seen to have increased recently, a trend also apparent in heterosexual relationships (see Chapter 3). While women in the oldest age group 45–59 reporting non-penetrative sex in the last year outnumber those reporting oral sex in this period by roughly 3:2, the ratio narrows with decreasing age and is ultimately reversed for the 16–24 age group, so that reports of oral sex outnumber those for non-penetrative sex (mutual masturbation). As Figures 5.16–18 show, the age group reporting the highest levels of sexual activity (as measured by most recent experience of particular sexual practices) is that of 25–34-year-olds. This is nearly a decade later than for those reporting on heterosexual partnerships, and is consistent with later age at first experience.

SUMMARY

The starting point for investigation into patterns of sexual orientation has been that homosexual and heterosexual behaviour are part of a broad range of sexual expression. Every effort has been made to avoid pigeon-holing people and to describe sexual behaviours rather than sexual identities.

Perhaps the most important proviso to be made in this chapter is that, since homosexuality is stigmatized in this and other societies, it is likely to be under- rather than over-reported. Again, every effort has been made, by avoiding stigmatizing labels, by including the questions in the self-completion component, etc., to facilitate disclosure. Nevertheless, the prevalence estimates of homosexual behaviour based on these data must be regarded as minima.

Several estimates of prevalence of homosexual behaviour are provided. These range from 6.1% of men and 3.4% of women reporting any homosexual experience in their lifetime to 1.1% of men and 0.4% of women reporting having had a homosexual partner in the past year. For many, it seems, homosexual experience is transitory and unlikely to lead to a permanent behaviour pattern. It is more likely to be reported by men than by women.

The data show clearly that there is no 'typical' homosexual profile. Homosexual behaviour is reported across a broad range of social and demographic backgrounds. The main exception to this is the higher prevalence in London, which seems likely to be attributable to the more hospitable climate and the greater range of amenities existing there.

Many of the findings from this large scale, cross-sectional survey support and reinforce those from other smaller-scale, focused studies of homosexual men. (Few empirical data on women exist for purposes of comparison.) There is some evidence that a minority of men report larger numbers of male partners than do men reporting female partners, but if partners with whom penetrative sex has occurred are compared, the differences may be less marked. Similarly, as evidenced in other surveys, there is no support for the popular stereotype of patterns of homosexual behaviour mimicking those of heterosexual behaviour. Men reporting anal sex do so as both the receptive and the insertive partner.

In at least one important respect though, these data paint a somewhat different picture of homosexual behaviour from that portrayed by surveys using purposive or focused samples of homosexual men. Exclusively homosexual behaviour is rare, and the proportion of men who report having had a male sexual partner also report having had a female sexual partner in specific time periods is high – higher than found in purposive samples. This suggests that the national survey is more likely to have recruited a higher proportion of men who are covert about their experience of sex with men.

REFERENCES

ACSF Investigators (1992). 'AIDS and Sexual Behaviour in France', *Nature*, 360: 407–9

Bancroft, J. (1989). *Human Sexuality and its Problems*. Edinburgh: Churchill Livingstone

Bayer, R. (1981). *Homosexuality and American Psychiatry: The Politics of Diagnosis*. New York: Basic Books

Bell, A. P., and M. S. Weinberg (1978). *Homosexualities: A Study of*

Diversity among Men and Women. New York: Simon and Schuster

Bell, A. P., M. S. Weinberg, and S. K. Hammersmith (1981). *Sexual Preference: Its Development in Men and Women*. Bloomington: Indiana University Press

Boulton, M., and P. Weatherburn (1990). *Literature Review on Bisexuality and HIV Transmission*. Report commissioned by the Global Programme on AIDS, World Health Organization

Coxon, A. P. M. (1985). *The 'Gay Lifestyle' and the Impact of AIDS*. London: Project Sigma Working Paper No. 1

Dank, B. M. (1971). 'Coming Out in the Gay World', *Psychiatry*, 34: 180–97

Davies, P. M. (1988). *Some Problems in Defining and Sampling Non-heterosexual Males*. London: Project Sigma Working Paper No. 3

Davies, P. M., P. Weatherburn, A. J. Hunt, S. C. Hickson, T. J. McManus, and A. P. M. Coxon (1992). 'The Sexual Behaviour of Young Gay Men in England and Wales', *AIDS Care* 4(3): 259-72

Ford, C. S., and F. A. Beach (1952). *Patterns of Sexual Behaviour*. London: Eyre and Spottiswoode

Forman, D., and C. Chilvers (1989). 'Sexual Behaviour of Young and Middle-aged Men in England and Wales', *British Medical Journal*, 298: 1137–42

Freud, S. (1953). '*Three Essays on the Theory of Sexuality*', in James Strachey (ed.), *The Standard Edition of the Complete Psychological Works of Sigmund Freud*, vol. 21. London: Hogarth Press and the Institute of Psychoanalysis, 24 vols (1953–74)

Gagnon, J., and W. Simon (1973). *Sexual Conduct: The Social Sources of Human Sexuality*. Chicago: Aldine

Harry, J., and W. B. DeVall (1978). *The Social Organisation of Gay Males*. New York: Praeger

Hunt, A. J., P. M. Davies, P. Weatherburn, A. P. Coxon, and T. J. McManus (1991). 'Sexual Partners, Penetrative Sexual Partners and HIV Risk', *AIDS*, 5 (6): 723–8.

Kinsey, A. C., W. B. Pomeroy, and C. E. Martin (1948) *Sexual Behavior in the Human Male*. Philadelphia: W. B. Saunders.

Kinsey, A. C., W. B. Pomeroy, C. E. Martin, and C. H. Gebhard

(1953). *Sexual Behavior in the Human Female.* Philadelphia: W. B. Saunders

Larson, P. (1982). 'Gay Male Relationships', in W. Paul *et al.* (eds), *Homosexuality: Social, Psychological and Biological Issues.* London: Sage Publications

McQueen, D. V., B. J. Robertson, and L. Nisbet (1991). *Data Update: AIDS-related Behaviour, Knowledge and Attitudes, Provisional Data.* No. 27 1991. RUHBC, University of Edinburgh

Paul, W. and J. D. Weinrich (1982). Introduction in Paul, W. *et al.* (eds), *Homosexuality.* Beverly Hills: Sage

Rogers, S. M., and C. F. Turner (1991). 'Male–Male Sexual Contact in the USA: Findings from Five Sample Surveys, 1970–1990', *Journal of Sex Research*, 28 (4): 491–519

Saghir, M. T., and E. Robins (1973). *Male and Female Homosexuality: A Comprehensive Investigation.* Baltimore: Williams and Wilkins

Spencer, L., A. Faulkner, and J. Keegan (1988). *Talking about Sex.* London: Social and Community Planning Research

Sundet, J. M., I. L. Kvalem, P. Magnus, and L. S. Bakketeig (1988). 'Prevalence of Risk-prone Behaviour in the Central Population of Norway', in A. F. Fleming, M. Carballo, and D. F. Fitzsimons (eds), *The Global Impact of Aids.* London: Alan R. Liss

Weatherburn, P., P. M. Davies, A. J. Hunt, A. P. M. Coxon, and T. J. McManus (1990). 'Heterosexual Behaviour in a Large Cohort of Homosexually Active Men in England and Wales', *AIDS Care*, 2 (4): 319–24

Weatherburn, P., A. J. Hunt, F. C. I. Hickson, and P. M. Davies (1992). *The Sexual Lifestyles of Gay and Bisexual Men in England and Wales.* London: Project Sigma

Weeks, J. (1986). *Sexuality.* London and New York: Tavistock Publications

Weinberg, M. S., and C. J. Williams (1974). *Male Homosexuals: Their Problems and Adaptations.* New York: Oxford University Press

Wellings, K., and J. Wadsworth (1990). 'AIDS and the Moral Climate', in R. Jowell *et al.* (eds), *British Social Attitudes: The 7th Report.* Aldershot: Gower

Wolfenden Report (1957). *Report of the Committee on Homosexual Offences and Prostitution*, London: HMSO: Cmnd 247

CHAPTER 6

Sexual Attitudes

Sex is heavily regulated in all societies (Ford and Beach, 1952). One measure of the strength of this regulation is the extent to which social rules governing sexual conduct are internalized into public attitudes and opinion. This chapter looks at moral values associated with and attitudes towards sexual behaviour during the course of life. Many of the conventions governing sex in our society can be traced to their religious origins. The equation of sex with procreation and its containment within marriage are central to the Judaeo-Christian religions (Russell, 1929), and, though less strongly expressed than hitherto, still colour our moral judgement. Even in secular societies, we can see a legacy of the traditional Christian view that sexual intercourse should take place within marriage for the purpose of reproduction.

Sexual relations that take place between those in monogamous, heterosexual and procreative couples are almost universally accepted in every culture. Social disapproval tends to be reserved for relationships that occur outside of this dyad, the degree of disapproval depending on the strength of taboos in particular cultures. Generally, the strongest regulation extends to those sexual relationships and practices that are not capable of being reproductive or in which reproduction is considered socially inappropriate. Sex between two people of the same sex is an obvious focus for opprobrium, but the stigma also extends to precocious sex, sex before and outside of marriage, non-exclusive sexual relationships, and so on.

Constraints usually take the form of social sanctions but in some instances the law is invoked to uphold and underpin moral norms. In England and Wales, anal sex between a man and a woman is legally prohibited, for example, and sex between two men is heavily legally circumscribed. Sexual relations before an age judged to be socially appropriate are legally regulated and sexual non-exclusivity still features among legal grounds for divorce. Abortion, the ultimate expression of the severance of sex from its reproductive consequences, although legalized more than 25 years ago, is still the subject of constant public debate.

Opinions were sought on the strength of marriage as an institution, as measured by views on the age at which it should be entered and the ease with which it should be dissolved; on an age before which sexual intercourse should not occur, on sex before and outside of marriage; and attitudes towards sexual exclusivity and homosexuality. Opinions on abortion are also included here – an important measure of the degree to which people are prepared to tolerate sex being separated from procreation.

There already exists a considerable body of data on sexual attitudes. This survey is unique in providing an opportunity to explore how attitudes correspond with behaviour. The exact nature of the relationship between the two must remain a matter for conjecture. The assumption that attitudes might predict behaviour needs to be viewed with caution. Attitudes may influence behaviour but it is equally plausible that those with experience of a particular pattern of behaviour will adopt an attitude in keeping with their experience.

Nevertheless some insight into the relationship between the two is useful, particularly in the context of advice on risk reduction in relation to sexual health. It is sometimes assumed that a change in attitudes is a necessary prerequisite to any modification in behaviour. Whether or not this is the case, there is a more important sense in which a knowledge of sexual attitudes can aid sexual health promotion. Plainly, health educational advice, if it is to be adopted, must contain messages that are acceptable to the audience, and consistent with their sexual preferences. There would seem little point, for example, in urging monogamy and sexual restraint on a population heavily committed to polygamy and sexual licence. Thus the value for health educators of insights into attitudes lies not in the possibility of manipulating attitudes to modify behaviour but in selecting and harnessing those attitudes most likely to support sexually healthy behaviour.

METHODOLOGICAL NOTE

Many of the questions used in this survey are taken from the stock of questions included in the annual British Social Attitudes Survey (Airey, 1984; Brook, 1988; Harding, 1988; Wellings and Wadsworth, 1990). A similar set is asked in the American General Social Survey (Smith, 1990). This decision was made partly on the grounds of expediency, since such questions have been extensively piloted and also because their repeated use has resulted in a good deal being known about the associations of their responses. Because they have been asked at regular intervals since their introduction in 1983, they have the additional advantage of allowing trends to be discerned.

Possible sources of response bias, such as social desirability, may be exacerbated and accentuated in the investigation of attitudes. Since the attitudinal questions were asked in the face-to-face section of the questionnaire, and since the topics are so value laden, there might have been considerable scope for the intrusion of this bias. In formulating these questions, every effort was made to avoid any form of labelling with moral connotations. Terms such as adultery, infidelity and promiscuity convey such strong moral reprobation that it is difficult to imagine responses not being influenced by their use in a question, and so these words were deliberately avoided in order to minimize the effect of a social desirability response. Instead, questions simply stated what was involved in practice. Fluency of style may sometimes have suffered as a result, but in the interests of validity and reliability neutral and accurate phraseology was used. A further preventive measure adopted in this context was the use of show-cards allowing respondents to provide answers without having to verbalize them.

Another response bias which applies particularly to attitude-scale items has been described as 'acquiescence' or 'agreement' bias, a general tendency towards assent rather than dissent with an expressed viewpoint. This applies particularly to the use of Likert-type scales in which subjects are asked to place themselves on a 5-point scale for each statement – running from 'strongly agree' to 'agree', 'uncertain', 'disagree' and 'strongly disagree'. Where the opportunity arises, responses to statements expressing opposite points of view on the same issue have been checked for consistency in an attempt to determine the extent of such bias (see p. 264 below).

ATTITUDES, BELIEFS AND KNOWLEDGE

For ease of understanding, social psychologists make a rough distinction between opinions, attitudes and beliefs according to the strength of conviction, whether it is chiefly cognitive or emotional in origin, and the extent to which it is related to action. Attitudes are reinforced by beliefs (the cognitive component) and often attract strong feelings (the emotional component) that will lead to particular forms of behaviour (the action tendency component).

The boundary between attitude and knowledge measurement is both fine and blurred, and it has to be said that we cannot always know whether respondents interpreted particular questions as attempts to test knowledge or elicit attitudes. A case in point is the example of sex before the age of 16. If a man has sexual intercourse with a woman under this age, he is acting unlawfully, and so a recommendation of a later age as the minimum for first intercourse may be influenced by both knowledge and opinion. In the case of any legally sanctioned activity, the choice of the response option 'sometimes wrong' may thus be more a reflection of knowledge of the law than of personal opinion.

VIEWS ON AGE AT FIRST INTERCOURSE

All respondents were asked for their views on a minimum age for first sexual intercourse. The question asked was

> In general, is there an age below which you think young people nowadays ought not to start having sexual intercourse . . . first, for boys? . . . and for girls?

Response options permitted respondents to cite a specific age or to express the view, 'Depends on the individual' or 'Not before marriage'. Of interest with respect to these data is the extent to which public opinion on a minimum age at first intercourse is in line with, firstly, legally imposed age limits and, secondly, the actual age at which this occurred for respondents and at which it occurs for most people today. Of interest too is the question of whether views on an appropriate age differ for men and women.

Recommended Minimum Age Compared with Legal Age

Roughly one in eight respondents (marginally more men than women, and marginally more in the case of boys than girls) took the view that an appropriate age at first intercourse would depend on individual readiness and gave no specific age (Table 6.1). Considerably fewer, around 4% of the sample, believed that, irrespective of age, intercourse should not occur before marriage. This view was some 4 times more likely to be volunteered by the oldest respondents (45–59) than by the youngest (16–24). This corresponds to age-related patterns of premarital experience described in Chapter 2.

According to the law governing the age of sexual consent, it is an offence for a man to have sex with a woman aged under 16 in Britain, though the woman commits no offence in participating. The age at which a man is permitted to have sex, or a woman to have sex with him, is not legally regulated, and the law is also silent on the matter of sex between two women. There seems to be no evidence from these data of widespread support for a lowering of the age of sexual consent (Tables 6.1 and 6.2). Only a minority of people – in the region of one in eight of the sample as a whole – are in favour of sexual intercourse being permitted before the age of 16 for boys or girls (Table 6.2). Marginally fewer women than men favour intercourse under 16 and there is a tendency for both men and women to believe that under 16 is more appropriate for boys than girls. 16.3% of men believe it acceptable for boys to have sexual intercourse before the age of 16, while only 9.9% of women do so; and the proportion of men viewing this to be right for girls is 13.9% compared with 8.7% of women.

In general, is there an age below which you think young people nowadays ought not to start having sexual intercourse?

views of . . .	. . . on ideal age for		under 13	13–15	16–17	18–19	20+
men	boys	%	0.7	15.6	48.6	11.8	1.8
men	girls	%	0.5	13.5	51.0	13.1	1.9
women	boys	%	0.3	9.6	48.0	18.8	2.5
women	girls	%	0.3	8.4	49.5	20.3	2.7

views of . . .	. . . on ideal age for		depends on individual not age	not before marriage	other	no view/ don't know	*base*
men	boys	%	13.8	3.2	0.9	3.7	*8268*
men	girls	%	12.6	3.5	0.8	3.1	*8262*
women	boys	%	12.4	4.3	0.9	3.2	*10349*
women	girls	%	11.2	4.9	1.0	1.9	*10348*

Table 6.1 Views on minimum age for first sexual intercourse. Source: Interview Questions 34a, 34b

			age group of respondent				
views of . . .	. . . on age for		16–24	25–34	35–44	45–59	total
men	boys	%	24.3	19.2	12.7	9.5	16.3
		base	*1951*	*2139*	*2019*	*2159*	*8268*
men	girls	%	21.0	15.9	11.5	7.9	13.9
		base	*1949*	*2138*	*2016*	*2159*	*8262*
women	boys	%	16.2	10.6	7.6	6.2	9.9
		base	*2207*	*2862*	*2538*	*2741*	*10348*
women	girls	%	14.4	9.2	6.6	5.5	8.7
		base	*2207*	*2863*	*2538*	*2741*	*10349*

Table 6.2 Views on minimum age for first sexual intercourse: proportion of respondents in each age group citing this age to be under 16. Source: Interview Questions 34a, 34b

Views differ markedly with the age of the respondent. Looking at responses for different age groups (Table 6.2), younger people are more likely than older ones to be in favour of intercourse occurring before the present legal age of sexual consent. The proportion of 16–24-year-olds who see a minimum age for sexual intercourse before the age of 16 is more than twice that among 45–59-year-olds, irrespective of whether the respondent is a man or a woman or whether the response relates to boys or girls. But even among the young this is still a minority view.

Knowledge of the Law Relating to the Age of Sexual Consent

The knowledge that it is unlawful for a man to have sex with a young woman aged under 16 is virtually universal (95.7% men and 96.8% women know this to be so). However, almost as large a majority (92.2% of men and 92.5% of women) mistakenly believe that the woman herself is committing an offence by having sex under the age of 16. Furthermore, a majority (69.0% men and 67.6% women) are under the misapprehension that it is against the law for a man aged under 16 to have sex, and that a *woman* who has sex with a *man* under 16 is also committing an offence (76.0% of men and 73.3% women) (Figure 6.1).

Considerable uncertainty also surrounds the legal age of sexual consent for same-gender sex. The 1967 Act made it lawful for two men over the age of 21 to have sexual relations together in private and with mutual consent. Sex between two women is neither legislated for nor against. One in three women, and one in four men, did not know the legal position on sexual relations between two women, and 20.1% women and 15.1% of men lack information on the law relating to men. 68.0% of men, and 61.3% of women, know that sex between two men under the age of 21 is illegal. Only a third of the sample was aware that sex between two women is not legislated against.

Figure 6.1 (*opposite*) Men's and women's knowledge of the law relating to age of sexual consent (*Figure continued on p. 238*). Source: Interview Question 35

Would you tell me whether you think each of these things is legal or illegal under the law . . .?

a) For a woman aged under 16 to have sex?

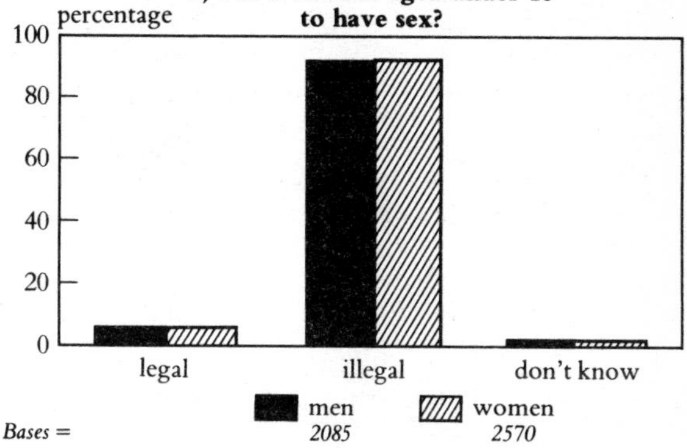

Bases =

Correct answer = legal

b) For a man aged under 16 to have sex?

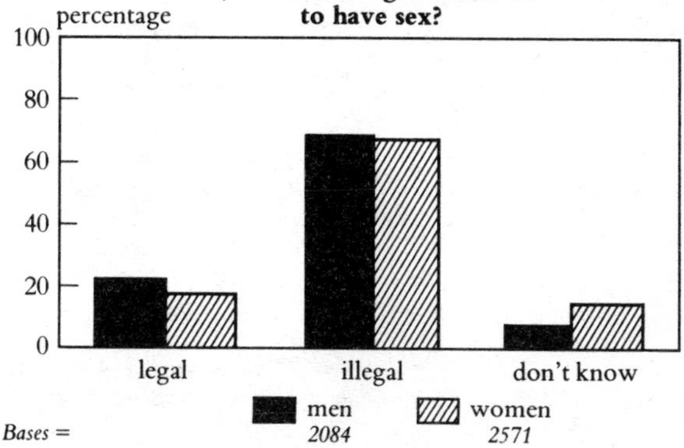

Bases =

Correct answer = legal

c) For a man to have sex with a woman of under 16?

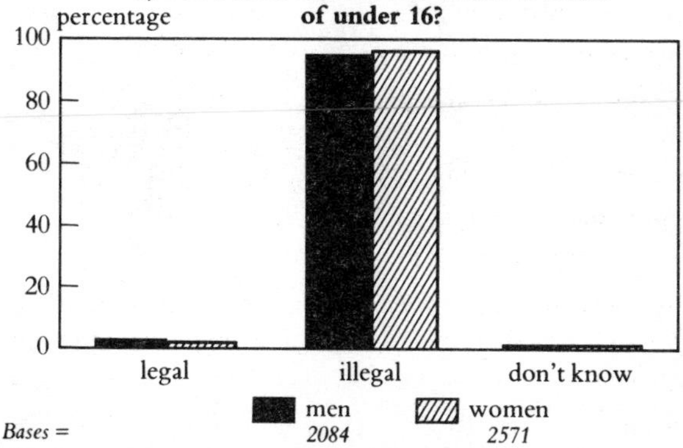

Bases =

Correct answer = illegal

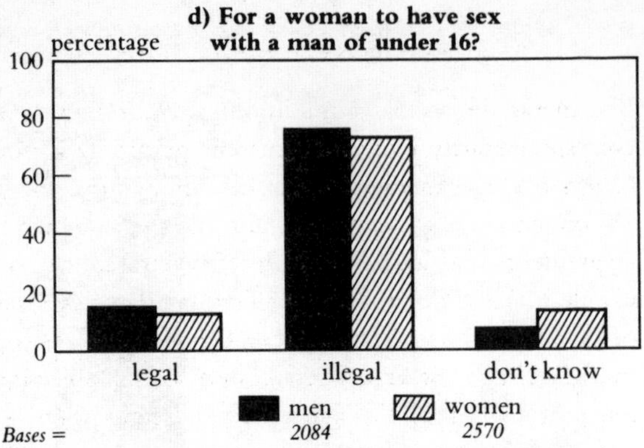

Correct answer = legal

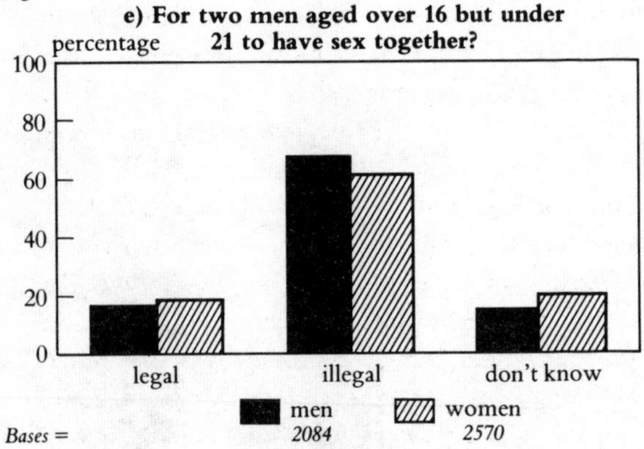

Correct answer = illegal

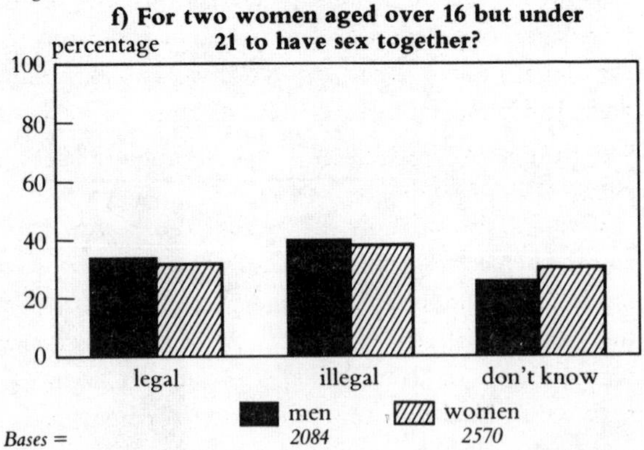

Correct answer = legal

Figure 6.1 *continued*

Ideal Age in Relation to Actual Age

In general, views on a minimum age for first sexual intercourse correspond fairly closely to current behavioural norms. Recalling Chapter 2, the median age at first intercourse for 16–24-year-old respondents was 17, and this is also the age at which the majority of respondents find it acceptable for first intercourse to have occurred (Table 6.1). Older respondents favour a later age than do younger ones but, even so, the majority of those aged 45–59 who specify a minimum age for sexual intercourse see no objection to its occurrence at or before the age of 17. It seems then as if people are providing responses more in line with present-day norms than with those that prevailed in their own youth. The median age at first intercourse for men aged 45–59, for example, was 20, yet 73.9% of men in this age group believe it acceptable for young men below that age to be having sexual intercourse.

Views on an appropriate minimum age for sexual intercourse are none the less related to personal experience. Predictably, those who themselves experienced first intercourse at a younger age were more likely to favour a lower age limit for others, and those who first experienced sexual intercourse at an older age were more likely to recommend a higher minimum age for others. The difference between actual age at first intercourse and recommended minimum age for young people of the same gender was calculated for each respondent and these results are summarized in Table 6.3. The proportion of people who themselves had intercourse before the age they regard today as the minimum varies with a number of factors, several of which are clearly related. Number of sexual partners, for example, varies with current age and also the age at which intercourse first takes place.

Overall, this analysis shows that those who experienced intercourse themselves before the minimum they now recommend for others are a minority. Women are less likely than men to do so but the gender differences are not marked. Fewer than one in five women aged 16–24 were experienced at a younger age than they now see as ideal, but this proportion is nevertheless nearly 3 times higher than among women aged 45–59. Interestingly, this reflects the higher proportion of women aged 16–24 who felt that they had

	%	*base**	%	*base**
age group				
16–24	17.8	*1199*	18.9	*1454*
25–34	19.4	*1699*	13.9	*2374*
35–44	15.8	*1563*	10.9	*2021*
45–59	12.4	*1573*	6.5	*2070*
marital status				
married	15.3	*3709*	9.8	*5020*
cohabiting	19.7	*481*	15.0	*698*
widowed/separated/divorced	21.0	*335*	16.4	*854*
single	16.7	*1510*	16.3	*1346*
social class				
I, II	11.1	*2165*	7.7	*2824*
III NM	15.0	*1197*	10.7	*1804*
III M	21.1	*1515*	14.2	*1475*
IV, V, other	21.4	*1154*	18.6	*1812*
education				
degree	7.1	*715*	4.9	*618*
A level	13.6	*2043*	8.6	*1778*
O level	17.4	*1773*	12.2	*3021*
other	11.9	*146*	11.7	*121*
none	24.6	*1349*	16.5	*2377*
no homosexual partner ever	16.4	*5818*	12.0	*7773*
1+ homosexual partner ever	15.1	*201*	19.8	*139*
heterosexual partners ever				
1	3.8	*1243*	5.9	*3155*
2	8.7	*680*	13.1	*1408*
3–4	13.9	*1184*	14.6	*1510*
5–9	17.7	*1259*	19.8	*1103*
10+	30.2	*1502*	23.0	*533*
overall	16.3	*6035*	12.1	*7920*

Table 6.3 Proportion of people who had intercourse before the age they would recommend for young people today. Source: Interview Questions 19a, 34a, 34b; Booklet Questions 7a, 8a

* includes only those who have had sexual intercourse and who specify a minimum age for sexual intercourse

had sex too soon (see Chapter 2, p. 80). The age gradient for men is less clear.

The number of heterosexual partners is a very important influence, as shown in Table 6.3, those with large numbers being much more likely to recommend a later starting age for others than they experienced themselves. Educational level also plays an important role, those with no qualifications being more than twice as likely to have had intercourse themselves at an age they now feel to be premature than those with education to A level or beyond. The social-class effect is slightly weaker than that of educational level for men and slightly stronger for women. Logistic regression was used to identify which of the factors mentioned above were significant. In order of importance of influence, the variables significantly associated with the tendency to recommend a later age for first intercourse than self-experienced were number of heterosexual partners, educational level, current age, social class, marital status and whether or not the respondent had had any homosexual partner.

Reasons for Choice of Age

Respondents who gave a minimum age for first intercourse were asked to give the main reason for their choice from a pre-formulated list and these are summarized in Figure 6.2. By far the most common reason identified (by 57.8% women and 54.0% men) was that, before the age given, young people are not sufficiently emotionally mature. Men were more likely to feel that those younger than the minimum age they stated had not learned enough about sex. Women were slightly more likely to mention risks to health, but these accounted for responses from small proportions overall. Even smaller proportions mentioned lack of physical maturity and that sex before the stated age was morally wrong. Older respondents were more likely to cite risks to health than were younger respondents but they were no more likely to state that sexual intercourse before a certain age was morally wrong.

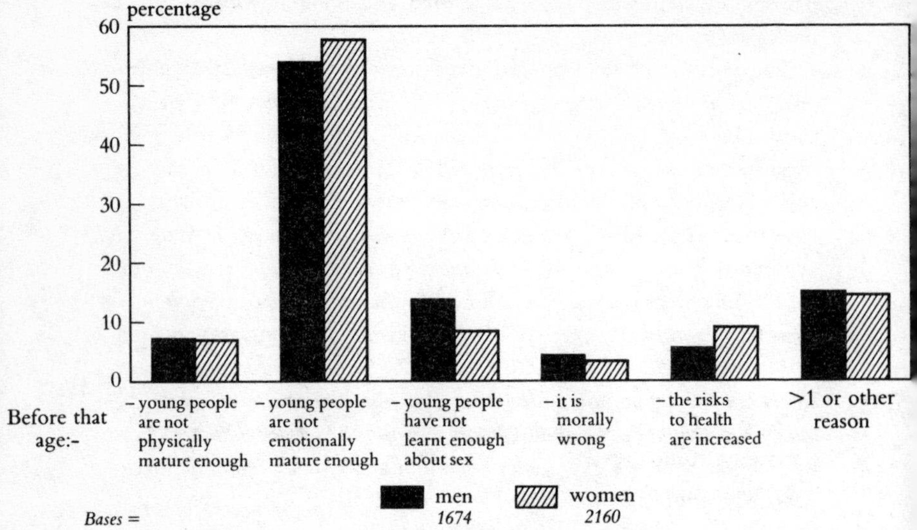

Figure 6.2 Main reason for opinions relating to minimum age at first intercourse. *What is the main reason you say that/those ages?* Source: Interview Question 34

A Good Age for Marriage

Respondents were asked what they thought was a good age for marriage for both men and women and their responses were notable more for their similarity than their differences. 25 was the age given for both sexes by more than a quarter of men and women (Table 6.4). However, for men, about equal proportions of men thought under 25, 25, or over 25 was an appropriate age for men, while women tended on average to favour a slightly older age for men. Men and women were more in accord about a 'good' age for women to marry, but on average it was a younger age than was thought appropriate for men: nearly half of both men and women thought an age below 25 was most appropriate.

How does this pattern of opinions about a good age for marriage compare with the actual ages at which people get married? 31% of men and 46% of women who married in 1989 were under the age of 25 (CSO, 1991). Overall, this accords reasonably well with the propor-

	men		women	
	(a) men %	(b) women %	(a) men %	(b) women %
younger than 25	28.0	44.6	24.9	45.7
25	29.4	24.9	33.3	26.7
older than 25	28.1	14.4	30.0	15.8
depends/varies	12.9	12.9	10.8	10.9
don't know/not answered	1.6	2.2	1.1	0.9
base *		*2088*		*2577*

Table 6.4 Opinions on a good age for marriage. *In general, what age do you think is a good age for (a) a man and (b) a woman to get married?* Source: Interview Question 38

* all respondents answering the long questionnaire

tions of respondents who felt marriage at a young age to be desirable. But, at the other end of the age range, 23% of men and 17% of women who married in 1989 were aged 35 or older while less than 2% of the sample had given desirable ages as high as this. This is not as surprising as it may seem at first sight because the figures for age at marriage include people marrying for the second (or subsequent) time while respondents were doubtless thinking only of first marriages in giving their views.

There has been a dramatic change in the distribution of ages at marriage over the past decade or so: in 1977 15% of men were under 21 at marriage and 48% (in total) under 25, compared with only 5% and 31% respectively by 1989. The equivalent figures for women were 34% under 21 in 1977 and 64% under 25, compared with only 14% and 46% in 1989 (*Annual Abstract of Statistics*, 1992). These increases in age at marriage can hardly be explained by the inclusion of second and subsequent marriages as there has been only a small increase in these over the period: in 1977 it was the first marriage for both partners in 68% of cases compared with 64% in 1989. The change in the age profile at marriage must be viewed in the context of a gradually diminishing absolute number of marriages per year (10% reduction between 1977 and 1989).

Given that the majority of both men and women accept that sex before marriage is not wrong (see below) and that an acceptable age to start having intercourse is 18 or younger, it would seem logical that it is also accepted that, for very many people, there will be a substantial number of years of premarital sexual activity.

VIEWS ON SELECTED SEXUAL RELATIONSHIPS AND EXPERIENCES

As indicated above, respondents were asked for their opinion on the morality of a number of different sexual relationships, described on show-cards using the phrasing reproduced in Figures 6.4–7. For each statement response options were presented on a 5-point scale from 'always wrong' through 'sometimes wrong', 'neither right nor wrong' to 'rarely wrong' and 'not wrong at all'.

Premarital Sex

As can be seen from Table 6.5 and Figure 6.3 the level of disapproval varies very much from one practice to another. Attitudes towards premarital sex, for example, vary markedly from those towards extramarital sexual relationships. Three-quarters of the sample consider sex before marriage not wrong at all (or only rarely so), while a similar and slightly higher proportion – nearly 80% – consider sex outside marriage to be always or mostly wrong.

It seems clear that the necessity of marriage as a precondition of sex is becoming very much a thing of the past. Acceptance of sex before marriage is now nearly universal, with nearly three-quarters of men and two-thirds of women condoning it as not wrong at all. Fewer than one in ten respondents (8.2% of men and 10.8% of women) believe it to be always or mostly wrong. Women are marginally less tolerant than men but the disparity diminishes with decreasing age. Age has a bearing on attitudes, though it is weaker than might be expected (Figure 6.4). Not surprisingly, premarital sex is viewed with greatest leniency in the age group in which it is most likely to occur. Only one in twenty men and women aged 16–24 consider premarital sex to be wrong, compared with nearly 3

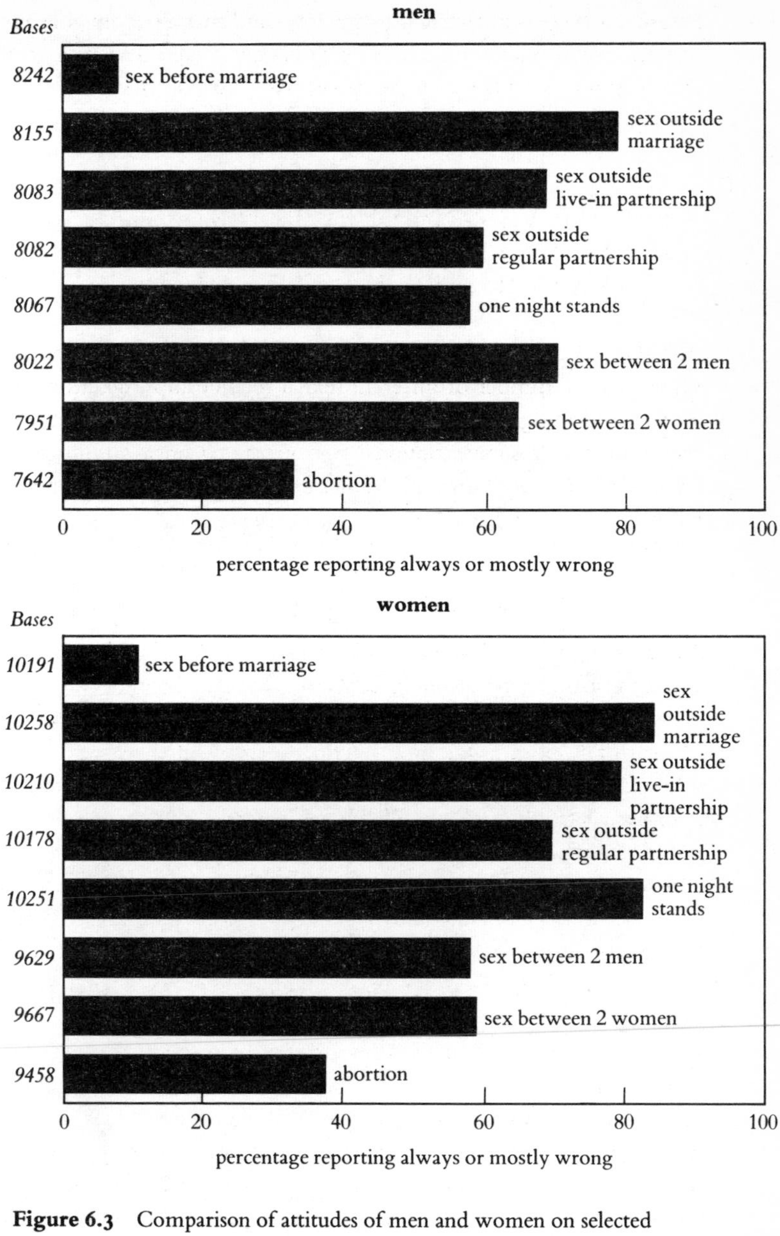

Figure 6.3 Comparison of attitudes of men and women on selected items. Source: Interview Questions 39a–h

	sex before marriage		sex outside marriage		sex outside live-in partnership		sex outside regular partnership		one-night stands		sex between 2 men		sex between 2 women		abortion	
	%	*base*	%	*base*	%	*base*	%	*base*	%	*base*	%	*base*	%	*base*	%	*base*
men																
total	8.2	*8242*	78.7	*8155*	68.5	*8083*	59.4	*8082*	57.5	*8067*	70.2	*8022*	64.5	*7951*	33.1	*7642*
age																
16–24	5.1	*1962*	81.5	*1960*	66.2	*1954*	61.0	*1950*	48.5	*1942*	68.6	*1930*	63.2	*1916*	36.5	*1837*
25–34	5.2	*2140*	76.8	*2110*	69.2	*2085*	61.0	*2102*	50.4	*2096*	64.7	*2069*	58.6	*2055*	33.1	*2018*
35–44	7.8	*2017*	74.7	*1987*	65.7	*1969*	56.0	*1975*	60.8	*1963*	67.9	*1952*	62.0	*1937*	33.0	*1869*
45–59	14.4	*2123*	82.0	*2099*	72.5	*2074*	60.0	*2055*	70.1	*2067*	79.3	*2072*	74.1	*2043*	30.1	*1918*
marital status																
married	10.5	*4704*	80.5	*4663*	70.1	*4605*	59.4	*4614*	62.8	*4598*	74.1	*4586*	68.5	*4546*	33.3	*4344*
cohabiting – opposite-sex partner	1.3	*604*	68.8	*591*	68.5	*588*	60.8	*582*	53.5	*589*	63.5	*578*	54.8	*575*	25.7	*559*
cohabiting – same-sex partner	0.0	*19*★	68.9	*18*★	67.3	*19*★	57.0	*19*★	20.2	*19*★	0.0	*20*	0.0	*20*	21.1	*19*★
widowed	10.9	*49*	88.2	*47*	85.5	*48*	68.8	*47*	70.9	*49*	84.7	*47*	82.2	*46*	29.5	*42*
divorced/separated	5.0	*393*	73.7	*383*	67.0	*385*	58.6	*382*	56.2	*382*	69.7	*376*	63.3	*372*	35.5	*359*
single	6.0	*2471*	78.5	*2452*	65.3	*2437*	59.2	*2437*	48.8	*2429*	64.7	*2414*	60.0	*2392*	34.3	*2318*

	women															
total	10.8	*10191*	84.3	*10258*	79.6	*10210*	69.9	*10178*	82.7	*10251*	57.9	*9629*	58.8	*9667*	37.7	*9458*
age																
16–24	5.2	*2225*	84.8	*2219*	77.7	*2208*	71.6	*2206*	76.1	*2193*	52.4	*2104*	54.0	*2115*	39.9	*2089*
25–34	6.0	*2851*	84.5	*2848*	80.8	*2848*	72.9	*2838*	75.5	*2834*	52.7	*2682*	53.5	*2685*	36.7	*2654*
35–44	9.5	*2497*	80.5	*2513*	76.5	*2497*	65.5	*2485*	85.2	*2512*	56.6	*2361*	57.0	*2363*	36.0	*2299*
45–59	22.1	*2619*	87.2	*2680*	82.9	*2657*	69.6	*2649*	93.3	*2711*	69.6	*2482*	70.4	*2503*	38.5	*2417*
marital status																
married	13.0	*6126*	85.7	*6210*	79.8	*6160*	68.7	*6142*	85.8	*6205*	62.1	*5805*	62.9	*5827*	38.9	*5671*
cohabiting – opposite-sex partner	1.6	*826*	76.3	*817*	80.2	*818*	70.5	*814*	75.7	*820*	48.1	*768*	47.6	*769*	34.0	*774*
cohabiting – same-sex partner	0.0	*11*★	72.1	*11*★	46.5	*11*★	54.3	*11*★	58.3	*10*★	22.7	*11*★	0.0	*11*★	50.8	*11*★
widowed	23.9	*193*	88.2	*193*	88.7	*193*	74.7	*193*	93.6	*198*	69.0	*179*	68.9	*182*	41.1	*176*
divorced/separated	8.2	*840*	82.8	*836*	82.0	*834*	72.2	*831*	81.1	*838*	55.8	*779*	56.4	*785*	35.5	*769*
single	8.0	*2193*	83.5	*2189*	77.3	*2191*	71.9	*2185*	76.2	*2178*	50.0	*2085*	51.9	*2092*	36.2	*2056*

Table 6.5 Attitudes towards selected relationships and behaviours – proportions considering them mostly or always wrong.
Source: Interview Questions 39a–h
★ note small base.

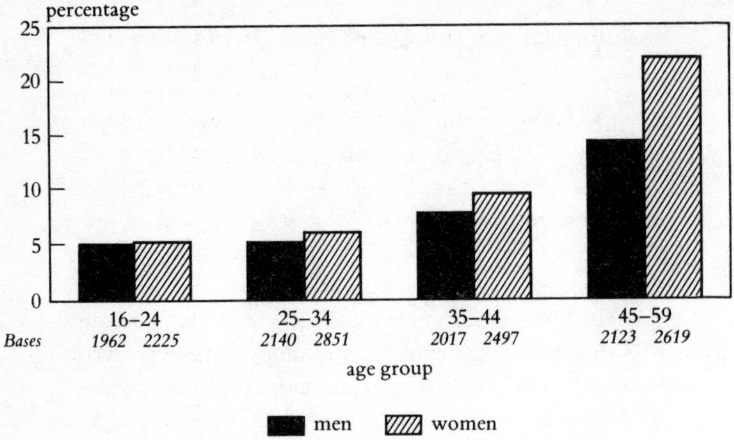

Figure 6.4 Views of sex before marriage: proportion stating always or mostly wrong. *If a man and a woman have sexual relations before marriage, what would your general opinion be?* Source: Interview Question 39a

times as many men and more than 4 times as many women in the oldest age group, 45–59. Yet, even among the oldest age group, those who disapprove are still in a minority.

There is now a considerable body of both US and British data indicating that intolerance of premarital sex has been stable at this low level for some time (Glenn and Weaver, 1979; Singh, 1980; Airey, 1984; Saunders and Edwards, 1984; Smith, 1990). On this issue, however, the British public appear to be less censorious than the US public, 36% of whom view premarital sex as always or mostly wrong (Smith, 1990).

Bivariate analysis shows religious affiliation strongly influencing attitudes towards premarital sex. Those affiliated to no religious denomination are less likely to disapprove of premarital sex (only 2.6% men and 3.8% women in this group do so), those of Christian faiths other than Anglican or Roman Catholic (mainly Baptist) more likely to do so (20.3% men and 22.0% of women), and those of non-Christian religious affiliation very much more likely to do so (46.2% of men and 41.3% women believe premarital sex to be always or mostly wrong).

Extramarital Sex and Other Non-exclusive Sexual Relationships

The pattern of responses to the question on sex outside marriage is the reverse of that relating to sex before marriage (Figure 6.3). Extramarital sex is regarded in an altogether stricter light. Only one respondent in fifty believes extramarital sex to be not at all wrong, and some four out of five people (78.7% men and 84.3% women) are of the opinion that it is always or mostly wrong. Only marginally fewer people – two-thirds of men and more than three-quarters of women – disapprove of sexual relationships outside a live-in relationship, and well over half of men and more than two-thirds of women see sexual relations outside a regular relationship as always or mostly wrong. In fact, the majority view on all these issues concerning exclusivity is that monogamy is the correct form of behaviour – the degree varying with the extent to which the relationship is formalized by marriage or common residence (Table 6.5).

Disapproval of extramarital sexual relationships extends to all age groups. The proportion of 16–24-year-olds who see it as wrong is as high as it is in the oldest age group, 81.5% of men and 84.8% of women aged 16–24 compared with 82.0% and 87.2% respectively among 45–59-year-olds. There is no clear age-related trend in these data (Figure 6.5). Neither the return to more traditional moral values documented in the trend literature of the mid-1980s (Airey, 1984; Harding, 1988) nor the slight reversal of this trend apparent towards the end of the decade (Wellings and Wadsworth, 1990) are evident from an analysis of these data by age.

In terms of marital status, those who are married or widowed have a greater commitment to the institution of marriage. They are more likely to see sex before and outside of marriage as wrong than are those who are cohabiting or divorced and separated, though the differences are not great. Bivariate analysis shows views on the value of exclusiveness in sexual relationships to vary with social class, those in lower social strata being more censorious than those in higher ones, though the gradient is clearer for women than for men.

What do these results tell us about sex in relation to marriage as an institution in contemporary Britain? It seems clear that marriage as a necessary precondition to having sex is a thing of the past. Yet

What about a married person having sexual relations with someone other than his or her partner?

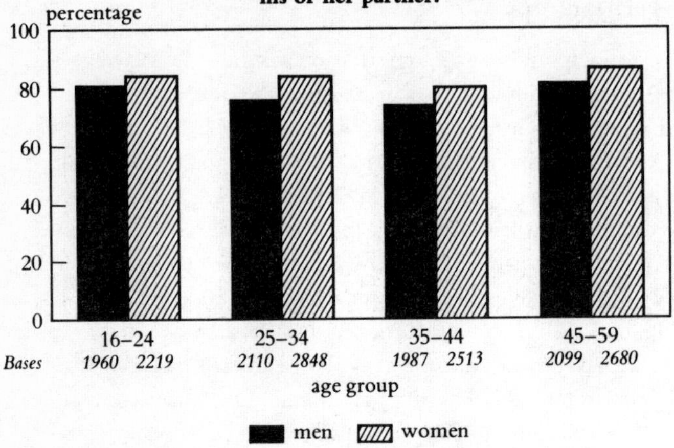

What about a person who is living with a partner, not married, having sexual relations with someone other than his or her partner?

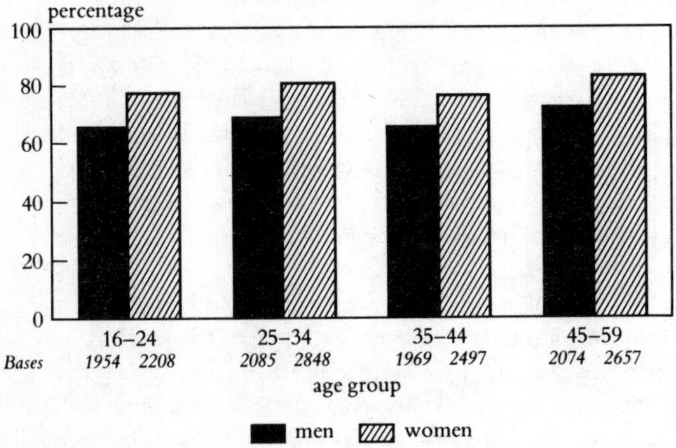

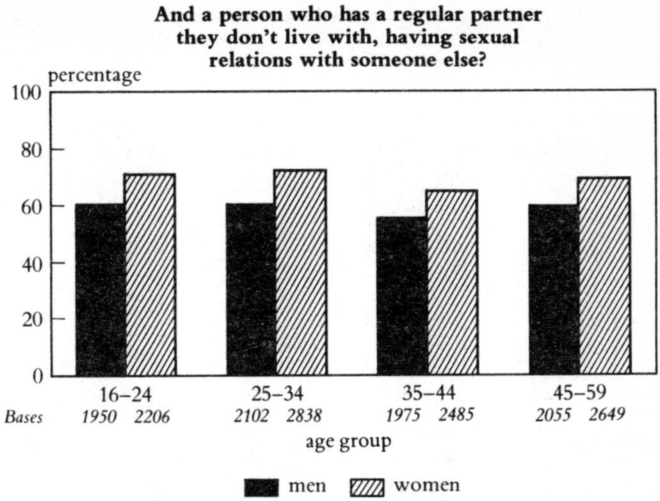

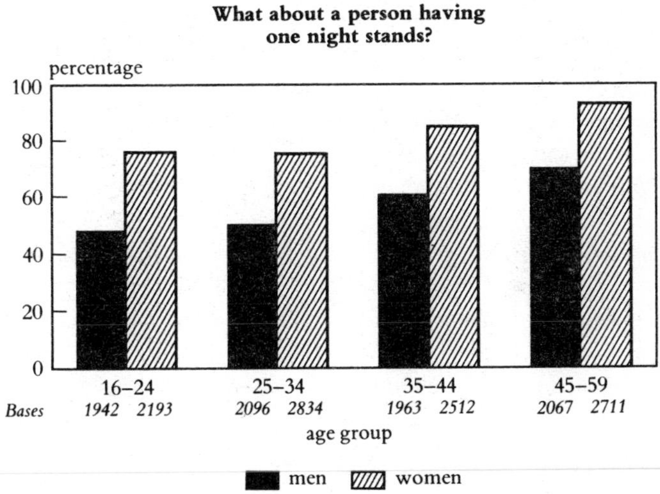

Figure 6.5 Views on non-exclusive sexual relationships: Proportion stating certain behaviours are always or mostly wrong. Source: Interview Questions 39b–e

these findings give little support to the assertion that marriage is losing its importance in Britain. While it is clear that it is no longer seen as the starting point of sexual relationships, once entered into, it is certainly viewed by the majority of the population as an exclusive relationship for men and women alike. Care needs to be taken here in distinguishing attitudes from behaviour. Disapproval of behaviour does not mean that people refrain from it. Adultery is still one of the most widely cited grounds for divorce in Britain. But, practice aside, the principle of monogamy is held in very high regard.

Casual Sex

One of the health promotional messages formulated for risk reduction in relation to HIV and sexual health generally has been to avoid casual sex. A question was therefore included to elicit opinions on 'one-night stands', which are commonly equated with casual sex (Spencer *et al.*, 1988). As with other attitude questions, whether the respondent should answer these questions in relation to him- or herself or to some generalized other was not specified. But the level of opprobrium attached to one-night stands is high.

Not only is it high, but it is the issue on which the views of men and women are most divided. On all questions relating to exclusivity, women are less tolerant than men of people having sexual relationships with partners in addition to their marital, cohabiting or regular partners, but they are especially censorious on the topic of one-night stands. While 35.8% of men view this as always wrong, 62.4% of women do so (Table 6.5, Figure 6.5). The greater difference in attitudes towards one-night stands persists in those aged 35 and under, among whom there is generally higher acceptance compared with the older age groups.

Ideals of monogamy seem to be more strongly held by women than men. This gender difference has been shown to be common to many other societies (Foa *et al.*, 1987). Views on why this may be so will depend on the particular theory of sexuality held. Those who subscribe to socio-biological theories of sexuality may see it as a biologically driven commitment on the part of women to monogamy and men to polygamy, tracing it back to the seeking of reproductive advantages by males and females in the distant past. Those favouring a Marxist–feminist perspective may see it as a reflection of the power base of our society in which male economic power and a property view of women nurtures and permits a double standard. Whatever the explanation, there seems little doubt that British women have a greater commitment to monogamy than men (see Chapter 3).

Homosexuality

In the late twentieth century, depending on the social circles one moves in, homosexuality may be viewed as a proud source of identity, a more or less tolerated 'alternative lifestyle', or as a perverse and bestial crime against God and nature (Scull, 1989). This attitudinal eclecticism is reflected in our data. Views are more strongly polarized on these kinds of sexual relationships than on any other. More of the responses fall into the 'not wrong at all' category at the extreme end of the scale compared with those on the issue of exclusivity; one in five respondents believes sex between people of the same gender to be not at all wrong (Table 6.5).

But, despite the spread of opinion, homophobic attitudes are widespread in Britain. More than two-thirds of men (70.2%) and more than half of women (57.9%) believe sex between two men to be always or mostly wrong, and there is only marginally less condemnation of sex between two women (which 64.5% of men and 58.8% of women see as always or mostly wrong). Younger respondents are not markedly more tolerant than older ones (Figure 6.6). Acceptance of homosexuality is scarcely greater in British society than it is in the US where the practice of homosexual acts is still illegal in some States. Three-quarters of US respondents in the 1989 General Social Survey judged such practice to be always or almost always wrong (Smith, 1990).

Comparing attitudes towards sexual exclusivity and homosexual relations, the pattern of the disparity between men and women is reversed (Figure 6.3). Women tend to be more accepting than men of same-gender relationships. This is more marked in attitudes towards sexual relations between two men than in attitudes towards sexual relations between two women. It has been noted that most

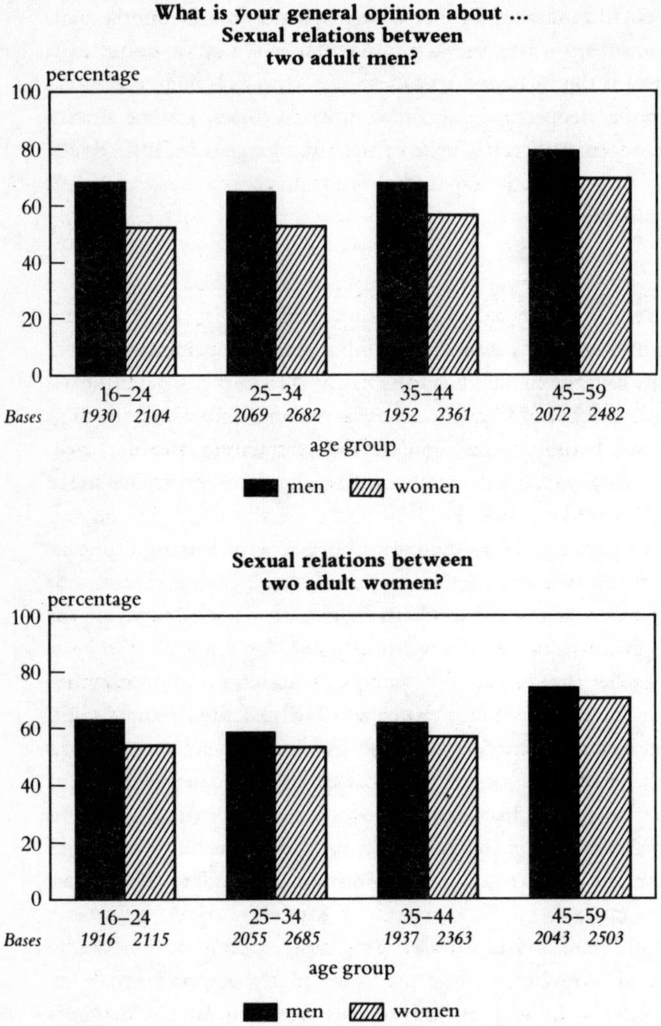

Figure 6.6 Views on homosexual relationship: Proportion stating always or mostly wrong. Source: Interview Questions 39f, 39g

researchers fail to distinguish between male and female homosexuality in inquiries into attitudes (Kite, 1984). The question on homosexuality asked in the British Social Attitudes Survey so far makes no distinction between female and male homosexuality, asking simply for views on sex between people of the same gender. Mindful of the possibility that attitudes may differ according to whether the couple are men or women, and also that homosexuality might be wrongly equated by some only with sex between men (see Chapter 5), separate questions were asked focusing on sex between men and sex between women. These data show (in common with the US data) that men, though not women, hold more negative attitudes towards male than towards female homosexuality. US surveys have shown that people are more likely to view as wrong sexual relationships between two people of the same gender as themselves (Kite, 1984; Whitley, 1988), and our findings bear this out for men but not for women (Table 6.5).

A higher prevalence of homosexual experience in London compared with the rest of Britain was noted in Chapter 5 and it was suggested that this resulted from migration of gay men to the capital. It is not clear whether this effect is the result of 'pull' – a response to the attractions of the capital city in terms of anonymity, together with the facilities and services for gay life, such as clubs and pubs, or whether it is the result of 'push' – escape from negative and hostile attitudes towards homosexuality outside London. An analysis of attitudes towards homosexuality by region confirms higher tolerance of sex between men in the capital than outside it. 61.4% of men in Greater London compared with 70.2% in the country as a whole see sex between two men as always or mostly wrong. Women's views on this issue vary even more markedly according to whether or not they live in the capital: 47.0% of women living in London compared with 57.9% in the country as a whole see sex between two men as always or mostly wrong. Once again, caution needs to be exercised in identifying cause and effect here, since it is equally plausible that more tolerant attitudes attract gay men as it is that the presence and higher profile of gay men in the capital increases familiarity and therefore tolerance.

Abortion

Of all the moral issues recently debated in the public arena, abortion has been perhaps most passionately contested. It has been the subject of intense political lobbying with well-organized and vociferous protest groups on each side. Although Britain was one of the first countries to liberalize the law relating to abortion – the 1967 Abortion Law Reform Act legalizing abortion in this country came into effect in April 1968 – some are of the view that it has fallen behind since (Lewis, 1987; Francome, 1988). In the 25 years since the law came into effect, many attempts have been made to amend or reform it. Most recently, the debate has focused on the latest stage in pregnancy at which a woman may be allowed by law to have an abortion.

On abortion, the responses of men and women are broadly similar. Women take a slightly less liberal view of abortion than do men (37.7% see abortion as always or mostly wrong compared with 33.1% of men, Figure 6.3) and this is a contrary result to that in almost all the polls except one in the past 10 years (Francome,

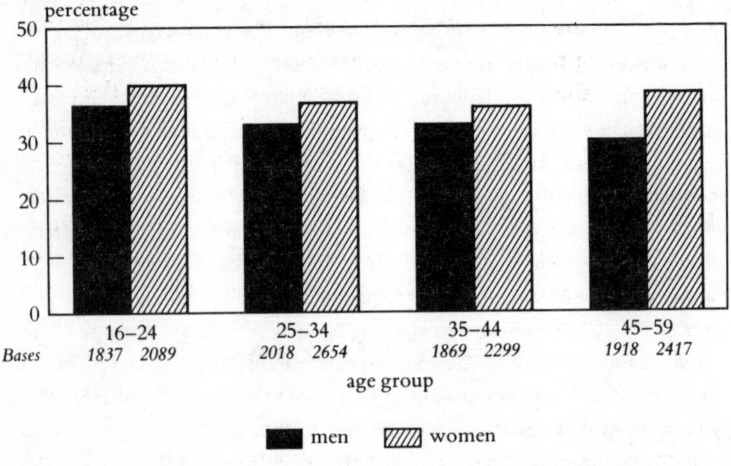

Figure 6.7 Views on abortion: Proportion stating abortion is always or mostly wrong. Source: Interview Question 39h

1988). Generally speaking, younger people are less sympathetic than older people towards abortion, though the age differences are not marked (Figure 6.7).

Bivariate analysis shows that respondents whose religious affiliation is Roman Catholic are very much more likely to oppose abortion than those of another affiliation or none. 58.9% of women reporting Roman Catholic affiliation believe abortion to be mostly or always wrong, compared with 33.7% of Anglicans and 31.7% of those with no affiliation; for men the comparable figures are 58.8%, 29.3% and 28.0%. Respondents of non-Christian and 'other' Christian denominations were also more likely to oppose abortion though the difference for these groups is less marked. These findings are not consistent with those from other surveys which have shown that only a small percentage of Roman Catholics follow their Church's position, which is for a total ban on abortion with the exception, nowadays, of cases that save the woman's life (Francome, 1988).

RELATIONSHIP BETWEEN ATTITUDES AND BEHAVIOUR

Table 6.6 shows the associations between attitudes and the behaviours that most closely correspond to them. In general, those without experience of behaviours on which views are sought are more likely to perceive them as wrong. This is especially marked in the case of premarital sex (these data were available only for respondents who completed the long questionnaire). Respondents who themselves had no sexual intercourse before marriage were nearly 10 times as likely to frown on this practice as those who had. The association was also marked for homosexual experience. Men who, in the self-completion component of the questionnaire, reported never having had sexual experience with a man were more than 3 times as likely to view such relationships as wrong as were those who had done so, and women who reported no sexual experience with a woman 5 times as likely to see such behaviour as wrong.

Attitudes to non-exclusive sexual relationships – sex outside marriage, sex outside a cohabiting relationship, and sex outside a regular partnership – varied less markedly with reporting of experience, but

	men				women			
	experience		no experience		experience		no experience	
	%	*base*	%	*base*	%	*base*	%	*base*
sex before marriage (respondents ever married (long questionnaire))	5.1	*1138*	46.2	*115*	4.2	*1428*	38.2	*374*
sex outside marriage (respondents married 5 + years)	47.7	*354*	80.7	*3371*	50.0	*198*	84.9	*4832*
sex outside cohabitation (respondents cohabiting 5 + years)	44.9	*30*	66.5	*125*	61.2	*25*	80.2	*211*
sex outside regular* partnership (single or widowed/separated/ divorced for 5 + years)	53.7	*1014*	63.8	*748*	61.6	*544*	73.4	*1067*
one-night stands† (2 + partners in the last 5 years)	38.0	*1450*	51.4	*882*	63.7	*941*	73.9	*892*
sex between 2 men	19.3	*301*	69.3	*7997*				
sex between 2 women					11.0	*197*	55.1	*10205*
abortion					12.0	*1229*	36.7	*8603*

Table 6.6 Concordance of sexual attitudes and sexual experience: proportions reporting behaviour as always or mostly wrong. Source: Interview Questions 39a–h

* comparison between those who have had sex with at least 1 non-regular partner and those who had sex only with regular partners in the last 5 years

† for those who have had 2 or more partners in the last 5 years, comparison between those who have had sex once only with any partner and those who have had sex more often

nevertheless a tendency towards greater lenience can be seen among those with some experience of the behaviours they were judging. Again it must be stressed that any direction of causal influence is unclear. In terms of chronological order, the experience – where it has occurred – clearly predates the attitudinal statement, which could suggest that attitudes are expressed to support the behaviour reported. However, it is also possible that respondent's attitudes have been constant over time and that particular views have led to certain types of behaviour.

A 'PERMISSIVENESS' AND HOMOSEXUAL ACCEPTANCE SCALE

There is evidence to suggest that respondents tend to treat most issues of sexuality in a conceptually similar manner. Permissive or censorious attitudes to the various categories of sexual relationships tend to be associated, so that individuals inclined to condemn extramarital sex or divorce, for example, tend also to be critical of homosexuality (Gorer, 1971; Airey, 1984; Harding, 1988). In order to explore patterns of responses to the various questions eliciting attitudes to sexual relationships and practices, principal component analysis was used.[1]

[1] This technique looks for common patterns of responses to each of the questions which account for as much of the variation in all the different answers as possible. More specifically, a pattern of responses is a weighting attached to the answer for each question, such that each individual's responses to all the questions can be summarized as a single weighted sum for each pattern. These patterns are called principal components. The first principal component is the weighting that will produce the greatest spread of scores among all the respondents, subject to certain technical constraints and is here used to reflect the underlying variable 'permissiveness'. The second principal component will be the weighting that will produce the greatest spread of scores after the first component has been subtracted, and so on for the third, fourth, etc.

The analysis will generate as many patterns of responses (principal components) as there are questions (in this case the eight items as listed on Table 8.5). Together, these eight principal components will account for all the variation in the original data. In general though, the first few principal components will account for most of the variation in responses and these will be of most interest.

The aim of this procedure was to see to what extent a general attribute of 'permissiveness' could be seen to exist across all these attitudinal items (see Table 6.5), relatively independently of the specific behaviour on which the view was elicited, and to what extent opinions were specific to each item or component, and were held relatively independently of one another. Responses to each of the attitudinal statements in this set (see Table 6.5) will be partly attributable to a general underlying permissiveness trait (which could be predicted to prompt similar answers to related questions), and partly to specific opinions on each individual item. This analysis allows us to see the extent to which items in the set are interrelated, one with another and each with the overall trait, the extent to which they contribute to an overall permissiveness 'score', and whether this score is associated with other selected attributes of the respondent.

The first principal component includes weights for the 8 variables, which are all positive and of the same order of magnitude. It simply measures how 'permissive' the respondent was in the sense that they were likely to choose answers at the 'not wrong' end of the scale for all questions. A high positive score indicates a very permissive attitude and a low negative score indicates a very censorious attitude. The second principal component measures views on homosexuality with positive weights for the two questions about sex between two men and between two women. Those who were less disapproving of homosexuality would get a high positive score for this principal component, and people whose opinions were the converse would get a low negative score.

In general, men's scores for permissiveness are higher (more liberal) than women's and this difference is reversed for attitudes towards homosexuality. The level of permissiveness as shown in Figure 6.8 highlights striking differences between men and women as well as age trends. Men under 45 show a relatively constant level of permissiveness, which reverses sharply after the age of 50. In contrast, women under 45 seem relatively neutral as far as a general attribute of sexual permissiveness can be measured on this scale, but become increasingly censorious with increasing years after the age of 45.

Attitudes towards homosexuality, while showing less marked age

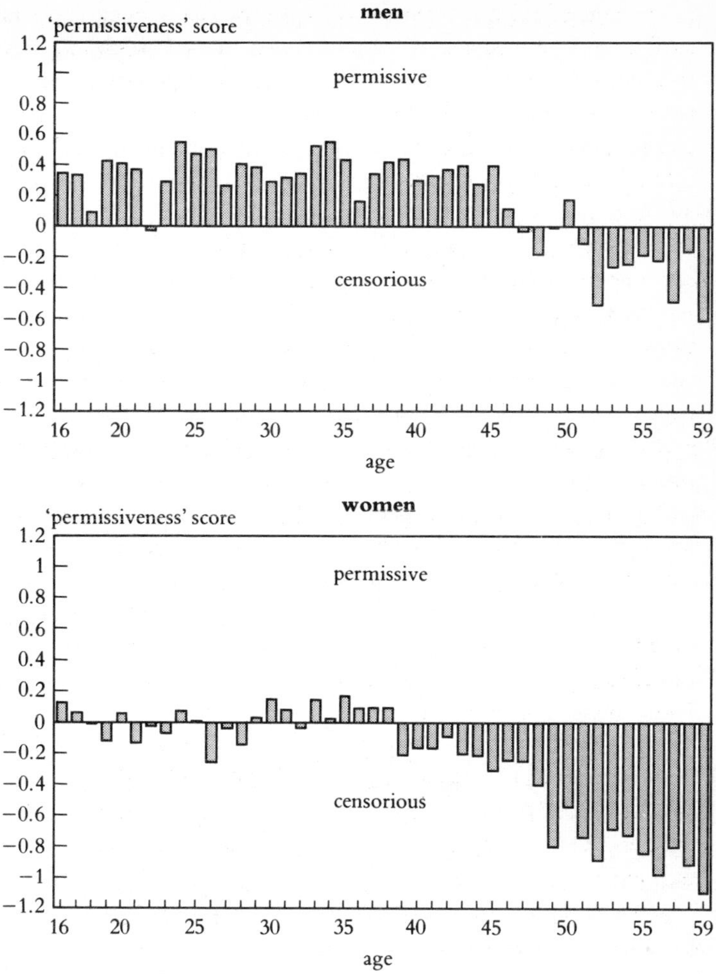

Figure 6.8 Relationship between 'permissiveness' and age. Source: Interview Questions 39a–h

trends, do show contrasting patterns for men and women. Men in general are quite intolerant of homosexuality, while women are more tolerant, particularly those in their twenties and thirties (Figure 6.9).

Other studies suggest a number of antecedent variables associated with attitudes towards homosexuality. Data from the 1981 European Values Study show that, in all countries, approval of homosexuality was greater among the young and better educated (Jensen *et al.* 1988). US research shows a higher prevalence of negative attitudes towards homosexuals in men than women; among older people and those of lower educational level (Hong, 1983, 1984; Herek, 1984; Kite, 1984; Kurdek, 1988). These findings are confirmed in our data.

We cannot tell to what extent these effects (Figures 6.8 and 6.9) can be attributed to cohort or life stage effects. Attitudes towards moral issues are shaped by an individual's social and personal experiences – those in certain age bands share a common experience, having been brought up in a particular moral climate, but views on sexual behaviour will also vary with different stages of life. These data do however testify to a strong influence of age on permissiveness.

OPINIONS ON THE SIGNIFICANCE OF SEX

In order to minimize the intrusiveness of the survey, no questions were asked about personal sexual satisfaction, the quality of sexual relationship or the importance attached to sex, in the behavioural section of the questionnaire. Instead, these areas were explored by means of attitudinal questions probing general opinions rather than personal experience. These questions were asked only in the long questionnaire so that data are available for the quarter of the sample who completed this part of the interview schedule.

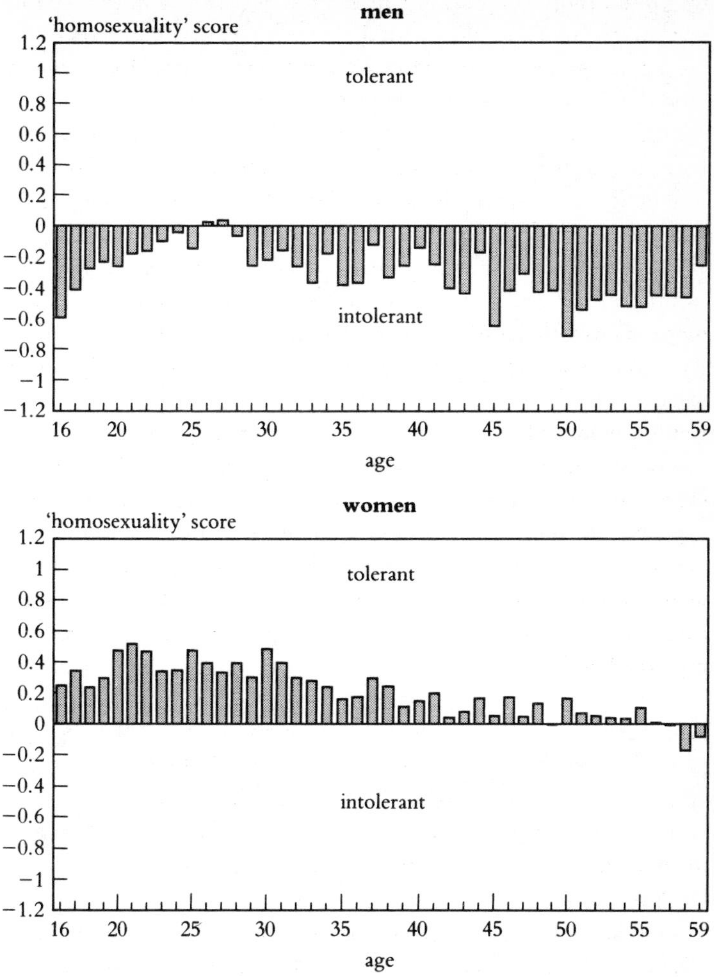

Figure 6.9 Relationship between attitude to homosexuality and age.
Source: Interview Questions 39a–h

The Importance of Sex within Marriage

Two statements were included in the set relating to the importance of sex within a marriage or relationship. These were

Companionship and affection are more important than sex in a marriage or relationship.

and

Sex is the most important part of any marriage or relationship.

Most noteworthy perhaps, given the emphasis placed on the importance of sex in some sections of the media (Brunt, 1982), is the sizeable majority of respondents who do not see sex as the most important part of a marriage or relationship. Two out of three respondents agree that companionship and affection are more important than sex in a marriage or relationship and only one in ten disagrees (Table 6.7). Reactions to a statement expressing the opposite view, that sex is the most important part of any marriage or relationship are generally consistent, though interestingly the proportion agreeing – 16.9% of men and 16.4% women – is higher than the 10.8% of men and 9.9% of women who disagree with the converse. Since agreement with the first statement is inconsistent with agreement with the second, a comparison of responses to this pair of statements provided an opportunity to gauge the extent of agreement or acquiescence bias. 58.4% of men and 60.1% of women gave consistent responses, that is their agreement or disagreement with the first statement was matched by the opposite response on the second.

Included in the attitudinal component was also a question seeking views on the importance of various factors in the making of a successful marriage (Figure 6.10). Responses showed that faithfulness and mutual respect ranked higher than all other factors. Sex emerged as the third most commonly mentioned in the rank ordering, followed by having children, shared interests, shared chores, adequate income and shared religious beliefs.

Table 6.7 (*opposite*) Views on sexual behaviour and sexual satisfaction. *Now please would you say how far you agree or disagree with each of these things . . .?* Source: Interview Questions 40a–h

		agree or agree strongly %	neither agree/ disagree %	disagree or disagree strongly %	*base*
It is natural for people to want sex less often as they get older.	**men**	37.9	28.3	33.8	*2082*
	women	37.7	28.5	33.7	*2567*
Having a sexual relationship outside a regular one doesn't necessarily harm that relationship.	**men**	17.2	11.6	71.2	*2079*
	women	13.2	8.2	78.6	*2566*
Companionship and affection are more important than sex in a marriage or relationship.	**men**	67.2	22.0	10.8	*2079*
	women	68.4	21.7	9.9	*2563*
Sex without orgasm, or climax, cannot be really satisfying for a man.	**men**	48.7	17.4	33.9	*2077*
	women	43.3	27.3	29.4	*2557*
Sex without orgasm, or climax, cannot be really satisfying for a woman.	**men**	37.4	27.7	34.9	*2078*
	women	28.6	21.5	49.9	*2562*
A person who sticks with one partner is likely to have a more satisfying sex life than someone who has many partners.	**men**	50.4	28.9	20.8	*2080*
	women	51.6	30.0	18.5	*2552*
Sex is the most important part of any marriage or relationship.	**men**	16.9	20.9	62.2	*2078*
	women	16.4	15.8	67.8	*2560*
Sex tends to get better the longer you know someone.	**men**	68.6	21.8	9.6	*2080*
	women	69.9	19.3	10.9	*2560*

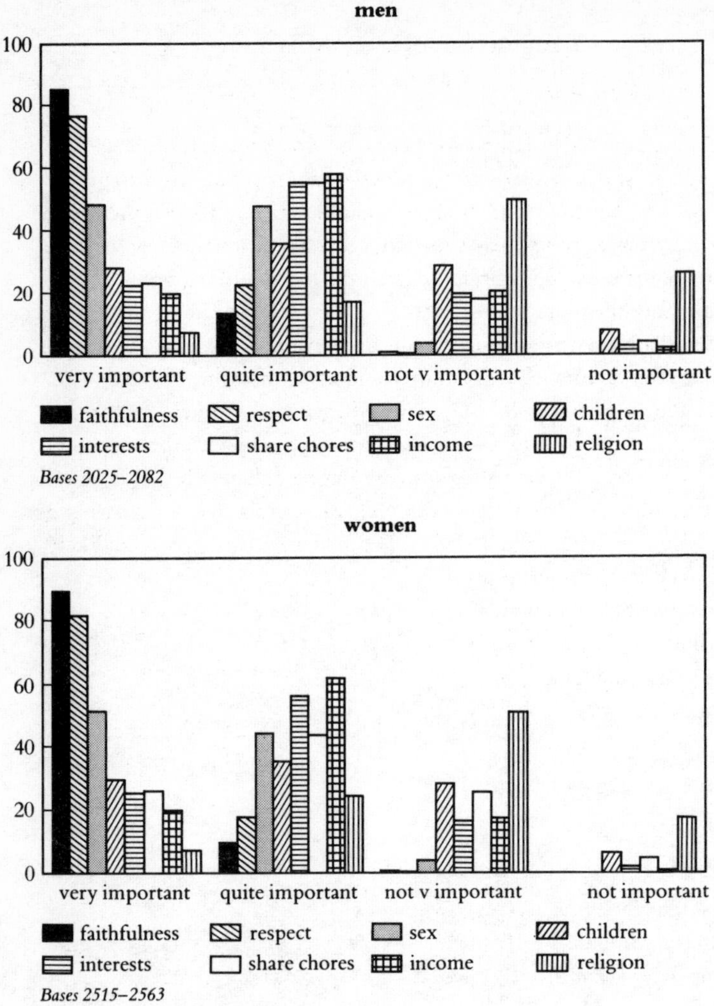

Figure 6.10 Factors associated with a happy marriage. Source: Interview Questions 37a–h

The Changing Importance of Sex

With Age

The statement 'it is natural for people to want sex less often as they get older' was intended to assess perceptions of the importance of sex with advancing years. It elicited neither strong disagreement nor agreement and responses were fairly evenly distributed across the scale (Table 6.8). Young people with no first-hand experience were predictably more likely to report that they 'didn't know' than were those in the oldest age group (10.8% of men and 8.1% of women aged 16–24, compared with 2.1% of men and 2.8% of women aged 45–59).

At the aggregate level, the views of men and women correspond well: almost 38% of both men and women agreed with the statement and 33.8% of both men and women disagreed. These broad findings conceal some variations between the sexes with marital status and age. Women who are married or living with a man are more likely to agree than men in these categories.

	men		**women**	
	%	*base**	%	*base**
age				
16–24	35.7	*508*	28.0	*531*
25–34	30.3	*543*	27.8	*720*
35–44	36.1	*536*	38.1	*634*
45–59	50.6	*494*	55.5	*682*
marital status				
married	39.6	*1162*	43.1	*1567*
cohabiting	26.9	*134*	31.7	*198*
widowed	30.8	*15**	46.6	*49*
separated/divorced	38.0	*103*	31.0	*212*
single	37.4	*669*	25.7	*539*

Table 6.8 Proportion of respondents agreeing or agreeing strongly with the statement: *It is natural for people to want sex less often as they get older.* Source: Interview Question 40a

* note small base.

Differences between the marital status groups – married and widowed people are more likely to hold that sexual appetite is dulled with age, those who are single or cohabiting less so – may well reflect age differences (Table 6.8). Contrary to the commonly held view that young people see themselves as having a monopoly on sex, and have difficulty in imagining older people having sexual needs, these data show few signs of ageism in the views of the younger respondents. More than half of all 45–59-year-olds agree that it is natural for people to want sex less often as they get older, compared with roughly a third of under-35s, and this difference is more marked for women than men.

With the Length of the Relationship

Two statements sought to elicit views relating to the effect of the duration and nature of relationships on sexual satisfaction:

A person who sticks with one partner is likely to have a more satisfying sex life than someone who has many partners.

and

Sex tends to get better the longer you know someone.

Both of these statements are of significance in the context of health educational advice in relation to HIV/AIDS and sexual health. Those seeking to promote monogamous and long-term relationships can be heartened by the fact that the majority view on both is that exclusivity and familiarity are more likely to lead to satisfying sex lives than short-term, multiple sexual partnerships. Half of the sample agreed or agreed strongly with the statement to the effect that monogamy brings greater sexual satisfaction than having multiple partners, and more than two-thirds that the quality of sexual satisfaction increases with the duration of the relationship. In view of the higher level of support for the second statement compared with the first, it might be productive for health educators and those concerned with effective communication aimed at stemming the spread of HIV and other sexually transmitted infections to harness this support in their efforts to secure healthier lifestyles.

Given the gender-related differences in attitudes to non-exclusive and casual sex (see above, pp. 249–53), it is perhaps surprising that gender-related differences are not shown in the responses to the attitudinal statement linking numbers of partners with the quality of sexual experience. Around 50% of both men and women agree that monogamy gives rise to greater sexual satisfaction and 20.8% men and 18.5% women disagree (Table 6.7).

The Importance of Monogamy

The statement 'Having a sexual relationship outside a regular one doesn't necessarily harm that relationship' required respondents to focus more on the consequences of infidelity than on its intrinsic morality. The nature of the relationship – whether it was marital, cohabiting or simply regular – was not specified. The pattern of responses varied little with the relationship status, except in so far as respondents were less likely to choose the extreme response option 'Disagree strongly'. None the less, aggregating the responses 'Disagree' and 'Disagree strongly', the majority of respondents, 71.2% of men and 78.9% of women, do not agree that no harm would be done to a regular sexual relationship by straying outside it.

Those who are married are more likely to regard sexual infidelity as potentially harmful than those who are single. Interestingly, among respondents who are cohabiting with a partner of the opposite sex, the pattern of responses by women is more similar to that of married women than single women; the same proportion of married as of cohabiting women (81%) disagree with the statement compared with 74% of single women. For men the reverse is true – 65% of cohabiting men are in disagreement, compared with 75% of married men and 68% of those who are single – revealing greater discordance between the sexes in couples who live together outside marriage.

The Role of Orgasm in Sexual Satisfaction

No questions were asked about orgasm or sexual satisfaction in the behavioural component of the questionnaire. Attitudes relating to a generalized 'other' rather than the respondent were considered to be less intrusive. The question of whether and to what extent orgasm is necessary to sexual satisfaction is of interest because of the role of ejaculation in the transmission of HIV. But in view of the proliferation of interest in and advice on how to achieve sexual satisfaction in women's journals and men's magazines it is also of interest to investigate how highly the sexual climax is rated in terms of sexual satisfaction.

Respondents were asked to express agreement or disagreement with the statement 'Sex without orgasm cannot be really satisfying for a man' and the statement was repeated in a subsequent version substituting 'for a woman'. Both were asked of both male and female respondents. This is not, apparently, an issue on which people generally tend to feel vehemently. Only a small minority selected the response options that allowed them to express the strongest agreement or disagreement.

In terms of gender differences in responses, men attach greater importance to orgasm in sexual satisfaction for either sex than do women, and both men and women see orgasm as more essential to a man's sexual satisfaction than to that of a woman. However, neither of these two views was held quite as strongly or as universally as could have been anticipated.

Nearly half (48.7%) of all men agree or agree strongly that orgasm is necessary to male sexual satisfaction, compared with 43.3% of women who hold this view in relation to men; but a third of all men disagree with the statement expressing this view. Orgasm is clearly not universally conceived as a prerequisite to male sexual satisfaction. This tends to run counter to the popular stereotype of men as sexually goal-seeking.

Moreover, while both men and women attach greater importance to the male orgasm than to the female orgasm in sexual satisfaction, the proportion of men who believe the female orgasm to be necessary to women's sexual satisfaction is higher than the proportion of women who themselves hold this view, so that it seems not to be the case that men put the achievement of their own satisfaction before that of their partners. 37.4% of men compared with 28.6% of women agree that sex without orgasm cannot be really satisfying for women (Table 6.7).

SUMMARY

The view which emerges predominantly from these data is one of the British as a nation strongly committed to the ideal of the heterosexual, monogamous union, but of considerable relaxation in attitudes towards teenage sexuality and, in particular, sex before marriage. Although there is no widespread support for a lowering of the age of sexual consent, views on the age before which sexual intercourse is thought to be inadvisable accord remarkably well with current patterns of behaviour. Nor is there apparent widespread opposition to the idea of sexual intercourse occurring before marriage. Acceptance of premarital sex is now nearly universal, as indeed is its practice (Chapter 2).

The pattern of response to questions relating to sexual exclusivity contrasts markedly. The consensus view is that sex outside a regular relationship is wrong and the strength of disapproval increases only slightly with the extent to which the relationship is formalized by marriage or common residence. Disapproval of infidelity extends to all age groups, the young being only marginally more tolerant than older respondents.

Ideals of monogamy seem to be more strongly held by women than men. Women are generally less tolerant than men of non-monogamous relationships. This is seen most clearly in relation to casual sex, the notion of which finds far greater acceptance among men than women.

Responses to attitudinal questions show widespread condemnation of homosexual relationships, and reporting of such relationships (see Chapter 5) must be seen in this context. Here the pattern of gender differences is reversed and greater tolerance is found among women. The use of principle component analysis provides some evidence of an underlying attitudinal trait of permissiveness. It does not, however, account for all differences in attitudes; people exhibit varying profiles across different issues.

Bringing together practices reported, and attitudes towards them, reveals some congruence between the two. Not surprisingly, those who practise particular behaviours are more likely to condone them and the converse is also true.

Responses to the questions on sexual satisfaction and the importance of sex within a relationship reveal the majority view to be that sex is not considered the most important part of a relationship; that a monogamous relationship is more likely to lead to greater sexual satisfaction; and that sexual appetite does not necessarily diminish with age.

REFERENCES

Airey, C. (1984). 'Social and Moral Values', in R. Jowell and C. Airey (eds), *British Social Attitudes Survey: The 1984 Report.* Aldershot: Gower

Annual Abstract of Statistics (1992), No. 128. London: HMSO

Brook, L. (1988). 'The Public's Response to AIDS', in R. Jowell, S. Witherspoon and L. Brook (eds), *British Social Attitudes Survey: The 5th Report.* Aldershot: Gower

Brunt, R. (1982). 'The Immense Verbosity: Permissive Sexual Advice in the 1970s', in R. Brunt and C. Rowan (eds), *Feminism, Culture and Politics* (pp. 143–70). London: Lawrence and Wishart

CSO (1991). *Social Trends 21; 1991 Edition.* London: HMSO

Foa, U. G., B. Anderson, J. Converse Jnr, W. A. Urbansky, M. J. Cawley III, S. M. Muhlhausen, and K. Y. Tornblom (1987). 'Gender-related Sexual Attitudes: Some Cross-cultural Similarities and Differences', *Sex Roles*, 16(9/10): 511–19

Ford, C. S., and F. A. Beach (1952). *Patterns of Sexual Behaviour.* London: Eyre and Spottiswoode

Francome, C. (1988). 'Public Support for the Right to Choose Abortion', *New Humanist*, 103: 15–16

Glenn, N., and C. N. Weaver (1979). 'Attitudes towards Premarital, Extramarital, and Homosexual Relations in the US in the 1970s', *Journal of Sex Research*, 15: 108–118

Gorer, G. (1971). *Sex and Marriage in England Today.* London: Nelson

Harding, S. (1988). 'Trends in Permissiveness', in R. Jowell, S. Witherspoon and L. Brook (eds), *British Social Attitudes: The 5th Report.* Aldershot: Gower

Herek, G. M. (1984). 'Beyond "Homophobia": A Social Psychological Perspective on Attitudes toward Lesbians and Gay Men', *Journal of Homosexuality*, 10: 1–22

Hong, S. M. (1983). 'Sex, Religion and Factor Analytically Derived Attitudes toward Homosexuality', *Australian Journal of Sex, Marriage and Family*, 4: 142–50

Hong, S. M. (1984). 'Australian Attitudes towards Homosexuality: A Comparison with College Students', *Journal of Psychology* 117: 89–95

Jensen, L., D. Gambles, and J. Olsen (1988). 'Attitudes toward Homosexuality: A Cross-Cultural Analysis of Predictors', *International Journal of Social Psychiatry*, 34 (1): 47–57

Kite, M. E. (1984). 'Sex Differences in Attitudes towards Homosexuals: A Meta-analytic Review', *Journal of Homosexuality*, 10: 69–82

Kurdek, L. A. (1988). 'Correlates of Negative Attitudes toward Homosexuals in Heterosexual College Students', *Sex Roles*, 18 (11/12): 727–38

Lewis, J. (1987). 'Abortion and the New Conservatism', *New Left Review*, March/April, 123–8

Russell, B. (1929). *Marriage and Morals*. London: Allen and Unwin

Saunders, J. M., and J. N. Edwards (1984). 'Extramarital Sexuality: A Predictive Model of Permissive Attitudes', *Journal of Marriage and the Family*, 46 (4): 825–35

Scull, A. (1989). 'Attitudes and Explanations', *The Times Literary Supplement*, 28 July, 820

Singh, B. K. (1980). 'Trends in Attitudes to Premarital Sexual Relations', *Journal of Marriage and the Family*, 42 (2): 387–93

Smith, T. W. (1990). 'The Polls – A Report: The Sexual Revolution', *Public Opinion Quarterly*, 54: 415–35

Spencer, L., A. Faulkner, and J. Keegan (1988). *Talking about Sex*. London: Social and Community Planning Research

Weeks, J. (1988). 'Clause for Concern', *Marxism Today*, February 1988

Wellings, K., and J. Wadsworth (1990). 'AIDS and the Moral Climate', in R. Jowell *et al.* (eds), *British Social Attitudes: The 7th Report*. Aldershot: Gower

Whitley, B. E., Jnr (1988). 'Sex Differences in Heterosexuals' Attitudes toward Homosexuals: It Depends upon What you Ask', *Journal of Sex Research*, 24: 287–91

CHAPTER 7

Physical Health and Sexual Behaviour

INTRODUCTION

The relationship between many aspects of lifestyle and health have been studied but sexual behaviour is a notable exception where little work has been undertaken. This chapter sets out to examine the relationship between sexual behaviour and perceived health, health behaviour, health service use and adverse outcomes related to fertility and infertility. In other areas of epidemiological research a great deal is known, for example, about the adverse influences of smoking on health and to a lesser extent the influences of diet, alcohol consumption and social environment (Shaper, 1980; Blaxter, 1987; Thorogood *et al.*, 1987; Barker *et al.*, 1989; Davey Smith *et al.*, 1990; Peto *et al.*, 1992). Follow-up studies have shed light on the long-term relationships between health and antecedent factors. Behaviour may influence health, but health may likewise influence behaviour. Unemployment may contribute to ill-health, but those who are sick may be less able to work (Moser *et al.*, 1990). Alcohol consumption may influence heart disease risk, while those who are sick may be more likely to give up drinking (Shaper *et al.*, 1990). In a cross-sectional survey, causality cannot be imputed in exploring relationships between physical well-being, health-related behaviour and sexual behaviour. Sexual expression is an essential component of human relationships and in itself may promote quality of life and a sense of physical, social and psychological well-being. Set against this are potential negative consequences such as sexually transmitted disease, unwanted pregnancy and infertility.

In relation to sexual health promotion, it is important to achieve a better understanding of the relationship between patterns of sexual and other health-related behaviour and health outcomes if characteristics of those at greater risk of unwanted pregnancy and sexually transmitted disease (STD) are to be identified. In this chapter, the relationship between perceived health, body mass index, smoking, alcohol consumption and sexual behaviour are explored. Patterns of injecting drug use are discussed in relation to the HIV epidemic. Sexual behaviour and health service use are explored in relation to STD clinic attendance and HIV antibody testing. Finally, the relationship between sexual lifestyle and infertility, miscarriage, stillbirth and abortion are discussed.

QUESTION FORMAT

Questions about perceived health and chronic illness, alcohol consumption, smoking, height and weight were asked in the face-to-face interview, and a question on injecting prescribed and non-prescribed drugs was completed in the booklet. Inquiry into sexual and reproductive health included questions on experience of fertility and infertility, and attendance at an STD clinic. Women only were asked about experience of miscarriage and termination of pregnancy (abortion). A question on HIV antibody testing was also included (Booklet Question 20). This inquired not only whether the respondent had had such a test but also the reason for testing. Men were also asked whether or not they were circumcised.

REPORTED HEALTH AND SEXUAL BEHAVIOUR

Questions on health included an item on self-reported health status on a 5-point scale (Interview Question 2a). As in other surveys (Cox *et al.*, 1987) the majority of men and women of all ages described their health as fairly good or very good for their age (Figure 7.1). Age trends show only a moderate effect with an increasing proportion reporting their health to be poor or very poor with increasing age, while at the same time the proportion

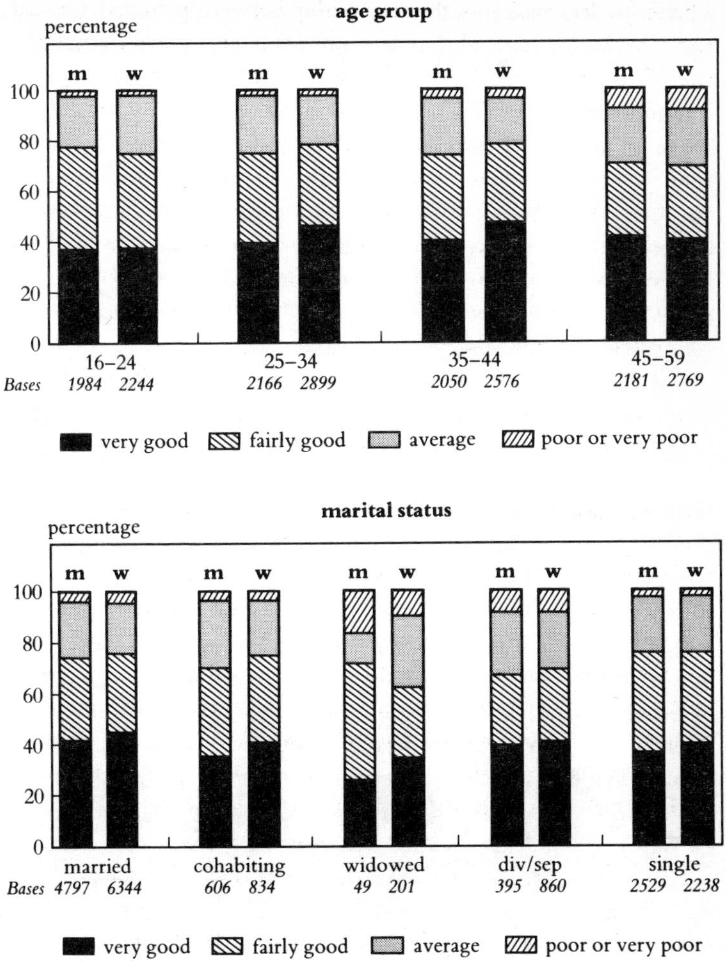

Figure 7.1 Reported health by age group and marital status. Source: Interview Question 2a

reporting very good health 'for your age' also increased (Figure 7.1). There were only minimal differences between men and women in self-reported health status.

Marital status was more closely related to reported health in bivariate analysis (Figure 7.1). While the proportion reporting very good health was relatively stable across the marital-status categories, there were quite marked differences in the proportion reporting poor or very poor health by marital-status group. Divorced and separated respondents were more likely to report poor health than married people (Figure 7.1). In a cross-sectional survey, the reasons for this association must remain speculative since ill-health may influence the likelihood of marriage or marital breakdown while the absence of a long-term relationship may in turn influence physical, economic or psychological well-being.

A more objective question on health was asked about disability, chronic medical condition and illness or accident in the last 5 years affecting the respondent's health for at least 3 months (Interview Questions 2b–d) (Table 7.1). The percentage of respondents reporting a permanent disability or chronic condition increased quite markedly with age, although the age trend for reported 3-month illness was more marked for women than for men. This is similar to age trends in other surveys (OPCS, 1992). The relationship between these three measures and reported health is complex. 13,130 respondents had no disability, no chronic condition and no illness whose effects lasted at least 3 months. Of these, 81.6% felt their health was good or very good and less than 1% felt their health was poor or very poor. Of 468 respondents who reported permanent disability as well as a chronic condition and a 3-month illness, 50.0% reported that their health was poor, while 23.9% felt their health was good or very good. In summary, most respondents with no identifiable serious medical problem felt that their health was good, while of those with problems, more than one in five took the view that their health was good.

Figure 7.2 illustrates the relationship between perceived health and sexual behaviour. Frequency of heterosexual intercourse was weakly related to perceived health. Those who experienced no intercourse in the last 4 weeks were more likely to report poor health. These respondents were also likely to include disproportion-

	permanent disability		chronic condition		3-month illness	
	%	*base*	%	*base*	%	*base*
age group						
			men			
16–24	6.5	*1979*	7.7	*1982*	12.6	*1984*
25–34	8.3	*2165*	10.7	*2165*	10.4	*2167*
35–44	10.9	*2050*	15.8	*2050*	13.9	*2051*
45–59	19.9	*2181*	26.2	*2182*	16.3	*2181*
all ages	11.5	*8376*	15.3	*8379*	13.3	*8382*
			women			
16–24	5.9	*2244*	11.1	*2244*	9.2	*2244*
25–34	6.7	*2898*	14.7	*2899*	11.4	*2895*
35–44	9.9	*2574*	19.5	*2570*	16.5	*2571*
45–59	20.1	*2768*	34.4	*2769*	20.0	*2769*
all ages	10.9	*10484*	20.3	*10482*	14.4	*10479*

Table 7.1 Proportions reporting permanent disability, chronic condition and illness lasting at least 3 months by age group. Source: Interview Questions 2b–d

ate numbers of older respondents without a current sexual partner. With increasing frequency of sexual intercourse, respondents were less likely to report poor health, although the effect is more marked for men than for women. Similar trends are evident when perceived health is analysed in relation to numbers of sexual partners in the last 5 years, with decreasing proportions reporting ill-health with increasing numbers of partners in bivariate analysis. In order to adjust for the effects of age and other social variables, multiple logistic regression was used (results not shown). This confirmed the very weak relationship between perceived health and sexual behaviour, suggesting that perceived health *per se* has little influence on overall patterns of sexual lifestyle.

Number of occasions of sex in the last 4 weeks

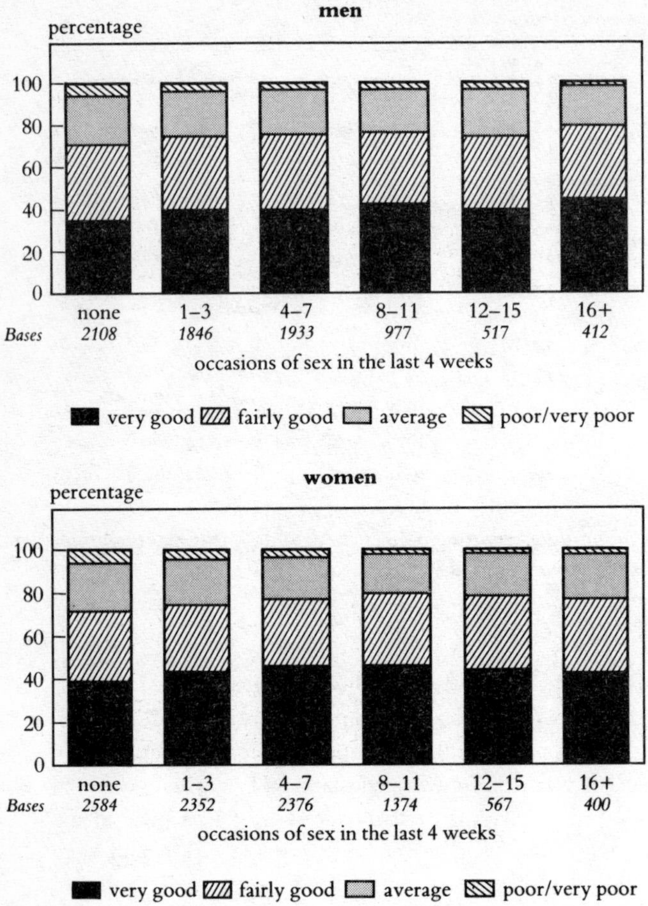

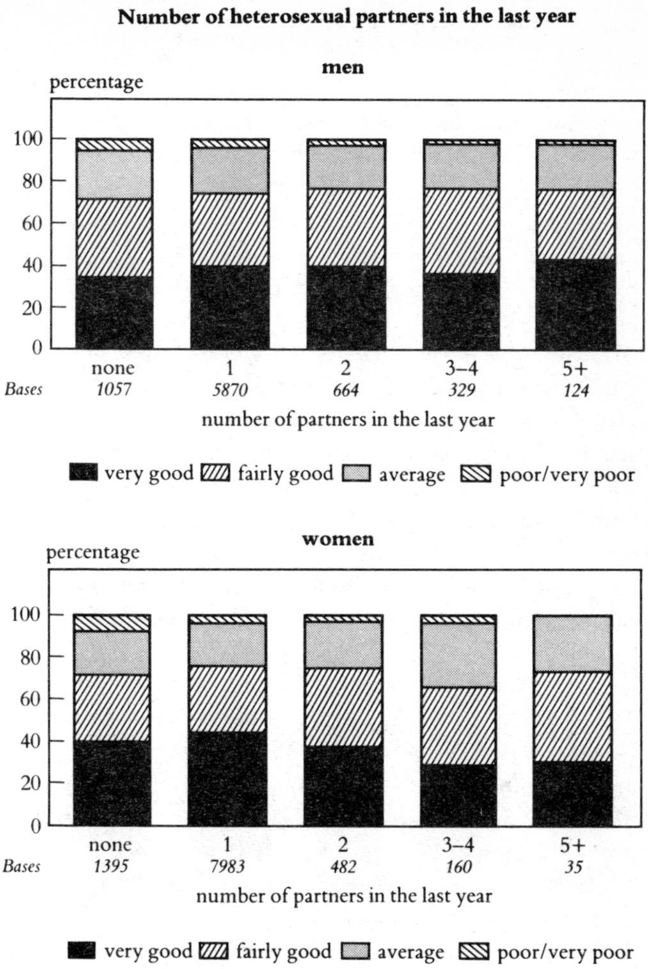

Figure 7.2 Heterosexual behaviour and reported health. Source: Interview Question 2a; Booklet Question 7d

Smoking and Sexual Behaviour

Smoking is known to be causally related to a number of serious conditions including lung cancer, lung disease and heart disease (Peto *et al.*, 1992), and has also been found to be associated with a number of outcomes related to sexual health. Early studies of adverse health outcomes among oral contraceptive users had to take careful account of potential confounding by smoking since oral contraceptive users are more likely to smoke than non-users, suggesting some relationship between sexual lifestyle and smoking (RCGP, 1974; Wright *et al.*, 1978). Oral contraceptive users may have different sexual lifestyles from non-users (see Chapter 8). Studies of cervical cancer have shown an increased risk associated with early age at first intercourse, numbers of sexual partners, and smoking (Boyd and Doll, 1964; Singer, 1979; Brown *et al.*, 1984). The strength of this association has led many to conclude that the relationship between smoking and cervical cancer risk is causal (Winkelstein, 1990) but the subject remains controversial and may still be confounded by the association between smoking and sexual behaviour.

Table 7.2 shows the reported pattern of smoking by age group. This is similar to that reported in other surveys (Cox *et al.*, 1987; OPCS, 1991). The proportion of those who have never smoked declines with age, most markedly for men. Those under 35 were more likely to be current smokers than those over 35, reflecting the increasing proportion who have given up in older age groups. The youngest age group, 16–24, were the least likely to be heavy smokers (15 or more cigarettes per day).

Figure 7.3 illustrates the relationship between smoking and number of heterosexual partners reported in the last year, showing a striking trend of increasing prevalence of current smoking with increasing numbers of sexual partners, a finding that is consistent with data from studies of contraceptive use and cervical cancer (Winkelstein, 1990). Such a bivariate relationship may be confounded by other influences on patterns of partnership formation and smoking, such as age (Chapter 3) and this relationship is explored in greater detail below.

In addition to a relationship between smoking and sexual partner-

age group	16–24 %	25–34 %	35–44 %	45–59 %	all ages
			men		
non-smoker	53.1	43.0	36.7	27.0	39.7
ex-smoker	6.3	15.4	25.4	39.7	22.0
smokes < 15 per day	22.8	15.8	11.7	9.5	14.8
smokes 15 + per day	17.8	25.8	26.2	23.9	23.5
base	*1963*	*2151*	*2031*	*2161*	*8306*
			women		
non-smoker	52.7	47.0	42.5	43.5	46.2
ex-smoker	6.4	14.3	20.8	22.5	16.4
smokes < 15 per day	25.5	16.9	13.1	11.5	16.4
smokes 15 + per day	15.3	21.9	23.7	22.5	21.1
base	*2215*	*2874*	*2544*	*2739*	*10372*

Table 7.2 Smoking behaviour by age group. Source: Interview Question 5

ships, there is also a weak relationship with the number of heterosexual acts in the last 4 weeks, those with a high frequency (12 or more) being more likely to smoke (Figure 7.3). Both these relationships remained after adjustment for age and marital status.

Alcohol Consumption and Sexual Behaviour

An association between alcohol consumption and sexual behaviour might be expected on a number of grounds, although the precise direction of the relationship may not be obvious. On the one hand the social circumstances in which alcohol is consumed and the lessening of inhibition resulting from consumption might be associated with higher levels of sexual activity or new sexual partnership. Conversely, the depressant effect of large quantities of alcohol might be expected to have the reverse effect. Health educators have expressed concern that individuals may increase their risk-taking behaviour as a result of intoxication by alcohol. Recent studies, particularly among gay men, have found little evidence that alcohol

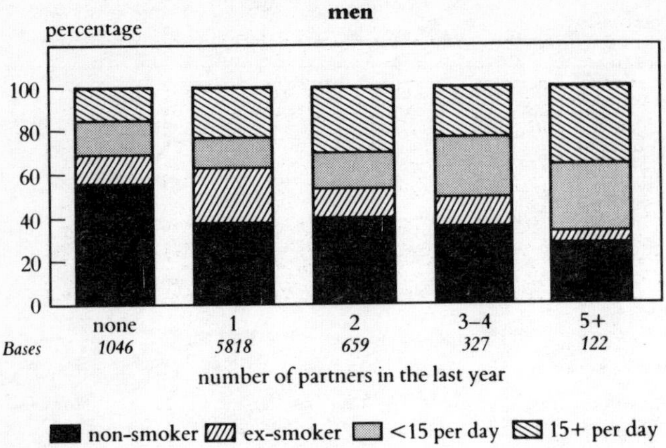
men
percentage
100
80
60
40
20
0
none
1
2
3–4
5+
Bases
1046
5818
659
327
122
number of partners in the last year
non-smoker
ex-smoker
<15 per day
15+ per day

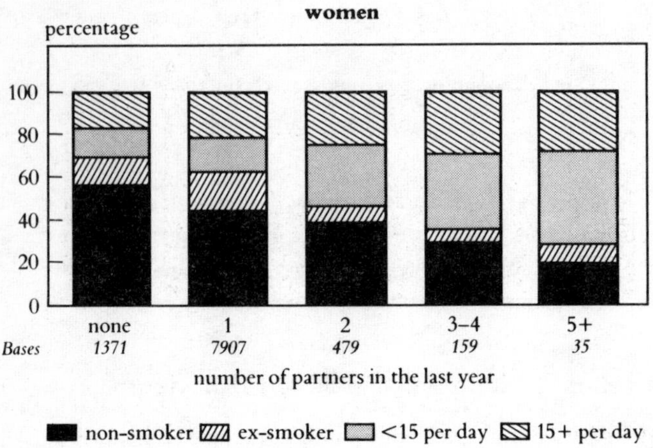
women
percentage
100
80
60
40
20
0
none
1
2
3–4
5+
Bases
1371
7907
479
159
35
number of partners in the last year
non-smoker
ex-smoker
<15 per day
15+ per day

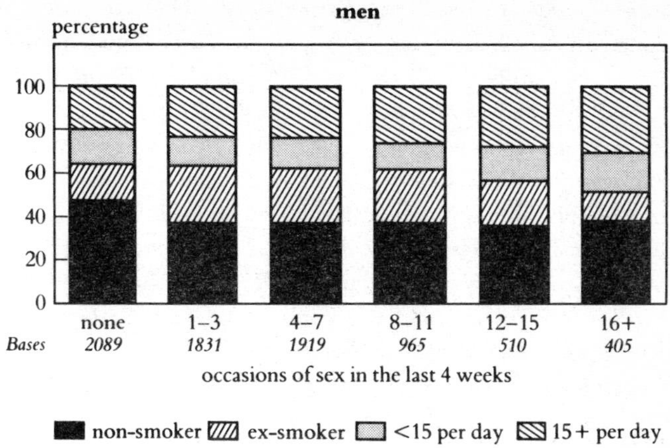

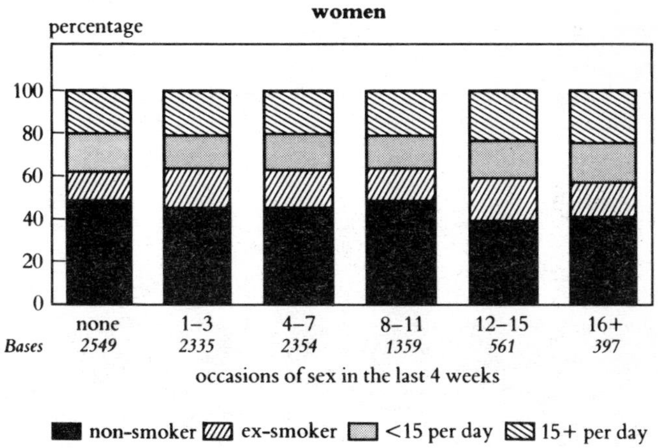

Figure 7.3 Heterosexual behaviour by smoking. Source: Interview Questions 5a–c; Booklet Question 2a

intake is associated with more risky sexual behaviour at the time of consumption (Weatherburn *et al.*, 1993). There is no evidence from the present study that alcohol consumption has a major role to play in decisions about first intercourse (see Chapter 2). It is not possible to examine the immediate relationship between consuming alcohol and levels of sexual activity under its influence, but overall patterns of alcohol consumption can be related to sexual behaviour. By so doing, it is not intended to impute a causal relationship between alcohol consumption and its immediate effects on sexual behaviour. Rather it is intended to examine the relationship between other aspects of lifestyle and sexual behaviour.

Table 7.3 shows patterns of estimated alcohol consumption by sex and age group. Estimates of number of units consumed were derived from a combination of frequency of drinking and number of drinks consumed. These were categorized into 4 groups similar to those used by the General Household Survey (GHS) (OPCS, 1992). Reported levels of consumption are slightly lower than in the 1990 GHS but this probably derives from differences in question

age group	16–24 %	25–34 %	35–44 %	45–59 %	all ages %
alcohol consumption			**men**		
none never drinks alcohol	10.4	6.9	7.4	10.8	8.9
low ≤ 20 units per week	71.5	77.9	73.6	72.7	74.0
moderate 21–50 units per week	15.9	12.1	15.0	12.3	13.8
high 51 + units per week	2.2	3.1	4.0	4.3	3.4
base	*1982*	*2162*	*2046*	*2179*	*8370*
			women		
none never drinks alcohol	14.3	12.7	11.7	17.7	14.1
low ≤ 14 units per week	70.9	77.5	80.7	76.7	76.7
moderate ≤ 15–35 units per week	4.5	9.5	7.0	5.2	8.8
high 36 + units per week	0.3	0.3	0.6	0.5	0.4
base	*2241*	*2896*	*2569*	*2767*	*10473*

Table 7.3 Estimated weekly alcohol consumption by age group. Source: Interview Question 4

wording and the less detailed data collection in the survey. The tendency for people to under-report alcohol consumption in surveys is well known. Age is not strongly related to alcohol consumption (Table 7.3), although among men high consumption (51 or more units per week) increased with increasing age.

The relationship between alcohol consumption and number of sexual partners is shown in Figure 7.4. As with smoking, there is a marked positive relationship between increasing alcohol consumption and numbers of sexual partners for both men and women. Only 5.8% of men and 3.1% of women who had 3 or more partners in the last year never drink alcohol, compared with over 20% of those with no partners. This is balanced by an increase in the proportions reporting 'moderate' or 'high' alcohol consumption by those with 3 or more partners compared to those with no partners (Figure 7.4).

Alcohol consumption was also related to the frequency of acts of heterosexual sex in the last four weeks (Figure 7.4). With increasing frequency of intercourse, the proportion of teetotallers declined while the proportion of moderate or heavy drinkers increased.

Body Mass Index and Sexual Behaviour

The distribution of self-reported height and weight in the sample was very similar to that derived from formal measurement in a similar population (Cox *et al.*, 1987). Given the concerns of fashion and culture with body size and sexual attractiveness, the relationship between body mass index (BMI, weight (kg) / height^2 (m)) and sexual behaviour was examined. Figure 7.5 shows a small decrease in height with age and a steady increase of weight with age. Taking account of both these effects, not surprisingly, BMI shows a pronounced increase with age. Figure 7.6 shows a strong relationship between the proportion of respondents reporting 2 or more partners in the last year and quartiles of BMI, with the likelihood of reporting 2 or more partners declining rapidly with increased BMI. This relationship is likely to be confounded by the relationship between BMI and age and is explored in greater detail in a logistic regression model.

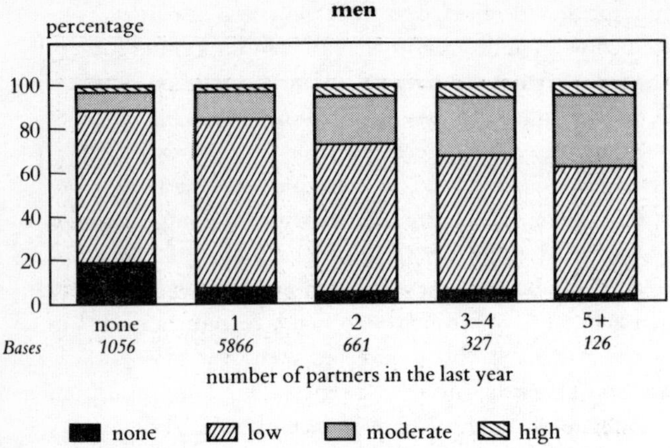
men
percentage
100
80
60
40
20
0
none
1
2
3–4
5+
Bases
1056
5866
661
327
126
number of partners in the last year
none
low
moderate
high

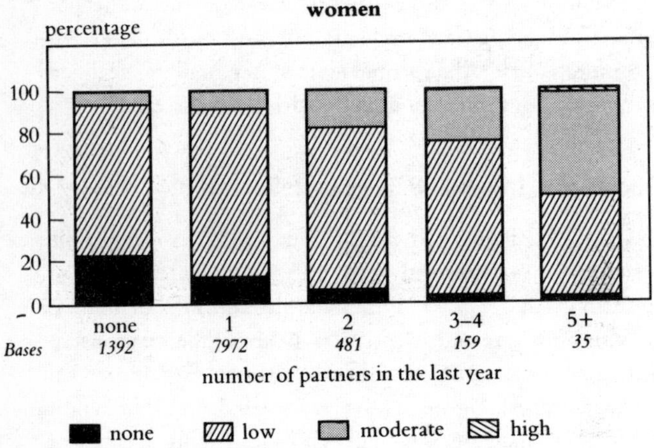
women
percentage
100
80
60
40
20
0
none
1
2
3–4
5+
Bases
1392
7972
481
159
35
number of partners in the last year
none
low
moderate
high

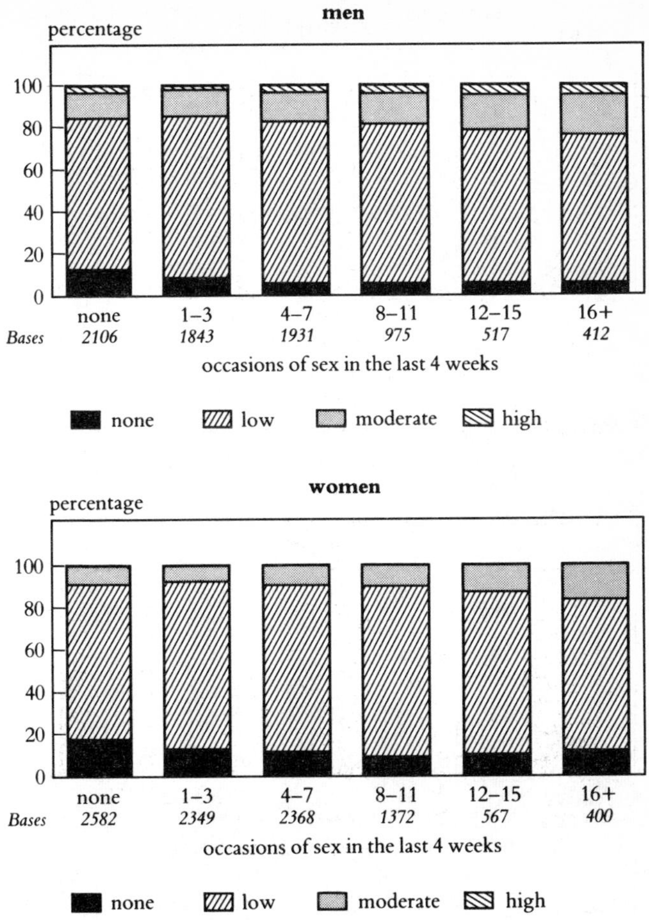

Figure 7.4 Heterosexual behaviour by alcohol consumption. Source: Interview Questions 4a, 4b; Booklet Question 2a

Body Mass Index

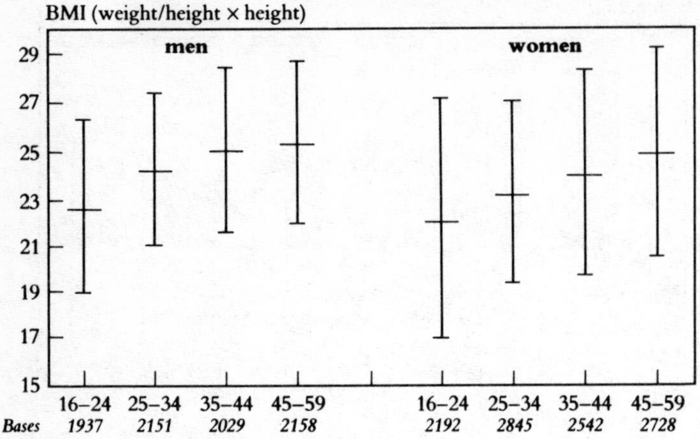

Height

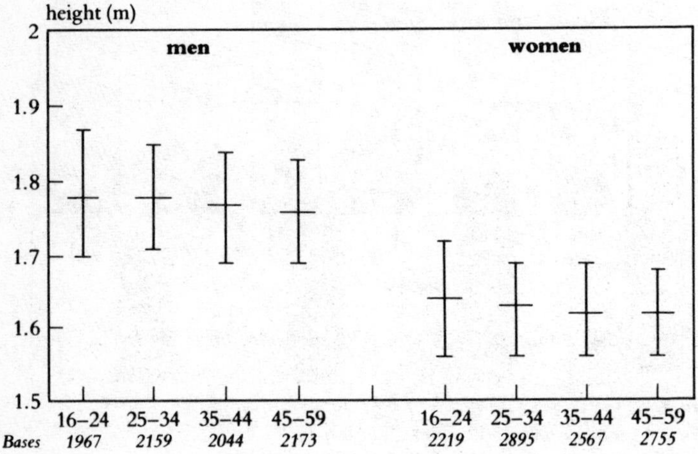

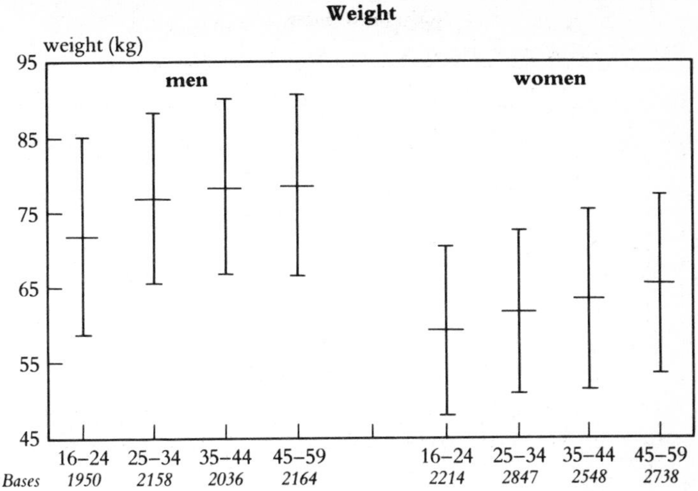

Figure 7.5 Mean and standard deviation of body mass index, height and weight. Source: Interview Question 6

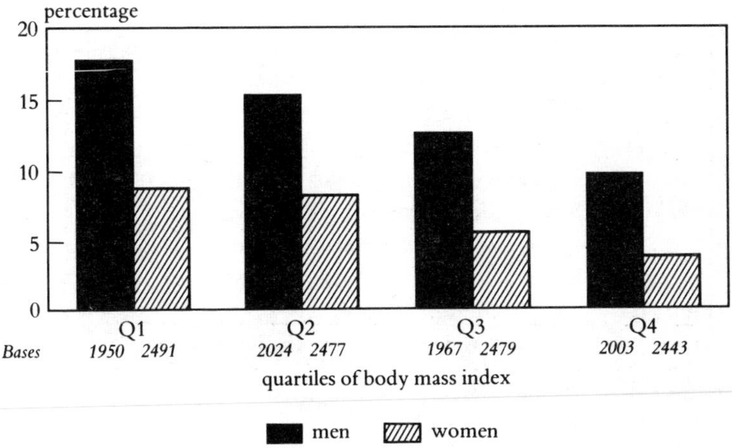

Figure 7.6 Proportion of respondents reporting 2 or more partners in the last year by body mass index. Source: Interview Question 6; Booklet Question 7d

The Relationship between Health-related Behaviour and Sexual Behaviour

The foregoing analysis indicates that there may be complex relationships between health-related behaviour, demographic variables and sexual behaviour. The health-related factors found to be associated with sexual behaviour in bivariate analysis were examined in a logistic regression model which also took account of the demographic factors associated with reporting increased numbers of sexual partners which were identified in Chapter 3. Variables included in the model were age group, social class, marital status, BMI, smoking and alcohol consumption. These were examined in relation to the likelihood of reporting 2 or more partners in the last year (Figure 7.7). Results are expressed as adjusted odds ratios with their 95% confidence intervals. As discussed in Chapter 3, age group and marital status exert strong influences on patterns of sexual partnership, but after taking account of these variables, those who smoked or drank alcohol were significantly more likely to report multiple partnerships. (BMI was not a significant factor in the model, largely due to its strong association with age.)

The data are consistent with the well-known association between smoking and drinking observed in other studies (Cox *et al.*, 1987). Our data clearly indicate a further association between smoking, drinking and multiple sexual partnerships. This confirms the notion that there is a relationship between a number of risk-taking behaviours. These effects appear to be independent of age and marital status. In the multivariate model, marital status remains the strongest effect, but the adjusted odds ratio for moderate or high alcohol consumption is in excess of 3 for both men and women reporting 2 or more partners in the last year.

Injecting Drug Use

In Europe and the US, one of the predominant modes of HIV transmission is through sharing syringes and needles by those injecting illicit drugs (Des Jarlais *et al.*, 1992). There are several important interactions between patterns of drug use, sexual behaviour and the epidemiology of HIV and other STDs. In the US and the countries

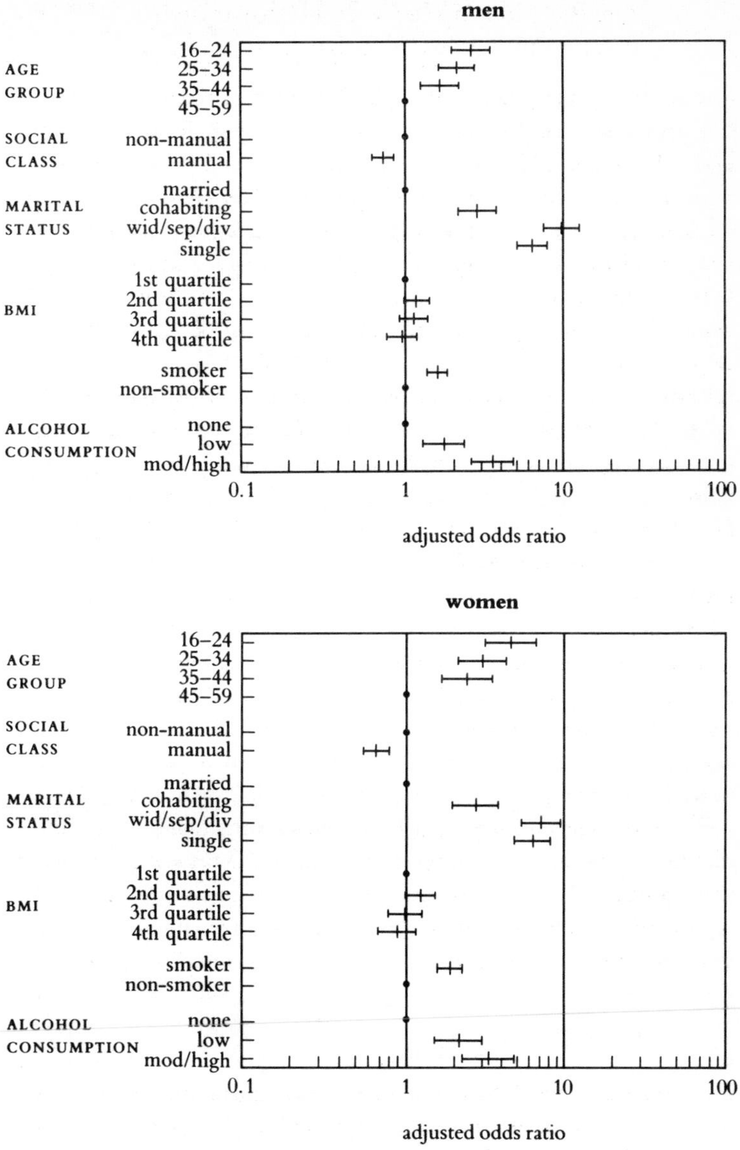

Figure 7.7 Adjusted odds ratios (95% confidence intervals) for 2 or more partners in the last year. Source: Booklet Question 7d

of southern Europe, a high proportion of heterosexually acquired HIV infection is through transmission from infected injecting drug users (IDUs) to their heterosexual partners, though in Britain transmission by this route has so far been limited (Des Jarlais *et al.*, 1992; Johnson, 1992). Both male and female drug users may sell sexual services to finance their drug habit so that there is a close interaction between the cultures of drug use and prostitution (Padian, 1988). In the US, the emergence of 'crack' cocaine addiction has been shown to be associated with outbreaks of STD and heterosexually acquired HIV (Chaisson *et al.*, 1989). This appears to be a result not only of prostitution but also of increased libido and more frequent partner change among users.

In assessing the potential impact of injecting drug use on the HIV epidemic, it is therefore important to estimate the extent of drug injecting and the frequency of needle sharing. While focused studies among IDUs have examined patterns of risk behaviour, none has been able to assess with accuracy the overall prevalence of injecting drug use in the population, although 'capture–recapture' methods combined with addiction notifications have been used to make estimates (Hartnoll *et al.*, 1985).

Since drug injecting involves only a small proportion of the population, it was not appropriate to include very detailed questions on this topic which are more appropriately obtained from specific studies of drug users. All respondents were asked whether they had ever injected drugs (Booklet Question 17). Those injecting drugs for medical purposes (e.g. diabetes) were distinguished from those injecting illicit drugs by asking respondents to report whether drugs were prescribed or non-prescribed. Table 7.4 shows prevalence of reported injecting non-prescribed drugs stratified by age and gender.

Overall 0.8% of men and 0.4% of women reported ever injecting non-prescribed drugs. These figures fell to 0.4% of men and 0.3% of women injecting in the last 5 years (Table 7.4). No respondents who had injected only prescribed drugs reported ever sharing a needle, while among those injecting non-prescribed drugs, 53% gave history of needle sharing. The prevalence of ever injecting non-prescribed drugs varied substantially with age (Table 7.4) rising to 1.4% among men aged 25–34 and to 0.8% among women aged 16–24. Only one respondent over the age of 44 reported

age group	16–24 %	25–34 %	35–44 %	45–59 %	all ages %
injected non-prescribed drugs			**men**		
ever	0.8	1.4	0.9	0.0	0.8
last 5 years	0.8	0.7	0.3	0.0	0.4
last year	0.2	0.6	0.2	0.0	0.3
ever shared needles	0.3	0.6	0.7	0.0	0.4
base	*1640*	*2065*	*1914*	*1963*	*7582*
injected non-prescribed drugs			**women**		
ever	0.8	0.6	0.2	0.0	0.4
last 5 years	0.8	0.3	0.1	0.0	0.3
last year	0.4	0.1	0.0	0.0	0.1
ever shared needles	0.3	0.4	0.1	0.0	0.2
base	*1857*	*2742*	*2443*	*2479*	*9520*

Table 7.4 Reported injecting drug use by age group. Source: Booklet Question 17

injecting drug use. For the population under 45, the proportion reporting ever injecting was 1.0% for men and 0.5% for women. The low rates of injecting among those over 45 accords with studies indicating the rarity of drug injecting in Britain before the late 1960s (Stimson and Oppenheimer, 1982). Regional variations were detectable with significantly higher rates of ever injecting among respondents in Greater London, 2.1% of men, 0.8% of women, (Table 7.5). The increased prevalence in London corresponds to the high proportion of Home Office notifications of drug addiction from the London area (Hartnoll *et al.*, 1985).

It should be emphasized that estimates of the prevalence of injecting drug use are likely to be minimum estimates for several reasons. Injecting illicit drugs is both a legally and socially censured behaviour which respondents might be particularly unwilling to report. Population estimates from the survey might also be lowered since those injecting drugs may be disproportionately represented among the homeless, who could not be included in the sampling frame. Because of the rules about who should complete the booklet, the question was

		Greater London %	Rest of England and Wales %	Scotland %	Great Britain %
ever	**men**	2.1	0.6	0.5	0.8
	women	0.8	0.3	0.6	0.4
in the last 5 years	**men**	1.4	0.3	0.3	0.4
	women	0.8	0.14	0.6	0.3
in the last year	**men**	1.0	0.15	0.0	0.3
	women	0.5	0.03	0.3	0.1
base	**men**	*993*	*5948*	*642*	*7582*
	women	*1165*	*7406*	*950*	*9520*

Table 7.5 Reported injecting drug use by geographical area. Source: Booklet Question 17

not asked of a relatively high proportion of those aged 16–24, mainly the sexually inexperienced, so that population estimates for this group may be subject to greater error. Given these caveats, applying these rates to the population of England and Wales gives an estimate of 100,000 people injecting in the last 5 years and 175,000 ever. These figures are of a similar order of magnitude to Hillier's who estimated 120,000 injecting drug users in England and Wales on the basis of scarce data from surveys of drug users and Home Office reports (Hillier, 1988).

HEALTH SERVICE USE AND SEXUAL BEHAVIOUR

STD-Clinic Attendance

Epidemiological studies indicate that the likelihood of acquiring a sexually transmitted disease increases with the number of sexual partners with whom unprotected sexual intercourse takes place (Aral and Holmes, 1990). No direct questions were asked about specific sexually acquired infections because of the difficulties of defining these in terms comprehensible to respondents. Attendance at an STD or special/VD clinic was used as a proxy indicator since open-access clinics, free at the time of use, are available throughout Great Britain, and are widely used by all sectors of the sexually active population (Belsey and Adler, 1981). Routine statistics on STD diagnoses are collected from these clinics and up to 90% of STDs in the country are thought to be diagnosed and treated in these settings rather than in general practice (Department of Health, 1991; Catchpole, 1992).

Although not all those who attend STD clinics have a sexually acquired infection, the majority are likely to perceive themselves to be at risk of infection. The probability of attendance should therefore be associated both with numbers of partners and the demographic and other factors shown to be related to partner change (see Chapter 3). Routine STD-clinic statistics have the disadvantage that they are based on 'episodes' of STD in a given time period rather than on the number of people with STD. Demographic data collected on attenders are restricted to age and gender and only recently has limited data on sexual orientation been collected (Belsey and Adler, 1981; Catchpole, 1992). No routine information is collected on the sexual behaviour of attenders.

8.3% of men and 5.6% of women reported visiting an STD clinic in their lifetime (so far) and less than 1% had attended in the last year (Figure 7.8). STD-clinic attendance was closely associated with age. Figure 7.8 indicates that the likelihood of attendance in the last 5 years for women is highest in the youngest age group (16–24) but for men peaks in the 25–34-year-old age group, thereafter declining in older age groups. This is consistent with data on age from STD clinic returns (KC60) for England and Wales. These show that for confirmed STD diagnoses the average age is approximately 3 years younger for women (24) than for men (27) (Department of Health, 1991). Similarly, the number of confirmed diagnoses in men exceeds those in women at all ages except for those under 25. The proportion of respondents reporting *ever* attending a clinic peaked in the 25–34-year-old age group and rapidly declined with increasing age. This corresponds to what is known about changing

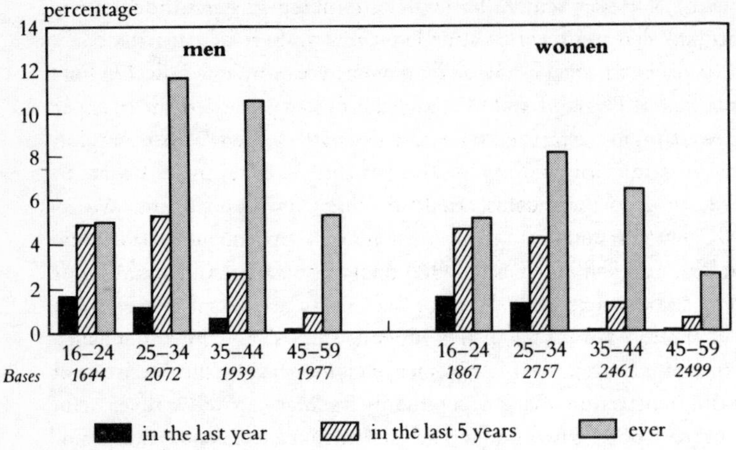

Figure 7.8 Reported STD-clinic attendance by age group. Source: Booklet Question 16

patterns of partnership formation over the preceding decades (see Chapter 3), the increased incidence of STDs through the 1960s, and the establishment of more STD clinics (Adler, 1982).

Substantial regional variation in frequency of STD-clinic attendance in the last 5 years is also evident. These differences are most marked for residents of Greater London. 7.4% of men and 6.7% of women reported STD-clinic attendance in the last 5 years as compared with 3.4% of men and 2.6% of women for the entire sample. The lowest levels of attendance were reported by men and women from the northern region (1.3% and 0.8% respectively) and women in Wales (0.5%). These findings are again consistent with data from KC60 returns which indicate the greatest number of attendances per head of the population in the Northern Thames Regional Health Authorities (Department of Health, 1991).

The proportion attending also varied markedly by marital status. Only 1.1% of married women and 1.5% of married men reported STD-clinic attendance in the last 5 years, with substantially higher incidence in all other marital-status categories with the exception of widowed women. This is entirely consistent with data on increased numbers of partners among those who are not married.

In 1978, Belsey and Adler (1981) attempted to assess the relationship between numbers of attenders and numbers of attendances by undertaking a survey of a representative sample of STD-clinic attenders in England and Wales. Attendances exceeded the number of attenders by a factor of 1.3 and this ratio varied both by region and by sexual orientation of the patient. They estimated that, in 1978, 332,000 individuals attended clinics in England and Wales. The equivalent estimate from our data was 261,000 attenders in the last year and just under 900,000 in the last 5 years. As the number of STD-clinic attendances (but not necessarily attenders) is known to have increased since 1978, this suggests that STD-clinic attendance may be under-reported in the survey. Other factors might also lead to different estimates, such as double counting of individuals who attended more than one clinic and the inclusion of those not resident in Britain in the Belsey and Adler survey as well as the substantial differences in methodology for deriving estimates.

STD-Clinic Attendance and Behaviour

The likelihood of attending an STD clinic increased markedly with increasing number of heterosexual partners (Table 7.6). Over one in seven of those with 5 or more heterosexual partners in the last 5 years had attended a clinic in that time and more than one in five of those reporting 10 or more, lifetime partners had ever attended. Among men reporting homosexual partners, more than half of those with 5 or more partners in the last year had attended a clinic in the same period. These may well be minimum estimates in view of the possible under-reporting of clinic attendance. Figure 7.9 demonstrates the very clear relationship between number of partners and STD-clinic attendance when both heterosexual and homosexual partnerships are taken into account. The proportion of men who report STD-clinic attendance but no heterosexual partners (Table 7.6) is largely accounted for by those with homosexual partners. The high proportion of individuals with multiple partnerships who attend STD clinics confirms the relationship between sexual lifestyle and probability of STD acquisition, but also underlines the importance of such clinics for assisting individuals to reduce their risk of acquiring further STD.

			number of homosexual partners ever					
			0	1	2	3–4	5–9	10+
ever attended STD clinic	men	%	7.4	20.3	15.1	33.9	44.3	67.3
		base	*7325*	*148*	*37*	*48*	*12*	*55*
	women	%	5.3	27.9	16.9	32.7	26.6	–
		base	*9409*	*120*	*32*	*13*★	*10*★	*3*★

			number of heterosexual partners ever					
			0	1	2	3–4	5–9	10+
ever attended STD clinic	men	%	9.2	1.7	2.8	3.8	7.8	20.2
		base	*184*	*1628*	*841*	*1447*	*1549*	*1943*
	women	%	0.5	1.3	2.4	6.1	12.2	26.7
		base	*182*	*3896*	*1679*	*1816*	*1308*	*678*

			number of homosexual partners in last 5 years				
			0	1	2	3–4	5+
attended STD clinic last 5 years	men	%	3.1	7.9	9.4	32.0	51.4
		base	*7505*	*49*	*11*★	*18*★	*41*
	women	%	2.6	8.1	5.2	–	–
		base	*9518*	*40*	*16*★	*3*★	*6*★

			number of heterosexual partners in last 5 years				
			0	1	2	3–4	5+
attended STD clinic last 5 years	men	%	7.5	0.7	2.9	4.5	13.7
		base	*357*	*4490*	*798*	*958*	*1017*
	women	%	0.3	1.2	4.1	8.0	15.7
		base	*510*	*6503*	*1062*	*771*	*431*

Table 7.6 Proportions of respondents attending an STD clinic in relation to number of homosexual and heterosexual partners. Source: Booklet Questions 7a, 7b, 8a, 8b, 16

★ note small base.

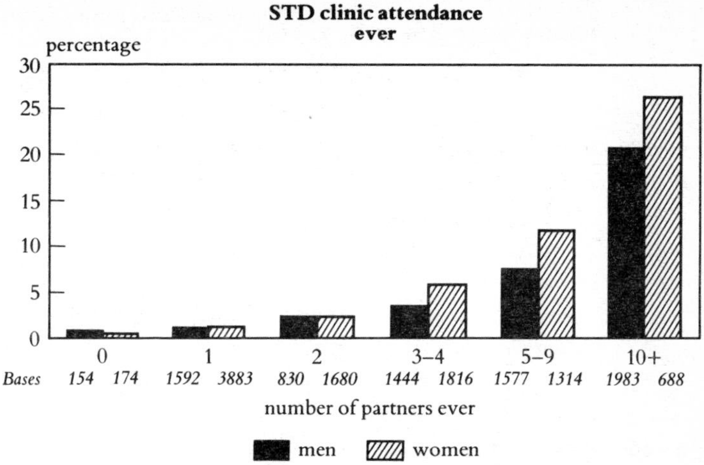

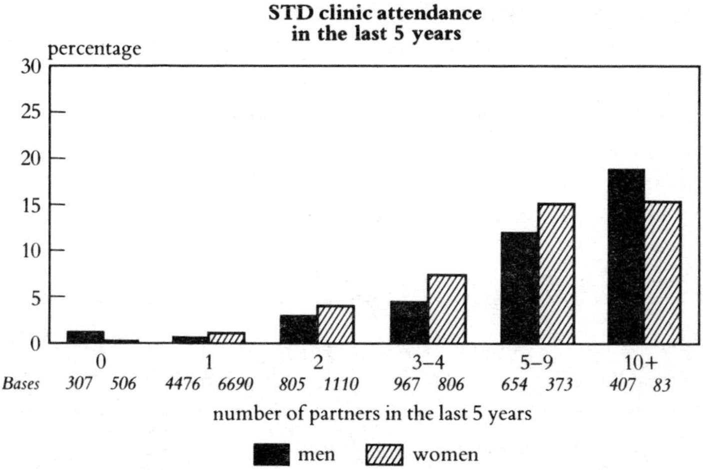

Figure 7.9 STD-clinic attendance by number of heterosexual and homosexual partners. Source: Booklet Questions 7a, 7b, 16

Multivariate Analysis

A logistic model was constructed to assess the simultaneous effects of age, marital status, numbers of heterosexual and homosexual partners and non-prescribed drug injecting on the likelihood of attendance at an STD clinic in the last 5 years (Figure 7.10).

After adjustments for other factors in the analysis, numbers of heterosexual partners in the last 5 years exerted the strongest effect in the model for both men and women. The adjusted odds ratio for STD attendance for women reporting 5 or more partners was in excess of 9 and for men more than 12. Homosexual partnerships exerted a strong effect in the model for men only (odds ratio 12:4) confirming the strong association between behaviour and clinic attendance. For women, injecting drug use was associated with a significantly increased likelihood of clinic attendance. The effects of age and marital status, after controlling for other variables in the model, were somewhat weaker. Men aged 25–44 were more likely to have been to an STD clinic in the last 5 years than older or younger men. For women, the age range was younger, those aged 16–34 being most likely to attend. Marital status had a weaker effect among men than among women, with only single status being associated with a significantly raised odds of clinic attendance.

HIV Antibody Testing

HIV antibody testing has been widely available in STD clinics, hospitals and other settings since 1985. All donated blood is routinely screened for HIV antibody. HIV screening is sometimes undertaken in other circumstances such as for life insurance, travel to certain countries and in connection with pregnancy. Understanding the proportion of the population who have undergone testing is important for assessing the likely extent of undiagnosed HIV infection and the degree to which those at high risk of infection have actively sought testing.

Respondents reported whether they had had an HIV test in the last 5 years and for what reason. Options given were 'being a blood donor (giving blood)', 'pregnancy' (for men 'a pregnancy of your wife/partner'), 'insurance, mortgage or travel', or 'other reason(s)'.

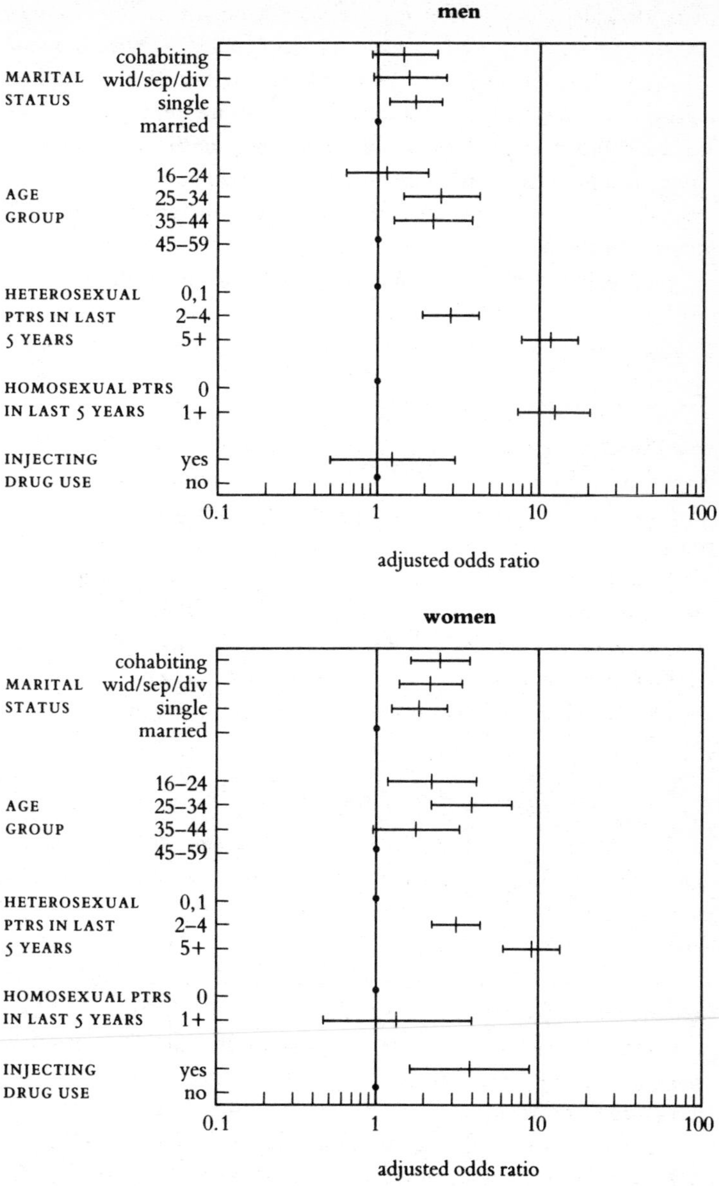

Figure 7.10 Adjusted odds ratios for attendance at an STD clinic in the last 5 years. Source: Interview Question 16

This last category was of particular interest because it was likely to include respondents who had actively sought HIV testing because they perceived themselves to be at risk of infection. Unless data on reasons for testing were collected, incidence of testing might be over-estimated because of confusion in the minds of respondents who had had blood tests in the last 5 years, as to whether this included HIV testing. Overall, more than 13% of the sample reported that they had had an HIV test (Table 7.7). The commonest reason for testing was blood donation (7.5% of men, 6.2% of

age group	16–24 %	25–34 %	35–44 %	45–59 %	all ages %
			men		
blood test					
yes	12.7	15.5	14.9	8.9	13.1
no	81.9	79.5	80.6	87.1	82.2
unsure	5.4	5.0	4.4	4.1	4.7
reason for test					
blood donor	7.4	8.9	9.1	4.4	7.5
pregnancy	0.4	0.6	0.3	0.0	0.3
insurance, mortgage, etc.	0.8	1.4	1.7	1.5	1.4
'other'	4.5	5.5	4.2	2.7	4.2
base	*1648*	*2066*	*1919*	*1939*	*7572*
			women		
blood test					
yes	15.9	18.9	12.8	7.0	13.7
no	77.2	74.2	81.1	89.7	80.6
unsure	6.9	6.9	6.1	3.3	5.8
reason for test					
blood donor	6.1	7.5	6.8	4.0	6.2
pregnancy	6.4	8.9	3.0	0.1	4.6
insurance, mortgage, etc.	0.6	0.7	0.5	0.4	0.5
'other'	3.6	3.3	2.7	2.1	2.9
base	*1852*	*2731*	*2439*	*2435*	*9456*

Table 7.7 HIV testing by age group. Source: Booklet Question 20

women) but 4.2% of men and 2.9% of women had an HIV test for reasons other than blood donation, pregnancy, or insurance/travel. Testing rates declined in those aged 45 or more.

HIV Testing and Sexual Behaviour

The relationship between reported behaviour and the likelihood of testing is shown in Table 7.8. More than one in five men (and one in four women) with 5 or more heterosexual partners in the last 5 years reported having an HIV test, and one in ten had done so other than for blood donation, etc. Among men with homosexual partners in the last 5 years, the proportion rose to over four out of ten, with more than one out of four seeking testing for an 'other' reason. For those injecting non-prescribed drugs, nearly half had been tested. All these rates are in excess of those of the population as a whole,

	HIV test for any reason				HIV test for 'other' reason			
	men		**women**		**men**		**women**	
	%	*base*	%	*base*	%	*base*	%	*base*
heterosexual partners in the last 5 years								
0, 1	11.1	*4791*	11.2	*7108*	3.1	*4777*	1.9	*7081*
2–4	13.8	*1752*	19.7	*1897*	3.9	*1747*	5.1	*1893*
5+	21.0	*1016*	26.7	*441*	10.2	*1016*	8.9	*441*
homosexual partners in the last 5 years								
0	12.6	*7446*	13.6	*9391*	3.9	*7427*	2.8	*9360*
1+	43.0	*118*	24.0	*64*	27.0	*118*	13.1	*65*
Injecting drug use								
ever	41.5	*58*	62.7	*35*	31.4	*58*	48.6	*35*
last 5 years	47.9	*33*	76.2	*24*	37.4	*33*	60.6	*24*
never	12.8	*7436*	13.5	*9344*	4.1	*7417*	2.7	*9310*

Table 7.8 HIV testing and sexual behaviour. Source: Booklet Questions 7b, 8b, 17, 20

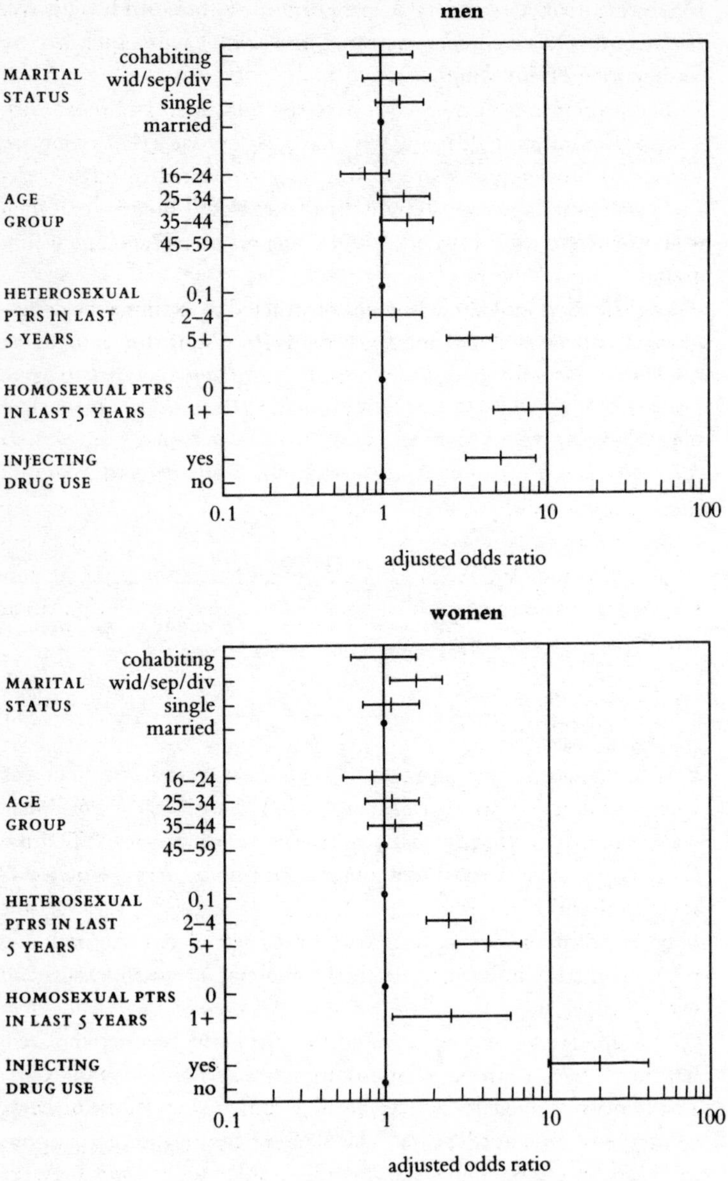

Figure 7.11 Adjusted odds ratios for HIV testing for 'other' reasons. Source: Interview Question 20

suggesting that a considerable proportion of those with high-risk behaviours perceive their increased risk and have responded by undertaking HIV testing.

The proportions of men who have sex with men and those with a history of injecting drug use who have undergone HIV testing are similar to those reported from drug users recruited through treatment and other agencies and volunteer samples of homosexual men (Dawson *et al.*, 1991; Hart *et al.*, 1991; Report of a Working Group, 1993).

Logistic regression models were constructed to examine the demographic and behavioural influence on HIV testing for any reason other than blood donation, pregnancy, insurance or travel (Figure 7.11). For men and women, the dominant effects were numbers of heterosexual partners, any homosexual partners and injecting drug use. After controlling for other variables in the model, age and marital status were not significantly associated with an HIV test for 'other' reasons. This analysis confirms the strong relationship between behaviour and seeking testing, since the demographic factors known to be associated with patterns of behaviour are not significant effects in the model.

Circumcision

The final question for men in the booklet (Question 21) inquired whether the respondent was circumcised. This question was included on the basis of evidence that the risk of acquisition of STD and HIV may be increased by the presence of the foreskin (Cameron *et al.*, 1989; Aral and Holmes, 1990). Studies examining this variable may be confounded by differing and interrelated cultural and religious factors influencing both the practice of circumcision and sexual behaviour.

Overall, 21.9% of men reported that they had been circumcised, but there was a strong relationship with age (Table 7.9). Only 12.5% of men aged 16–24 had been circumcised and this increased to 32.3% of men aged 45–59. This striking age relationship appears to reflect changing public health policy on circumcision between the 1930s (Gairdner, 1949) and the 1970s.

The data were examined by religious denomination on account

	%	*base*
age group		
16–24	12.5	*1874*
25–34	15.9	*2111*
35–44	26.4	*1956*
45–59	32.3	*2049*
religion		
none	18.4	*4120*
Church of England	24.7	*2011*
Roman Catholic	18.6	*678*
other Christian	22.1	*863*
non-Christian	55.8	*312*
ethnic group		
white	20.9	*7551*
black	34.1	*150*
Asian	35.3	*165*
other	51.5	*107*
all men	21.9	*7990*

Table 7.9 Proportion of men circumcised by age, religion and ethnic groups. Source: Interview Question 33a; Booklet Question 21

of varying views on the practice of circumcision (Table 7.9). Circumcision rates were markedly higher in non-Christian religions, reflecting in particular the routine religious practice of circumcision among Jews and Muslims. Analysis by ethnic group shows white males to be the least likely to be circumcised.

In our data there was no relationship in bivariate analysis between circumcision and rates of attendance at an STD clinic.

INFERTILITY, ADVERSE PREGNANCY OUTCOMES AND SEXUAL BEHAVIOUR

The relationships between sexual behaviour and a number of adverse outcomes with respect to fertility are explored here. These include infertility, loss of pregnancy through miscarriage or stillbirth and termination of an unwanted or abnormal pregnancy. In this section patterns of infertility, miscarriage and abortion are examined in relation to demographic and behavioural characteristics of the sampled population.

Infertility

The incidence of infertility was measured by two questions (Booklet Questions 15a and 15b):

Have you ever had a time lasting 6 months or longer when you (and your partner) were trying to get pregnant but it did not happen?

This measure was used as an indicator of delay in conception. Any time cut-off, however, has its drawbacks. Studies of couples of proven fertility indicate that a significant minority will conceive within 6 months and 1 year of first trying and a further minority will conceive after 1 year (Tietze, 1956; Tietze, 1968). To assess action taken in response to infertility a second question was asked:

Have you (or your partner) ever sought medical or professional help about infertility?

The reported incidence of both infertility for 6 months and professional help-seeking are shown in Figure 7.12. Women were more likely than men to report both infertility for at least 6 months and seeking professional help. This may reflect more accurate recall among women than men of the time taken to conceive, related to awareness of the menstrual cycle. The discrepancies between male and female reporting of professional help-seeking are smaller. What differences there are may arise either from lack of awareness of their

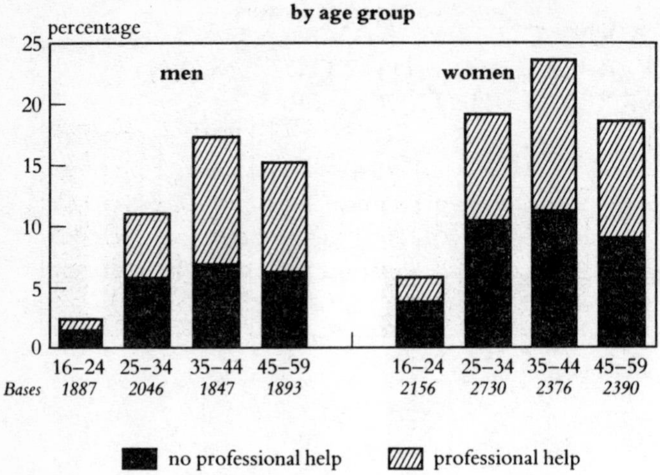
by age group
percentage
25
20
15
10
5
0
men
women
16–24
25–34
35–44
45–59
16–24
25–34
35–44
45–59
Bases
1887
2046
1847
1893
2156
2730
2376
2390
no professional help
professional help

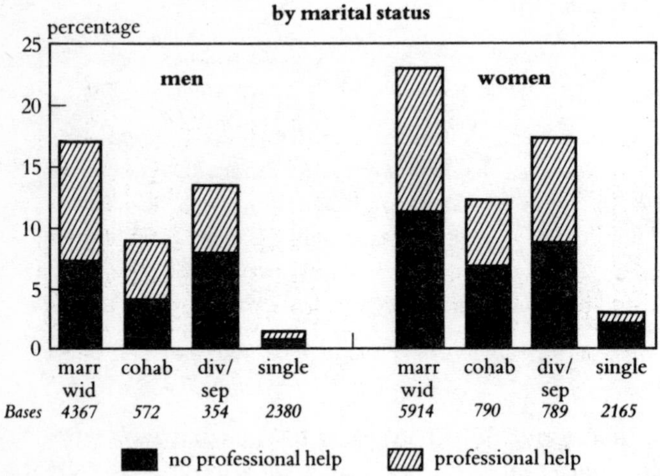
by marital status
percentage
25
20
15
10
5
0
men
women
marr wid
cohab
div/ sep
single
marr wid
cohab
div/ sep
single
Bases
4367
572
354
2380
5914
790
789
2165
no professional help
professional help

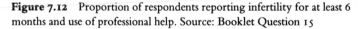

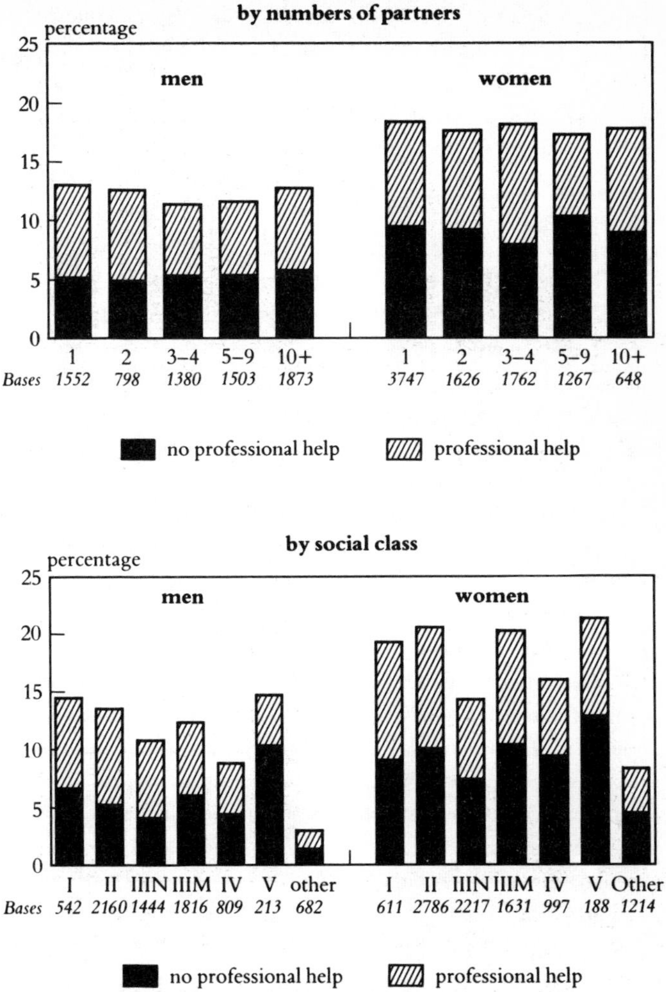

Figure 7.12 Proportion of respondents reporting infertility for at least 6 months and use of professional help. Source: Booklet Question 15

partner's seeking advice or a tendency for respondents to consider that the majority of fertility problems lie with women.

Figure 7.12 indicates marked variability in experience of infertility and use of professional help by age group with the incidence peaking in men and women aged 35–44. The lower apparent incidence in the oldest age group may reflect either a genuine increase in infertility in younger cohorts or simply a changing awareness of infertility and the professional help available. Several studies have shown that the proportion of women seeking professional help for infertility has increased over recent decades (Johnson *et al.*, 1987; Aral and Cates, 1983). Johnson *et al.* estimated that 7% of women born in 1950 had consulted an infertility specialist by the time they were 35, a figure that is consistent with the 12.3% of 35–44-year-olds and 9.5% of 45–59-year-old women seeking professional help in this sample. On the basis of general practice records, Johnson *et al.* (1987) estimated that there had been no significant increase in rates of primary infertility *per se* although rates of voluntary childlessness had increased. Templeton *et al.* (1990), on the basis of a postal survey, estimated that 14% of women aged 46–50 in Aberdeen had experienced difficulty in becoming pregnant for more than 2 years as compared with 17% for more than 6 months for 45–59-year-olds in this sample. Since approximately one-fifth of couples who do not conceive within 6 months can be expected to conceive by 24 months, the survey figures are of similar order of magnitude. A very much more detailed history was taken in that survey than was available in this dataset.

Not surprisingly, experience of involuntary infertility was strongly related to marital status, with rates being very much lower among single people than among those who were currently or had ever been married or who were currently cohabiting with an opposite sex partner (Figure 7.12). There was no obvious relationship with social class or with number of lifetime partners in bivariate analysis (Figure 7.12). The latter finding is perhaps surprising since tubal damage due to prior pelvic infection accounted for some 14% of cases of infertility seen in one infertility clinic (Hull *et al.*, 1985) and this is in turn likely to be related to previous sexually acquired infection. The relationship however is complex and likely to be confounded by age and marital status since the youngest and single respondents are least likely to have tried to become pregnant.

A logistic regression model exploring the relationship between age, marital status, a history of having one or more child and infertility confirmed the findings of the bivariate analysis (Figure 7.13). The likelihood of reporting and seeking help for infertility was greatest in women aged 35–44; the single were those least likely to have sought help, although cohabitees and the widowed, separated and divorced were less likely than the married to report infertility problems.

Stillbirth, Miscarriage and Abortion

Miscarriage and stillbirth are unwanted outcomes of pregnancy while abortion (or the therapeutic termination of pregnancy) is generally a response to unwanted pregnancy. Secular changes in rates of reported abortion must be expected following the legalization of termination of pregnancy by the Abortion Act of 1967. Reporting of abortion is a sensitive matter and, in her 1976 survey, Dunnell (1979) estimated that only half the abortions expected from official statistics were reported. Results from this survey indicate that although age-specific reporting rates of abortions consistently lay slightly below those expected from official statistics for 1990, the 95% confidence limits for the rates reported in the survey always included the recorded national rates (Wadsworth, Field, *et al.*, 1993).

As Figure 7.14 indicates, there are substantial variations in rates of reporting by age and the patterns for miscarriage and stillbirth differ substantially from those for abortion. Lifetime reporting of miscarriage is extremely common for women (20.7% of all respondents) and, as expected, increases with age as women accumulate experience of pregnancy. Nearly one-third of women aged 45–59 reported experience of miscarriage or stillbirth in their lifetime. Recent experience (in the last 5 years) was most common (10.9%) among women in the most active reproductive years, 25–34. In contrast, lifetime experience of abortion was highest (15.4%) among women aged 35–44, the majority of whom would have had therapeutic abortion available to them throughout their sexually active careers. For those aged over 45, abortion would have become

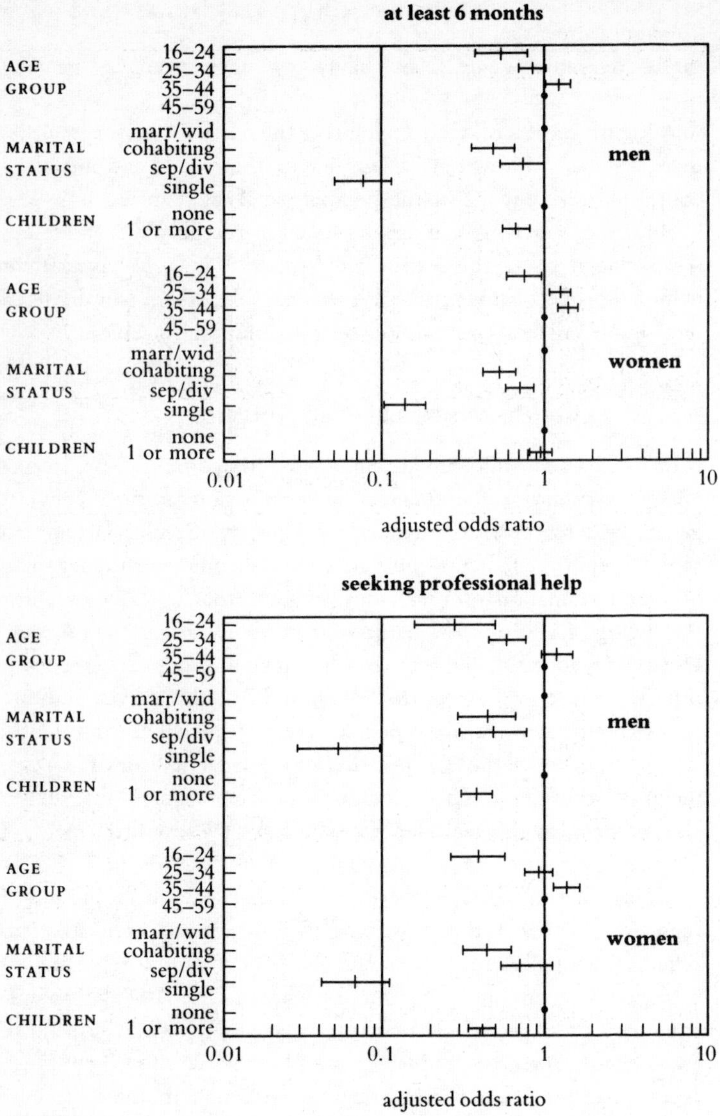

Figure 7.13 Adjusted odds ratios for infertility. Source: Booklet Question 15

Figure 7.14 *(opposite)* Proportion of women reporting miscarriage or stillbirth and abortion. Source: Booklet Questions 13, 14

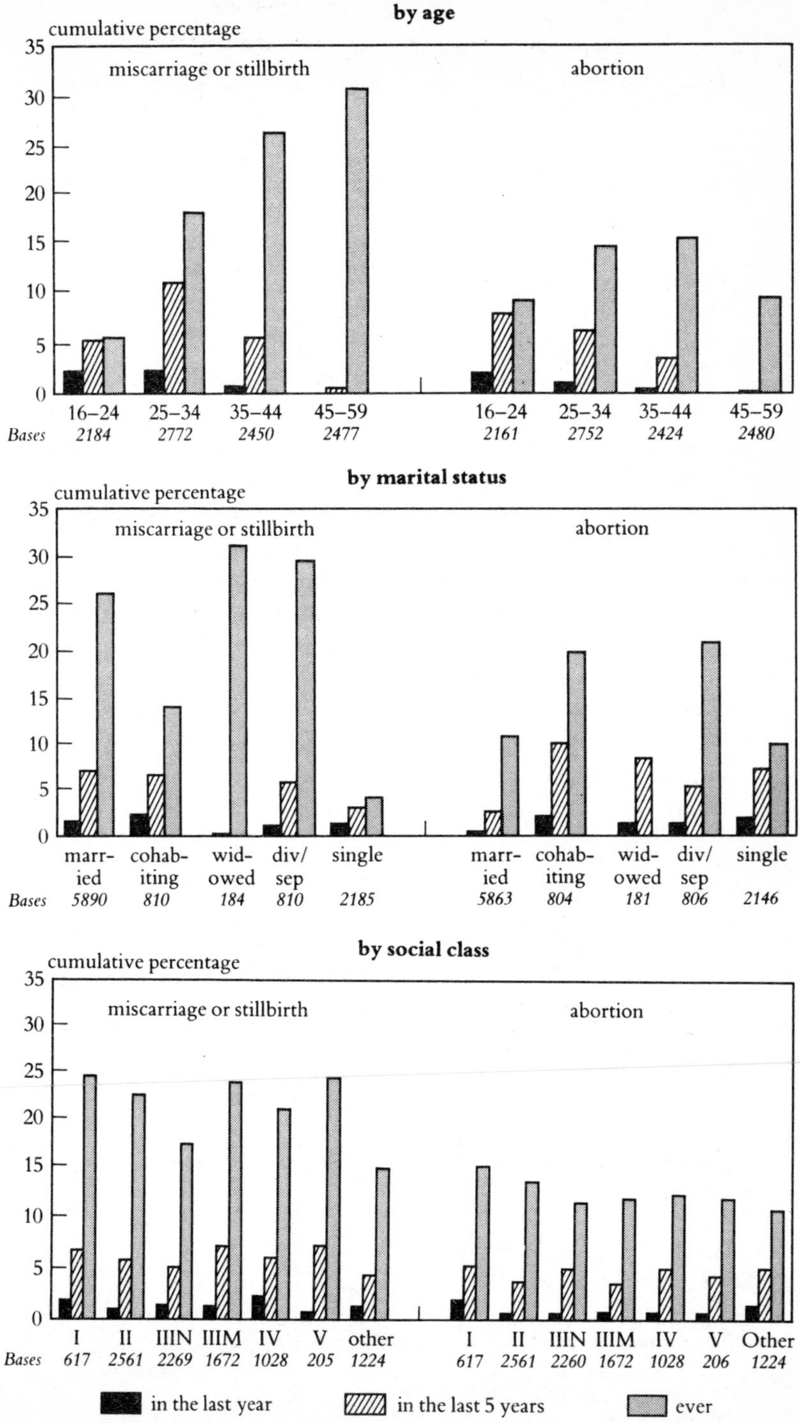
by age
cumulative percentage
35
30
25
20
15
10
5
0
miscarriage or stillbirth
abortion
16–24
25–34
35–44
45–59
Bases
2184
2772
2450
2477
16–24
25–34
35–44
45–59
2161
2752
2424
2480
by marital status
cumulative percentage
miscarriage or stillbirth
abortion
marr- ied
cohab- iting
wid- owed
div/ sep
single
Bases
5890
810
184
810
2185
marr- ied
cohab- iting
wid- owed
div/ sep
single
5863
804
181
806
2146
by social class
cumulative percentage
miscarriage or stillbirth
abortion
I
II
IIIN
IIIM
IV
V
other
Bases
617
2561
2269
1672
1028
205
1224
I
II
IIIN
IIIM
IV
V
Other
617
2561
2260
1672
1028
206
1224
in the last year
in the last 5 years
ever

available after their most sexually experimental period and this is reflected in less frequent experience of abortion (9.4%). Recent abortion (in the last 5 years) was most common among those aged 16–24 (7.9%), possibly reflecting poor use of contraception, greater numbers of sexual partners and a higher prevalence of uncommitted relationships.

The pattern of miscarriage, stillbirth and abortion in relation to marital status is entirely consistent with known demographic patterns in relation to childbirth (Botting, 1991; OPCS, 1993). Miscarriage, both in the last 5 years and ever, is least common among the single, although this relationship will also be affected by current age. Different patterns are seen for abortion in the last 5 years, which was least common among the widowed (1.3%) and married (2.6%). Single women reported higher rates (7.3% in the last 5 years) but the highest rates were among cohabiting women (10.2%). This last finding can be compared with data reported in Chapters 3 and 4 showing the less monogamous lifestyles of those cohabiting. Though making sufficient commitment to a relationship to live with a partner, they appear to have a less exclusive attitude to that relationship, and possibly also to the responsibilities of childcare.

Miscarriage and stillbirth show no relationship with social class (Figure 7.14). There were no differences in reporting of abortion in the last 5 years by social class, but the proportion of women who had *ever* had an abortion decreased with lower social class.

Miscarriage, Stillbirth and Abortion in Relation to Sexual Partners

Experience of miscarriage, stillbirth and abortion is examined in relation to numbers of sexual partners in Figure 7.15. Reporting of stillbirth and miscarriage shows no relationship with number of partners in any time interval, but the likelihood of abortion in any given time period is strongly related to the number of sexual partners in the same time period. For example, women reporting 10 or more partners in their lifetime were more than 5 times more likely to have an abortion than those who had only one partner (34.4% and 6.0% respectively).

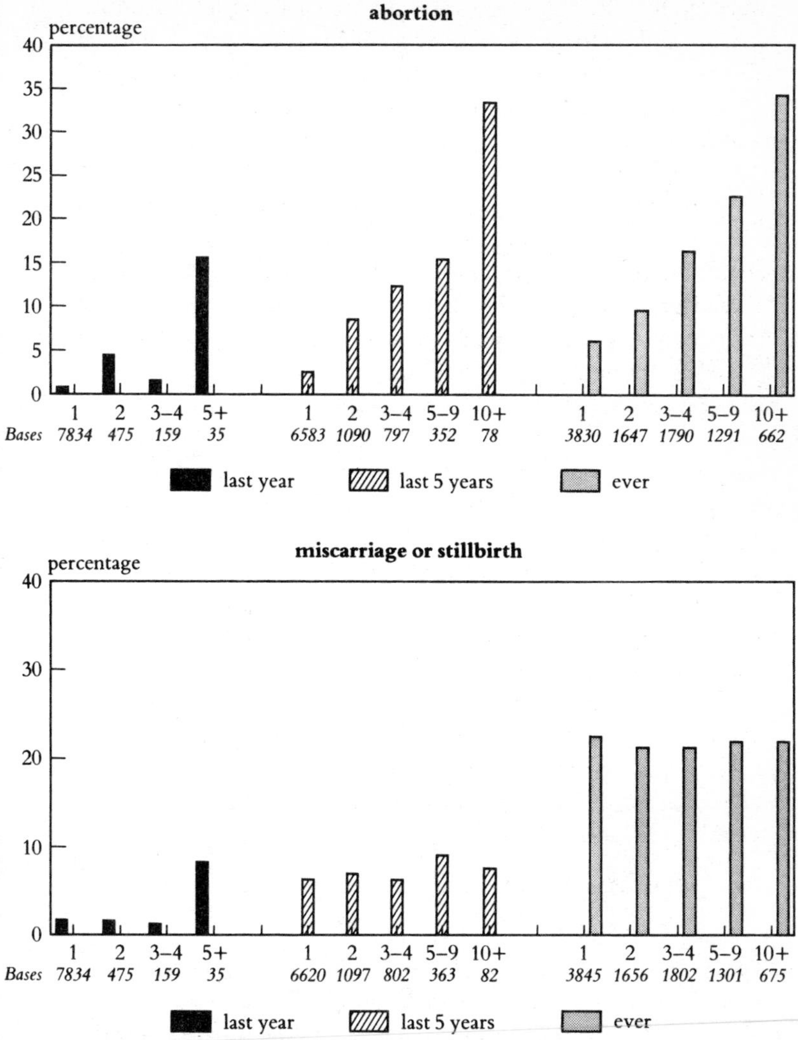

Figure 7.15 Proportions of women reporting abortion and miscarriage or stillbirth by numbers of heterosexual partners in 3 time intervals. Source: Booklet Questions 7a, 7b, 7d, 13, 14

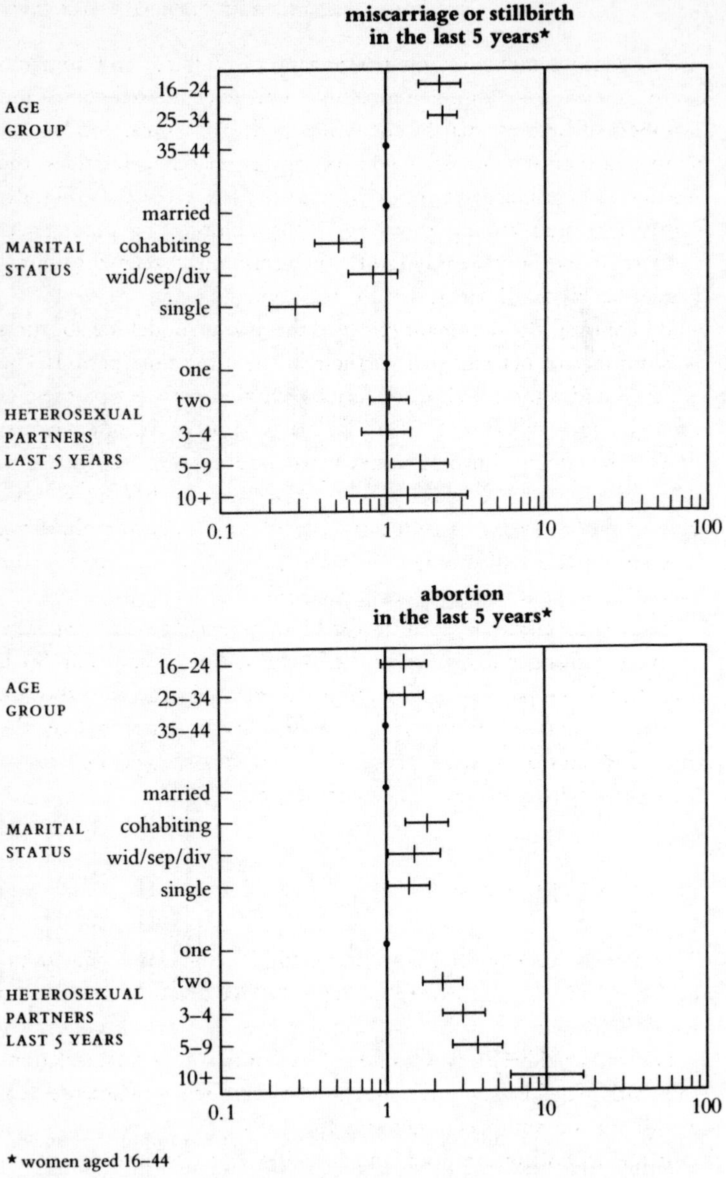

Figure 7.16 Adjusted odds ratios for reported miscarriage or stillbirth and abortion in the last 5 years. Source: Booklet Questions 13, 14

The various influences on miscarriage or stillbirth and abortion were examined in logistic regression with age, marital status and numbers of heterosexual partners included. The 5-year models are shown in Figure 7.16. After controlling for all other variables, the likelihood of stillbirth or miscarriage in the last 5 years was significantly increased among those aged 16–34, decreased among the unmarried and only weakly (and non-significantly) related to numbers of heterosexual partners in the last 5 years.

By contrast, the dominant effect in the 5-year model for abortion was number of heterosexual partners in the same time period. The adjusted odds ratio for abortion among women with 5–9 partners in the last 5 years was close to 4 and for those with 10 or more in excess of 10. The effects of both age and marital status were attenuated, so that age effects were weak and non-significant, while only those cohabiting showed a significantly raised odds ratio for abortion. The strong effect of numbers of partners was also sustained in the model when lifetime data were considered.

Thus, sexual lifestyle, as measured by numbers of partners, appears to exert a strong influence over the likelihood of an abortion. Such a relationship is not unexpected, both in terms of increased exposure to risk and less commitment to partners, and is supported by the increased rates of sexually acquired infections observed in women attending abortion clinics (Cohn and Stewart, 1992).

SUMMARY

This chapter has explored physical health, health-related behaviour, health service use and aspects of reproductive health in relation to sexual behaviour.

Self-reported health was found to have only a very weak relationship with sexual behaviour as measured by frequency of heterosexual acts of sex and numbers of heterosexual partners.

Both alcohol consumption and smoking were found to be associated with patterns of sexual behaviour. After controlling for age, social class and marital status, reporting of multiple partnerships was significantly associated with smoking and with increasing levels of alcohol consumption.

A history of injecting non-prescribed drugs was reported by less than 1% of the sample. Reporting rates were, however, higher among those under 45 and those resident in London. More than half those injecting non-prescribed drugs had shared a needle at some time. Although these estimates should be regarded as minima, they are consistent with limited data from other sources.

A history of attendance at an STD clinic was strongly associated with number of heterosexual partners and with a history of homosexual partnership, even after controlling for age and marital status. Over one in seven of those with 5 or more heterosexual partners in the last 5 years had attended a clinic in that time. Among men reporting 5 or more homosexual partners in the last 5 years, more than half had attended. This finding indicates that a high proportion of those at risk of STD and HIV are attending STD clinics and emphasizes the importance of these health service settings for assisting individuals in risk-reduction strategies.

Over 13% of respondents reported that they had had an HIV test, showing that a relatively high proportion of the population has already been tested. After excluding those tested for blood donation, pregnancy, insurance or travel, a history of HIV testing was strongly associated with patterns of HIV risk behaviour. In particular, a history of HIV testing was much more likely among those with 5 or more heterosexual partners in the last 5 years, any homosexual partners in the last 5 years or a history of injecting non-prescribed drugs. These findings suggest that those at increased risk of HIV infection have perceived their risk and opted to undergo HIV testing.

21.9% of men had been circumcised. The prevalence of circumcision increased markedly with age and was also related to religious denomination and ethnic group. White men were the least likely to be circumcised.

Experience of infertility and seeking help for it were, not surprisingly related to age and marital status. No relationship was detected between numbers of heterosexual partners and experience of infertility.

A history of miscarriage or stillbirth was common, involving more than one in five women of all ages and nearly one in three women aged 45–59. While the likelihood of miscarriage or stillbirth was related to age and marital status, no relationship was found with numbers of heterosexual partners. In contrast, the likelihood of termination of pregnancy increased markedly with increasing numbers of heterosexual partners independent of age and marital status.

The findings in this chapter indicate close associations between a number of risk-taking behaviours. They confirm the strong relationship between sexual behaviour and the probability of STD clinic attendance, abortion and HIV testing. These findings both indicate general awareness of the risk of HIV infection and other adverse outcomes for sexual health and also emphasize the importance of health service provision in the design and implementation of sexual health programmes.

REFERENCES

Adler, M. W. (1982). 'Sexually Transmitted Disease', in: D. L. Miller and R. D. T. Farmer (eds) *Epidemiology of Diseases*. Oxford: Blackwell Scientific Publications

Aral, S. O., and W. Cates (1983). 'The Increasing Concern with Infertility – Why Now?', *Journal of American Medical Association*, 250, 2327–31

Aral, S. O., and K. K. Holmes (1990). 'Epidemiology of Sexual Behavior and Sexually Transmitted Diseases', in K. K. Holmes, P. A. Mardh, P. F. Sparling, and P. J. Weisner (eds), *Sexually Transmitted Diseases*, 2nd edn (pp. 19–36). New York: McGraw-Hill.

Barker, D. J. P., P. D. Winter, C. Osmond, B. Margetts, and S. J. Simmonds (1989). 'Weight in Infancy and Death from Ischemic Heart Disease, *Lancet*, ii, 577–80

Belsey, E. M., and M. W. Adler (1981). 'Study of STD Clinic Attenders in England and Wales 1978: 1. Patients versus Cases', *British Journal of Venereal Disease*, 57, 285–9

Blaxter, M. (1987). 'Evidence on Inequality in Health from a National Survey', *Lancet*, ii, 30–33

Botting, B. (1991). 'Trends in Abortion', *Population Trends*, 64, 19–29

Boyd, J. T., and R. Doll (1964). 'A Study of the Aetiology of

Carcinoma of the Cervix Uteri', *British Journal of Cancer*, 18, 419–34

Brown, S., M. Vessey, and R. Harris (1984). 'Social Class, Sexual Habits and Cancer of the Cervix', *Community Medicine*, 6, 281–6

Cameron, D. W., J. N. Simonsen, and J. L. D'Costa (1989). 'Female to Male Transmission of Human Immunodeficiency Virus Type I', *Lancet*, ii, 403–7

Catchpole, M. (1992). 'Sexually Transmitted Diseases in England and Wales: 1981–1990', *Communicable Diseases Report*, 2, R1–12

Chaisson, R. E., P. Bacchetti, D. Osmond, B. Brodie, M. A. Sande, and A. R. Moss (1989). 'Cocaine Use and HIV Infection in Intravenous Drug Users in San Francisco', *Journal of American AIDS*, 261, 561–5

Cohn, M., and P. Stewart (1992). 'Prevalence of Potential Pathogens in Cervical Canal before Termination of Pregnancy', *British Medical Journal*, 304, 1479

Cox, B. D., M. Blaxter, A. L. J. Buckle, N. P. Fenner, J. P. Golding, M. Gore, *et al.* (1987). *The Health and Lifestyle Survey*. London: Health Promotion Research Trust

Davey Smith, G., M. Bartley, and D. Blane (1990). 'The Black Report on Socioeconomic Inequalities in Health 10 Years On', *British Medical Journal*, 301, 373–7

Dawson, J., R. Fitzpatrick, J. McLean, G. Hart, and M. Boulton (1991). 'The HIV Test and Sexual Behaviour in a Sample of Homosexually Active Men', *Social Science and Medicine*, 32, 683–8

Department of Health (1991). *New Cases Seen at NHS Genito Urinary Medicine Clinics in England. Years 1988/89 and 1989/90. Summary Information from Form KC60*. London: Department of Health, SM12B

Des Jarlais, D. C., S. R. Friedman, K. Choopanya, S. Vanicheseni, and T. P. Ward (1992). 'International Epidemiology of HIV and AIDS among Injecting Drug Users', *AIDS*, 6, 1053–68

Dunnell, K. (1979). *Family Formation 1976*. London: HMSO

Gairdner, D. (1949). 'The Fate of the Foreskin', *British Medical Journal*, 4, 1433–5

Hart, G. J., N. Woodward, A. M. Johnson, J. Tighe, J. V. Parry, and M. W. Adler (1991). 'Prevalence of HIV, Hepatitis B and

Associated Risk Behaviours in Clients of a Needle-exchange in Central London', *AIDS*, 5, 543–7

Hartnoll R., R. Lewis, M. Mitcheson, and S. Bryer (1985). 'Estimating the Prevalence of Opioid Dependence', *Lancet*, i, 203–5

Hillier, H. (1988). 'Estimation of HIV Prevalence in England and Wales – The Direct Approach', in *Short-term Prediction of HIV Infection and AIDS in England and Wales* (pp. 48–52). London: Department of Health

Hull, M. G. R., C. M. A. Glazener, N. J. Kelly, D. I. Conway, P. A. Foster, R. A. Hinton, *et al.* (1985). 'Population Study of Causes, Treatment and Outcome of Infertility', *British Medical Journal*, 291, 1693–7

Johnson, A. M. (1992). 'Home-grown Heterosexually Acquired HIV Infection', *British Medical Journal*, 304, 1125–6

Johnson, G., D. Roberts, R. Brown, E. Cox, Z. Evershed, P. Goutam, *et al.* (1987). 'Infertile or Childless by Choice? A Multipractice Survey of Women aged 35 and 50', *British Medical Journal*, 294, 804–6

Moser, K., P. Goldblatt, J. Fox, and D. Jones (1990). 'Unemployment and Mortality', in P. Goldblatt (ed.), *Longitudinal Study: Mortality and Social Organisation* (pp. 81–97). London: HMSO

Office of Population Censuses and Surveys (1991). *General Household Survey 1989*. London: HMSO

Office of Population Censuses and Surveys (1992). *General Household Survey GHS21 1990*. London: HMSO

Office of Population Censuses and Surveys (1993). *Birth Statistics 1991. England and Wales. Series FMI No. 20*. London: HMSO

Padian, N. S. (1988). 'Prostitute Women and AIDS: Epidemiology', *AIDS*, 2, 413–19

Peto, R., A. D. Lopez, J. Boreham, M. Thun, J. R. C. Heath (1992). 'Mortality from Tobacco in Developed Countries: Indirect Estimation from National Vital Statistics', *Lancet*, 339, 1268–78

Report of a working group (Chairman N. E. Day) (1993). 'AIDS Projections to 1997, England and Wales', *Communicable Diseases Report*, 1–12

Royal College of General Practitioners (1974). *Oral Contraceptives and Health*. London: Pitman Medical

Shaper, A. G. (1980). 'Alcohol and Mortality: A Review of Prospective Studies', *British Journal of Addiction*, 85, 837–47

Shaper, A. G., G. Wannametree, and M. Walker (1990). 'Alcohol and Mortality in British Men: Explaining the J-shaped Curve', *Lancet*, ii, 1267–74

Singer, A. (1979). 'Further Evidence for High-risk Male and Female Groups in the Development of Cervical Carcinoma', *Obstetrical and Gynecological Surveys*, 34, 867

Stimson, G. V., and E. Oppenheimer (1982). *Heroin Addiction: Treatment and Control in Britain*. London: Tavistock

Templeton, A., C. Fraser, and B. Thompson (1990). 'The Epidemiology of Infertility in Aberdeen', *British Medical Journal*, 301, 148–52

Thorogood, M., R. Carter, L. Benfield, K. McPherson, and J. J. Mann (1987). 'Plasma Lipid and Lipoprotein Cholesterol Concentrations in People with Different Diets in Britain', *British Medical Journal*, 292, 351–3

Tietze, C. (1956). 'Statistical Contributions to the Study of Human Infertility', *Fertility and Sterility*, 7, 88–95.

Tietze, C. (1968). 'Fertility after the Discontinuation of Intrauterine and Oral Contraception', *International Journal of Fertility*, 13, 385–9

Wadsworth, J., J. Field, A. M., Johnson, S. Bradshaw, and K. Wellings (1993). 'Methodology of the National Survey of Sexual Attitudes and Lifestyles', *Journal of the Royal Statistical Society*, series A, 156:3: 407–21

Weatherburn, P., P. M. Davies, F. C. I. Hickson, A. J. Hunt, T. J. McManus, and A. P. M. Coxon (1993). 'No Connection between Alcohol Use and Unsafe Sex among Gay and Bisexual Men', *AIDS*, 7, 115–19

Winkelstein, W. (1990). 'Smoking and Cervical Cancer – Current Status: A Review', *American Journal of Epidemiology*, 131, 945–57

Wright, N. H., M. P. Vessey, K. Kenwood, K. McPherson, and R. Doll (1978). 'Neoplasia and Dysplasia of the Cervix Uteri and Contraception. A Possible Protective Effect of the Diaphragm', *British Journal of Cancer*, 38, 273–9

CHAPTER 8

Risk-Reduction Strategies

INTRODUCTION

This chapter looks at aspects of sexual attitudes and behaviour in the context of prevention, describing evidence of strategies used to reduce the risk of adverse effects of sexual activity. In terms of sexual health, these adverse effects can be principally identified as unplanned pregnancy and STD (sexually transmitted disease), and the preventive practices as contraception and prophylaxis.

Safer-sex practices vary in the extent to which they confer protection, and strategies that may be effective in one context do not always transfer to another. Behaviour adopted to prevent infection will not necessarily serve to prevent pregnancy and the reverse is also true. With the exception of the condom, methods of contraception do not normally protect against infection, and although condom use may be the best available strategy for reducing the risk of infection, there are more effective means of preventing conception. Reducing the number of partners may lower the probability of infection but not that of pregnancy. Avoiding penetrative sex reduces the risk of HIV transmission and pregnancy but not necessarily of some other sexually transmitted infections, such as herpes.

The preventive practices described here have relevance for many areas of sexual health but the questions asked in this survey concerned mostly safer sex in the context of preventing pregnancy and HIV transmission. The first part of this chapter describes patterns of contraceptive use among different subgroups of the population. The second looks at knowledge of risk-reduction strategies, awareness of risk of HIV, and reported behaviour change in response to the threat of AIDS.

CONTRACEPTIVE USE

Two questions on contraception were asked in the face-to-face interview of all those with experience of sexual intercourse with someone of the opposite sex after the age of 13. The questions were phrased similarly to those of the General Household Survey (GHS) (OPCS, 1991). The term 'contraception' does not feature in the question, though the response options clearly have in common that they are all contraceptive methods.

Respondents were presented with a show-card listing contraceptive methods, including 'other' and 'no method' options, and asked which, if any, they had used with a partner ever, and which in the past year. (The method used on the occasion of first intercourse is described in Chapter 2). In addition, the self-completion booklet contained questions on condom use in the past 4 weeks and on the last occasion of sex.

Contraceptive Users and Non-users

21.1% of women and 17.6% of men reported having used no method of contraception in the past year (Figure 8.1). These data are based on responses from those with at least one heterosexual partner in the past year and therefore exclude the 13.9% of women and 13.1% of men who reported no partner during that period. It cannot be assumed that those who were not sexually active in that recent period were not using some method of contraception, but it can be assumed that they were not at risk of heterosexually acquired infection or pregnancy.

Among those using no method, it is not possible to distinguish between those who were sexually active and at risk of an unplanned pregnancy, and those who were pregnant, seeking pregnancy, or sterile for non-contraceptive reasons, and therefore not at risk. Even on the most conservative estimate of these categories, the residual category of those sexually active and not protected against unplanned pregnancy is probably well under 10% of the total. Just how much progress has been made in contraceptive practice in Britain can be appreciated when we recall that at the turn of the century only 10% of women used any contraceptive method at all (Wellings, 1986a).

Contraceptive use decreases with age. More than nine out of ten sexually active 16–24-year-old men and women reported the use of at least one method in the past year, compared with two-thirds of men and just over half of women in the oldest age group, (many of whom will no longer be of childbearing age) (Figure 8.1). Compared with those who were married, contraceptive use was higher among the single or cohabiting, lower among those who were divorced or separated and lowest among the widowed, reflecting varying levels of sexual activity and need for protection against pregnancy in these different groups (Table 8.1).

Contraceptive Methods Used

Respondents were asked to list *all* methods used in the past year, so that more than one method could have been reported and used concurrently or sequentially in this time period. Some methods, especially those conferring lower levels of protection against pregnancy, are more likely to be used in conjunction with another than others – barrier methods (diaphragms, condoms and spermicides) and natural family planning (the rhythm method, or 'safe-period'), for example. But even those with higher effectiveness rates, such as sterilization and oral contraception, may be reported in addition to another – for those with more than one sexual relationship in the last year, for example, or for those who seek prophylactic as well as contraceptive protection. Analysis of highly effective methods of contraception together with condom use in the past year is described below (see p. 356).

According to reports of use in the past year, the three contraceptive methods most commonly relied on are the pill (reported by 28.8% women and 30.4% of men), the condom (25.9% of women

16–24

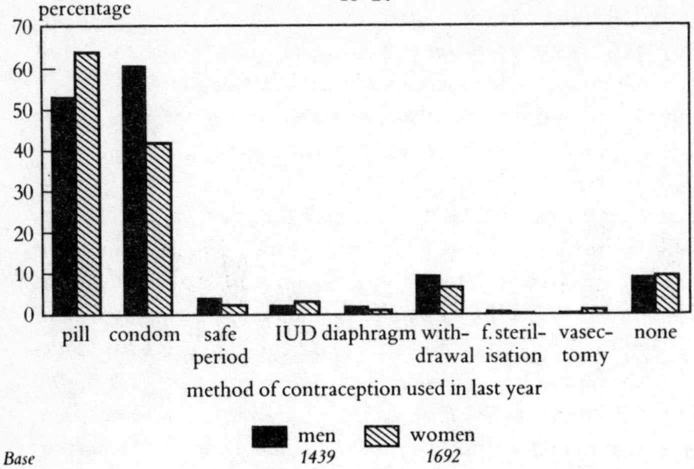
percentage
70
60
50
40
30
20
10
0
pill
condom
safe period
IUD
diaphragm
with-drawal
f. steril-isation
vasec-tomy
none
method of contraception used in last year
men
women
Base
1439
1692

25–34

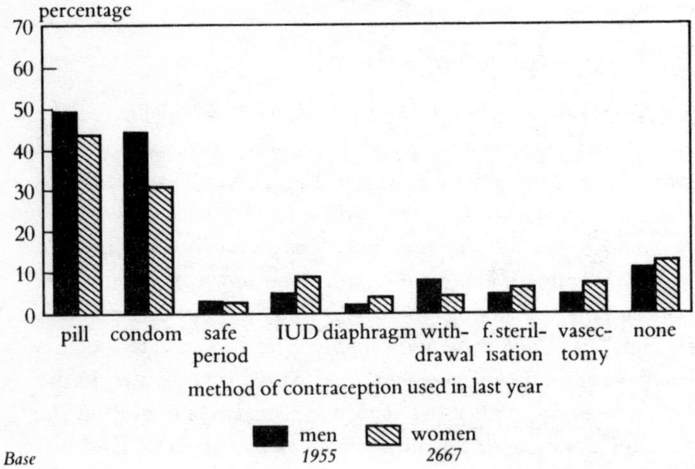
percentage
70
60
50
40
30
20
10
0
pill
condom
safe period
IUD
diaphragm
with-drawal
f. steril-isation
vasec-tomy
none
method of contraception used in last year
men
women
Base
1955
2667

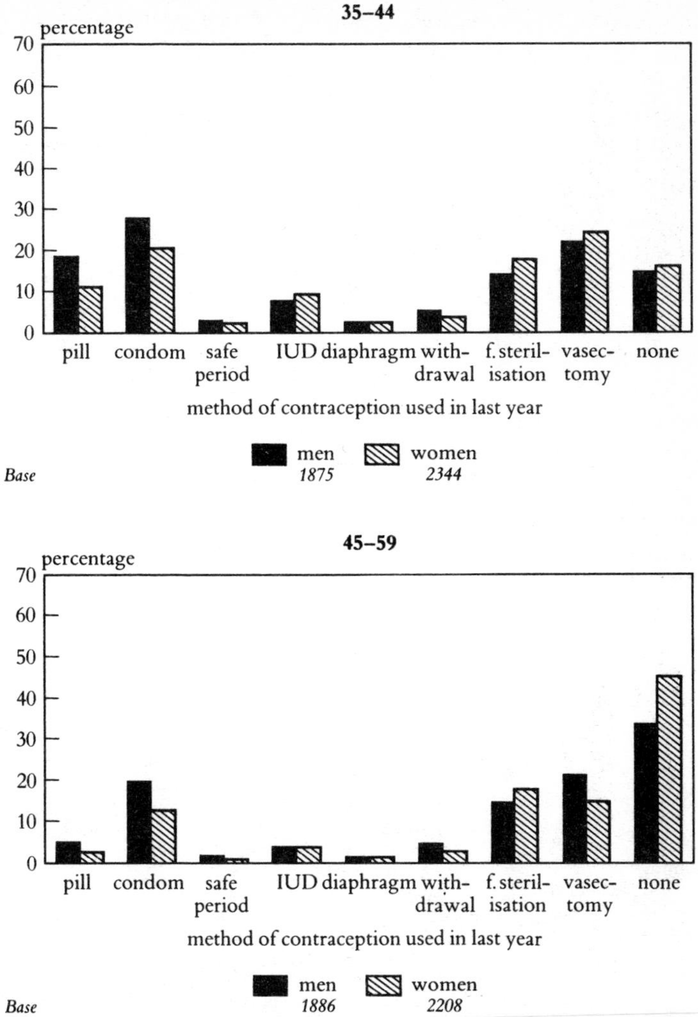

Figure 8.1 Contraceptive method used in the last year by age group.
Source: Interview Question 30b

	married %	cohabiting opposite sex %	widowed %	divorced/ separated %	single %	all %
			men			
pill	21.3	51.9	15.7	26.7	48.7	30.4
IUD	5.6	5.7	5.0	5.9	2.5	4.9
condom	27.9	31.0	32.4	37.1	64.2	36.9
diaphragm	1.8	2.9	0.0	1.6	2.1	2.0
pessaries	0.7	1.3	0.0	0.2	0.3	0.6
sponge	0.0	0.2	0.0	0.2	0.3	0.1
douche	0.0	0.5	0.0	1.3	0.3	0.2
safe period	2.1	3.8	7.7	3.2	3.9	2.7
withdrawal	5.4	10.0	7.3	8.5	9.3	6.8
female sterilization	11.9	7.8	0.0	12.6	1.1	9.1
vasectomy	18.2	7.5	6.8	9.2	0.1	12.8
abstinence	1.0	2.5	0.0	1.7	2.4	1.5
other method	0.2	0.3	0.0	0.6	0.4	0.3
none	20.4	11.4	40.1	24.9	10.3	17.6
*base**	*4584*	*597*	*21*	*307*	*1639*	*7149*
			women			
pill	19.7	48.7	4.6	24.5	59.0	28.8
IUD	7.1	5.7	4.4	12.0	3.2	6.6
condom	21.8	26.2	2.2	19.1	46.7	25.9
diaphragm	2.1	3.5	0.8	3.4	2.0	2.3
pessaries	0.8	0.8	0.0	0.5	0.8	0.8
sponge	0.1	0.1	0.0	0.2	0.2	0.1
douche	0.1	0.0	0.0	0.3	0.2	0.1
safe period	1.7	2.7	0.0	1.3	2.6	1.9
withdrawal	3.5	4.5	0.0	3.7	7.5	4.2
female sterilization	13.1	9.8	16.8	16.7	0.5	11.0
vasectomy	17.1	4.9	3.5	5.7	0.6	12.6
abstinence	0.6	1.8	0.7	0.8	2.4	1.0
other method	0.5	1.3	0.0	1.4	0.9	0.7
none	23.9	12.4	67.7	26.7	9.9	21.1
*base**	*6053*	*816*	*64*	*544*	*1429*	*8906*

Table 8.1 Contraception used in the last year by marital status. Source: Interview Question 30b; Booklet Question 7d

* excludes respondents with no heterosexual partner in the last year

and 36.9% of men) and male or female sterilization (23.3% of women and 21.4% of men) (Figure 8.1). No other single method is reported by more than 10% of respondents.

Oral Contraception

Although the pill is the method of choice for a quarter of British women, reliance on this method varies markedly with age group and marital status (Table 8.1 and Figure 8.1). Oral contraceptive use declines steeply with age. Nearly two thirds (64.1%) of women aged 16–24 reported the use of this method in the past year, but scarcely more than one in ten of those aged 35–44 did so and the proportion falls to one in forty (2.5%) in the age group 45–59 (Figure 8.1). Similarly, well over half of single women and nearly half of those cohabiting reported the use of oral contraceptives in the past year, compared with fewer than one in five of those who were married (Table 8.1).

The sharpest fall in level of oral contraceptive use occurred between women in the 25–34 age group (43.6% of whom reported pill use in the past year) and those in the 35–44 age group (11.3% of whom did so). This may well concur with DHSS guidelines relating to use of the combined pill for those aged 40 and over (DHSS, 1979).

Although age and marital status are clearly related, each exerts a separate effect on method choice, as shown in Table 8.2. The decline in use of the pill with increasing age, however, is more marked at an earlier age for married women than it is for those who are single, reflecting a diminishing need among married women for reliable contraception in the peak childbearing years, and a continuing need among single women (Table 8.2).

Sterilization

While the pill is more commonly the method of choice among single women, and decreases in use with age, surgical methods of birth control find favour with married women and increase in popularity with age. The proportion of women relying on their own sterilization or that of their partner increased with age up to 44

men

16–24 years

	married	cohabiting opposite sex	widowed	separated/ divorced	single	total
pill	57.7	71.4	–	57.9	50.0	53.1
condom	38.9	37.9	–	20.0	67.6	60.8
total sterilization	2.4	1.3	–	0.0	0.3	0.6
female sterilization	1.8	1.3	–	0.0	0.3	0.5
vasectomy	0.6	0.0	–	0.0	0.0	0.1
none	13.5	7.5	–	2.0	73.7	9.0
base†	*163*	*146*	*0*	*16*‡	*1114*	*1439*

25–34 years

	married	cohabiting opposite sex	widowed	separated/ divorced	single	total
pill	45.5	66.5	–	45.9	52.0	49.4
condom	40.2	37.0	–	46.7	61.3	44.4
total sterilization	12.8	2.1	–	11.4	2.7	9.4
female sterilization	5.7	1.7	–	10.3	2.6	4.8
vasectomy	7.2	0.4	–	1.1	0.1	4.7
none	11.8	8.7	–	18.1	9.0	11.2
base†	*1224*	*240*	*0*	*96*	*396*	*1955*

	35–44 years					
	married	cohabiting opposite sex	widowed	separated/ divorced	single	total
pill	17.0	27.7	–	19.2	31.5	18.7
condom	26.5	20.1	–	44.2	47.7	28.1
total sterilization	38.6	32.9	–	24.9	4.0	35.7
female sterilization	14.8	16.1	–	14.9	3.1	14.3
vasectomy	24.2	20.8	–	10.4	0.9	22.0
none	13.8	12.9	–	22.8	24.3	14.7
base †	*1549*	*130*	*4*‡	*94*	*96*	*1873*

	45–59 years					
	married	cohabiting opposite sex	widowed	separated/ divorced	single	total
pill	3.8	12.8	3.1	13.4	15.2	4.9
condom	18.9	18.7	34.5	24.0	36.5	19.6
total sterilization	36.5	39.2	8.4	31.0	6.0	35.5
female sterilization	14.7	24.3	0.0	14.8	4.6	14.8
vasectomy	22.5	20.2	8.4	17.2	1.3	21.6
none	33.7	25.4	47.9	34.7	42.9	33.7
base†	*1648*	*82*	*17*‡	*101*	*33*	*1882*

Table 8.2 *continued overleaf*

† excludes respondents with no heterosexual partners in the last year
‡ note small base

women

16–24 years

	married	cohabiting opposite sex	widowed	separated/ divorced	single	total
pill	61.3	70.1	–	48.7	63.9	64.1
condom	29.1	35.3	–	31.5	48.8	41.9
total sterilization	2.0	4.0	–	0.0	0.6	1.5
female sterilization	0.5	0.9	–	0.0	0.2	0.4
vasectomy	1.5	3.1	–	0.0	0.4	1.1
none	17.6	5.7	–	21.0	7.2	9.4
base†	*353*	*302*	*1*‡	*33*	*1000*	*1689*

25–34 years

	married	cohabiting opposite sex	widowed	separated/ divorced	single	total
pill	40.2	51.8	–	39.8	56.0	43.6
condom	30.2	28.4	–	22.3	42.3	31.0
total sterilization	16.6	8.6	–	12.9	2.1	13.5
female sterilization	6.9	6.1	–	9.6	1.0	6.2
vasectomy	9.8	2.8	–	3.6	1.2	7.4
none	12.7	12.1	–	17.3	11.0	12.7
base†	*1822*	*313*	*2*‡	*185*	*343*	*2666*

	35–44 years					
	married	cohabiting opposite sex	widowed	separated/ divorced	single	total
pill	10.1	14.6	9.1	19.7	18.5	11.3
condom	20.9	10.7	0.0	19.8	46.3	20.7
total sterilization	44.0	43.5	34.7	28.4	4.3	41.6
female sterilization	17.0	30.8	34.7	19.7	2.6	17.8
vasectomy	27.5	14.1	0.0	9.0	1.7	24.3
none	15.6	14.3	52.0	18.7	24.2	16.2
base †	*1935*	*147*	*11*‡	*187*	*63*	*2344*

	45–59 years					
	married	cohabiting opposite sex	widowed	separated/ divorced	single	total
pill	2.4	4.2	0.0	4.7	0.0	2.5
condom	13.4	4.6	1.8	10.7	20.7	12.8
total sterilization	33.5	25.7	18.3	30.1	2.6	32.4
female sterilization	17.5	23.9	13.8	26.1	2.6	17.9
vasectomy	16.5	1.9	4.5	5.4	0.0	15.0
none	43.8	46.9	74.2	51.6	68.0	45.3
base†	*1942*	*54*	*50*	*138*	*23*	*2207*

Table 8.2 Contraceptive method ★ used in the past year by age and marital status. Source: Interview Question 30b; Booklet Question 7d

★ 3 most commonly used methods only

† excludes respondents with no heterosexual partners in the last year

‡ note small base

years (Table 8.2 and Figure 8.1). Reliance on female sterilization or vasectomy was reported by very small proportions of men and women aged 16–24. Use of these methods peaks in the age group 35–44, falling slightly in the oldest age group, 45–59.

As shown in Table 8.2, sterilization is far more common among married than single women, and vies with the pill as the method of choice for married women as a whole. There is, however, an abrupt reversal in the popularity of the two methods in the middle years of the lives of married women. While pill users outnumber those who rely on sterilization in the 25–34 age range, they are heavily outnumbered in the 35–44 age group. Reports of reliance on sterilization peaked among married women aged 35–44, 44% of whom are protected by their partners' or their own sterilization. The prevalence of sterilization in the 45–59 age group of women was lower than among those aged 35–44, but the proportion using no method was higher – 43.8% cf. 15.6% – so that sterilization accounted for more than half of all contraceptive use in the 45–59 age range.

The ratio of male to female sterilization also varies with age. For women, reliance on vasectomy is more common than reliance on female sterilization in all age groups save the oldest. For men, reliance on female sterilization is more common in those aged under 35 and vasectomy in those of 35 and older. The trend towards greater reliance on male than female sterilization in recent decades documented elsewhere (Bone, 1985; Wellings, 1986b) is also demonstrated here.

Condoms

Condom use is described among contraceptive methods but it should be borne in mind that the question wording made no mention of contraception as such, so that respondents might be equally likely to be reporting prophylactic use of condoms here. Condom use on the last occasion of heterosexual sex and in the last 4 weeks was also probed in the booklet, and these data are described below (p. 370).

Until recently, the method of contraception that showed the most striking rise in popularity was sterilization, reflecting the decline of the pill, since for those looking for a highly effective method free from side-effects, this is the only serious alternative (Wellings, 1986b). However, following the wide publicity given to the advantages of condom use in response to the HIV epidemic, the condom has increased in prominence among contraceptive methods.

Overall, 25.9% of women and 36.9% of men report having used a condom in the past year. Generally speaking, the popularity of condoms declines with age (Figure 8.1). The proportion of young women aged 16–24 who reported condom use in the past year is twice that of 35–44-year-old women and more than 3 times that of those aged 45–59. Similar trends are evident for men, although a higher proportion of men than women in all age groups report condom use in the last year. Despite the pattern of decreasing use with increasing age, reports of condom use at least once in the past year outnumber reports of pill use in men and women aged 35 and over.

Other Methods

Methods of contraception other than those described above are reported by far fewer respondents. The next most commonly reported method, the IUD, is more popular among women in their middle years, 25–44, 9.1% of whom report its use (Figure 8.1), but the proportions fall markedly among younger and older women. The IUD is twice as popular among married women as it is among those who are single (Table 8.1). This variation may reflect contra-indications of IUD use for nulliparous women (women who have not borne children) and for those for whom the risk of STD might be greater. The increased risk of pelvic inflammatory disease associated with the use of this method is greater, and has more serious implications in terms of a possible adverse effect on fertility, for those who have not had children. Menopausal women are advised to have IUDs removed within a year of the menopause because of narrowing of the cervical canal.

6.8% of men and 4.2% of women reported having relied on withdrawal as a method of contraception in the past year, and these are much more likely to be young. 2.7% of men and 1.9% of women reported having calculated the safe period to prevent conception. Female barrier methods are used by very small proportions of respondents; the diaphragm is used by little more than 2% of women. Use of the diaphragm is highest among cohabiting women and those women who are divorced and separated.

Contraceptive Use by Social Class

Earlier surveys have shown some variation in contraceptive method use by social class. In 1970, Bone (1973) found significant variation in use between women in manual and non-manual social classes. In particular women in the lowest socio-economic groups were most likely to report abstinence or the use of no method. Differences in contraceptive practice between social classes were still just perceptible in 1975 (the year in which contraceptive provision was made freely available to all under the NHS), but they had diminished (Bone, 1978). Dunnell's data (1979) showed that when only those who were currently sexually active were considered, there was little social-class difference in contraceptive behaviour among single women.

In common with these findings, these data show the association with social class to be more marked for whether a method is used at all than for specific choice of method. In bivariate analysis, the data show a social-class gradient for use of any contraceptive method in the past year, particularly for men (Table 8.3). 14.2% of men in social classes I and II reported the use of no method in this time period compared with 20.7% of those in social classes IV and V. For women, the comparable figures were 19.4% and 23.6%.

Social-class variation is apparent for some but not all methods used. Use seems to be differentiated more in terms of intrusiveness. Those in non-manual groups, for example, seem to be more likely to use intercourse-related methods. Women in upper socio-economic groups were more likely to have used female barrier methods in the past year – the diaphragm and pessaries – and also to have used the safe period.

The ratio of male to female sterilization also varies with social class. Women reporting reliance on male sterilization outnumber

	I %	II %	III NM %	III M %	IV %	V %	all social classes %
				women			
pill	21.9	23.7	36.0	24.2	33.4	36.6	28.8
IUD	6.7	7.0	6.4	6.6	7.0	6.0	6.7
condom	28.6	27.0	27.3	19.5	23.1	31.8	25.9
diaphragm	5.8	3.1	2.1	1.1	0.7	2.1	2.3
pessaries	1.8	1.1	0.3	0.4	0.3	1.1	0.8
sponge	0.2	0.1	0.2	0.2	0.0	0.1	0.1
douche	0.3	0.1	0.2	0.1	0.2	0.2	0.1
safe period	4.0	2.0	1.9	1.6	1.6	1.2	1.9
withdrawal	4.4	3.3	4.4	4.3	5.2	5.6	4.2
female sterilization	8.2	12.1	9.6	13.1	11.3	9.0	11.1
vasectomy	15.0	15.8	11.5	14.9	7.8	4.2	12.5
abstinence	1.4	1.0	0.6	0.7	1.0	2.0	1.0
other method	0.0	0.4	0.5	1.0	1.2	1.3	0.7
none	19.2	19.4	18.6	24.7	24.2	23.0	21.1
base★	*607*	*2730*	*2044*	*1683*	*899*	*934*	*8897*
				men			
pill	28.9	27.9	32.3	30.4	30.5	36.0	30.4
IUD	4.9	5.3	5.4	5.1	4.0	2.6	4.9
condom	40.1	35.4	33.8	34.3	36.1	55.7	36.9
diaphragm	4.6	3.3	1.3	0.8	1.3	0.8	2.0
pessaries	1.2	1.2	0.4	0.2	0.3	0.0	0.6
sponge	0.3	0.1	0.0	0.1	0.0	0.3	0.1
douche	0.0	0.1	0.0	0.1	0.5	0.9	0.2
safe period	5.1	3.2	2.6	1.7	1.7	3.8	2.7
withdrawal	7.6	5.8	6.0	7.6	6.9	9.2	6.8
female sterilization	7.7	11.2	9.6	8.6	9.0	2.9	9.1
vasectomy	13.9	16.4	14.7	11.5	8.4	3.3	12.8
abstinence	2.6	1.5	1.5	0.9	1.6	1.9	1.5
other method	0.2	0.2	0.2	0.2	0.5	0.7	0.3
none	14.2	14.2	15.9	21.7	22.7	18.0	17.6
base★	*505*	*2127*	*1393*	*1771*	*764*	*584*	*7145*

Table 8.3 Contraceptive method used by social class. Source: Interview Question 30b; Booklet Question 7d

★ excludes respondents with no heterosexual partners in the last year

those reporting reliance on female sterilization in all social classes except IV and V, in which the reverse holds. This finding from bivariate analysis is consistent with that of Hunt and Annandale (1990), i.e. that women who were sterilized themselves were of lower social class than those with a sterilized partner. The difference may be partly explained by parity; women in manual groups being more likely to have a larger number of children (see below, p. 342). Bivariate analysis shows no consistent social-class effect on pill use, though women in social class I seem less likely than those in other social-class groups to report its use (Table 8.3).

Contraceptive Use and Religion

The relationship between contraceptive use and religious affiliation has been analysed and the data are summarized in Table 8.4. In the case of some faiths, canons contained within the scriptures militate against the use of particular contraceptive methods, or even of the use of any at all. The papal encyclical, *Humanae Vitae* (1968), for example, opposes all forms of contraception except for the rhythm method or safe period, forbidding practising Catholics, in theory at least, to control their fertility artificially. Similarly, although reversible contraceptive methods are acceptable to most in the Islamic faith (Sachedina, 1990), vasectomy is prohibited in Islam and female sterilization permitted only in limited circumstances (Mujahidul Islam, 1989). Religious affiliation may also be linked to contraceptive use through cultural values relating to gender and family roles, and the power of community influence.

With increasing secularization, these influences on contraceptive behaviour might be expected to have weakened. Few data exist on religion and contraceptive usage in Britain. US data from Cycle IV of the National Survey of Family Growth carried out in 1988 (Goldscheider and Mosher, 1988; 1991) show that despite evidence of convergence, contraceptive use patterns still show a continuing effect of religion. Protestants report a higher level of sterilization; Catholics higher pill use; while the Jewish pattern is distinctive for its significantly higher levels of female compared with male sterilization, and higher levels of diaphragm and condom use.

As shown in Table 8.4, bivariate analysis of the data supports a

	no religion %	Christian: C of E %	Christian: RC %	Christian: other %	non-Christian %	total %
			men			
pill	36.0	23.3	28.5	23.9	23.1	30.4
IUD	4.5	5.0	5.5	5.0	6.8	4.9
condom	40.0	31.2	35.4	35.3	42.8	36.9
diaphragm	2.2	1.6	0.8	2.4	2.3	2.0
pessaries	0.6	0.7	0.7	0.4	0.5	0.6
sponge	0.1	0.1	0.1	0.1	0.4	0.1
douche	0.2	0.2	0.5	0.0	0.0	0.2
safe period	3.0	2.7	2.8	2.1	1.6	2.7
withdrawal	7.4	5.6	8.3	5.5	6.1	6.8
female sterilization	8.4	10.9	7.5	10.5	4.6	9.0
vasectomy	10.8	18.6	9.0	14.4	4.5	12.8
abstinence	1.8	0.9	1.6	1.9	0.4	1.5
other method	0.2	0.2	0.6	0.4	0.4	0.3
none	15.1	18.7	22.6	19.8	26.5	17.6
base *	*3676*	*1823*	*639*	*736*	*274*	*7148*
			women			
pill	37.7	21.4	31.0	29.0	17.0	28.8
IUD	6.9	6.3	7.1	5.8	8.8	6.6
condom	27.7	23.8	25.8	25.6	27.6	25.9
diaphragm	2.6	2.0	1.9	2.3	3.2	2.3
pessaries	0.8	0.6	0.5	1.0	1.2	0.8
sponge	0.2	0.0	0.2	0.1	0.0	0.1
douche	0.1	0.1	0.2	0.2	0.2	0.1
safe period	2.1	1.2	2.9	2.1	2.6	1.9
withdrawal	4.2	4.1	5.3	3.7	4.8	4.2
female sterilization	9.4	13.4	7.0	13.7	8.6	11.1
vasectomy	10.3	16.4	8.8	13.8	7.0	12.6
abstinence	1.0	0.8	1.7	0.8	1.8	1.0
other method	0.5	0.7	1.4	0.6	1.9	0.7
none	16.9	22.6	24.3	23.0	32.1	21.0
base *	*3339*	*2978*	*1004*	*1277*	*299*	*8897*

Table 8.4 Contraceptive method used by religion. Source: Interview Question 30b; Booklet Question 7d

* excludes respondents with no heterosexual partners in the last year

view of a continuing though weak effect of religion on contraceptive practice. Those of non-Christian religion are more likely to have used no method at all in the past year compared with those of another religious denomination and nearly twice as likely as those with no religious denomination, among whom reports of no method use are lowest.

Overall, those with a religious denomination seemed less likely to be pill users than those who report no denomination. As documented in the US literature, distinctive patterns of contraceptive use continue to characterize a general comparison of Catholics and Protestants. Pill use is higher among Catholics than Anglicans (28.5% cf. 23.3% men and 31.0% cf. 21.4% women) and reports of surgical methods of contraception lower. The ratio of female to male sterilizations also varies with religious affiliation. Compared with those with no religious affiliation, male sterilization is marginally more common among Anglicans and less common among Catholics. Compared with Anglicans, Catholic women are more likely to use the safe period.

Contraceptive Method Use by Numbers of Children

To some extent the effects of parity and age are confounded since the number of children increases with age. Looking at number of children within age group, however, Table 8.5 shows that reports of female sterilization are strikingly higher among those with more children.

Contraceptive Method Use and Number of Heterosexual Partners

Data on risk and preventive practice can be used to explore whether risk reduction strategies are related to current or past patterns of behaviour. In this context those with multiple sexual partners are clearly of interest, and method use was examined in relation to partner numbers in the last year (Table 8.6). Those with 1 or more partner are less likely to have used no method than those who report having been monogamous in the past year. Pill use increases with numbers of partners. This is particularly marked for women. 70.2%

of women reporting 5 or more partners in the past year used oral contraception compared with 27.6% of those reporting only one partner.

Condom use also increased markedly with number of partners. More than half (55.9%) of men with 2 female partners reported condom use in the past year and 71.6% of those with 5 or more. For women, the comparable figures were 39.6% and 60.4%. Nevertheless a substantial proportion of the small number of those with 5 or more heterosexual partners, 39.6% of women and 28.4% of men, do not report any condom use in the past year. The use of almost all non-surgical methods – IUD, condom, diaphragm, safe period, withdrawal – seems to show little variation with increase in numbers of partners. Use of sterilization and vasectomy is highest among those with only one partner.

Multivariate Analysis

Logistic regression models were used to explore the relationship between age, marital status, social class, parity, numbers of partners, and contraceptive method (Figures 8.2 and 8.3). Age exerts a strong effect on any use of contraception, increasing for both men and women after controlling for other factors (Figure 8.2). The social-class effect was sustained – men in manual social-class groups were twice as likely as those in non-manual social-class groups to report use of no method, though for women this effect was weaker. The effect of numbers of partners was more marked for men than for women, those with more than one sexual partner in the past year being 4 times less likely to report no method use than those with one. For both men and women, having children was significantly associated with using some method of contraception.

Looking at the pattern for the main methods used (Figure 8.3), oral contraception is positively associated, for both men and women, with younger current age, with cohabiting or once-married status and, for men, with having 3 or more sexual partners. Those with children are less likely to use oral contraception. The age effect is reflected in condom use, though it is less marked, and the effect of marital status is reversed for condom use for women. Those with 2

	men					
	16–24 years					
number of children	0 %	1 %	2 %	3 %	4+ %	total %
pill	53.1	55.7	41.5	–	–	53.1
condom	63.9	33.4	31.2	–	–	60.8
total sterilization	0.5	1.7	3.9	–	–	0.6
female sterilization	0.4	1.7	3.9	–	–	0.5
vasectomy	0.1	0.0	0.0	–	–	0.1
base †	*1285*	*119*	*23*	*9‡*	*1‡*	*1438*
	25–34 years					
number of children	0 %	1 %	2 %	3 %	4+ %	total %
pill	57.4	49.4	39.9	30.3	39.1	49.4
condom	49.7	42.5	40.9	30.7	31.5	44.4
total sterilization	2.9	3.0	18.0	35.2	39.0	9.4
female sterilization	2.6	2.1	7.0	15.8	20.8	4.8
vasectomy	0.3	0.9	11.0	20.9	18.3	4.7
base †	*905*	*432*	*437*	*126*	*55*	*1955*

	35–44 years					
number of children	0 %	1 %	2 %	3 %	4+ %	total %
pill	30.3	19.9	15.6	17.3	9.4	18.7
condom	33.5	35.6	26.6	23.0	22.2	28.0
total sterilization	15.0	27.0	42.8	45.6	36.2	35.8
female sterilization	10.1	15.4	12.0	20.7	18.5	14.3
vasectomy	4.9	12.0	31.6	26.0	17.7	22.1
base †	*342*	*237*	*791*	*360*	*142*	*1872*

	45–59 years					
number of children	0 %	1 %	2 %	3 %	4+ %	total %
pill	6.5	7.6	4.3	3.6	5.4	4.9
condom	23.1	27.0	19.3	16.0	16.9	19.6
total sterilization	9.7	24.9	41.2	43.9	33.7	35.6
female sterilization	6.8	12.6	14.9	15.4	21.6	14.8
vasectomy	2.9	13.3	27.6	29.1	12.8	21.7
base †	*189*	*240*	*771*	*430*	*252*	*1882*

Table 8.5 *continued overleaf*

† excludes respondents with no heterosexual partners in the last year
‡ note small base

	women					
	16–24 years					
number of children	0 %	1 %	2 %	3 %	4+ %	total %
pill	66.8	58.4	53.5	45.2	–	64.1
condom	47.8	24.2	27.4	18.8	–	41.8
total sterilization	1.1	0.7	4.3	17.0	–	1.5
female sterilization	0.2	0.2	0.9	10.9	–	0.4
vasectomy	0.9	0.5	3.4	6.1	–	1.1
base †	*1253*	*295*	*109*	*28*	*4*‡	*1690*
	25–34 years					
number of children	0 %	1 %	2 %	3 %	4+ %	total %
pill	56.7	48.5	37.5	25.3	19.3	43.7
condom	39.4	29.7	28.2	20.9	23.4	31.0
total sterilization	1.9	3.3	20.9	33.3	41.9	13.5
female sterilization	0.4	1.7	8.5	16.6	26.2	6.2
vasectomy	1.6	1.7	12.5	16.8	15.7	7.4
base †	*837*	*564*	*841*	*313*	*111*	*2665*

	35–44 years					
number of children	0	1	2	3	4+	total
	%	%	%	%	%	%
pill	19.5	16.7	8.0	11.4	11.5	11.3
condom	24.7	22.7	21.8	18.1	14.5	20.7
total sterilization	15.5	24.8	47.7	49.8	43.8	41.7
female sterilization	6.1	10.1	17.7	24.7	25.1	17.8
vasectomy	9.4	14.7	30.7	25.8	18.7	24.4
base †	*224*	*303*	*1086*	*487*	*242*	*2341*

	45–59 years					
number of children	0	1	2	3	4+	total
	%	%	%	%	%	%
pill	4.0	3.0	2.0	2.9	2.1	2.5
condom	19.5	15.7	14.7	11.5	5.0	12.8
total sterilization	11.6	20.0	35.4	36.8	37.7	32.4
female sterilization	7.8	8.9	17.1	20.7	27.3	17.9
vasectomy	3.8	11.5	18.9	16.5	11.4	15.0
base †	*165*	*278*	*851*	*555*	*358*	*2207*

Table 8.5 Contraceptive method★ used in the past year by age group and number of children. Source: Interview Question 30b; Booklet Question 7d

★ 3 most commonly used methods only

† excludes respondents with no heterosexual partners in the last year

‡ note small base

number of partners	1	2	3–4	5+
	%	%	%	%
		men		
pill	28.0	38.4	56.8	54.6
IUD	5.1	4.9	2.6	5.2
condom	33.2	55.9	61.8	71.6
diaphragm	1.9	1.9	4.2	3.2
pessaries	0.6	0.5	0.9	0.5
sponge	0.1	0.5	0.1	0.9
douche	0.1	0.3	1.1	2.4
safe period	2.3	5.1	7.4	1.7
withdrawal	5.6	10.5	15.5	22.7
female sterilization	10.0	5.3	4.6	4.6
vasectomy	14.2	8.0	4.9	0.7
abstinence	1.5	1.3	1.8	4.7
other method	0.3	0.4	0.3	0.0
none	18.0	9.2	8.3	8.9
base *	*5799*	*655*	*328*	*125*
		women		
pill	27.6	46.2	53.4	70.2
IUD	6.6	7.0	7.7	4.4
condom	24.8	39.6	52.3	60.4
diaphragm	2.3	3.8	1.3	2.7
pessaries	0.7	1.2	1.8	1.4
sponge	0.1	0.3	1.0	0.0
douche	0.1	0.3	0.0	0.0
safe period	2.0	1.3	5.9	1.4
withdrawal	4.1	6.7	8.3	4.4
female sterilization	11.5	9.2	4.2	0.0
vasectomy	13.4	6.1	4.2	2.8
abstinence	1.0	1.2	1.3	4.6
other method	0.8	0.1	0.0	0.0
none	20.8	11.3	8.0	0.0
*base**	*7914*	*476*	*159*	*35*

Table 8.6 Contraceptive method used in the last year by number of heterosexual partners in the last year. Source: Interview Question 30b; Booklet Question 7d

* excludes respondents with no heterosexual partners last year

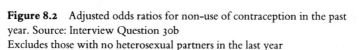

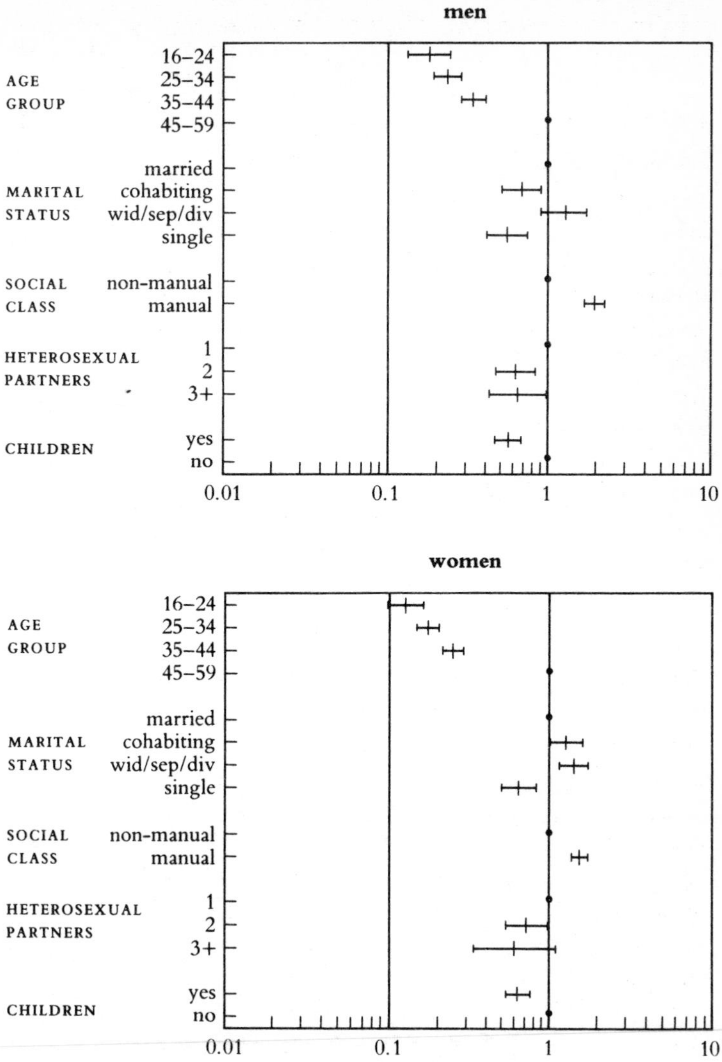

Figure 8.2 Adjusted odds ratios for non-use of contraception in the past year. Source: Interview Question 30b
Excludes those with no heterosexual partners in the last year

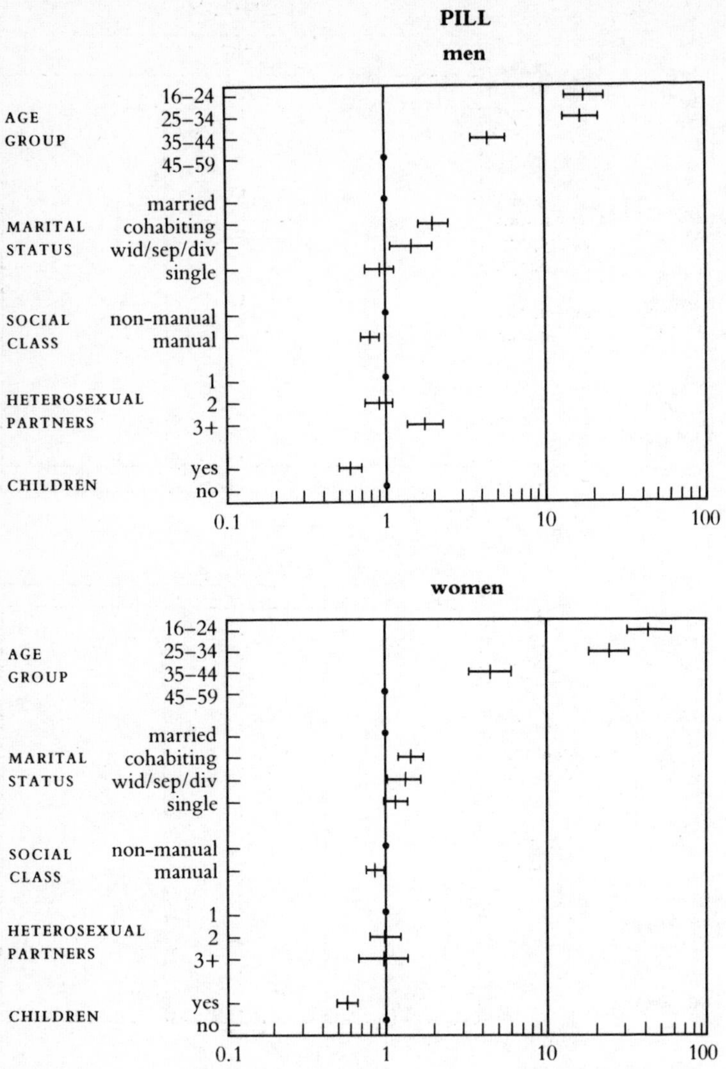
PILL
men
AGE GROUP
16–24
25–34
35–44
45–59
MARITAL STATUS
married
cohabiting
wid/sep/div
single
SOCIAL CLASS
non-manual
manual
HETEROSEXUAL PARTNERS
1
2
3+
CHILDREN
yes
no
0.1
1
10
100
women
AGE GROUP
16–24
25–34
35–44
45–59
MARITAL STATUS
married
cohabiting
wid/sep/div
single
SOCIAL CLASS
non-manual
manual
HETEROSEXUAL PARTNERS
1
2
3+
CHILDREN
yes
no
0.1
1
10
100

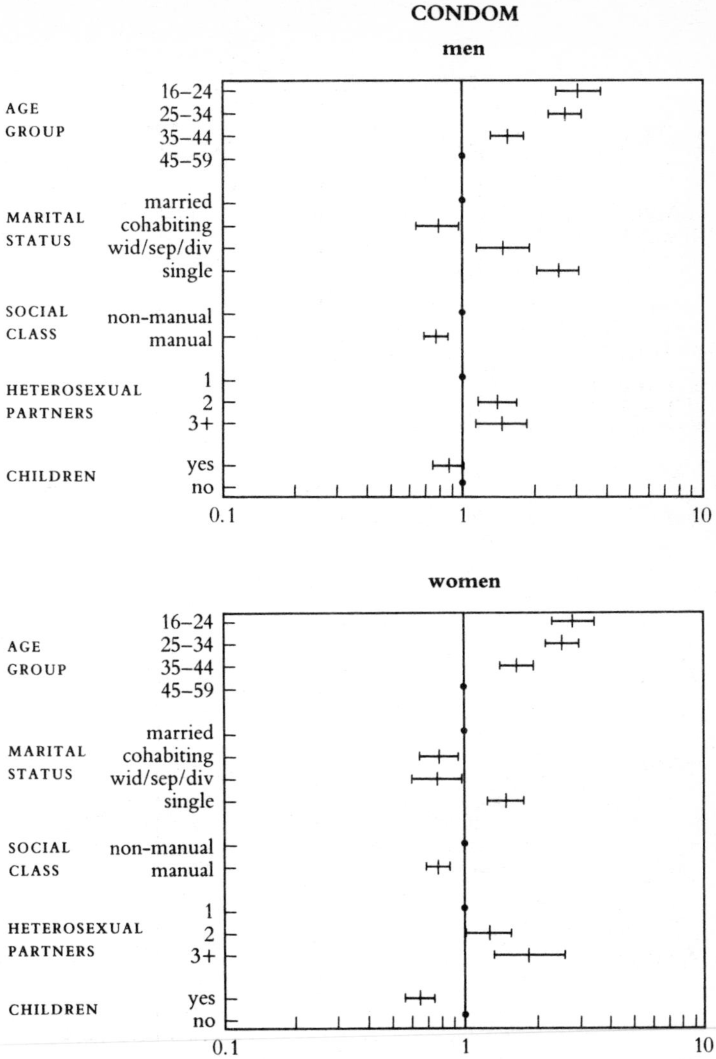

Figure 8.3 *continued overleaf*

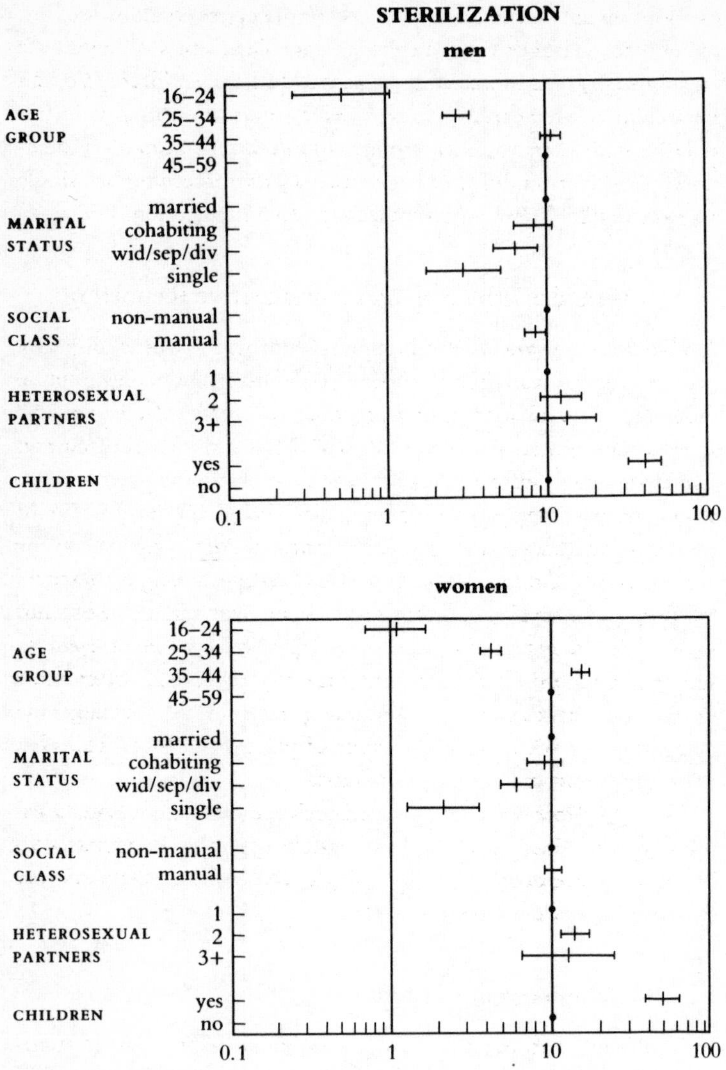

Figure 8.3 Adjusted odds ratios for contraceptive method used in the last year. Source: Interview Question 30b

or more sexual partners are more likely to report condom use, but the effect is weaker than the effect of age. The most striking effects on sterilization are those of age, marital status and children. Women with children are nearly 5 times as likely, and men 4 times as likely, as those with none to rely on sterilization for contraceptive protection. Not surprisingly, those aged 16–24 and those who are single are very unlikely to rely on sterilization for contraception.

Gender Differences in Contraceptive Reporting

As shown in Table 8.1 and Figure 8.1, there is some disparity between the sexes in their reporting of the use of any contraceptive methods. Several factors might account for gender differences. The age difference between partners is such that a proportion of men in each age range will report the method used by women 2 or 3 years younger, on average, than themselves. The lower proportion of men in the younger age group reporting partner's pill use may be explained by the fact that a proportion of these younger men will be having a sexual relationship with young women who have not yet started taking the pill. The higher proportion of men aged 35–44 reporting pill use in the last year may reflect the fact that a proportion of these men will have partners in the younger age range among whom the prevalence of pill use is higher. This effect is also apparent in the sterilization data.

Lack of familiarity with the partner's method might also explain some of the discrepancy, and so the difference could be expected to be more pronounced for the single than the married and for younger rather than older respondents.

Contraceptive Trends

It is difficult to determine to what extent these cross-sectional patterns of contraceptive use should be interpreted in terms of life-stage effects and to what extent in terms of historical trends. Needs relating to fertility control vary throughout the life course. At the start of the sexual career, before childbearing, the need is for a reliable and reversible method of contraception. During the period of starting and spacing a family, a concern for efficacy may take second place to a need for safety and acceptability. On completion of childbearing and possible resumption of a woman's employment the need for a reliable method returns, but this time the need for reversibility is less, and with advancing years the concern for side-effects greater.

Among older women, the decline of pill use no doubt reflects declining fertility and the decreasing need for a totally efficacious contraceptive method, together with increasing awareness of adverse side-effects with advancing years, and is therefore to some extent a function of life stage. Similarly the increase in popularity of sterilization with parity and age reflects a continuing need for a high degree of efficacy together with a greater tolerance for a method that is irreversible, on completion of family size.

Yet the notion of an orderly 'reproductive career' has not gone unchallenged. The concept of a linear life course comprising three consecutive stages – a sexually active period before childbearing, a period of childbearing during which pregnancies are spaced, and the remaining fertile years when no further children are wanted – is oversimplified and ignores changes in marital status (Hunt, 1991). Age is the only reliably progressive variable; marital status and even family spacing do not dependably follow a sequential course.

At any one point in the life of an individual, a decision relating to contraceptive use will reflect not only personal needs and circumstances but also the social and historical context in which it is made. Thus patterns of contraceptive use reflect both biographical and secular changes. The last 30 years have witnessed marked changes in contraceptive use, the most dramatic being the rapid increase in female sterilization and vasectomy in the 1970s and early 1980s, the changing prevalence in oral contraceptive use, the decline in the use of less effective methods and, more recently, the growing awareness of the prophylactic effect of condoms. The general effect of legislation and other developments relating to family planning since 1960 has been to increase the accessibility of the most effective methods of birth control.

As service barriers to the provision of medically prescribed methods have been progressively removed, availability seems gradually to have given way to considerations of efficacy, safety and acceptability in contraceptive decision-making. Reappraisal of the relative importance of these criteria changes throughout the life course, but also through time as different factors conspire to change the balance of costs and benefits.

Concern for the side-effects of different methods of contraception undoubtedly increases with age, as advancing years and a heightened sense of mortality sensitizes women to health risks. These health concerns have also increased over time, as shown in recent surveys of contraceptive practice and attitudes in Britain and other West European countries (Coulter, 1985; Riphagen and Lehert, 1989). Evidence of possible adverse effects of methods such as the pill and the IUD has been accumulating in the past 15 years. Publicity given to papers published in the mid-1970s, linking the pill with an increased risk of cardio-vascular disease (RCGP, 1977; Vessey *et al.*, 1977) and in the early 1980s with breast and cervical cancer (Pike *et al.*, 1983; Vessey *et al.*, 1983) have steadily eroded the appeal of this method in the past decade or so, firstly among older women but more recently among younger women too (OPCS, 1991).

Access to the pill has raised women's expectations of a guarantee of high protection against unwanted pregnancy after achievement of desired family size. 70% of mothers with children of ten and over are now in full- or part-time employment and this long-term commitment to work has increased the need for highly effective methods of contraception. These factors may explain the increasing popularity of permanent methods of contraception.

Increase in male sterilization reflects an increasing need for a reliable method of contraception but also a change in the availability and simplicity of the operation. The number of operations increased rapidly during the later 1960s with the more widespread use of simpler techniques (Jackson, 1969). The increase may also be attributable to an erosion of the traditional resistance on the part of men to the curtailment of what is normally a lifelong capacity and an increasing awareness on the part of younger men of the need to share contraceptive responsibility.

Thus the increase in reliance on sterilization with age is clearly life-stage related since the majority of those who resort to it will have first completed their families. But it is also a function of a trend towards increasing popularity of this method of fertility control over the past two decades (Bone, 1973; Dunnell, 1979;

OPCS, 1985; OPCS, 1991). Evidence of a trend towards increasing popularity of surgical methods of contraception is also discernible within these data in the higher proportions of men and women aged 35–44 reporting sterilization compared with those older than themselves (Figure 8.1).

The advantages of condom use have been highlighted during the HIV epidemic because of their dual role in prophylaxis and contraception and more is said about this below. General Household Survey (GHS) data show that between 1986 and 1989 there was an increase in the percentage of women aged 18–24 who had partners who used the condom so that the relative proportions of pill and condom users among those aged 20–24 has altered quite radically (OPCS, 1991).

Condom Use and Use of Other Methods

Respondents were not asked to distinguish whether condoms were used to protect against pregnancy or infection, or both, although reporting was in the context of contraception. Identifying respondents who have reported the use of condoms and at least one other method of contraception in the last year is clearly of interest in the context of sexual health. While reporting of both cannot be taken to indicate that those reporting use of both another contraceptive method as well as a condom would have used them together on the same occasion of sex (Table 8.7), it is reasonable to assume that a proportion would have done so.

These data show sizeable proportions reporting both a reliable method of contraception and a condom, particularly among the young and those with 2–4 partners (though clearly the variety of contraceptive methods encountered by both men and women will increase with the number of sexual partners).

SAFER SEX

The focus in this section of the chapter is on behaviour that tends to reduce the likelihood of transmission of sexually transmitted infection. Of interest in this context is awareness of personal risk

age group	16–24		25–34		35–44		45–59		all ages	
	%	*base*	%	*base*	%	*base*	%	*base*	%	*base*
heterosexual partners in the last year					**men**					
1	25.3	*889*	17.2	*1601*	6.4	*1638*	1.4	*1671*	10.9	*5799*
2	27.5	*274*	30.5	*178*	11.9	*121*	5.3	*83*	22.6	*655*
3–4	42.1	*176*	36.0	*87*	30.8	*42*	26.3	*23*	37.9	*328*
5+	35.0	*68*	54.8	*40*	13.1	*16*†	–	*1*†	38.2	*125*
total	28.3	*1407*	20.1	*1905*	7.4	*1817*	1.9	*1778*	13.8	*6907*
heterosexual partners in the last year					**women**					
1	21.0	*1322*	12.1	*2408*	3.3	*2172*	1.2	*2012*	8.4	*7914*
2	30.1	*217*	24.5	*135*	6.5	*82*	3.7	*41*	22.2	*476*
3–4	32.0	*98*	24.7	*37*	41.7	*19*†	–	*5*†	30.4	*159*
5+	27.8	*23*	–	*9*†	–	*3*†	–	*0*	39.4	*35*
total	22.9	*1660*	13.1	*2589*	3.8	*2276*	1.2	*2058*	9.7	*8584*

Table 8.7 Proportions of respondents using a highly effective method of contraception* and a condom in the last year. Source: Interview Question 30b; Booklet Question 7d

* vasectomy, female sterilization, pill, IUD
† note small base.

and knowledge of the means by which to reduce it, whether people take preventive health action and what strategies are adopted. The exact relationship between these variables is unclear. It has long been accepted that information is insufficient to prompt behaviour change (Gatherer *et al.*, 1979) and others have noted an absence of any clear association between awareness of unsafe sexual practices and a change to safer sex (Joseph *et al.*, 1987; Becker and Joseph, 1988; Memon, 1991).

Questions asked in the survey relate to several of these variables. Respondents were asked, for example, to describe their understanding of safer sex; to assess their own risk status in relation to HIV transmission; and to report any behaviour change made because of the AIDS epidemic. Information provided elsewhere in the questionnaire enables the relationship between self-perceived risk and risky behaviour to be explored, together with the extent of adoption of risk-reduction strategies. These data also afford an opportunity for exploring the relationship between reported behaviour change and actual practice.

Meaning of Safer Sex

The question relating to safer sex was included in the context of the AIDS epidemic. Respondents were asked,

> There has been a lot of publicity about AIDS in the last year or two. From what you have heard or read, what does the phrase 'safer sex' mean to you?

Respondents' answers were recorded verbatim and interviewers were instructed to probe until no further responses were forthcoming. This was the only open-ended question in the schedule and responses were subsequently post-coded according to the categories that emerged from respondents. These are summarized in Table 8.8.

The dominant messages of the British AIDS public education campaigns have been to remain within a sexually exclusive relationship or where this is not feasible to use a condom. Choosing a partner carefully has been implied rather than explicit in the messages to avoid casual sex, but there has been no real attempt to promote non-penetrative sex among heterosexuals except in a few advertisements in the women's press, and in campaigns mounted by voluntary agencies (Wellings, 1992). This has, however, been a prominent message for risk-reduction among homosexual men.

Responses to the survey question tend to correspond fairly closely with official advice. What the data show most strikingly is the widespread equation of safer sex with condom use (Table 8.8). More than three-quarters of respondents saw safer sex in terms of condom use. No other single strategy was mentioned by more than 36% of respondents. The next most common (in order of frequency) were sexual exclusivity, reducing the number of partners and knowing a partner well, mentioned by approximately a quarter of

age group	16–24 %	25–34 %	35–44 %	45–59 %	all ages %
			men		
use of condom	75.6	79.0	74.5	72.1	75.3
use of other contraception	14.5	7.2	6.5	4.9	8.2
safer-sex practices	6.8	9.6	9.2	4.7	7.7
monogamy	19.3	25.9	32.3	33.9	27.9
restrict number of partners	31.8	28.6	26.8	21.2	27.1
know partner	21.5	22.8	22.0	14.8	20.4
abstain from sex	2.2	3.9	4.1	4.9	3.8
avoid drug use	5.8	4.8	7.3	4.4	5.6
avoid STDs/pregnancy	5.8	5.9	3.5	6.0	5.3
other	5.1	4.7	6.0	8.8	6.1
*base**	*508*	*546*	*537*	*497*	*2088*
			women		
use of condom	80.5	84.8	79.2	79.0	81.0
use of other contraception	13.5	5.0	4.6	3.5	6.3
safer-sex practices	2.8	4.9	4.4	3.5	4.0
monogamy	21.2	27.8	33.4	33.8	29.4
restrict number of partners	44.5	37.3	30.6	31.5	35.6
know partner	28.4	26.1	20.7	18.8	23.3
abstain from sex	4.2	5.8	6.9	7.8	6.3
avoid drug use	6.8	4.2	4.3	3.0	4.4
avoid STDs/pregnancy	4.0	4.9	4.4	4.3	4.4
other	1.2	4.7	4.8	3.9	3.8
*base**	*536*	*721*	*634*	*686*	*2577*

Table 8.8 Meaning of the phrase 'safer sex' by age group. Source: Interview Question 43

* all respondents given long questionnaire

respondents in each case. Restricting numbers of partners was mentioned more often by women than men; younger respondents were more likely to report restricting numbers of partners, while older respondents interpreted safer sex more in terms of monogamy.

Comparatively few references were made to sexual practices, including non-penetrative sex, which is perhaps not surprising given its relative rarity in the heterosexual repertoire (see Chapter 4). Nor is it surprising, since the question was asked within the context of the AIDS epidemic, that use of contraception (other than condoms) does not feature prominently among responses. It is mentioned by only 8.2% of men and 6.3% of women. Interestingly, this meaning was more likely to be given by younger respondents, aged 16–24 (14.5% men and 13.5% of women), who were brought up in the era in which safer sex was almost synonymous with the prevention of transmission of HIV.

Perceived Risk

An important question here is to what extent subjective ratings relate to actual behaviour. Respondents were asked for their assessment of whether they felt themselves to be at risk of HIV. Interviewers told them,

> Nobody yet knows for sure how many people are at risk of becoming infected with the AIDS virus, but we would like to know what you think about . . .
>
> (a) the risks to you personally with your present sexual lifestyle?

Response options were: 'Greatly at risk'; 'Quite a lot'; 'Not very much'; 'Not at all at risk'. The proportion of respondents who chose any but the last of these were aggregated to form a category of those who saw themselves as at any risk. The results are summarized in Table 8.9 in relation to number of heterosexual partners, homosexual partners and injecting drug use in the last 5 years.

Six out of ten men and women with 5 or more partners in the past 5 years see their current lifestyle as presenting some risk – more than 4 times as many as those with only one partner. Men who report 5 or more heterosexual partners in the past 5 years are less

	men		women	
	%	*base*	%	*base*
heterosexual partners in the last 5 years				
0	25.7	*689*	12.4	*910*
1	14.1	*4536*	15.0	*6750*
2	33.9	*802*	31.5	*1104*
3–4	46.0	*964*	44.3	*808*
9	58.2	*630*	61.9	*362*
10+	61.6	*388*	63.3	*81*
homosexual partners in the last 5 years				
0	26.0	*8153*	20.5	*10294*
1	51.4	*49*	53.8	*40*
2	–	*9★*	52.5	*16★*
3–4	56.9	*18★*	–	*3★*
5–9	74.2	*11★*	–	*5★*
10+	82.0	*30*	–	*1★*
injecting drug use in the last 5 years				
yes	59.0	*33*	70.0	*23*
no	26.9	*7522*	21.3	*9462*
total	26.5	*8318*	20.7	*10419*

Table 8.9 Proportions of respondents who perceive themselves to be at some risk of AIDS. Source: Interview Question 45a

★ note small base

likely to see themselves as at risk for HIV than are those with 5 or more homosexual partners (Table 8.9). The numbers of women with homosexual partners are too small to make the same comparison. 59.0% of men and 70.0% of women reporting injecting non-prescribed drugs consider themselves to be at some risk. These data show that risk perception is higher among those reporting behaviours that carry a higher risk of HIV infection.

Prevalence and Distribution of Unsafe Sex

Since an important aim of this survey was to identify the size and nature of the section of the population at higher risk of adverse outcomes, we sought to construct a variable measuring unsafe heterosexual sex. A broad measure of risk-taking behaviour is obtained by defining a group of people who have had 'unsafe' sex as those who have had 2 or more heterosexual partners in the last year but *never* used a condom in that time. This is not an all-inclusive definition of unsafe sexual behaviour. It excludes those who use a condom inconsistently, and those who have had only one partner but who may have been at risk as a result of their partner's behaviour, and so is likely to underestimate the prevalence of unsafe sex. These uncertainties are difficult to resolve in a large-scale quantitative survey and are better addressed by means of other investigative techniques. Nevertheless, defining a group in this way provides an indicator for the likely attributes of those who may be at increased risk.

From Table 8.10, it is clear that the likelihood of having unsafe sex decreases with age. In all age groups, men were more likely to have had unsafe sex than women (6.0% cf. 4.0%). More than 9% of men and women under 25 reported 2 or more partners and no condom use in the last year. These proportions decreased very noticeably with age for women; only 1.6% of those over 44 had 'unsafe' sex in the last year.

Marital status also has a strong effect, with only 3.0% of married men and 1.3% of married women reporting 'unsafe' sex in the last year. Men who were cohabiting were 3 times as likely to report 'unsafe' sex as were those who were married. 9.6% of single men and 10.6% of single women had 'unsafe' sex, but the highest proportions

	men		women	
	%	*base**	%	*base**
age group				
16–24	9.7	*1534*	9.2	*1732*
25–34	5.8	*2029*	3.8	*2729*
35–44	5.7	*1929*	3.1	*2453*
45–59	3.7	*1983*	1.6	*2534*
marital status				
married	3.0	*4545*	1.3	*6003*
cohabiting	10.4	*593*	5.7	*817*
widowed/separated/divorced	15.7	*421*	8.0	*1013*
single	9.6	*1914*	10.6	*1613*
social class				
I, II	5.5	*2734*	2.6	*3455*
III NM	5.0	*1453*	5.4	*2164*
III M	7.7	*1838*	1.7	*1696*
IV, V, other	5.9	*1444*	6.6	*2126*
homosexual partners in the last year				
0	6.0	*7404*	4.0	*9415*
1 +	7.4	*64*	11.0	*32*
all respondents	6.0	*7476*	4.0	*9448*

Table 8.10 Proportions of respondents reporting 'unsafe' sex (2 or more heterosexual partners and no condom use) in the last year. Source: Interview Question 30b; Booklet Question 7d

* all respondents who have had sexual intercourse

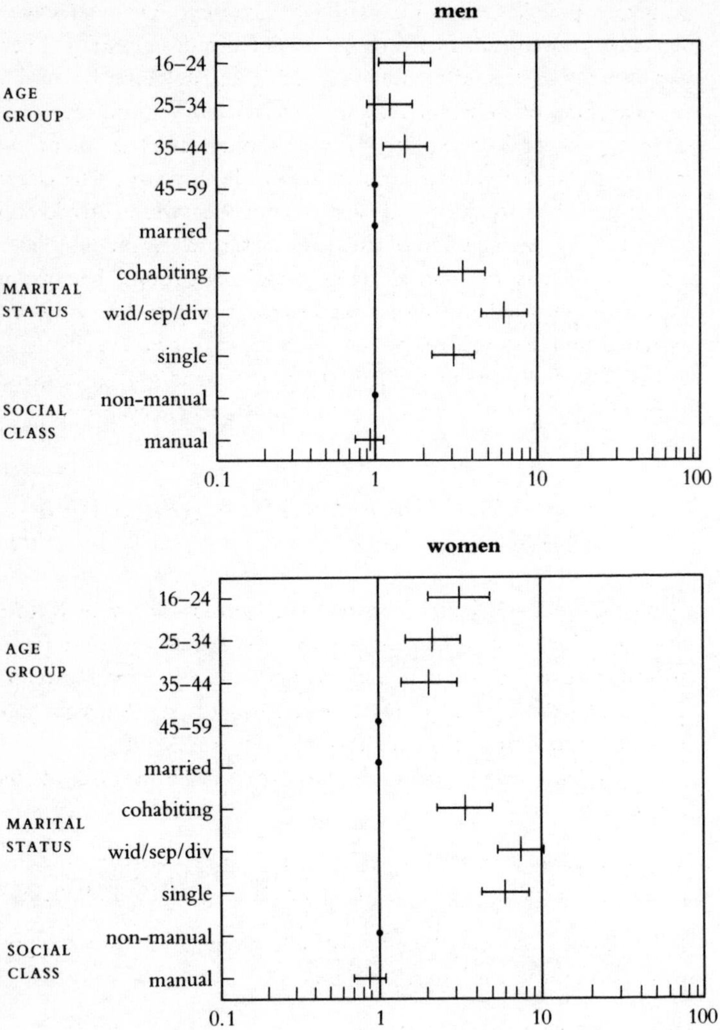

Figure 8.4 Adjusted odds ratios for 'unsafe'★ heterosexual sex in the last year. Source: Interview Question 30b; Booklet Question 7d

★ 2 or more heterosexual partners and no condom use in the last year

of unsafe practice were reported by men who were widowed, separated or divorced, 15.7% of whom fall into this category. There was little social-class difference in reporting 'unsafe' sex.

Since some of these variables are interrelated, logistic regression models were used to explore the relationships between them and the likelihood of reporting 'unsafe' sex in the last year. The effects of age remained for men and women, but they were considerably attenuated by the inclusion of the other factors in the model (Figure 8.4). The effects of marital status remained strong. The group apparently most likely to be exposed to risk are the widowed, separated and divorced, who are more than 5 times as likely to report 'unsafe' sex as those who were married, and so might form a neglected audience in terms of health educational intervention.

BEHAVIOUR CHANGE BECAUSE OF AIDS

Change in sexual behaviour may result from a variety of factors, most of which are not amenable to exploration in this type of study. However, responses to a series of questions probing behaviour change, and the type of changes made, provide some insight into the extent and nature of the response to HIV and AIDS.

Respondents were asked, in the face-to-face section of the questionnaire,

> Have you changed your own sexual lifestyle in any way or made any decisions about sex because of concern about catching AIDS or HIV virus?

If the answer was yes, the following response options were presented, on a show-card, to the respondent:

Having fewer partners
Finding out more about a person before having sex
Using a condom
Not having sex
Sticking to one partner
Avoiding some sexual practices
Other change(s)

age group	16–24 %	25–34 %	35–44 %	45–59 %	all ages %
			men		
having fewer partners	12.0	8.0	4.1	1.8	6.4
know partner before having sex	20.1	11.1	5.5	2.0	9.5
using a condom	26.4	13.7	7.0	2.1	12.1
not having sex	3.6	3.2	1.7	0.9	2.3
sticking to one partner	15.6	11.2	6.5	3.0	9.0
avoid some sexual practices	5.0	3.6	2.4	0.8	2.9
other change(s)	1.1	0.8	0.8	0.2	0.7
base	*1983*	*2153*	*2042*	*2172*	*8350*
any change in sexual lifestyle	36.2	22.9	13.9	6.2	19.5
base	*1983*	*2154*	*2042*	*2173*	*8352*
			women		
having fewer partners	9.1	4.6	2.0	0.8	3.9
know partner before having sex	18.0	7.5	3.9	1.8	7.4
using a condom	16.8	7.5	4.1	1.5	7.1
not having sex	4.2	2.8	1.6	1.4	2.4
sticking to one partner	16.3	9.2	4.7	1.7	7.6
avoid some sexual practices	3.2	1.3	1.1	0.6	1.5
other change(s)	1.0	1.1	0.7	0.2	0.7
base	*2233*	*2889*	*2572*	*2754*	*10448*
any change in sexual lifestyle	29.7	15.7	9.4	4.5	14.2
base	*2236*	*2892*	*2572*	*2758*	*10458*

Table 8.11 Proportions of respondents who report sexual lifestyle change because of AIDS by age group. Source: Interview Question 44b

19.5% of men and 14.2% of women reported some behaviour change because of AIDS. Not surprisingly, the proportions of people doing so decreased with increasing age (Table 8.11). There are marked differences in reporting with sexual lifestyle. Those at apparently greater risk are more likely to have adopted preventive strategies in the context of AIDS. Reporting of changes increases with numbers of partners for both men and women reporting heterosexual partners in the past 5 years, and also for men reporting homosexual partners in that time period (Table 8.12). 48.5% men with 5 or more heterosexual partners in the last 5 years reported having made changes compared with 7.8% of those with only one, and for women the comparable proportions were 51.0% and 6.2%.

Men reporting homosexual partners were generally more likely to have made changes; nearly half of those with only one partner in the last 5 years having done so. Evidence of the most widespread behaviour modification was found among the small number of men reporting 10 or more homosexual partners in the last 5 years, nearly 90% of whom reported having made changes. Those who reported having injected non-prescribed drugs were much more likely to have made lifestyle changes than those who had never done so (Table 8.12).

Looking at preferred options for behaviour change for all respondents, there are clear gender differences in preferences for different strategies (Table 8.11). The lifestyle change most commonly reported by men was the use of condoms (12.1%), and by women 'sticking to one partner' (7.6%). 'Finding out more about a person before having sex' was next most commonly cited by both men and women (9.5% and 7.4% respectively), followed by 'sticking to one partner' for men (9.0%) and 'using a condom' for women (7.1%). 'Having fewer partners' was less commonly reported, possibly because the majority of respondents have not had more than one partner in the last 5 years. 'Not having sex' and 'avoiding some sexual practices' were rare behaviour changes reported by fewer than 3% of respondents. When these responses were analysed by age, this overall pattern was reflected for each age group (Table 8.11).

Table 8.13 summarizes patterns of reported behaviour change made in response to AIDS by different behaviours. Selected strategies varied widely according to whether respondents reported

	men		women	
	%	*base*	%	*base*
total	19.5	*8352*	14.2	*10458*
heterosexual partners in the last 5 years				
0	25.0	*696*	19.1	*914*
1	7.8	*4539*	6.2	*6768*
2	27.2	*804*	28.1	*1106*
3–4	36.7	*967*	40.8	*810*
5–9	50.5	*635*	49.0	*364*
10+	45.2	*388*	60.1	*82*
homosexual partners in the last 5 years				
0	18.9	*8180*	14.1	*10326*
1	49.1	*49*	44.4	*40*
2	58.2	*11★*	26.9	*16★*
3–4	66.6	*18*	–	*3★*
5–9	73.1	*11★*	–	*5★*
10+	89.7	*30*	–	*1★*
injecting drug use in the last 5 years				
yes	38.4	*33*	64.6	*24*
no	19.8	*7336*	14.2	*9487*

Table 8.12 Proportions of respondents reporting lifestyle change because of AIDS. Source: Interview Question 44a; Booklet Questions 7b, 8b, 17

★ note small base

	homosexual partner %	2 or more heterosexual partners %	injecting drug use %
		men	
having fewer partners	29.2	15.1	28.1
know partner before having sex	29.7	21.1	21.7
using a condom	44.2	26.2	31.0
not having sex	11.6	3.9	14.0
sticking to one partner	17.8	15.8	18.9
avoid some sexual practices	40.2	5.5	23.9
other change(s)	3.6	1.2	0.0
any change in sexual lifestyle	65.0	38.3	38.4
base	*118*	*2795*	*33*
		women	
having fewer partners	8.8	13.9	32.4
know partner before having sex	18.9	20.9	9.5
using a condom	14.9	20.5	37.1
not having sex	4.7	5.6	1.9
sticking to one partner	22.6	20.3	23.4
avoid some sexual practices	7.5	3.5	3.6
other change(s)	2.5	1.2	1.8
any change in sexual lifestyle	37.3	36.8	64.6
base	*65*	*2361*	*24*

Table 8.13 Reported behaviour change for those with any homosexual partners, 2 or more heterosexual partners, or injecting drug use in the last 5 years. Source: Interview Question 44; Booklet Questions 7b, 8b, 17

having homosexual partners, having more than one heterosexual partner or injecting drugs in the last 5 years. Men with homosexual partners are considerably more likely to report behaviour changes than are those with 2 or more heterosexual partners or who report injecting drug use, reflecting their perception of their risk status. In particular, they are far more likely to report avoiding some sexual practices, again very probably reflecting the perceived risk attached to anal sex and the emphasis of health educational messages on non-penetrative sex rather than reduction in number of partners. They are also more likely to report using a condom. In terms of reducing numbers of partners however, the difference is less marked and men with homosexual partners are no more or less likely than men in other groups to report 'sticking to one partner' as their preferred prevention strategy. This tends to suggest that gay men see risk reduction more in terms of safer sexual practice and less in terms of sexual exclusivity. The preventive strategies of women reporting a homosexual partner and women with more than one heterosexual partner are very similar, with the emphasis on sticking to one partner, using a condom, and knowing your partner before having sex.

These data permit some exploration of consistency between claimed risk-reduction practice in response to the threat of AIDS and reported behaviour. Claims of adopted condom use in response to AIDS can be compared with reports of recent use (Table 8.14). 49.7% of men and 41.3% of women who reported having adopted this risk-reduction strategy used a condom on the last occasion of sex, compared with 19.6% of men and 15.6% of women who reported no such change. Women who reported having taken up condom use as a preventive strategy were almost 3 times more likely to have reported using a condom on every occasion in the last 4 weeks than those reporting no such change. Nevertheless, 45.7% of men and 50.6% of women did not use a condom at all in the last 4 weeks despite claims of having adopted this preventive measure.

The data also allow a comparison of claims of avoiding certain (unspecified) sexual practices with reports of experience of sexual practices over different time periods. Vaginal intercourse, for example, was reported less frequently by those who claimed to be avoiding certain practices (Figure 8.5) than by those who did not and this difference is more marked in recent time intervals for men.

	men		women	
	'use a condom' mentioned		'use a condom' mentioned	
	no %	yes %	no %	yes %
condom used on last occasion*	19.6	49.7	15.6	41.3
base	*6484*	*887*	*8614*	*660*
condom use in last 4 weeks†				
always	14.8	35.3	12.5	36.8
sometimes	5.4	19.0	4.3	12.6
never	79.8	45.7	83.2	50.6
base	*5235*	*514*	*6795*	*356*

Table 8.14 Condom use by change in sexual lifestyle: 'use a condom'. Source: Interview Question 44b

* sexually active in the last 5 years
† sexually active in the last 4 weeks

The numbers of those reporting anal sex are small, but there are noticeable changes in reporting of both ever experience and more recent experience, with claims of avoiding some sexual practices. Those reporting avoidance of some practices are markedly more likely to have reported experience of anal sex at some time in their life, compared with those making no such claim, but the excess diminishes steadily over decreasing time periods and for reports of behaviour in the last 6 months it is negligible. No comparable differences were found between those who did and did not claim to have avoided certain practices, in reporting oral or non-penetrative sex, which carry no practical risk of HIV transmission.

Taken as a whole, there is evidence that respondents who felt the need to modify their sexual practices in response to AIDS are aware of the difference in likelihood of transmission between different practices. Vaginal and anal sex carry a higher risk of HIV transmission than oral and non-penetrative sex and the observed differences in behaviour reflect the avoidance of the practices carrying the highest risk.

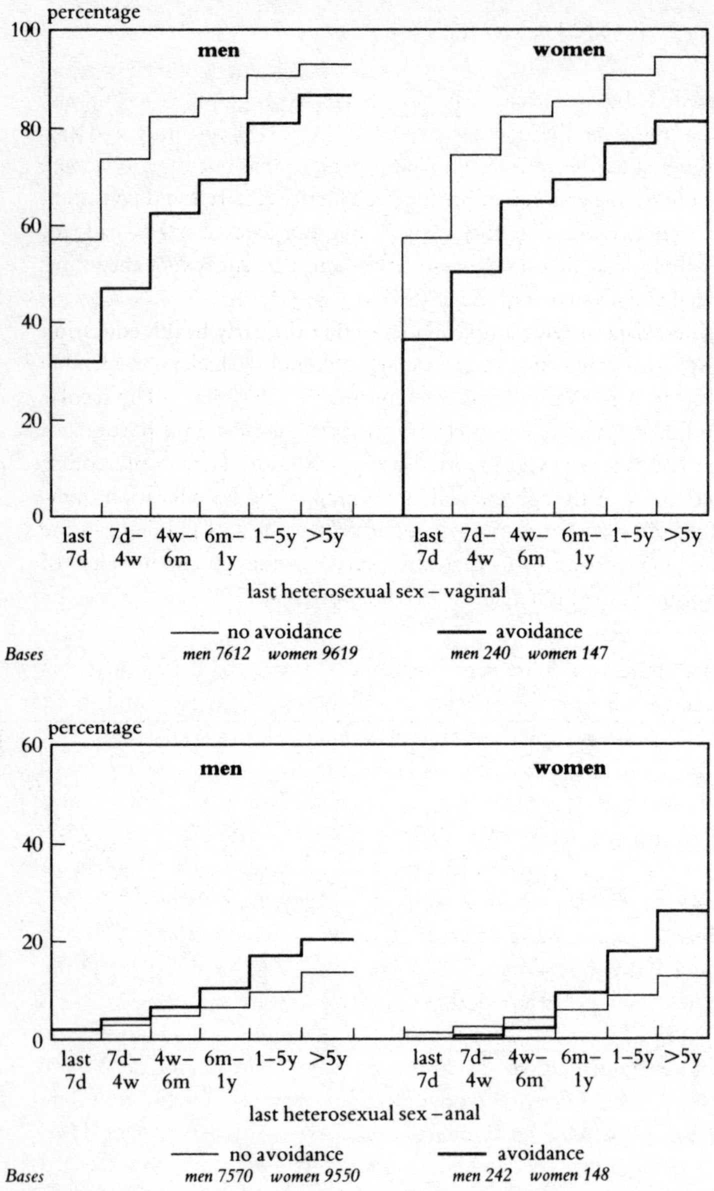

Figure 8.5 Relationship between sexual practices and reported avoidance of certain practices. Source: Interview Question 44b; Booklet Questions 3a, 3d

CONDOM USE

As stated above, a great deal of emphasis has been placed on the use of condoms in the context of the AIDS/HIV epidemic and this traditional barrier to infection and pregnancy has once again become one of the cornerstones of preventive practice. Correct and consistent use is not assessed in this survey, but estimates can be made of reported use at first intercourse, at the most recent sexual encounter as well as consistency of use in the last 4 weeks.

These data provide ample evidence that the early health education campaigns which encouraged the use of condoms had a considerable effect on behaviour at first intercourse (see Chapter 2). The secular trend in Figure 8.6 shows clearly the increase in the proportions of men and women who reported using a condom at first intercourse since 1985. Although official government public education campaigns did not start until early 1986, a good deal of publicity in the print and broadcast media was given to the potential value of condoms in the fight against AIDS before that.

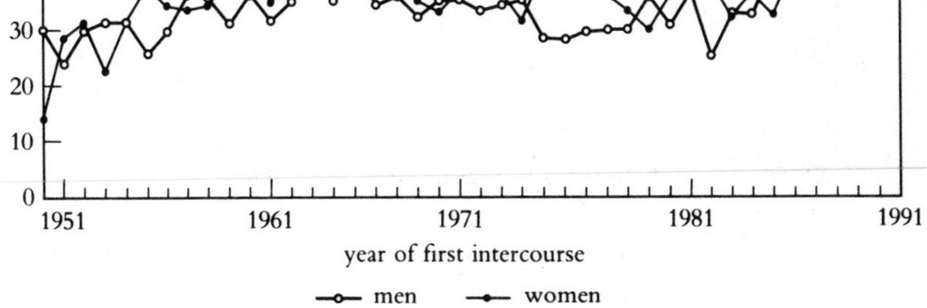

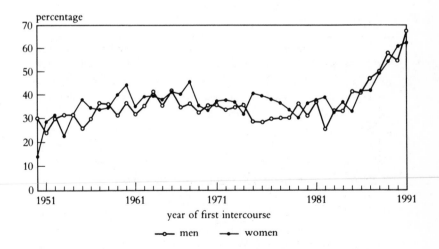

Figure 8.6 Proportions of respondents who used a condom at first sexual intercourse. Source: Interview Question 23

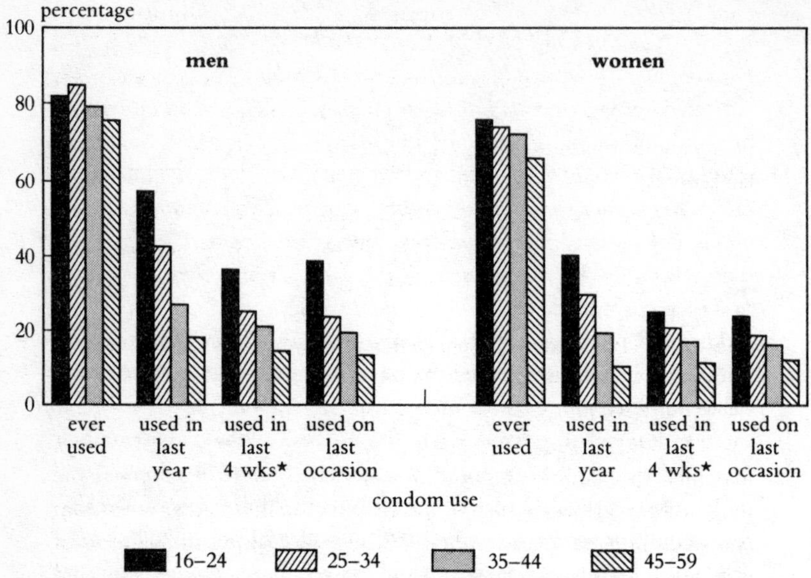

* respondents who were sexually active in the last 4 weeks

Figure 8.7 Condom use by age. Source: Interview Questions 30a, 30b; Booklet Questions 1c, 2d

In general, condoms are more commonly used by young people and this is clearly seen in Figure 8.7. Condom use ever, in the last year, in the last 4 weeks, and on the last occasion all show similar trends: a decrease in their use with increasing age. This pattern is not found for ever use in men aged under 25 and this is probably accounted for by the proportion of young men with no heterosexual experience. Given that older men, especially those aged 45–59, would have lived through an era in which condoms were one of the few contraceptive options available, these age-related differences are even more notable.

Condom use is clearly of greatest importance in preventing the occurrence of sexually transmitted infections in new and non-exclusive relationships. Looking in some detail at the last 4 weeks, reported use of condoms has been examined in relation to numbers of partners and numbers of new partners. 4 weeks is a short interval

	men			women		
	numbers of new partners			numbers of new partners		
	none	1+	*base*	none	1+	*base*
partners in the last 4 weeks	%	%	%	%	%	%
1	97.7	2.3	*5554*	99.0	1.0	*7044*
2	54.3	45.8	*122*	65.5	34.5	*75*
3+	38.1	61.9	*20*	–	–	*5**

Table 8.15 Proportion of respondents with new partners in the last 4 weeks. Source: Booklet Questions 2b, 2c

* note small base

in which to examine multiple or new partnerships, but it was the longest interval over which it was realistic to ask whether a condom was used on every occasion of sex. Table 8.15 shows the patterns of new partner formation in the last 4 weeks. For 2.3% of men and 1.0% of women with 1 partner in the last 4 weeks, that partner was a new one with whom the respondent had never previously had sexual intercourse. For those who reported more than 1 partner in the last 4 weeks, 48% of men and 36% of women reported that at least one of their partners was a new one. It could be expected that people in both these categories might be more aware of the importance of using condoms or adopting non-penetrative sexual practices.

By comparing respondents who reported using a condom on every occasion in the last 4 weeks with those who used them occasionally or not at all, safe sexual behaviour with multiple or new partners can be evaluated. Among those reporting only 1 partner in the last 4 weeks, 16.4% of men and 13.4% of women for whom that partner was someone with whom sex had taken place on a previous occasion used a condom on every occasion of sex in that time (Table 8.16). These proportions increased to 34.2% and 41.4% for men and women respectively whose only partner in the last 4 weeks was a new one. For men who had 2 or more partners in the last 4 weeks, the proportion who used condoms on every occasion of sex dropped to 5.7% (no new partners) and 17.5% (at least 1 new partner(s)). Women showed a somewhat different

partners in the last 4 weeks	men				women			
	new partner				new partner			
	yes		no		yes		no	
	%	*base*	%	*base*	%	*base*	%	*base*
1	34.2	*127*	16.4	*5401*	41.4	*68*	13.4	*6924*
2+	17.5	*68*	5.7	*74*	10.1	*29*	14.3	*51*

Table 8.16 Proportion of respondents who used a condom on all occasions of sex in the last 4 weeks. Source: Booklet Question 2

pattern. Of those with 2 or more partners in the last 4 weeks, none of whom were new, 14.3% used a condom on every occasion of sex whereas for those who had at least 1 new partner, only 10.1% reported using a condom on every occasion.

A logistic regression model was constructed to assess the relationship between consistent condom use in the last 4 weeks with age group, multiple partners and new partners in the same time interval (Figure 8.8). For men and women, those under 45 were significantly more likely to use a condom on every occasion of sex than older people, even after patterns of new partnerships had been taken into account. For men, those with a new partner were significantly more likely to have used a condom every time than those with no new partner, but those with 2 or more partners in the last 4 weeks were significantly less likely to use a condom than those with only 1 partner. For women the picture is slightly less clear cut. They are significantly more likely to use condoms on every occasion if they have a new partner, but there is no significant effect of numbers of partners. This model needs to be interpreted with caution because of the small number of women with multiple or new partners in the last 4 weeks.

Decisions about condom use rest on a multitude of factors, not all of which bear rational examination after the event. Nevertheless, the demographic and behavioural characteristics of those who used a condom on the last occasion of sex can be compared with those who did not. Age and marital status are obvious variables to choose

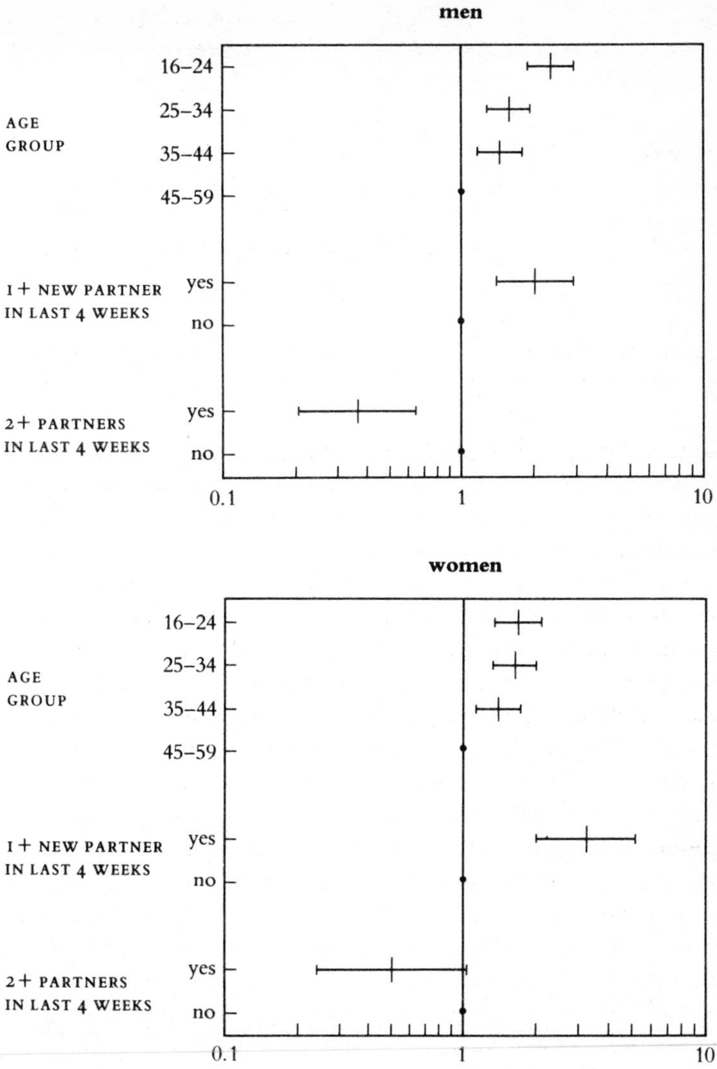

Figure 8.8 Adjusted odds ratios for condom use in the last 4 weeks.
Source: Booklet Question 2d

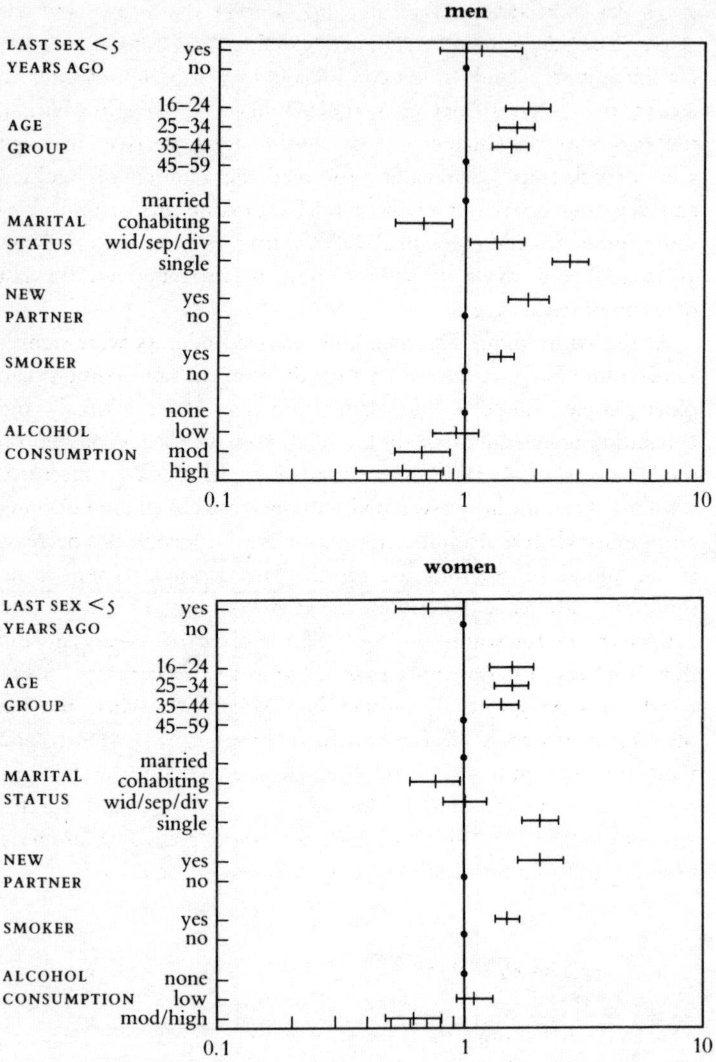

Figure 8.9 Adjusted odds ratios for condom use on the last occasion of sex. Source: Booklet Question 1c

given the expectation of greater risk among the young and the single. The selection of behavioural variables was guided by other considerations. Failure to use condoms has often been attributed to alcohol use (Leigh, 1990; Gillies, 1991; Gold *et al.*, 1991). In addition, the suggestion in Chapter 7 of a consistent profile over different areas of risk-taking behaviour prompted the addition of smoking and drinking behaviour to the model. Smoking and alcohol consumption have been combined with the timing (more or less than 5 years ago) and status of partner (new or not new) on the last occasion of sex.

As shown in Figure 8.9, men and women under 45 were significantly more likely to have used a condom on the last occasion than older people. Single people were more than twice as likely and cohabiting people significantly less likely to have used a condom on the last occasion. As far as behavioural characteristics are concerned, smoking is significantly associated with increased likelihood of using a condom, whereas alcohol consumption is associated with a decrease in likelihood of condom use on the last occasion. There is no significant difference in condom use at last occasion of sex for men between those for whom this took place more than 5 years ago and those for whom it was more recent. For women there was a weak trend showing greater likelihood of condom use when the last occasion of sex took place more than 5 years ago. Both men and women were significantly more likely to use a condom with a new partner, but the size of the odds ratio (1:8 for men and 2:1 for women) indicates that this difference was not as great as might have been hoped for in the light of recent health education efforts.

SUMMARY

This chapter has looked at awareness of possible adverse outcomes of sexual activity in terms of physical health consequences (sexually transmitted disease and unplanned pregnancy), and at strategies adopted to prevent them, (i.e. contraception and prophylaxis).

The evidence from these data is that the proportion of the British population at risk of unplanned pregnancy is low – probably below 10%. The choice of contraception used reflects varying levels of sexual activity and needs for protection against pregnancy. The three methods most commonly relied on are the pill, the condom, and male or female sterilization. No other single method is reported by more than 10% of respondents. The use of oral contraception declines steeply with age, and condom use is more prevalent among the young. Reliance on sterilization, by contrast, increases with age. Contraceptive use is also higher among those reporting more than one partner in the past year than it is among those reporting only one, and condom use increases markedly with numbers of partners.

The advantages of condom use have been emphasized since the advent of the HIV epidemic because of their dual role in contraception and prophylaxis. There is evidence here of the concurrent use of both a highly effective method of contraception and a condom, reflecting awareness of the role of condoms in preventing infection. This is also confirmed in the widespread equation of safer sex with condom use. The message to use condoms seems to have been more acceptable than messages to restrict numbers of partners. This traditional barrier to infection and pregnancy seems once again to have resumed a key role in preventive practice.

Perceived risk of HIV infection is higher among those reporting behaviours which carry a higher risk of infection. There is also an observable consistency between reporting of lifestyle change in response to HIV/AIDS, and actual behaviours reported. Those who feel the need to modify their sexual practices are aware of the difference in the likelihood of HIV transmission between different sexual practices. Nevertheless, despite the encouraging uptake of messages relating to condom use, there is little sign as yet of widespread adoption of other safer-sex practices among those reporting heterosexual behaviour. There is clearly still ample scope for further progress to be made in this respect.

REFERENCES

Becker, M., and J. Joseph (1988). 'AIDS and Behavioural Change to Reduce Risk: A Review', *American Journal of Public Health*, 778(4): 394–410

Bone, M. (1973). *Family Planning Services in England and Wales.* London: HMSO

Bone, M. (1978). *The Family Planning Services: Changes and Effects.* London: HMSO

Bone, M. (1985). *Family Planning in Scotland in 1982.* London: HMSO

Coulter, A. (1985). 'Decision-making and the Pill', *British Journal of Family Planning* 11: 98–103

Department of Health and Social Security (1979). *Handbook of Contraceptive Practice*, 1979 edn. London: HMSO

Dunnell, K. (1979). *Family Formation 1976.* London: HMSO

Gatherer, A., J. Parfit, E. Porter, and M. Vessey (1979). *Is Health Education Effective?* London: Health Education Council

Gillies, P. (1991). 'HIV Information, Alcohol Use and Illicit Drugs', *Current Opinion in Psychiatry*, 4: 448–53

Gold, R. S., A. Karmiloff-Smith, M. J. Skinner, and J. Morton (1991). 'Situational Factors and Thought Processes Associated with Unprotected Intercourse in Heterosexual Students', *AIDS Care* 4 (3): 305–23

Goldscheider, C., and W. D. Mosher (1988). 'Religious Affiliation and Contraceptive Usage: Changing American Patterns, 1955–82', *Studies in Family Planning*, 19: 1: 48–57

Goldscheider, C., and W. D. Mosher (1991). 'Patterns of Contraceptive Use in the United States: The Importance of Religious Factors', *Studies in Family Planning*, 22: 2: 102–15

Hunt, K. (1991). 'The First Pill-taking Generation: Past and Present Use of Contraception amongst a Cohort of Women Born in the Early 1950s', *British Journal of Family Planning*, 16: 3–15

Hunt, K., and E. Annandale (1990). 'Predicting Contraceptive Method Usage among Women in West Scotland', *Journal of Biosocial Science*, 22: 405–21

Jackson, L. N. (1969). *Vasectomy Follow-up of a Thousand Cases.* London: Simon Population Trust

Joseph, J., S. Montgomery, and C. Emmons (1987). 'Magnitude and Determinants of Behavioural Risk Reduction: Longitudinal Analysis of a Cohort at Risk for AIDS', *Psychology and Health*, 1: 73–95

Leigh, B. (1990). 'The Relationship between Substance Use during

Sex to High-risk Sex Behaviour', *Journal of Sex Research*, 27: 199–213

Memon, A. (1991). 'Perceptions of AIDS Vulnerability: The Role of Attributions and Social Context', in P. Aggleton, G. Hart, and P. Davies (eds), *AIDS: Responses, Interventions and Care*. Basingstoke: Falmer Press

Mujahidul Islam, Q. (1989). *Family Planning and Abortion: An Islamic Viewpoint*. Mobeni: Islamic Medical Association

Office of Population Censuses and Surveys (1985). *General Household Survey 1983*. London: HMSO

Office of Population Censuses and Surveys (1991). *General Household Survey 1989*. London: HMSO

Pike, M. C., D. E. Henderson, M. D. Krailo, *et al.* (1983). 'Breast Cancer in Young Women and Use of Oral Contraceptives, Possible Modifying Effect of Formulation and Age of Use', *Lancet*, ii: 926–30

RCGP (1977). 'Oral Contraceptive Study, Mortality among Oral Contraceptive Users', *Lancet*, (ii): 727–31

Riphagen, F. E., and P. Lehert (1989). 'A Survey of Contraception in Five West European Countries', *Journal of Biosocial Science*, 21: 23–46

Sachedina, Z. (1990). 'Islam, Procreation and the Law', *International Family Planning Perspectives*, 16: 3: 107–11

Vessey, M. P., K. McPherson, and B. Johnson (1977). 'Mortality among Women Participating in the Oxford FPA Study', *Lancet*, ii: 731–3

Vessey, M. P., M. Lawless, K. McPherson, *et al.* (1983). 'Neoplasia of the Cervix Uteri: A Possible Adverse Effect of the Pill', *Lancet*, 2: 930–34

Wellings, K. (1986a). 'Trends in Contraceptive Method Usage since 1970', *British Journal of Family Planning*, 12: 15–22

Wellings, K. (1986b). 'Sterilization Trends', *British Medical Journal*, 292: 1029

Wellings, K. (1992). 'Assessing HIV/AIDS Preventive Strategies in the General Population', in F. Paccaud, J. P. Vader, and F. Gurtzwiller (eds), *Assessing AIDS Prevention*. Switzerland: Birkhauser

Appendix: Survey Questionnaires

THE NATIONAL SURVEY OF SEXUAL ATTITUDES AND LIFESTYLES, 1990

LONG QUESTIONNAIRE

SECTION ONE: HEALTH, FAMILY AND LEARNING ABOUT SEX

ASK ALL

I would like to start by asking you a few questions about health, but may I check first:

1.a) What was your age last birthday? 16 – 59 ONLY

ENTER AGE | 1 | 7 |

b) **INTERVIEWER:** RECORD WHETHER RESPONDENT IS MALE OR FEMALE

Male . . . 1
Female . . . 2 ✓

2.a) For your age, would you describe your state of health as . . . **READ OUT**

. . . very good . . . 1 ✓
fairly good . . . 2
average . . . 3
rather poor . . . 4
or very poor? . . . 5

b) Do you have any permanent disability that restricts the kind of work you can do or your leisure activities?

Yes . . . 1
No . . . 2 ✓

c) Do you have any long term medical condition that needs regular treatment or check ups?

Yes . . . 1
No . . . 2 ✓

d) In the last *five* years have you had any (other) illness or accident that affected your health for at least 3 months?

Yes . . . 1
No . . . 2 ✓

ASK ALL

3.a) I am going to read out two statements; please say which one comes closest to how you feel about things, . . . **READ OUT**

. . . there is a lot that people can do to keep themselves in good health, . . . 1 ✓
or, when it comes down to it, good health is mostly a matter of luck? . . . 2
(Can't choose/Don't know) . . . 8

b) Now which of these two comes closest to how you feel, . . . **READ OUT**

. . . on the whole I am happy with the way I am . . . 1
or, I often wish I could be a different sort of person? . . . 2 ✓
(Can't choose/Don't know) . . . 8

c) And which of these two comes closest to how you feel, . . . **READ OUT**

. . . I mostly find that things just happen in my life . . . 1
or, I usually feel that I control what happens to me in life? . . . 2
(Can't choose/Don't know) . . . 8

d) What about this statement: 'To have good health is the most important thing in life.' Do you . . . **READ OUT**

strongly agree, . . . 1
agree, . . . 2
disagree, . . . 4
or, strongly disagree? . . . 5
(All depends/Don't know) . . . 3

4.a) On average, how often do you drink alcohol, is it . . . **READ OUT**

. . every day or nearly every day 1
several days a week 2
at least once a week 3
less than once a week 4
} **ASK b)**

or, never? 5 **GO TO Q.5**

(Varies a great deal) 6 **ASK b)**

b) About how many drinks do you usually have on the days when you have any, apart from parties or special occasions?

(PROBE BY READING OUT IF NECESSARY)

ONE DRINK IS:-
½ pint of beer/lager
1 glass of wine
1 tot of spirits (gin/whisky)

One or two . . . 1
Three or four . . . 2
More than four . . . 3
Other answer, AFTER PROBE (STATE) . . . 7
____

ASK ALL

5.a) Do you ever smoke cigarettes?

Yes 1 **ASK b)**
No 2 **GO TO c)**

b) About how many do you smoke a day?

ENTER NUMBER PER DAY [ ][ ]
Doesn't smoke every day 96
Varies (STATE RANGE) ____________ 97
} **GO TO Q.6**

c) Have you ever smoked as much as a cigarette a day for as long as a year?

Yes . . . 1
No . . . 2

ASK ALL

6.a) About how much do you weigh? (st.) (lbs)

ENTER WEIGHT AS:- Stones/pounds [0 9] [0 2] **ASK b)**

OR AS:- Pounds [| |] (lbs) **ASK b)**

OR AS:- Kilograms [| |] (kg) **ASK b)**

OR:- Weight not known 998 **GO TO c)**

b) Are you fairly sure of your weight or is that an estimate?
Fairly sure . . . 1
Estimate ✓. . 2

c) And how tall are you?

ENTER HEIGHT AS:- Feet/inches [5] (ft) [0 5] (ins)

OR AS:- Centimetres [| |] (cms)

Height not known 998

ASK ALL

7. Now a few questions about you and your family when you were growing up:

a) Do you have, or did you have any brothers or sisters, including adopted, half- or step-brothers or sisters?
Yes – Brother(s) 1
– Sister(s) 2 ✓ } **ASK b)**
– Both 3
No, none 4 **GO TO Q.8**

b) How many *full*, *half* or *adopted* brothers/and/sisters) do, or did, you have?

ENTER NUMBER (EXCLUDING RESPONDENT) [0 2] **ASK c)**

None (ie. has step-sibling(s) only) 00 **GO TO e)**

c) Were you the oldest or youngest (ADD IF 2 OR MORE: or in between)?
Oldest ✓. . 1
Youngest . . . 2
In between (ONLY IF 2+) . . . 3

d) When you were about 13 or 14 (was your/were any of these) brother(s) or sister(s) still living with you, in the same family or household?
Yes ✓. . 1
No . . . 2

e) How many *step*-brothers or sisters do, or did, you have (if any)?

ENTER NUMBER [0 2] **ASK f)**

None 00 **GO TO g)**

f) And when you were about 13 or 14 (was your/were any of these) step-brother(s) or sister(s) living with you, in the same family or household?
Yes ✓. . 1
No . . . 2

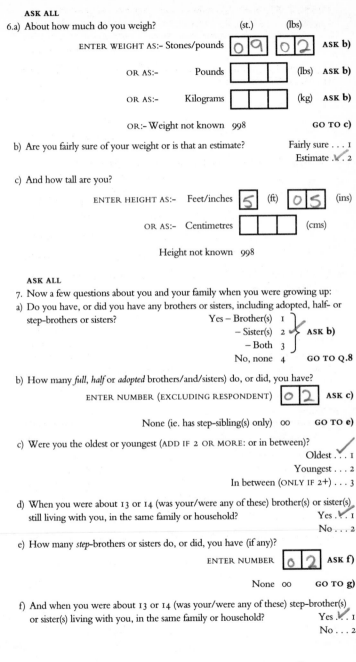

g) Still thinking of when you were about 13 or 14 would you say you felt specially close to (your/any of your) brother(s) or sister(s), or not?
(REFERS TO FULL, HALF, ADOPTED AND/OR STEP)

Yes (specially close to one or more) ✓. . 1
No (not specially close to any) . . . 2

ASK ALL

8.a) Did you live more or less continuously with *both* of your 'natural' parents at home until you were 16, that is with your parents at birth?
(*'YES' TO INCLUDE BOTH PARENTS BUT RESPONDENT AT BOARDING SCHOOL OR AWAY TEMPORARILY)

Yes* 1 **GO TO Q.9**
No 2 ✓ **ASK b)**

b) Is that because there was . . . **READ OUT**

. . . a divorce or separation ✓. 1
or, a death . . . 2
or, are you adopted . . . 3
or, is there another reason? (RECORD REASON IF GIVEN) . . . 7

____

c) How old were you when that happened (first)?

ENTER AGE ('00' IF LESS THAN ONE) [0|4]

d) And may I check, after that did you live more or less continuously with (*one* of your parents/both your adoptive parents) until you were 16?
IF YES, ONE: Your mother or your father (mainly)?

Yes, one:– Mother (natural or adoptive) 1 ✓ } **ASK Q.9**
– Father (natural or adoptive) 2 }
Yes, both adoptive parents 3 }
No, neither parent continuously till 16 4 **GO TO Q.12b)**

ASK ALL WHO LIVED WITH ONE OR BOTH PARENTS TO 16

9.a) How old were you when you first lived or stayed away from home for any length of time*, including boarding school or college, (or are you still living in your parents' home)?
(*MORE THAN 4 MONTHS IN THE YEAR)

ENTER AGE OF FIRST LIVING AWAY [|] **ASK b)**

Still living in parental home and has never lived away 00 ✓ **GO TO Q.10**

b) Did you first live away from home
because you . . . **READ OUT** . . . went to boarding school . . . 01
or, went away to college (or university) . . . 02
or, got married . . . 03
or, went to live with someone as married . . . 04
or, set up on your own with friends in
a flat or rooms (eg. for work/starting job) . . . 05
or, what? (CODE OTHER ANSWERS BELOW)
(National Service/Joined Services) . . . 06
(Live in job eg. nursing/au pair/hotel) . . . 07
(Went to live with relatives) . . . 08
(Came to Britain from abroad) . . . 10
(Evacuated during the war) . . . 11
(In care/children's home/fostered) . . . 12
(Other: STATE) ______________________ . . . 13

ASK ALL WHO LIVED WITH ONE OR BOTH PARENTS TO 16

10.a) When you were about 14, comparing your (parents/mother/father) with the parents of your friends, would you say that your (parents/mother/father) (were/was) *more strict* or *more easy going* about allowing you to go out at night, to parties, social events, and so on?
IF MORE STRICT/EASY GOING, PROBE: Much more or a little more (strict/easy going)?
Much more strict . . . 1
A little more strict . . . 2
About the same as others . . . 3
A little more easy going . . . 4
Much more easy going . . . 5
Didn't apply (eg. I didn't want to go out) . . . 6
Can't say/Can't remember . . . 8

b) Also when you were about 14, did you find it easy or difficult to talk to your (parents/mother/father) about sexual matters, or didn't you discuss sexual matters with (them/her/him) at that age?
Easy (with one or both) . . . 1
Difficult . . . 2
Didn't discuss (with either) . . . 3
Varied/depended on topic . . . 4
Can't remember . . . 8

11.a) **IF AGED 16/17 NOW**: Can you tell me what are . . .
IF AGED 18+: Now think of when you were about 16, can you remember what were . . .

. . . the views of your (parents/mother/father) on young people having sex before marriage; could you say whether, in general, (they/she/he) approve(d) or disapprove(d) or (have/had) mixed feelings?

IF MIXED, PROBE: Would you say (they/she/he) were more inclined to approve or to disapprove, or were (they/she/he) equally balanced?

b) What about your own views { **IF AGED 16/17**: now .... / **IF AGED 18+**: when you were about 16, } on young people having sex before marriage. In general (do/did) you approve or disapprove, or have mixed feelings?

IF MIXED, PROBE: (Are/were) you more inclined to approve or to disapprove or (are/were) you equally balanced?

		(a) Parents	*(b)* Self at 16
	Approve(d)	1	1 ✓
Mixed feelings (**PROBE**) →	Inclined to approve	2	2
	Equally balanced	3	3
	Inclined to disapprove	✓ 4	4
	Disapprove(d)	5	5
Other answers:	Disapprove(d) for girls	6	6
	Disapprove(d) for me	✓ 7	7
	Parents had different views	8	–
	Don't know/Can't remember	9	9

ASK ALL WHO LIVED WITH ONE OR BOTH PARENTS TO 16

CARD A

12.a) { **IF AGED 16/17**: Now................................ / **IF AGED 18+**: When you were about 16. } how important would you say religion and religious beliefs (are/were) to your (parents/mother/father)?

Very important	1
Fairly important	2
Not very important	✓ 3
Not important at all	4
Important to one parent, not the other	5
Don't know/Can't remember	8

12.b) INTERVIEWER CHECK CODE: FOR **ALL RESPONDENTS**

Respondent is aged 16/17	1	**GO TO d)**
Respondent is aged 18+	2	**ASK c)**

CARD A

c) When you were about 16, how important were religion and religious beliefs to *you*?

Very important	1
Fairly important	2
Not very important	3
Not important at all	4
Don't know/Can't remember	8

ASK ALL

CARD A

d) How important are religion and religious beliefs to you, now?

Very important	1
Fairly important	✓ 2
Not very important	3
Not at all important	4

ASK ALL

13.a) Do you regard yourself as belonging to any particular religion?

Yes A **ASK b)**
No, none 00 **GO TO Q.14**

b) Which one?

CHRISTIAN DENOMINATIONS:
- Christian – no denomination . . . 01
- Roman Catholic . . . 02
- Church of England/Anglican . . . 03
- United Reform Church (URC) . . . 04
- Congregational . . . 05
- Baptist . . . 06
- Methodist . . . 07
- Presbyterian/Church of Scotland . . . 08

Other Christian (SPECIFY) ________ . . . 09

OTHER RELIGIONS:
- Hindu . . . 10
- Jew . . . 11
- Islam/Muslim . . . 12
- Sikh . . . 13
- Buddhist . . . 14

Other non-Christian (SPECIFY) ________ . . . 15

c) Apart from such special occasions as weddings, funerals and baptisms, how often nowadays do you attend services or meetings connected with your religion?

- Once a week or more . . . 1
- Less often but at least once in two weeks . . . 2
- Less often but at least once a month . . . 3
- Less often but at least twice a year . . . 4
- Less often but at least once a year . . . 5
- Less often . . . 6
- Never or practically never . . . 7
- Varies . . . 8

ASK ALL

14.a) Do you have, or have you had any children of your own, that you are the natural {**MEN**: father of; **WOMEN**: mother of:} please include any who don't know, or never did live with you as part of your household? (IF MENTIONED, EXCLUDE MISCARRIAGE/ABORTION/ADOPTED)

Yes 1 **ASK b)**
No 2 **GO TO Q.15**

b) How old were you when your first child was born? (INCLUDE STILLBIRTH/DIED)

ENTER AGE [ ][ ]

c) How many children have you had?

One only 01 **GO TO Q.15**

More than one:- ENTER NUMBER [ ][ ] **ASK d)**

d) How old is the youngest now? ENTER AGE [ ][ ]

e) Do (both/all) your children have the same
MEN: mother?
WOMEN: father?

Yes; both/all the same . . . 1
No; different . . . 2

ASK ALL

15.a) Do you have any adopted or stepchildren?

Yes – adopted 1
– step 2
– both 3 } **ASK b)**
No – none 4 ✓ **GO TO Q.16**

b) How many (adopted/step) children do you have? ENTER NUMBER [ ][ ]

16.a) **ALL**: INTERVIEWER CHECK CODE: TOTAL NUMBER OF NATURAL AND NATURAL AND ADOPTED/STEP CHILDREN IS:

None ('No' at Q14a *and* Q15a) 1 ✓ **GO TO Q.17**
One ('01' at Q14c *or* Q15b) 2
Two (at Q14c and/or Q15b) 3
Three or more (at Q14c and/or Q15b) 4 } **ASK b)**

b) May I check, is (the child/either/any of the children) (including your own and adopted or stepchildren) aged 14 or over now?

Yes: one or more aged 14+ 1 **ASK c)**
No: none aged 14+ 2 **GO TO Q.17**

c) When your child(ren) were about 14, comparing yourself with other parents, would you say you were more strict or more easy going about allowing your child(ren) to go out at night, to parties, social events, and so on?
IF MORE STRICT/EASY GOING, PROBE:
Much more or a little more (strict/easy going)?

Much more strict . . . 1
A little more strict . . . 2
About the same as others . . . 3
A little more easy going . . . 4
Much more easy going . . . 5
Doesn't apply (eg. child(ren) don't want to go out yet/none living with me when aged 14/not responsible for stepchildren, etc.) . . . 6

ASK ALL

CARD B (M OR W)

17.a) When you were growing up, in which of the ways listed on this card did you learn about sexual matters:

(**EXPLAIN**: You can just tell me the code letters.)

PROBE: What other ways: (UNTIL 'NO OTHERS')

CODE ALL THAT APPLY

Mother	(P)	01	IF TWO OR MORE CODES, ASK **b)**; IF ONE CODE ONLY, GO TO Q.18
Father	(Z)	02	
Brother(s)	(X)	03	
Sister(s)	(L)	04	
Other relative(s)	(N)	05	
Lessons at school	(D)	06	
Friends of about my own age	(J)	07	
MEN: First girlfriend or sexual partner / **WOMEN**: First boyfriend or sexual partner	(S)	08	
A doctor, nurse or clinic	(A)	09	
Television	(K)	10	
Radio	(E)	11	
Books	(G)	12	
Magazines or newspapers	(V)	13	
Other (SPECIFY) ______	(Q)	14	
Can't remember at all (PROBE BEFORE CODING)		98	**GO TO Q.18**

(*CARD B*)

b) From which *one* of those did you learn most?

ONE CODE ONLY

Mother	(P)	01
Father	(Z)	02
Brother(s)	(X)	03
Sister(s)	(L)	04
Other relative(s)	(N)	05
Lessons at school	(D)	06
Friends of about my own age	(J)	07
MEN: First girlfriend or sexual partner / **WOMEN**: First boyfriend or sexual partner	(S)	08
A doctor, nurse or clinic	(A)	09
Television	(K)	10
Radio	(E)	11
Books	(G)	12
Magazines or Newspapers	(V)	13
Other (SPECIFY) ______	(Q)	14
Can't choose just one (STATE MAIN ONES) ______		96
Don't know/Can't remember at all		98

ASK ALL

CARD C

18.a) Looking back to the time when you first felt ready to have some sexual experience yourself, is there anything on this list that you *now* feel you ought to have known more about?

Yes (ought to have known more) I ✓**ASK b)**

No/none – felt I knew enough at the time 2

No/None – not ready for sexual experience yet 3 } **GO TO Q.19**

b) Which ones?

PROBE: What others?

CODE ALL

THAT APPLY

How girls' bodies develop	(A)	. . . 01
How boys' bodies develop	(Q)	. . . 02
How a baby is born	(B)	. . . 03
Sexual intercourse	(H)	. ✓ 04
Contraception, birth control	(R)	. . . 05
Homosexuality, lesbianism	(L)	. ✓ 06
Masturbation	(T)	. ✓ 07
How to make sex more satisfying	(K)	. ✓ 08
How to be able to say 'No'	(S)	. ✓ 09
Sexual feelings, emotions and relationships	(M)	. ✓ 10
Sexually transmitted diseases (eg. VD/AIDS/HIV infection)	(D)	. . . 11
All of them		. . . 97
Would have liked to know more but can't specify which		. . . 98

CARD B (AGAIN)

c) Looking at this list again, in which one or two of these ways would you have liked to learn more, at the time (you felt ready for some sexual experience) just about the sexual matters you've just mentioned?

CODE ONE OR TWO ONLY

Mother	(P)	. . . 01
Father	(Z)	. . . 02
Brother(s)	(X)	. . . 03
Sister(s)	(L)	. . . 04
Other relative(s)	(N)	. . . 05
Lessons at school	(D)	. ✓ 06
Friends of about my own age	(J)	. . . 07
{ **MEN**: First girlfriend or sexual partner { **WOMEN**: First boyfriend or sexual partner }	(S)	. . . 08
A doctor, nurse or clinic	(A)	. ✓ 09
Television	(K)	. . . 10
Radio	(E)	. . . 11
Books	(G)	. . . 12
Magazines or Newspapers	(V)	. . . 13
Other (SPECIFY) _____	(Q)	. . . 14
Don't know		. . . 98

SECTION TWO: FIRST EXPERIENCES

ASK ALL

CARD D

19. On this card are two questions about your own experience. For each question would you tell me your age at the time, or just say, 'this hasn't ever happened'.
PAUSE, TO GIVE RESPONDENT TIME TO READ CARD. DO NOT READ OUT THE QUESTIONS IN ITALICS (WHICH ARE ON THE CARD) UNLESS THE RESPONDENT NEEDS HELP.

> *A. How old were you when you first had sexual intercourse with someone of the opposite sex, or hasn't this happened?*
>
> *B.*How old were you when you first had any type of experience of a sexual kind – for example, kissing, cuddling, petting – with someone of the opposite sex (or hasn't this happened either)?*

*IF RESPONDENT QUERIES MEANING OF 'B', EXPLAIN: *Any* kind of experience that *you* feel is sexual.

a) **ASK**: How about question 'A'? — **RING LETTER**

RECORD ANSWER AND RING LETTER CODE

ENTER EXACT AGE, IF 13+	16	(A)
Not sure of age – PROBE: About how old? WRITE IN ESTIMATE/RANGE IF 13+	______	A
Age 12 or under: ENTER	☐☐	X
Hasn't ever happened	. . . 96 . . .	C
Refused to answer	. . . 97 . . .	D

b) **ASK**: And how about question 'B'?

RECORD ANSWER

ENTER EXACT AGE	11
Not sure of age – PROBE: About how old? WRITE IN ESTIMATE/RANGE	______
Hasn't ever happened	. . . 96
Refused to answer	. . . 97

INTERVIEWER CHECK:

c) **LETTER CODE AT a) IS . . .**

(A)	1	**GO TO Q.20**
X	2	**ASK d)**
C or D	3	**GO TO Q.31; RING 'C' OR 'D' AT Q.31c) BEFORE ASKING Q.31a)**

d) Looking at question 'A' again, has this happened with anybody *else* since you were 13?

RECORD ANSWER AND RING LETTER CODE

Yes – ENTER EXACT AGE, IF 13+ [ ][ ] A } ASK Q.20

Yes, not sure of age – PROBE About how old?
WRITE IN ESTIMATE RANGE IF 13+ ________ A } ASK Q.20

No, not with anybody else since age 13 (RING 96 AND 'B') . . . 96 B } **GO TO Q.31; RING 'B' or 'D' at Q.31c)**

Refused to answer (RING 97 AND 'D') . . . 97 D } **BEFORE ASKING Q.31a)**

ALL WHO HAD (FIRST) INTERCOURSE AT AGE 13+

20.a) **INTERVIEWER** CODE YOUR ASSESSMENT OF INTERVIEW CIRCUMSTANCES:

Private enough to ask Q.21–29 1 **GO TO Q.21**

Definitely *not* private enough to ask Q.21–29 2 **ASK b)**

ONLY RING CODE 2 IF ABSOLUTELY NECESSARY

b) HAND SELF-COMPLETION 'FIRST EXPERIENCES' SHEET–MEN'S/WOMEN'S VERSION

You may prefer to answer the next few questions yourself, on this sheet. You just need to tick boxes opposite the answers that apply to you.

CODE Sheet accepted 1 **ANSWER c)**

Prefers to be *asked* the questions 2 **ASK Q.21–29**

c) WHILE RESPONDENT COMPLETING, WRITE IN YOUR REASON FOR DECIDING ON USE OF SELF-COMPLETION

____

d) WHEN COMPLETED, TAKE SHEET BACK AND SAY:

Thank you. Was there anything you weren't sure about that you'd like to check with me? EXPLAIN IF NECESSARY.

CODE: Sheet completed and attached – no queries 1 } **NOW GO TO Q.30**

Sheet completed and attached – after query 2 } **NOW GO TO Q.30**

Sheet not completed/Refused (STATE WHY) 3 } **NOW GO TO Q.30**

21. The next few questions are about the first time you had sexual intercourse with someone of the opposite sex (ADD IF Q.19d) WAS ASKED: that is, the first new partner you had sex with after you were 13):

a) How old was your partner at that time? ENTER AGE [1][7]

Not sure of age – PROBE: About how old?

WRITE IN ESTIMATE/RANGE ________

Never knew partner's age . . . 97

Can't remember partner's age . . . 98

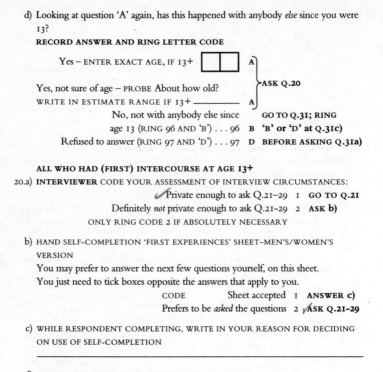

b) As far as you *now* know, was it (also) your partner's first time ever, or not?
IF DON'T KNOW, PROBE:
Do you *think* it was {MEN: her / WOMEN: his} first time, or not?

Yes, first time	1
Think it was first time	2
Think it was not first time	3
No, not first time	4
Don't know	8

ALL WHO HAD (FIRST) INTERCOURSE AT AGE 13+

22.a. Would you say that you were both equally willing to have intercourse that first time, or was one of you more willing than the other?
IF ONE MORE WILLING: Who was more willing?

Both equally willing	1	**GO TO Q.23**
Respondent more	2	**GO TO Q.23**
Partner more	3	**ASK b)**
Can't remember	8	**GO TO Q.23**

b) Would you say . . . READ OUT

. . . that you were also willing	1
or, that you had to be persuaded	2
or, that you were forced?	3

CARD E (M OR W)

23. Did you or your partner use any form of contraception or take any precautions that first time, or not?

Condom (Sheath/Durex)	(1)	1
Other contraception	(2)	2
{MEN: I withdrew / WOMEN: Partner withdrew}	(3)	3
Made sure it was a 'safe period'	(4)	4
No precaution by me, don't know about partner	(5)	5
No precautions by either of us	(6)	6
Can't remember		8

24. *CARD F* (M OR W)
Which one of these descriptions applies best to you and your partner at the time you first had intercourse?

(**MEN ONLY**) She was a prostitute	(N)	01	**ASK Q.25**
We had just met for the first time	(T)	02	**ASK Q.25**
We had met recently	(X)	03	**ASK Q.25**
We had known each other for a while, but didn't have a steady relationship at the time	(D)	04	**ASK Q.25**
We had a steady relationship at the time	(Q)	05	**ASK Q.25**
We were living together (but not married or engaged)	(J)	06	**ASK Q.25**
We were engaged to be married	(B)	07	**ASK Q.25**
We were married	(H)	08	**GO TO Q.72**
Other (SPECIFY) ______	(S)	97	**ASK Q.25**

ALL WHO WERE NOT MARRIED AT FIRST INTERCOURSE

CARD G

25. Which of these statements is closest to how that first time of having intercourse came about?

It just happened on the spur of the moment	(A)	. . . 1
I expected it would happen soon, but wasn't sure when	(B)	. . . 2
I expected it to happen at that time	(C)	. . . 3
I planned it to happen at that time	(D)	. . . 4
We planned it together beforehand	(E)	. . . 5
Can't remember		. . . 8

CARD H

26.a) Which, if any, of these things applied to you *at the time*? Please choose *all* that applied.

CODE ALL THAT APPLY

I was curious about what it would be like	(M)	01	**ASK b) IF *TWO+* CODES. GO TO Q.27 IF *ONE* CODE ONLY.**
I got carried away by my feelings	(C)	02	
Most people in my age group seemed to be doing it	(F)	03	
It seemed like a natural 'follow on' in the relationship	(L)	04	
I was a bit drunk at the time	(R)	05	
I wanted to lose my virginity	(H)	06	
I was in love	(D)	07	
Other particular factor (SPECIFY) ______________	(S)	08	
None of these applied		97	**GO TO Q.27**
Can't remember		98	

b) Which *one* was the main one that applied at the time?

NB. CODE HERE MUST BE SAME AS ONE OF THOSE RINGED AT a)

CODE ONE ONLY

I was curious about what it would be like	(M)	. . . 01
I got carried away by my feelings	(C)	. . . 02
Most people in my age group seemed to be doing it	(F)	. . . 03
It seemed like a natural 'follow on' in the relationship	(L)	. . . 04
I was a bit drunk at the time	(R)	. . . 05
I wanted to lose my virginity	(H)	. . . 06
I was in love	(D)	. . . 07
Other particular factor (SPECIFY) ______________	(S)	. . . 08
Can't choose/more than one main factor		. . . 97
Can't remember		. . . 98

ALL WHO HAD (FIRST) INTERCOURSE AT 13+

27. How long did the *sexual* relationship with your (first) partner continue after the first time you had sex, or is it still continuing now, or did it not continue at all?

Still continuing now . . . 01

Did not continue at all (i.e. once only with first partner) . ✓. 02

Continued, but ended after:-

1 month or less . . . 03
Over 1 month to 3 months . . . 04
Over 3 to 6 months . . . 05
Over 6 to 12 months . . . 06
Over 1 to 5 years . . . 07
Over 5 to 10 years . . . 08
Over 10 years (STATE) ________ . . . 09
Can't remember how long . . . 98

28. Looking back *now* to the first time you had sexual intercourse, do you think . . .
READ OUT

. . . you should have waited longer before having sex with anyone . . . 1
or, that you should not have waited so long ✓. . 2
or, was it at about the right time? . . . 3
(Don't know/No opinion) . . . 8

29.a) About how long was it after the *first* time you had intercourse with your (*first*) partner till you had intercourse with a second partner, that is, with a different {MEN: woman / WOMEN: man} or hasn't that happened?

Hasn't happened 02 **GO TO Q.30**

Happened after:-

1 month or less	03 ✓	**ASK b)**
Over 1 to 3 months	04	
Over 3 to 6 months	05	
Over 6 to 12 months	06	
Over 1 to 5 years	07	
Over 5 to 10 years	08	
Over 10 years (STATE) ________	09	
Can't remember how long after	98	

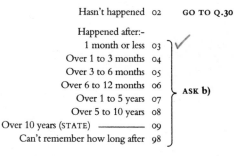

b) And for how long did the relationship with that (second) person continue, or is it still continuing now, or did it not continue at all?

Still continuing now . . . 01

Did not continue at all (i.e. once only with second partner) ✓ . 02

Continued, but ended after:-
1 month or less . . . 03
Over 1 to 3 months . . . 04
Over 3 to 6 months . . . 05
Over 6 to 12 months . . . 06
Over 1 to 5 years . . . 07
Over 5 to 10 years . . . 08
Over 10 years (STATE) _____ . . . 09
Can't remember how long . . . 98

SECTION THREE: LIFESTYLE

ALL WHO HAD (FIRST) INTERCOURSE AT AGE 13+

30. Now I'd like to ask you a few more general questions about things affecting sex.

CARD J (M OR W)

a) First, from this list, could you tell me which you or a partner have *ever* used, together? Just tell me the code letters.
PROBE: Any others?
CODE ALL THAT APPLY UNDER a).

b) And which have you used at all with a partner in the past year?
PROBE: Any others?
CODE ALL THAT APPLY UNDER b)

		a) *Ever*		b) *Past year*		
The pill	(J)	01		(J)	01	
The coil/IUD/Intra-uterine device	(R)	02		(R)	02	
Condom/sheath/Durex	(D)	03	✓	(D)	03	✓
Cap/diaphragm/Dutch cap	(Q)	04		(Q)	04	
Foam tablets/jellies/creams/suppositories/ pessaries/aerosol foam	(L)	05		(L)	05	
Sponge	(U)	06		(U)	06	
Douching, washing	(T)	07		(T)	07	
Safe period/rhythm method	(K)	08	ASK	(K)	08	
MEN: I have / WOMEN: partner has been careful / withdrawn	(S)	09	b)	(S)	09	
MEN: Partner / WOMEN: I am sterilized	(C)	10		(C)	10	
MEN: I am / WOMEN: Partner is sterilized (had vasectomy)	(M)	11		(M)	11	
Going without sexual intercourse to avoid pregnancy	(B)	12		(B)	12	
Other method of protection	(W)	13		(W)	13	
None of these – ever	(F)	14		–	–	
None of these – past year	(F)	–		(F)	14	

GO TO Q.31, BUT FIRST RING
CODE 'A' AT Q.31c) BEFORE
ASKING

IF RESPONDENT NEEDS HELP WITH Q.31, SHOW CARDS K AND/OR L, YOU MAY READ OUT FROM HERE, USING *MEN'S* OR *WOMEN'S* VERSIONS AS APPROPRIATE.

MEN

CARD K (M) (Q.31a)

I have felt sexually attracted . . .

. . . only to females, never to males	*(K)*
. . . more often to females, and at least once to a male	*(C)*
. . . about equally often to females and to males	*(F)*
. . . more often to males, and at least once to a female	*(L)*
. . . only ever to males, never to females	*(D)*
I have never felt sexually attracted to anyone at all	*(N)*

CARD L (M) (Q.31b)

Sexual experience *is any kind of contact with another person that you felt was sexual (it could be just kissing or touching, or intercourse, or any other form of sex).*

I have had some sexual experience . . .

. . . only with females (or a female), never with a male	*(R)*
. . . more often with females, and at least once with a male	*(Q)*
. . . about equally often with females and with males	*(T)*
. . . more often with males, and at least once with a female	*(O)*
. . . only with males (or a male), never with a female	*(Z)*
I have never had any sexual experience with anyone at all	*(W)*

WOMEN

CARD K (W) (Q.31a)

I have felt sexually attracted . . .

. . . only to males, never to females	*(K)*
. . . more often to males, and at least once to a female	*(C)*
. . . about equally often to males and to females	*(F)*
. . . more often to females, and at least once to a male	*(L)*
. . . only ever to females, never to males	*(D)*
I have never felt sexually attracted to anyone at all	*(N)*

CARD L (W) (Q.31b)

Sexual experience *is any kind of contact with another person that you felt was sexual (it could be just kissing or touching, or intercourse, or any other form of sex).*

I have had some sexual experience . . .

. . . only with males (or a male), never with a female	*(R)*
. . . more often with males, and at least once with a female	*(Q)*
. . . about equally often with males and with females	*(T)*
. . . more often with females, and at least once with a male	*(O)*
. . . only with females (or a female), never with a male	*(Z)*
I have never had any sexual experience with anyone at all	*(W)*

ASK ALL

CARD K (M) – MEN [DO NOT READ OUT CARD UNLESS RESPONDENT NEEDS HELP]

CARD K (W) – WOMEN

31.a) Now please read this card carefully as it is important that you understand it and are as honest as you can be in your answer.

PAUSE TILL RESPONDENT HAS READ CARD, THEN ASK:

Which letter represents your answer?

	K	C	F	L	D	N	Refused
RING ONE CODE FOR a) →	1	2	3	4	5	6	7

CARD L (M) – MEN [DO NOT READ OUT CARD UNLESS RESPONDENT NEEDS HELP]

CARD L (W) – WOMEN

b) As before, please read *this* card carefully and be as honest as you can be in your answer.

PAUSE TILL RESPONDENT HAS READ CARD, THEN ASK:

Which letter represents your answer?

	R	Q	T	O	Z	W	Refused
RING ONE CODE FOR b) →	1	2	3	4	5	6	7

TRANSFER LETTER CODE FROM Q.19 (*BEFORE* ASKING Q.31 a)

c) RING ONE							
A	01	05	09	13	17	21	25
B	02	06	10	14	18	22	26
C	03	07	11	15	19	23	27
D	04	08	12	16	20	24	28

d) **NOW**, IN GRID AVOVE, FOLLOW THE LINE FROM THE RINGED LETTER CODE AT c) TO THE POINT BELOW THE RINGED b) CODE: RING THE GRID CODE AT THAT POINT.

e) **IF THE GRID CODE IS:-**

- 22, 23, 24 (RESPONDENT ANY AGE) 1
- 02, 03, 04 or 26, 27, 28 *AND* RESPONDENT IS AGED 16/17 2

} **BOOKLET IS *NOT* TO BE GIVEN, GO TO Q.33**

- 02, 03, 04 or 26, 27, 28 *AND* RESPONDENT IS AGED 18+ .. 3
- 01, 05–20, 21, 25 (RESPONDENT ANY AGE) 4

} **BOOKLET *IS* TO BE GIVEN, GO TO Q.32**

ALL WHO ARE TO COMPLETE BOOKLET

32. **HAVE READY TO HAND TO RESPONDENT DURING INTRODUCTION:-**

- GREY BOOKLET (MEN) OR TURQUOISE BOOKLET (WOMEN) – ENTER SERIAL NUMBER
- ENVELOPE – ENTER SERIAL NUMBER
- PEN OR PENCIL
- SCRIBBLE PAPER

KEEP ANOTHER COPY OF BOOKLET BY YOU, TO REFER TO IF RESPONDENT ASKS FOR HELP.

INTRODUCE BOOKLET:

a) The next set of questions, which are in this booklet, will probably be easier if you read and answer them yourself. Some questions may not apply to you at all, so it shouldn't take long to do. When you have finished, *put the booklet in the envelope and seal it.*

ADD IF 'FIRST EXPERIENCES' SELF-COMPLETION SHEET USED (OTHERWISE ADD IF NECESSARY)	• The questions are quite personal and this way your answers will be *completely confidential and I won't see them.* • We need to have a number on it in case it gets separated from the questionnaire. Our office can then check that all documents for one person are completed, but names are never attached to answers.

It is very important to the study that you answer honestly and accurately, so please take your time. There is a piece of scribble paper in case you find it useful for jotting things down to help you remember.

Most questions can be answered by ticking a box, or by entering a number; SHOW Q.2a IN BOOKLET AND DEMONSTRATE BY POINTING – here, for example, if you were to answer 'none' you'd tick this box and go on to Question 3. Or you'd write in a number here, or here, and follow the arrow to b). *CLOSE* BOOKLET AND HAND TO RESPONDENT.

I should add that the booklet contains certain terms, like oral sex, anal sex and vaginal intercourse. So that everyone attaches the same meaning to these terms, they are defined in the front of the booklet. I'd like you to read them first.

If you need any help or explanations, do please ask. I will just be doing some paper work while you do the booklet.

WHEN RESPONDENT HAS FINISHED, BUT BEFORE ENVELOPE IS SEALED, ASK:

b) May I ask you whether you understood how to answer all the questions, or is there anything you would like me to explain, just to be sure?

Booklet *not* completed (STATE WHY) ________________ ________________	1	**ASK Q.33 – a) MEN b) WOMEN**
Booklet completed and attached:		**TAKE BACK**
– all understood/no help given	2	***SEALED***
– help given *during* completed (STATE BELOW)	3	**ENVELOPE;**
– help given *after* completion (STATE BELOW)	4	**CHECK THAT**
(Q.No.'s) ________________		***SERIAL NO.***
________________		**IS ENTERED;**
		GO TO Q.34

33.a) **MEN**: Now may I just ask, are you circumcised?

Yes	1	**ASK Q.34**
No	2	
Question not understood	3	

b) **WOMEN**: Now may I just ask, at what age did you start menstruating (having periods)? ENTER AGE [\ | \ ] **ASK Q.34**

SECTION FOUR: ATTITUDES

ASK ALL

34. Now I would like to ask you some questions on your *views* about sexual relationships.

In general, is there an age below which you think young people nowadays ought not to start having sexual intercourse . . .

a) . . . first, for boys? ENTER AGE [1][4] **ASK b)** **ASK c)**

Depends on individual, not age	95	**ASK b)**
Not before marriage	96	
Other (SPECIFY) ______	97	
No view/Don't know	98	

b) . . . and for girls? ENTER AGE [1][3] **ASK c)**

Depends on individual, not age	95	**IF 95–98 AT a) AND b) GO TO Q.35**
Not before marriage	96	
Other (SPECIFY) ______	97	
No view/Don't know	98	

CARD M

c) What is the *main* reason you say (that/those) ages?

Before that age:-
- young people are not *physically* mature enough . . . 1
- young people are not *emotionally* mature enough . . . 2
- young people have not *learnt* enough about sex . . . 3
- it is *morally* wrong . . . 4
- the risks to *health* are increased . . . 5

2(+) of the above equally/different ones for boys and girls (SPECIFY) ______ . . . 6

Other reason (SPECIFY) ______ . . . 7

Don't know . . . 8

35. Would you tell me whether you think each of these things is legal or illegal under the law . . .

READ OUT

	LEGAL	ILLEGAL	DON'T KNOW
a) . . . For a woman aged under 16 to have sex?	1	2	8
b) For a man aged under 16 to have sex?	1	2	8
c) For a man to have sex with a woman of under 16?	1	2	8
d) For a woman to have sex with a man of under 16?	1	2	8
e) For two men aged over 16 but under 21 to have sex together?	1	2	8
f) For two women aged over 16 but under 21 to have sex together?	1	2	8

ASK ALL

IF INTERVIEWING IN ENGLAND OR WALES, ASK ABOUT "BRITAIN"

IF INTERVIEWING IN SCOTLAND, ASK ABOUT "SCOTLAND"

36. Do you think that divorce in (Britain/Scotland) should be . . . **READ OUT**

. . . easier to obtain than it is now, . . . 1
or, more difficult, . . . 2
or, should things remain as they are? . . . 3
(Don't know) . . . 8

37. *CARD N*

As I read from this list, please look at the card and tell me how important you think each one is to a successful marriage . . . **READ OUT**

		very important	*quite important*	*not very important*	*not at all important*	*(don't know)*
a)	. . . Faithfulness?	1	2	3	4	8
b)	An adequate income?	1	2	3	4	8
c)	Mutual respect and appreciation?	1	2	3	4	8
d)	Shared religious beliefs?	1	2	3	4	8
e)	A happy sexual relationship?	1	2	3	4	8
f)	Sharing household chores?	1	2	3	4	8
g)	Having children?	1	2	3	4	8
h)	Tastes and interests in common?	1	2	3	4	8

38.a) In general, what age do you think is a good age for a man to get married?

ENTER AGE [ ][ ]

Varies/Depends/No particular age . . . 96
Other answer including age range (STATE BELOW)
____________________ . . . 97
Don't know . . . 98

b) And for a woman to get married?

ENTER AGE [ ][ ]

Varies/Depends/No particular age . . . 96
Other answer including age range (STATE BELOW)
____________________ . . . 97
Don't know . . . 98

ASK ALL

CARD O

39. From this card, what are your opinions about the following sexual relationships . . .
READ OUT

	always wrong	*mostly wrong*	*some-times wrong*	*rarely wrong*	*not wrong at all*	*depends/ don't know*
a) . . . If a man and a woman have sexual relations before marriage, what would your general opinion be?	1	2	3	4	5	8
b) What about a married person having sexual relations with someone other than his or her partner?	1	2	3	4	5	8
c) What about a person who is living with a partner, not married, having sexual relations with someone other than his or her partner?	1	2	3	4	5	8
d) And a person who has a regular partner they don't live with, having sexual relations with someone else?	1	2	3	4	5	8
e) What about a person having one night stands?	1	2	3	4	5	8
What is your general opinion about . . .						
f) Sexual relations between two adult men?	1	2	3	4	5	8
g) And sexual relations between two adult women?	1	2	3	4	5	8
h) Lastly, what is your general opinion about abortion?	1	2	3	4	5	8

ASK ALL

CARD P

40. Now please would you say how far you agree or disagree with each of these things . . . **READ OUT**

	agree strongly	*agree*	*neither agree nor disagree*	*dis-agree*	*dis-agree strongly*	*don't know*
a) . . . It is natural for people to want sex less often as they get older?	1	2	3	4	5	8
b) Having a sexual relationship outside a regular one doesn't necessarily harm that relationship?	1	2	3	4	5	8

c) Companionship and affection are more important than sex in a marriage or relationship?	1	2	3	4	5	8
d) Sex without orgasm, or climax, cannot be really satisfying for a man?	1	2	3	4	5	8
e) Sex without orgasm, or climax, cannot be really satisfying for a woman?	1	2	3	4	5	8
f) A person who sticks with one partner is likely to have a more satisfying sex life than someone who has many partners?	1	2	3	4	5	8
g) Sex is the most important part of any marriage or relationship.	1	2	3	4	5	8
h) Sex tends to get better the longer you know someone?	1	2	3	4	5	8

ASK ALL

CARD Q

41.a) In general, do you think it is *easy* or *difficult* for two people who have sex together to talk openly about it, for example, to tell each other what they like and dislike in sex?

b) What about you, how easy or difficult would it be for you?

	(a) *General*	(b) *You*
Easy with a husband, wife or regular partner, but difficult with a new partner	(C) . . . 1	(C) . . . 1
Easy with a new partner, but difficult with a husband, wife or regular partner	(L) . . . 2	(L) . . . 2
Easy with *any* partner	(B) . . . 3	(B) . . . 3
Difficult with *any* partner	(K) . . . 4	(K) . . . 4
Depends/Would vary/Can't say/Don't know	. . . 8	. . . 8

ASK ALL

CARD R

42.a) Which of these lifestyles would you regard as the ideal one for *you* at this stage of your life?

b) What about the future, say in five years time, which one do you think will be *your* ideal then?

	(a) *Now*	(b) *Future*
Prefer to have no sex activity	(T) . . . 01	(T) . . . 01
No regular partners but casual partner when I feel like it	(Q) . . . 02	(Q) . . . 02
A few regular partners	(B) . . . 03	(B) . . . 03
One regular partner but not living together	(S) . . . 04	(S) . . . 04
Living with a partner (not married) with some sex activity outside the partnership	(L) . . . 05	(L) . . . 05
Living with a partner (not married) and no other sex partners	(Z) . . . 06	(Z) . . . 06
Married, with some sex activity outside the marriage	(O) . . . 07	(O) . . . 07
Married, with no other sex partners	(H) . . . 08	(H) . . . 08
Have no ideal/None of these/Don't know	. . . 98	. . . 98

43. There has been a lot of publicity about AIDS in the last year or two. From what you have heard or read, what does the phrase 'safer sex' mean to you?
PROBE: What else? (UNTIL 'NOTHING'). *DO NOT PROMPT: RECORD VERBATIM*

ASK ALL

44.a) Have you changed your own sexual lifestyle in any way, or made any decisions about sex, because of concern about catching AIDS or HIV virus?

Yes	1	**ASK b)**
No	2	**GO TO Q.45**
Lifestyle has changed but *not* because of AIDS	3	**GO TO Q.45**

IF YES AT a)

CARD S

b) In which of these ways have you changed?
Please tell me the letters of all those that apply to you.

Having fewer partners	(D) . . . 1
Finding out more about a person before having sex	(L) . . . 2
Using a condom	(K) . . . 3
Not having sex	(C) . . . 4
Sticking to one partner	(X) . . . 5
Avoiding some sexual practices	(Q) . . . 6
Other change(s)	(N) . . . 7

ASK ALL

CARD T

45. Nobody yet knows for sure how many people are at risk of becoming infected with the AIDS virus, but we would like to know what *you* think about . . .
READ OUT

	greatly at risk (A)	*quite a lot* (B)	*not very much* (C)	*not at all at risk* (D)	*don't know*
a) . . . the risks to you, personally, with your present sexual lifestyle?	1	2	3	4	8

Now please choose a phrase from the card to tell me how much at risk you think each of these groups is from AIDS . . . **READ OUT**	(A)	(B)	(C)	(D)	Don't know
b) . . . People who have many different partners of the opposite sex?	1	2	3	4	8
c) Married couples who only have sex with each other?	1	2	3	4	8
d) Married couples who occasionally have sex with someone other than their regular partner?	1	2	3	4	8
e) Male homosexuals – that is gay men?	1	2	3	4	8
f) Female homosexuals – that is lesbians?	1	2	3	4	8

SECTION FIVE: CLASSIFICATION

ASK ALL

1. Finally, a few questions about you and your household.

a) At present are you . . . READ OUT AS FAR AS NECESSARY TO CODE

	. . . married (and living with spouse)	1	**ASK b)**
living with a partner	of opposite sex	2	**ASK b)**
	of same sex	3	**ASK b)**
	widowed	4	**GO TO Q.3**
	divorced	5	**GO TO Q.3**
	separated	6	**GO TO Q.3**
	or, single?	7	**GO TO Q.2**

b) What was your (husband's/wife's/partner's) age last birthday?

ENTER AGE ☐☐

c) For how long have you been married/living with your partner?

Less than 6 months . . . 95

6 months, but less than 1 year . . . 96

1 year or longer: ENTER NUMBER OF YEARS ☐☐

d) And may I check, is this

(EITHER) your first marriage . . .

(OR) the first partner you have lived with . . .

. . . or have you been married or lived with another partner before?

This is *first* marriage/partner . . . 1

Not the first:

– been married before . . . 2

– lived with (another) partner before . . . 3

– married before *and* lived with a partner before (i.e. different people) . . . 4

e) How old were you when you (got married/started living with a partner) (ADD IF (NOT FIRST: the *first* time)?

ENTER AGE ☐☐ **GO TO Q.4**

ASK ALL WHO ARE SINGLE

2.a) Have you ever lived with a partner* (as married)? **IF YES, PROBE**: Just once or more than once?

Yes, once 1

Yes, more than once: ENTER NUMBER ☐☐ **ASK b)**

No 0 **GO TO Q.4**

b) Hold old were you when you first started to live with a partner?*

*Partner may be opposite sex *or* same sex. ENTER AGE ☐☐ **GO TO Q.4**

ASK ALL WHO ARE WIDOWED/DIVORCED/SEPARATED

3.a) How long ago were you widowed/separated?*

*NOTE: IF DIVORCED, CODE HOW LONG AGO *SEPARATION* HAPPENED, *ACTUAL* SEPARATION (RATHER THAN LEGAL)

Less than 6 months ago . . . 95
6 months, but less than 1 year ago . . . 96
1 year or longer ago: ENTER NUMBER OF YEARS ☐☐

b) And for how long were you married? (LAST MARRIAGE)

Less than 6 months . . . 95
6 months, but less than 1 year . . . 96
1 year or longer: ENTER NUMBER OF YEARS ☐☐

c) And may I check, was that your first marriage or had you been married or lived with another partner before?

First marriage and not lived with any other partner . . . 1
Not the first – had been married before . . . 2
– lived with a partner before . . . 3
– married before and lived with a partner before (i.e. different people) . . . 4

d) How old were you when you got married (or lived with a partner) (ADD IF NOT THE FIRST: the *first* time)? ENTER AGE ☐☐

ASK ALL

4.a) Including yourself, how many people live here regularly members of this household? ENTER TOTAL ☐☐

b) How many are . . . READ OUT

. . . *children* aged under 2? ☐
– aged 2 to 5? ☐
– aged 6 to 15? ☐
Men aged 16 to 24? ☐
Women aged 16 to 24? ☐
Men aged 25 to 59? ☐
Women aged 25 to 59? ☐
Men aged 60 or older? ☐
Women aged 60 or older? ☐

ASK ALL

5. Do you (or your household) own or rent this (house/flat/accommodation)?

Own – outright or with mortgage/loan	1
Rent, from: – Council	2
– Housing Assoc.	3
– Private landlord	4
Tied to job (inc. rent free)	5
Squat	6
Other (STATE) ________________	7

6.a) For how long have you lived in this (city/town/village)?

Always (i.e. since birth and never lived elsewhere	1	**GO TO Q.7**
1 year or less	2	**ASK b)**
Over 1–5 years	3	
Over 5–10 years	4	
Over 10–20 years	5	
Over 20 years (but not always)	6	

b) Were you born in . . . READ OUT AS FAR AS NECESSARY

. . . England	1	**GO TO Q.7**
Wales	2	
Scotland	3	
Northern Ireland/Eire	4	**ASK c)**
or, another country? (STATE)	7	

c) How old were you when you (first came to live in Britain?

ENTER AGE [ ][ ]

ASK ALL

CARD C1

7. Which of these descriptions applies to what you were doing last week, that is, in the seven days ending last Sunday?

PROBE: Any others? **RING ALL LETTER CODES THAT APPLY IF ONLY ONE LETTER CODE, TRANSFER IT TO NUMBER CODE IF MORE THAN ONE, TRANSFER HIGHEST ON LIST TO NUMBER CODE**

In full-time education (not paid for by employer, including on vacation	A	01	**ASK Q.8**
On government training/employment scheme (e.g. Employment Training, Youth Training Scheme, etc.)	B	02	
In paid work (or away temporarily) for at least 10 hours in the week	C	03	**GO TO Q.9**
Waiting to take up paid work already accepted	D	04	
Unemployed and registered for benefit	E	05	**ASK Q.8**
Unemployed, not registered, but actively looking for a job	F	06	
Unemployed, wanting a job (of at least 10 hrs per week), but not actively looking for a job	G	07	
Permanently sick or disabled	H	08	
Wholly retired from work	J	09	
Looking after the home	K	10	
Doing something else (**SPECIFY**)	L	11	

ASK ALL NOT IN PAID WORK

8. When did you last have a paid job of at least 10 hours a week (or have you never had a paid job since leaving full-time education/other than the government schemes you mentioned)?

Never had a paid job	1	**GO TO Q.11**
Within past 3 months	2	**ASK Q.10**
Over 3-6 months ago	3	
Over 6 months – 1 year ago	4	
Over 1-5 years ago	5	
Over 5-10 years ago	6	
Over 10-20 years ago	7	**GO TO Q.11**
Over 20 years ago	8	

ASK ALL IN PAID WORK OR WAITING TO TAKE UP PAID WORK

9.a) How many hours a week do you normally (expect to) work in your (main) job, including any *paid* overtime?

(10+ ONLY)

IF VARIES, TAKE LAST WEEK — ENTER NUMBER OF HOURS [ ][ ]

b) Do (will) you do any shift work or night work in your (main) job?

Yes . . . 1
No . . . 2

c) Does (will) your job ever take you away from home for more than one night at a time?

IF YES: Is this often or just occasionally?

NOW ASK Q.10

Yes, often . . . 1
Yes, occasionally . . . 2
No . . . 3

ASK ALL *EXCEPT* THOSE WHO HAVE NEVER HAD A PAID JOB OR WHOSE LAST JOB WAS OVER 10 YEARS AGO (i.e. ALL EXCEPT Q.8 CODE 1, 7, 8)

- IF IN PAID WORK NOW, ASK ABOUT PRESENT (MAIN) JOB
- IF WAITING TO TAKE UP A JOB OFFERED, ASK ABOUT FUTURE JOB
- OTHERS, ASK ABOUT LAST (MAIN) JOB

Now I want to ask you about your (present/future/last) job.

CHANGE TENSES FOR (BRACKETED) WORDS AS APPROPRIATE

10.a) What (is) your job? PROBE AS NECESSARY:

What (is) the name or title of the job? ____________________

____

____

b) What kind of work (do) you do most of the time? IF RELEVANT: What materials/machinery (do) you use? ____________________

____

____

____

c) What training or qualifications do you have that (are) needed for that job?

____

____

____

d) (Do) you supervise or (are) you responsible for the work of any other people?
IF YES: How many: Yes: WRITE IN NO.: ________
No: (RING): 00

e) Can I just check: (are) you . . . **READ OUT** . . . . . . an employee, . . . 1
or, self-employed? . . . 2

f) What (does) your employer (IF SELF-EMPLOYED: you) make or do at the place where you usually work: IF FARM, GIVE NO. OF ACRES ________

____

____

____

g) Including yourself, how many people (are) employed at the place you usually (work) from? IF SELF EMPLOYED: (Do) you have any employees? IF YES: How many?

(No employees)	0
Under 10	1
10–24	2
25–99	3
100–499	4
500 or more	5

IF RESPONDENT IS MARRIED OR LIVING WITH A PARTNER (Q.1a CODE 1–3), ASK Q.11 ABOUT HUSBAND/WIFE/PARTNER. OTHERS GO TO Q.15 (on page 8)

CARD C1

11. Which of these descriptions applied to what your (husband/wife/partner) was doing last week, that is in the seven days ending last Sunday?
PROBE: Any others? RING ALL LETTER CODES THAT APPLY
IF ONLY ONE LETTER CODE, TRANSFER IT TO NUMBER CODE
IF MORE THAN ONE, TRANSFER HIGHEST ON LIST TO NUMBER CODE

In full-time education (not paid for by employer including on vacation	A	01	**ASK Q.12**
On government training/employment scheme (eg. Employment Training, Youth Training Scheme etc.)	B	02	
In paid work (or away temporarily) for at least 10 hours in the week	C	03	**GO TO Q.13**
Waiting to take up paid work already accepted	D	04	
Unemployed and registered for benefit	E	05	**ASK Q.12**
Unemployed, not registered, but actively looking for a job	F	06	
Unemployed, wanting a job (of at least 10 hrs per week), but not actively looking for a job	G	07	
Permanently sick or disabled	H	08	
Wholly retired from work	J	09	
Looking after the home	K	10	
Doing something else (SPECIFY) ________	L	11	

IF SPOUSE/PARTNER *NOT* IN PAID WORK

12. How long ago did your (husband/wife/partner) last have a paid job of at least 10 hours a week or has he/she never had a paid job since leaving full-time education/ other than the government scheme you mentioned)?

Never had a paid job	1	GO TO Q.15
Within past 3 months	2	GO TO Q.14
Over 3-6 months ago	3	GO TO Q.14
Over 6 months – 1 year ago	4	GO TO Q.14
Over 1-5 years ago	5	GO TO Q.14
Over 5-10 years ago	6	GO TO Q.14
Over 10-20 years ago	7	GO TO Q.15
Over 20 years ago	8	GO TO Q.15

IF SPOUSE/PARTNER IN PAID WORK OR WAITING TO TAKE UP PAID WORK

13.a) How many hours a week does (he/she) normally (expect to) work in (his/her) job, including any paid overtime?

(10+ONLY)

IF VARIES, TAKE LAST WEEK ENTER NUMBER OF HOURS [ ][ ]

b) Does (will) (he/she) do any shift work or night work in his/her (main) job?

Yes . . . 1
No . . . 2

c) Does (will) (his/her) job ever take him/her away from home for more than one night at a time?

IF YES: Is this often or just occasionally?

Yes, often . . . 1
Yes, occasionally . . . 2
No . . . 3

NOW ASK Q.14

ASK IF SPOUSE/PARTNER

- **IS IN A PAID JOB (Q.11 CODE 03) – ASK ABOUT PRESENT MAIN JOB**
- **IS WAITING TO TAKE UP A PAID JOB (Q.11 CODE 04) – ASK ABOUT *FUTURE* JOB**
- **HAD A PAID JOB IN PAST 10 YEARS (Q.12 CODES 2–6) – ASK ABOUT LAST MAIN PAID JOB**

14.a) Now I want to ask you about your (husband's/wife's/partner's) job. CHANGE TENSES FOR (BRACKETED) WORDS AS APPROPRIATE

What (is) the name or title of that job? ____________________

____

____

b) What kind of work (does) he/she do most of the time? IF RELEVANT: What materials/machinery (does) he/she use? ____________________

____

____

c) What training or qualifications does he/she have that (are) needed for that job?

____

____

____

d) (Does) he/she supervise or (is) he/she responsible for the work of any other people? IF YES: How many?

Yes: WRITE IN NO.: ____________

No: (RING): 00

e) (Is) he/she . . . READ OUT . . .

. . . an employee, . . . 1

or, self-employed? . . . 2

f) What (does) your employer (IF SELF-EMPLOYED: he/she) make or do at the place where he/she usually works: IF FARM, GIVE NO. OF ACRES

____

____

____

g) Including him/herself, roughly how many people (are) employed at the place where he/she usually (works) from? IF SELF-EMPLOYED: (Does) he/she have any employees? IF YES: How many?

(No employees) . . . 0

Under 10 . . . 1

10–24 . . . 2

25–99 . . . 3

100–499 . . . 4

500 or more . . . 5

ASK ALL

CARD C2

15.a) Have you passed any exams or got any of the qualifications on this card?

Yes 1 **ASK b)**

No, none 2 **GO TO Q.16**

b) Which ones? Any others? CODE ALL THAT APPLY

GCSE Grades D-G / CSE Grades 2-5	... 01
GCSE Grades A-C / CSE Grade 1 / GCE 'O' level / School certificate / Scottish (SCE) Ordinary	... 02
GCE 'A' level/'S' level / Higher certificate / Matriculation / Scottish (SCE) Higher	... 03
Overseas School Leaving Exam/Certificate	... 04
Recognised trade apprenticeship completed	... 05
RSA/other clerical, commercial qualification	... 06
City & Guilds Certificate – Craft/Intermediate/Ordinary/Part I	... 07
City & Guilds Certificate – Advanced/Final/Part II or Part III	... 08
City & Guilds Certificate – Full technological	... 09
BEC/TEC General/Ordinary National (ONC) or Diploma (OND)	... 10
BEC/TEC Higher/Higher National Certificate (HNC) or Diploma (HND)	... 11
Teacher's training qualification	... 12
Nursing qualification	... 13
Other technical or business qualification/certificate	... 14
University or CNAA degree or diploma	... 15

Other (SPECIFY) ______________________________

ASK ALL

16. Was the last school you attended a mixed school or for boys/girls only? (EXCLUDE 6TH FORM COLLEGE; INCLUDE 6TH FORM AT A SCHOOL *IF* RESPONDENT WAS IN 6TH FORM

Mixed school	... 1
Single sex school	... 2
Single sex up to 6th form but mixed 6th form	... 3

ASK ALL

CARD C3

17. To which of the groups on this card do you consider you belong?

	BLACK	... 01
	WHITE	... 02
ASIAN (origin/descent)	Indian	... 03
	Pakistani	... 04
	Bangladeshi	... 05
	Chinese	... 06
	Other Asian (STATE) ______________	... 07
ANY OTHER RACE OR ETHNIC GROUP (STATE) ______________		... 08
	Refused	... 98

18.a) Is there a telephone in (your part of) this accommodation? Yes 1 **GO TO c)**
No 2 **ASK b)**

b) Do you have easy access to a 'phone where you can receive incoming calls? IF YES, ASK: Is this a home or a work number? IF BOTH, CODE HOME ONLY
Yes – home 1 } **ASK c)**
No – work 2 }
No 3 **GO TO Q.19)**

c) A few interviews on any survey are checked by a supervisor to make sure that people are satisfied with the way the interview was carried out. In case my supervisor needs to contact you, it would be helpful if we could have your telephone number.
Number given* . . . 1
Number refused . . . 2

*RECORD HOME OR WORK NUMBER ON 'ARF' ADDRESS SLIP ONLY – NOT HERE

ASK ALL

19. We may be doing surveys on similar subjects in future and we may wish to include you again. Would this be all right?
Yes . . . 1
No . . . 2

TIME INTERVIEW COMPLETED ________ TOTAL DURATION OF INTERVIEW (MINUTES) [| |]

DATE OF INTERVIEW [|] [|]
Day Month

Interviewer's Name ________________ NUMBER [| | | |]

THANK RESPONDENT FOR HIS/HER HELP

INTERVIEWER TO COMPLETE

20.a) Were any other people in the home at all during the interview?

Yes	1	**ANSWER b)**
No	2	**GO TO Q.21**
Interview conducted outside (e.g. in garden, car)	3	**GO TO Q.21**

b) Was anyone else present in the room, *or* passing through, *or* nearby during any part of the interview and (possibly) able to overhear?

Yes	1	**ANSWER c)**
No	1	**GO TO Q.21**

c) Who was present/passing through etc? RING ONE CODE BELOW EACH CATEGORY OF PERSON

	Spouse/ partner	*Parent(s)*	*Child(ren) (approx. age) 0-5*	*6-15*	*Young adult(s) 16-21*	*Other adult(s)*	
Present throughout	1	1	1	1	1	1	**ANSWER d) IF ANY 1-2**
Present some of time	2	2	2	2	2	2	
May have overheard all/part*	3	3	3	3	3	3	**GO TO Q.21 (IF NONE CODED 1-2)**
Passing through only	4	4	4	4	4	4	
Not present (inc. not applicable)	5	5	5	5	5	5	

*NOT IN ROOM BUT PASSING THROUGH OFTEN, OR NEARBY, SO MAY HAVE LISTENED/OVERHEARD ALL/PART

d) Did anyone else look at or discuss any part of the self-completion booklet during completion?

Yes – looked at/read fill in together . . . 1
Yes – discussed only . . . 2
No . . . 3
Booklet not given . . . 4

21.a) In your view, did the respondent have any difficulty during the interview because of . . .

	Yes severe	*Yes some*	*No problem*
Language problems?	1	2	3
Literacy problems?	1	2	3
Other problems in understanding?	1	2	3

b) Did you need to read out any of the show cards?

Yes, all/most . . . 1
Yes, some . . . 2
No . . .3

c) In your view was the respondent . . .

. . . very embarrassed/ill at ease . . . 1
somewhat embarrassed/ill at ease . . . 2
only slightly embarrassed/ill at ease . . . 3
or, not at all embarrassed/ill at ease . . . 4

SELF-COMPLETION QUESTIONNAIRES

Confidentiality

The questions in this booklet are mostly very personal. Your answers will be treated in strict confidence; the interviewer does not need to see them.

When you have finished, put the booklet in the envelope and seal it. Your name will not be on the booklet or envelope.

How to answer

Just put a tick in the box opposite the appropriate answer like this ☑, OR write in a number on a line like this 19 ...90...

Not all the questions will apply to you; follow arrows and instructions.

Please ask for help or explanations if you are not sure.

Importance

It is very important to the whole study that you answer these questions completely honestly and as accurately as you can.

Some things may be hard to remember, so please take your time.

Please read these notes before answering the questions.

They are just to make sure everyone applies the same meaning to certain terms we use.

Partners
People who have had sex together – whether just once, or a few times, or as regular partners, or as married partners.

Genital area
A man's penis or a woman's vagina – that is, the sex organs.

Vaginal sexual intercourse
A man's penis entering a woman's vagina.

Oral sex (oral sexual intercourse)
A man's or a woman's mouth on a partner's genital area.

Anal sex (anal sexual intercourse)
A man's penis entering a partner's anus (rectum or back passage)

Genital contact NOT involving intercourse
Forms of contact with the genital area NOT leading to intercourse (vaginal, oral or anal), but intended to achieve orgasm, for example, stimulating by hand.

Any sexual contact or experience
This is a wider term and can include just kissing or cuddling, not necessarily leading to genital contact or intercourse.

WOMEN

QUESTION 1

a) When, if ever, was the last occasion you had sex with a man?
This means vaginal intercourse, oral sex, anal sex.

(Tick one box)

Have never had sex with a man ☐ → **GO TO QUESTION 4**

Last occasion was:

In the last 7 days ☐
Between 7 days and 4 weeks ago ☐
Between 4 weeks and 3 months ago ☐
Between 3 months and 6 months ago ☐
Between 6 months and 1 year ago ☐
Between 1 year and 5 years ago ☐
Longer than 5 years ago ☐

b) Was this the **first** occasion with that partner, or not?

(Tick one box)

Yes, first occasion with that partner ☐
No, not the first occasion ☐

c) Was a condom (sheath) used on that occasion?

(Tick one box)

Yes ☐
No ☐

d) What was his age (at that time)? *Write in age* ....

NOW PLEASE ANSWER QUESTION 2

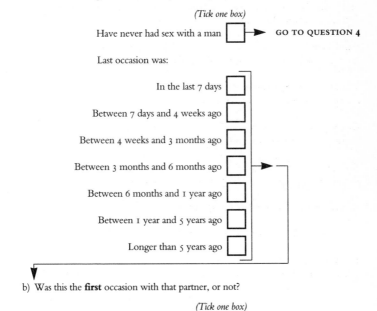

QUESTION 2

a) On how many occasions in the last **4 weeks** have you had sex with a man?

*Tick this box if **none*** ☐ → **AND GO TO QUESTION 3**

Or**, if **any**, write in the number of occasions in last **4 weeks ....

***Or**, give your best estimate here* ....

b) With how many men have you had sex in the last 4 weeks?

Write in the number ....

c) How many of these were new partners with whom you had not had sex before?

Write in the number ....
(If none, enter '0')

d) Was a condom (sheath) used on any occasions in the last 4 weeks?

(Tick one box)

Yes, on all the occasions ☐

Yes, on some occasions ☐

No, not in the last 4 weeks ☐

e) On how many occasions in the last **7 days** have you had sex with a man?

*Write in the number of occasions in last **7 days*** ....
(If none, enter '0')

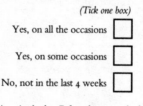

QUESTION 3

This is about different kinds of sex with men. In case you are not sure of the meanings, they are defined in the front of this booklet.

a) When, if ever, was the last occasion you had **vaginal sexual intercourse** with a man?

(Tick one box)

If never, tick the last box

- In the last 7 days ☐
- Between 7 days and 4 weeks ago ☐
- Between 4 weeks and 6 months ago ☐
- Between 6 months and 1 year ago ☐
- Between 1 year and 5 years ago ☐
- Longer than 5 years ago ☐
- Never had vaginal intercourse ☐

b) When, if ever, was the last occasion you had **oral sex** with a man – **by you to a partner?**

(Tick one box)

If never, tick the last box

- In the last 7 days ☐
- Between 7 days and 4 weeks ago ☐
- Between 4 weeks and 6 months ago ☐
- Between 6 months and 1 year ago ☐
- Between 1 year and 5 years ago ☐
- Longer than 5 years ago ☐
- Never had oral sex – by me to partner ☐

(Question 3 continued)

c) When, if ever, was the last occasion you had **oral sex** with a man – **by a partner to you?** *(Tick one box)*

If never, tick the last box

- In the last 7 days ☐
- Between 7 days and 4 weeks ago ☐
- Between 4 weeks and 6 months ago ☐
- Between 6 months and 1 year ago ☐
- Between 1 year and 5 years ago ☐
- Longer than 5 years ago ☐
- Never had oral sex – by partner to me ☐

d) When, if ever, was the last occasion you had **anal sex** with a man? *(Tick one box)*

If never, tick the last box

- In the last 7 days ☐
- Between 7 days and 4 weeks ago ☐
- Between 4 weeks and 6 months ago ☐
- Between 6 months and 1 year ago ☐
- Between 1 year and 5 years ago ☐
- Longer than 5 years ago ☐
- Never had anal sex ☐

e) When was the last occasion you had **genital contact** with a man **NOT involving intercourse?** (For example, stimulating sex organs by hand but not leading to vaginal, oral or anal intercourse) *(Tick one box)*

If never, tick the last box

- In the last 7 days ☐
- Between 7 days and 4 weeks ago ☐
- Between 4 weeks and 6 months ago ☐
- Between 6 months and 1 year ago ☐
- Between 1 year and 5 years ago ☐
- Longer than 5 years ago ☐
- Never had genital contact without intercourse as well ☐

QUESTION 4

a) Have you ever had ANY kind of sexual experience or sexual contact with a **female**?

*Please tick 'yes' here, even if it was a long time ago or did **not** involve contact with the genital area/vagina*

Yes ☐ No ☐ → **GO TO QUESTION 7**

b) How old were you the first time that ever happened?

Write in age ....

c) Have you ever had sex with a woman involving genital area/vaginal contact?

Yes ☐ No ☐ → **GO TO QUESTION 7**

d) When was the last occasion? *(Tick one box)*

In the last 7 days ☐

Between 7 days and 4 weeks ago ☐

Between 4 weeks and 3 months ago ☐

Between 3 months and 6 months ago ☐

Between 6 months and 1 year ago ☐

Between 1 year and 5 years ago ☐

Longer than 5 years ago ☐

e) Was this the first occasion with that partner, or not? *(Tick one box)*

Yes, **first** occasion with that partner ☐

No, not first occasion ☐

f) What was her age (at that time)?

Write in age ....

NOW PLEASE ANSWER QUESTION 5

QUESTION 5

a) On how many occasions in the last **4 weeks** have you had sex with a woman?

*Tick this box if **none*** ☐ → **AND GO TO QUESTION 6**

Or**, if **any**, write in the number of occasions in last **4 weeks ....

***Or**, give your best estimate here* ....

b) With how many women have you had sex in the last 4 weeks?

Write in the number ....

c) How many of these were new partners with whom you had not had sex before?

Write in the number ....
(If none, enter '0')

d) On how many occasions in the last **7 days** have you had sex with a woman?

*Write in the number of occasions in last **7 days*** ....
(If none, enter '0')

QUESTION 6

This question is about different kinds of sex with **women** partners, involving contact with the genital/vaginal area. In case you are not sure of the meanings, they are defined in the front of this booklet.

a) When, if ever, was the last occasion you had **oral sex** with a woman – **by you to a partner?** *(Tick one box)*

If never, tick the last box

In the last 7 days ☐
Between 7 days and 4 weeks ago ☐
Between 4 weeks and 6 months ago ☐
Between 6 months and 1 year ago ☐
Between 1 year and 5 years ago ☐
Longer than 5 years ago ☐
Never had oral sex – by me to partner ☐

(Question 6 continued)

b) When, if ever, was the last occasion you had **oral sex** with a woman – **by a partner to you?** *(Tick one box)*

If never, tick the last box

- In the last 7 days ☐
- Between 7 days and 4 weeks ago ☐
- Between 4 weeks and 6 months ago ☐
- Between 6 months and 1 year ago ☐
- Between 1 year and 5 years ago ☐
- Longer than 5 years ago ☐
- Never had oral sex – by partner to me ☐

c) When was the last occasion you had any **other form of sex** with a woman that involved genital contact but not also oral sex?
(For example, stimulating sex organs by hand) *(Tick one box)*

If never, tick the last box

- In the last 7 days ☐
- Between 7 days and 4 weeks ago ☐
- Between 4 weeks and 6 months ago ☐
- Between 6 months and 1 year ago ☐
- Between 1 year and 5 years ago ☐
- Longer than 5 years ago ☐
- Never had genital contact without oral sex as well ☐

QUESTION 7 AND QUESTION 8

These questions are about the number of people you have had sex with at different times in your life.
Please include everyone you have ever had sex with, whether it was just once, a few times, a regular partner or your husband.
Be as accurate as you can: give your best estimate if you can't remember exactly.

QUESTION 7: MALE PARTNERS

a) Altogether, in your life so far, with how many **men** have you had sexual intercourse (vaginal, oral or anal)?

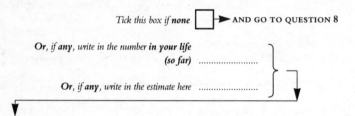

*Tick this box if **none*** ☐ → **AND GO TO QUESTION 8**

Or**, if **any**, write in the number **in your life (so far) ....

***Or**, if **any**, write in the estimate here* ....

If any, please answer b) and c) and d)

b) Altogether, in the last **5 years**, with how many men have you had sexual intercourse?

*Write in the number in the last **5 years*** ....

(If none, enter '0')

and –

c) Altogether, in the last **2 years**, with how many men have you had sexual intercourse?

*Write in the number in the last **2 years*** ....

(If none, enter '0')

and –

d) Altogether, in the last **year**, with how many men have you had sexual intercourse?

*Write in the number in the last **year*** ....

(If none, enter '0')

NOW PLEASE ANSWER QUESTION 8

Everyone please answer:

QUESTION 8: FEMALE PARTNERS

a) Altogether, in your life so far, with how many **women** have you had sex (that is oral sex or other forms of genital contact)?

Tick this box if ***none*** ☐ → AND GO TO QUESTION 9

Or, if ***any****, write in the number* ***in your life (so far)*** ....

Or*, give your best estimate here* ....

If any, please answer b) and c) and d)

b) Altogether, in the last **5 years**, with how many women have you had sex?

Write in the number in the last ***5 years*** ....
(If none, enter '0')

and –

c) Altogether, in the last **2 years**, with how many women have you had sex?

Write in the number in the last ***2 years*** ....
(If none, enter '0')

and –

d) Altogether, in the last **year**, with how many women have you had sex?

Write in the number in the last ***year*** ....
(If none, enter '0')

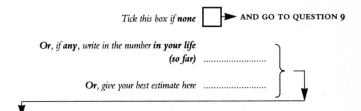

QUESTION 9

Thinking now of male and/or female partners you have had sex with in the last 5 years (whether just once, a few times, a regular partner or husband) . . .

. . . if **one** partner or **no** partners in the last 5 years, tick here ☐ → AND GO TO QUESTION 13

Or . . . if **two or more** partners in the last 5 years, tick here ☐ → AND GO TO QUESTION 10

QUESTION 10

These questions are about the partner you had sex with most recently.

a) When was the most recent occasion you had sex with that partner?

Write in: Month .... Year 19 ....

b) Was this the first occasion with that partner, or not?

Yes, the first ☐ → GO TO **d)**

No, not the first ☐ → ANSWER **c)**

c) When was the first occasion with that partner?

Write in: Month .... Year 19 ....

d) How old was that partner on the first occasion?

Write in age ....

e) Is that partner . . . . . . male ☐

or, female? ☐

f) Are you (or were you ever) . . .

. . . married to each other ☐

or, living together (but never married) ☐

or, regular partners (but never lived together) ☐

or, not regular partners (so far)? ☐

NOW PLEASE ANSWER QUESTION 11

QUESTION 11

These questions are about your 2nd most recent partner in the last 5 years.

a) When was the most recent occasion you had sex with that partner?

Write in: Month .... Year 19 ....

b) Was this the first occasion with that partner, or not?

Yes, the first ☐ → GO TO **d)**

No, not the first ☐ → ANSWER **c)**

c) When was the first occasion with that partner?

Write in: Month .... Year 19 ....

d) How old was that partner on the first occasion?

Write in age ....

e) Is that partner . . .

. . . male ☐

or, female? ☐

f) Are you (or were you ever) . . .

. . . married to each other ☐

or, living together (but never married) ☐

or, regular partners (but never lived together) ☐

or, not regular partners (so far)? ☐

g) In the last 5 years have you had sex with anyone else in addition to the two most recent partners?

Yes ☐ → PLEASE ANSWER QUESTION 12

No ☐ → GO TO QUESTION 13

QUESTION 12

These questions are about your 3rd most recent partner in the last 5 years.

a) When was the most recent occasion you had sex with that partner?

Write in: Month .... Year 19 ....

b) Was this the first occasion with that partner, or not?

Yes, the first ☐ → **GO TO d)**

No, not the first ☐ → **ANSWER c)**

c) When was the first occasion with that partner?

Write in: Month .... Year 19 ....

d) How old was that partner on the first occasion?

Write in age ....

e) Is that partner . . .

. . . male ☐

or, female? ☐

f) Are you (or were you ever) . . .

. . . married to each other ☐

or, living together (but never married) ☐

or, regular partners (but never lived together) ☐

or, not regular partners (so far)? ☐

QUESTION 13

a) Have you ever had a pregnancy that ended in miscarriage or still birth?

(Tick one box)

Yes ☐ No ☐ → GO TO QUESTION 14

b) When was that? (The last time, if more than once) *(Tick one box)*

In the last year ☐

Between 1 year and 5 years ago ☐

Longer than 5 years ago ☐

QUESTION 14

a) Have you ever had a termination of pregnancy (abortion)?

(Tick one box)

Yes ☐ No ☐ → GO TO QUESTION 15

b) When was that? (The last time, if more than once) *(Tick one box)*

In the last year ☐

Between 1 year and 5 years ago ☐

Longer than 5 years ago ☐

QUESTION 15

a) Have you ever had a time, lasting 6 months or longer, when you were trying to get pregnant but it didn't happen? *(Tick one box)*

Yes ☐ No ☐

b) Have you (or your partner) ever sought medical or professional help about infertility?

(Tick one box)

Yes ☐ No ☐

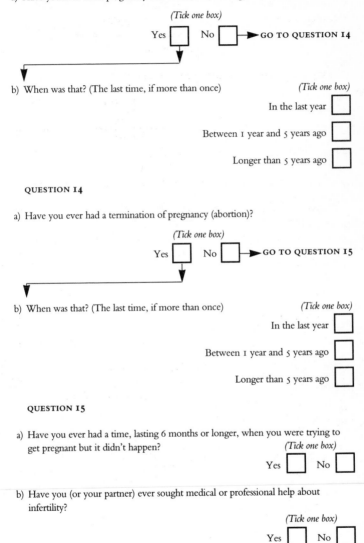

QUESTION 16

a) Have you ever attended a sexually transmitted disease (STD) clinic or special (VD) clinic? *(Tick one box)*

Yes ☐ No ☐ → **GO TO QUESTION 17**

b) When was that? (the last time, if more than once) *(Tick one box)*

In the last year ☐

Between 1 year and 5 years ago ☐

Longer than 5 years ago ☐

QUESTION 17

a) Have you ever injected yourself with any drugs or other substances, medical or otherwise. *(Tick one box)*

Yes ☐ No ☐ → **GO TO QUESTION 18**

b) Were any of these drugs or other substances prescribed for you, by a doctor, for a medical condition, and if so, for what condition? *(Tick one box)*

Yes, **all** prescribed ☐

Some prescribed, some not ☐

No, none prescribed ☐

Medical condition (*please write in*) ....

c) When was the last time you injected yourself with drugs or other substances?

(Tick one box)

In the last 7 days ☐

Between 7 days and 4 weeks ago ☐

Between 4 weeks and 1 year ago ☐

(Question 17 continued)

(Tick one box)

Between 1 year and 5 years ago ☐

Longer than 5 years ago ☐

e) Have you ever shared a needle – used for injecting – with someone else?

(Tick one box)

Yes ☐ No ☐

QUESTION 18

a) Have you ever avoided having sex to prevent the possibility of getting any infection or disease transmitted through having sex?

(Tick one box)

Yes ☐ No ☐ → GO TO QUESTION 19

b) Have you done this at any time in the last year?

(Tick one box)

Yes ☐ No ☐

QUESTION 19

As far as you know, have you ever met anyone who was confirmed as having the virus that causes AIDS (the HIV virus)?

(Tick one box)

Yes ☐ No ☐

QUESTION 20

a) In the last five years have you had a blood test that involved testing for the virus that causes AIDS (an HIV test)?

(Tick one box)

Yes ☐ → GO TO QUESTION 20b)

No ☐

Maybe/Not sure ☐

Prefer not to answer ☐

→ GO TO QUESTION 21

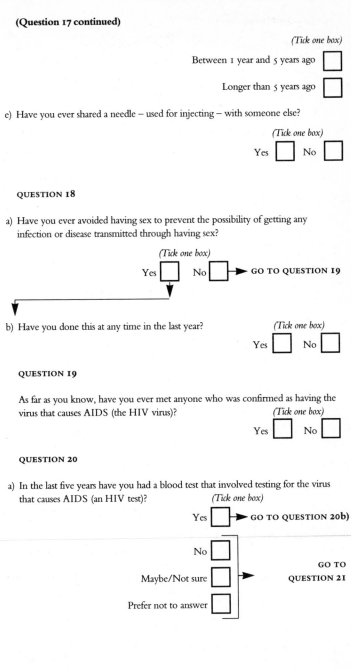

(Question 20 continued)

b) Has this been in connection with . . .

(Tick all that apply)

. . . being a blood donor (giving blood) ☐

being pregnant ☐

insurance, mortgage, or travel ☐

Other reason(s) ☐

c) When was that test? (the last HIV test if more than one)

(Tick one box)

In the past year ☐

Between 1 and 2 years ago ☐

Longer than 2 years ago ☐

QUESTION 21

How old were you when you started menstruating (having periods)?

Write in age ....

Thank you very much for your help in answering these questions.

MEN

QUESTION 1

a) When, if ever, was the last occasion you had sex with a woman?
This means vaginal intercourse, oral sex, anal sex.

(Tick one box)

Have never had sex with a woman ☐ → **GO TO QUESTION 4**

Last occasion was: In the last 7 days ☐

Between 7 days and 4 weeks ago ☐

Between 4 weeks and 3 months ago ☐

Between 3 months and 6 months ago ☐

Between 6 months and 1 year ago ☐

Between 1 year and 5 years ago ☐

Longer than 5 years ago ☐

b) Was this the **first** occasion with that partner, or not?

(Tick one box)

Yes, first occasion with that partner ☐

No, not the first occasion ☐

c) Did you use a condom (sheath) on that occasion?

(Tick one box)

Yes ☐

No ☐

d) What was her age (at that time)? *Write in age* ....

NOW PLEASE ANSWER QUESTION 2

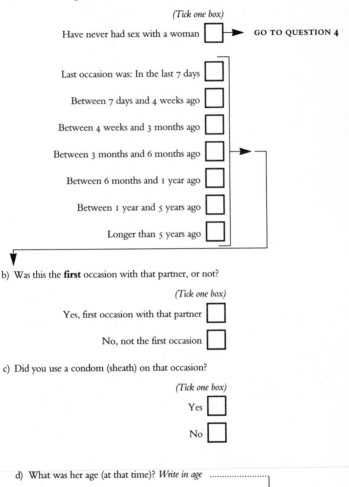

QUESTION 2

a) On how many occasions in the last **4 weeks** have you had sex with a woman?

Tick this box if ***none*** ☐ → **AND GO TO QUESTION 3**

Or*, if* ***any****, write in the number of occasions in last* ***4 weeks*** ....

Or*, give your best estimate here* ....

b) With how many women have you had sex in the last 4 weeks?

Write in the number ....

c) How many of these were new partners with whom you had not had sex before?

Write in the number ....
(If none, enter '0')

d) Did you use a condom (sheath) on any occasions in the last 4 weeks?

(Tick one box)

Yes, on all the occasions ☐

Yes, on some occasions ☐

No, not in the last 4 weeks ☐

e) On how many occasions in the last **7 days** have you had sex with a woman?

Write in the number of occasions in last ***7 days*** ....
(If none, enter '0')

QUESTION 3

This is about different kinds of sex with women. In case you are not sure of the meanings, they are defined in the front of this booklet.

a) When, if ever, was the last occasion you had **vaginal sexual intercourse** with a woman? *(Tick one box)*

If never, tick the last box

In the last 7 days ☐

Between 7 days and 4 weeks ago ☐

Between 4 weeks and 6 months ago ☐

Between 6 months and 1 year ago ☐

Between 1 year and 5 years ago ☐

Longer than 5 years ago ☐

Never had vaginal intercourse ☐

b) When, if ever, was the last occasion you had **oral sex** with a woman – **by you to a partner?** *(Tick one box)*

If never, tick the last box

In the last 7 days ☐

Between 7 days and 4 weeks ago ☐

Between 4 weeks and 6 months ago ☐

Between 6 months and 1 year ago ☐

Between 1 year and 5 years ago ☐

Longer than 5 years ago ☐

Never had oral sex – by me to partner ☐

(Question 3 continued)

c) When, if ever, was the last occasion you had **oral sex** with a woman – **by a partner to you?** *(Tick one box)*

If never, tick the last box

In the last 7 days ☐

Between 7 days and 4 weeks ago ☐

Between 4 weeks and 6 months ago ☐

Between 6 months and 1 year ago ☐

Between 1 year and 5 years ago ☐

Longer than 5 years ago ☐

Never had oral sex – by partner to me ☐

d) When, if ever, was the last occasion you had **anal sex** with a woman? *(Tick one box)*

If never, tick the last box

In the last 7 days ☐

Between 7 days and 4 weeks ago ☐

Between 4 weeks and 6 months ago ☐

Between 6 months and 1 year ago ☐

Between 1 year and 5 years ago ☐

Longer than 5 years ago ☐

Never had anal sex ☐

e) When was the last occasion you had **genital contact** with a woman **NOT involving intercourse?** (For example, stimulating sex organs by hand but not leading to vaginal, oral or anal intercourse) *(Tick one box)*

If never, tick the last box

In the last 7 days ☐

Between 7 days and 4 weeks ago ☐

Between 4 weeks and 6 months ago ☐

Between 6 months and 1 year ago ☐

Between 1 year and 5 years ago ☐

Longer than 5 years ago ☐

Never had genital contact without intercourse as well ☐

QUESTION 4

a) Have you ever had ANY kind of sexual experience or sexual contact with a **male**?
*Please tick 'yes' here, even if it was a long time ago or did **not** involve contact with the genital area/penis*

Yes ☐ No ☐ → **GO TO QUESTION 7**

b) How old were you the first time that ever happened?

Write in age ....

c) Have you ever had sex with a man involving genital area/penis contact?

Yes ☐ No ☐ → **GO TO QUESTION 7**

d) When was the last occasion? *(Tick one box)*

In the last 7 days ☐

Between 7 days and 4 weeks ago ☐

Between 4 weeks and 3 months ago ☐

Between 3 months and 6 months ago ☐

Between 6 months and 1 year ago ☐

Between 1 year and 5 years ago ☐

Longer than 5 years ago ☐

e) Was this the first occasion with that partner, or not? *(Tick one box)*

Yes, **first** occasion with that partner ☐

No, not first occasion ☐

f) Was a condom (sheath) used on that occasion? *(Tick one box)*

Yes ☐

No ☐

g) What was his age (at that time)?

Write in age ....

NOW PLEASE ANSWER QUESTION 5

QUESTION 5

a) On how many occasions in the last **4 weeks** have you had sex with a man?

Tick this box if ***none*** ☐ → **AND GO TO QUESTION 6**

Or*, if* ***any****, write in the number of occasions in last* ***4 weeks*** ....

Or*, give your best estimate here* ....

b) With how many men have you had sex in the last 4 weeks?

Write in the number ....

c) How many of these were new partners with whom you had not had sex before?

Write in the number ....
(If none, enter '0')

d) Was a condom (sheath) used on any occasions in the last 4 weeks *(Tick one box)*

Yes, on all the occasions ☐

Yes, on some occasions ☐

No, not in the last 4 weeks ☐

e) On how many occasions in the last **7 days** have you had sex with a man?

Write in the number of occasions in last ***7 days*** ....
(If none, enter '0')

QUESTION 6

This question is about different kinds of sex with **male** partners, involving contact with the genital/penis area. In case you are not sure of the meanings, they are defined in the front of this booklet.

a) When, if ever, was the last occasion you had **oral sex** with a man – **by you to a partner?**
(Tick one box)

If never, tick the last box

In the last 7 days ☐

Between 7 days and 4 weeks ago ☐

Between 4 weeks and 6 months ago ☐

Between 6 months and 1 year ago ☐

Between 1 year and 5 years ago ☐

Longer than 5 years ago ☐

Never had oral sex – by me to partner ☐

b) When, if ever, was the last occasion you had **oral sex** with a man – **by a partner to you?**
(Tick one box)

If never, tick the last box

In the last 7 days ☐

Between 7 days and 4 weeks ago ☐

Between 4 weeks and 6 months ago ☐

Between 6 months and 1 year ago ☐

Between 1 year and 5 years ago ☐

Longer than 5 years ago ☐

Never had oral sex – by partner to me ☐

c) When, if ever, was the last occasion you had **anal sex** with a man – **by you to a partner.**
(Tick one box)

If never, tick the last box

In the last 7 days ☐

Between 7 days and 4 weeks ago ☐

Between 4 weeks and 6 months ago ☐

(Question 6 continued)

(Tick one box)

Between 6 months and 1 year ago ☐

Between 1 year and 5 years ago ☐

Longer than 5 years ago ☐

Never had anal sex – by me to partner ☐

d) When, if ever, was the last occasion you had **anal sex** with a man – **by a partner to you.**

(Tick one box)

If never, tick the last box

In the last 7 days ☐

Between 7 days and 4 weeks ago ☐

Between 4 weeks and 6 months ago ☐

Between 6 months and 1 year ago ☐

Between 1 year and 5 years ago ☐

Longer than 5 years ago ☐

Never had anal sex – by partner to me ☐

e) When was the last occasion you had any **other form of sex** with a man that involved genital contact but NOT also oral or anal sex? (For example, stimulating sex organs by hand)

(Tick one box)

If never, tick the last box

In the last 7 days ☐

Between 7 days and 4 weeks ago ☐

Between 4 weeks and 6 months ago ☐

Between 6 months and 1 year ago ☐

Between 1 year and 5 years ago ☐

Longer than 5 years ago ☐

Never had genital contact without oral/anal sex as well ☐

QUESTION 7 AND QUESTION 8

These questions are about the number of people you have had sex with at different times in your life.
Please include everyone you have ever had sex with, whether it was just once, a few times, a regular partner or your wife.
Be as accurate as you can: give your best estimate if you can't remember exactly.

QUESTION 7: FEMALE PARTNERS

a) Altogether, in your life so far, with how many **women** have you had sexual intercourse (vaginal, oral or anal)?

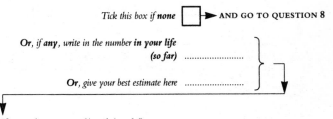

Tick this box if ***none*** ☐ → **AND GO TO QUESTION 8**

Or, if ***any****, write in the number* ***in your life (so far)*** ....

Or*, give your best estimate here* ....

If any, please answer b) and c) and d)

b) Altogether, in the last **5 years**, with how many women have you had sexual intercourse?

Write in the number in the last ***5 years*** ....
(If none, enter '0')

and –

c) Altogether, in the last **2 years**, with how many women have you had sexual intercourse?

Write in the number in the last ***2 years*** ....
(If none, enter '0')

and –

d) Altogether, in the last **year**, with how many women have you had sexual intercourse?

Write in the number in the last ***year*** ....
(If none, enter '0')

NOW PLEASE ANSWER QUESTION 8

Everyone please answer:

QUESTION 8: MALE PARTNERS

a) Altogether, in your life so far, with how many **men** have you had sex (that is oral, anal or other forms of genital contact)?

Tick this box if ***none*** ☐ → **AND GO TO QUESTION 9**

Or*, if* ***any****, write in the number* ***in your life (so far)*** ....

Or*, give your best estimate here* ....

If any, please answer b) and c) and d)

b) Altogether, in the last **5 years**, with how many men have you had sex?

Write in the number in the last ***5 years*** ....
(If none, enter '0')

and –

c) Altogether, in the last **2 years**, with how many men have you had sex?

Write in the number in the last ***2 years*** ....
(If none, enter '0')

and –

d) Altogether, in the last **year**, with how many men have you had sex?

Write in the number in the last ***year*** ....
(If none, enter '0')

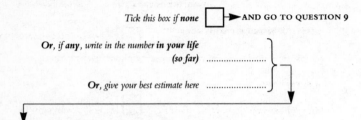

QUESTION 9

Thinking now of female and/or male partners you have had sex with in the last 5 years (whether just once, a few times, a regular partner or wife) . . .

. . . if **one** partner or **no** partners in the last 5 years, tick here ☐ → **AND GO TO QUESTION 13**

Or . . . if **two or more** partners in the last 5 years, tick here ☐ → **AND GO TO QUESTION 10**

QUESTION 10

These questions are about the partner you had sex with most recently.

a) When was the most recent occasion you had sex with that partner?

Write in: Month .... Year 19 ....

b) Was this the first occasion with that partner, or not?

Yes, the first ☐ → **GO TO d)**

No, not the first ☐ → **ANSWER c)**

c) When was the first occasion with that partner?

Write in: Month .... Year 19 ....

d) How old was that partner on the first occasion?

Write in age ....

e) Is that partner . . .

. . . female ☐

or, male? ☐

f) Are you (or were you ever) . . .

. . . married to each other ☐

or, living together (but never married) ☐

or, regular partners (but never lived together) ☐

or, not regular partners (so far)? ☐

NOW PLEASE ANSWER QUESTION 11

QUESTION 11

These questions are about your 2nd most recent partner in the last 5 years.

a) When was the most recent occasion you had sex with that partner?

Write in: Month .... Year 19 ....

b) Was this the first occasion with that partner, or not?

Yes, the first ☐ → **GO TO d)**

No, not the first ☐ → **ANSWER c)**

c) When was the first occasion with that partner?

Write in: Month .... Year 19 ....

d) How old was that partner on the first occasion?

Write in age ....

e) Is that partner . . .

. . . female ☐

or, male? ☐

f) Are you (or were you ever) . . .

. . . married to each other ☐

or, living together (but never married) ☐

or, regular partners (but never lived together) ☐

or, not regular partners (so far)? ☐

g) In the last 5 years have you had sex with anyone else in addition to the two most recent partners?

Yes ☐ → **PLEASE ANSWER QUESTION 12**

No ☐ → **GO TO QUESTION 13**

QUESTION 12

These questions are about your 3rd most recent partner in the last 5 years.

a) When was the most recent occasion you had sex with that partner?

Write in: Month .... Year 19 ....

b) Was this the first occasion with that partner, or not?

Yes, the first ☐ → GO TO d)

No, not the first ☐ → ANSWER c)

c) When was the first occasion with that partner?

Write in: Month .... Year 19 ....

d) How old was that partner on the first occasion?

Write in age ....

e) Is that partner . . .

. . . female ☐

or, male? ☐

f) Are you (or were you ever) . . .

. . . married to each other ☐

or, living together (but never married) ☐

or, regular partners (but never lived together) ☐

or, not regular partners (so far)? ☐

QUESTION 13

a) Have you ever paid money for sex with a woman?

(Tick one box)

Yes ☐ No ☐ → GO TO QUESTION 14

↓

GO TO QUESTION 13b)

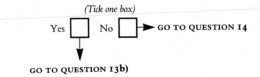

(Question 13 continued)

b) When was the last time you paid money for sex with a woman? *(Tick one box)*

In the last 7 days ☐

Between 7 days and 4 weeks ago ☐

Between 4 weeks and 1 year ago ☐

Between 1 year and 5 years ago ☐

Longer than 5 years ago ☐

c) In your lifetime, to about how many women altogether have you paid money for sex?

Write in the number ....

QUESTION 14

a) Have you ever paid money for sex with a man?

(Tick one box)

Yes ☐ No ☐ → **GO TO QUESTION 15**

b) When was the last time you paid money for sex with a man? *(Tick one box)*

In the last 7 days ☐

Between 7 days and 4 weeks ago ☐

Between 4 weeks and 1 year ago ☐

Between 1 year and 5 years ago ☐

Longer than 5 years ago ☐

c) In your lifetime, to about how many men altogether have you paid money for sex?

Write in the number ....

QUESTION 15

a) Have you ever had a time, lasting 6 months or longer, when you and your partner were trying to get pregnant but it didn't happen? *(Tick one box)*

Yes ☐ No ☐

b) Have you (or your partner) ever sought medical or professional help about infertility?

(Tick one box)

Yes ☐ No ☐

QUESTION 16

a) Have you ever attended a sexually transmitted disease (STD) clinic or special (VD) clinic? *(Tick one box)*

Yes ☐ No ☐ → **GO TO QUESTION 17**

b) When was that?
(the last time, if more than once)

(Tick one box)

In the last year ☐

Between 1 year and 5 years ago ☐

Longer than 5 years ago ☐

QUESTION 17

a) Have you ever injected yourself with any drugs or other substances, medical or otherwise. *(Tick one box)*

Yes ☐ No ☐ → **GO TO QUESTION 18**

b) Were any of these drugs or other substances prescribed for you, by a doctor, for a medical condition, and if so, for what condition? *(Tick one box)*

Yes, **all** prescribed ☐

Some prescribed, some not ☐

No, none prescribed ☐

Medical condition (*please write in*) ....

c) When was the last time you injected yourself with drugs or other substances?

(Tick one box)

In the last 7 days ☐

Between 7 days and 4 weeks ago ☐

Between 4 weeks and 1 year ago ☐

(Question 17 continued)

(Tick one box)

Between 1 year and 5 years ago ☐

Longer than 5 years ago ☐

e) Have you ever shared a needle – used for injecting – with someone else?

(Tick one box)

Yes ☐ No ☐

QUESTION 18

a) Have you ever avoided having sex to prevent the possibility of getting any infection or disease transmitted through having sex?

(Tick one box)

Yes ☐ No ☐ → GO TO QUESTION 19

b) Have you done this at any time in the last year? *(Tick one box)*

Yes ☐ No ☐

QUESTION 19

As far as you know, have you ever met anyone who was confirmed as having the virus that causes AIDS (the HIV virus)? *(Tick one box)*

Yes ☐ No ☐

QUESTION 20

a) In the last five years have you had a blood test that involved testing for the virus that causes AIDS (an HIV test)? *(Tick one box)*

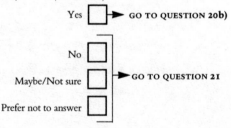

Yes ☐ → GO TO QUESTION 20b)

No ☐

Maybe/Not sure ☐ → GO TO QUESTION 21

Prefer not to answer ☐

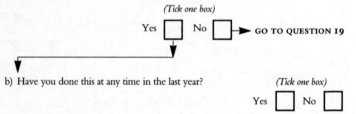

b) Has this been in connection with . . .

(Tick all that apply)

. . . being a blood donor (giving blood) ☐

a pregnancy of your wife/partner ☐

insurance, mortgage, or travel ☐

other reason(s) ☐

c) When was that test? (the last HIV test if more than one)

(Tick one box)

In the past year ☐

Between 1 and 2 years ago ☐

Longer than 2 years ago ☐

QUESTION 21

Are you circumcised ? *(Tick one box)*

Yes ☐ No ☐

Thank you very much for your help in answering these questions.

Index